Ghana

THE BRADT TRAVEL GUIDE

THE BRADT STORY

The first Bradt travel guide was written by Hilary and George Bradt in 1974 on a river barge floating down a tributary of the Amazon in Bolivia. From their base in Boston, Massachusetts, they went on to write and publish four other backpacking guides to the Americas and one to Africa.

In the 1980s Hilary continued to develop the Bradt list in England, and also established herself as a travel writer and tour leader. The company's publishing emphasis evolved towards broader-based guides to new destinations – usually the first to be published on those countries – complemented by hiking, rail and wildlife guides.

Since winning *The Sunday Times* Small Publisher of the Year Award in 1997, we have continued to fill the demand for detailed, well-written guides to unusual destinations, while maintaining the company's original ethos of low-impact travel.

Travel guides are by their nature continuously evolving. If you experience anything which you would like to share with us, or if you have any amendments to make to this guide, please write; all your letters are read and passed on to the author. Most importantly, do remember to travel with an open mind and to respect the customs of your hosts – it will add immeasurably to your enjoyment.

Happy travelling!

Hilary Bradt

19 High Street, Chalfont St Peter, Bucks SL9 9QE, England
Tel: 01753 893444 Fax: 01753 892333

Ghana

THE BRADT TRAVEL GUIDE
Second Edition

Philip Briggs

Bradt Travel Guides Ltd, UK
The Globe Pequot Press Inc, USA

First published in 1998 by Bradt Publications.
This second edition published in 2001 by Bradt Travel Guides Ltd,
19 High Street, Chalfont St Peter, Bucks SL9 9QE, England
Published in the USA by The Globe Pequot Press Inc,
246 Goose Lane, PO Box 480, Guilford, Connecticut 06437-0480

Text copyright © 2001 Philip Briggs
Maps copyright © 2001 Bradt Travel Guides Ltd
Photographs copyright © 2001 Ariadne Van Zandbergen

The author and publishers have made every effort to ensure the accuracy of the
information in this book at the time of going to press. However, the publishers
cannot accept any responsibility for any loss, injury or inconvenience resulting
from the use of information contained in this guide.

British Library Cataloguing in Publication Data
A catalogue record for this book is available from the British Library
ISBN 1 84162 030 0

Library of Congress Cataloging-in-Publication Data applied for

Photographs
Ariadne Van Zandbergen

Illustrations Annabel Milne
Maps Steve Munns

Typeset from the author's disc by Wakewing, High Wycombe
Printed and bound in Italy by Legoprint SpA, Trento

Author

Philip Briggs (philari@hixnet.co.za) is a travel writer and tour leader specialising in equatorial and southern Africa. Born in Britain and raised in South Africa, he first travelled in equatorial Africa in 1986, and since becoming a full-time writer in 1992 has spent half of his time exploring the highways and back-roads of the continent. His first book *Guide to South Africa* was published by Bradt in 1991. Subsequently, Philip has written seven other Bradt guides, covering Tanzania, Uganda, Ethiopia, Malawi, Mozambique, Ghana, and East and southern Africa. He has recently co-authored a new Bradt guide to Rwanda, is the author of the *Visitors' Guide to Kenya and East Africa* (Southern Books), and has contributed chapters to various Insight Discovery and AA travel guides. He is a regular contributor to several British and South African periodicals including *Travel Africa*, *Africa Environment & Wildlife*, *Africa Birds & Birding* and *Wanderlust*.

Ariadne Van Zandbergen (philari@hixnet.co.za), who took the photographs for this book and contributed to the research, is a freelance photographer and tour guide. Born and raised in Belgium, she travelled through Africa from Morocco to South Africa in 1994/5 and is now resident in Johannesburg. She has visited 25 African countries and her photographs have appeared in numerous books, magazines, newspapers, maps, periodicals and pamphlets.

Contents

LIST OF MAPS

Introduction

As travel destinations go, Ghana is difficult to flaw. When a few years back somebody coined the phrase 'Africa for Beginners' to describe Malawi, that most laid-back of southern African countries, they might as easily have been talking about Ghana today. Doubly so. Not only can Ghana, like Malawi, be recommended without reservation to even the most nervous of first-time independent travellers for being as amiable, affordable and hassle-free as practically any country on the African continent; just as important, Ghana boasts a travel circuit so varied and compact that it might almost be seen as offering a microcosmic first taste of Africa.

The southern part of Ghana is much as you'd expect of West Africa, all lush jungle, banana plantations and bone-white beaches, albeit with a unique dimension in the form of the string of 500-year-old European forts and castles that line the former Gold Coast. But the real surprises begin as you travel further north, for instance to the game-rich savannah of Mole National Park, a setting that evokes East Africa more than West Africa, or to the deeply Muslim Burkina Faso border region, where both mood and architecture have unexpected overtones of North Africa.

For English-speaking travellers, Ghana must certainly be regarded as the obvious first port of call in West Africa. Of only five anglophone countries in the region, it's the only one that really caters for independent travellers – granted, not necessarily a major commendation from a shortlist which also includes such potential 'holiday' venues as Liberia, Nigeria and Sierra Leone. Fairer to say that you're unlikely to meet an English speaker who's travelled in West Africa in recent years and has anything negative to say about Ghana by comparison with its more expensive (and generally less well-equipped) francophone neighbours.

What Ghana does not have is one drop-dead, big-name attraction, the sort of place that friends who've visited will say you simply have to see once in your lifetime. Zimbabwe has Victoria Falls, Tanzania has Kilimanjaro, South Africa has Cape Town, Ethiopia its rock-hewn churches. The closest thing Ghana has to offer in the not-to-be-missed stakes are the above-mentioned castles. Not quite the pyramids in terms of impact, I grant you, but nevertheless a unique and chilling memorial to an episode as sickening as any in the recorded history of Africa: the cruel trade in human life that resulted in several millions of Africans being displaced to a life of bondage in the plantations of the Americas and the Caribbean.

If Ghana lacks one truly great tourist attraction, then it is equally true that during the four rapidly paced months we spent researching two editions of this guide, barely a day went by without at least one memorable highlight, be it swimming below one of the gorgeous waterfalls of the eastern highlands, the thrill of getting closer on foot to a wild elephant than I ever have in East Africa, climbing to the roof of one of the surreal mosques that dot the northwest, taking a dugout canoe through papyrus swamps to the stilted village of Mzulezu, or watching colourful mona monkeys play between the houses of Baobeng village.

Ghana is a perfect travel destination, not least because it is so mercifully free of the trappings associated with mass tourism. Nowhere in the country are you made to feel part of some tourist treadmill, and – even if it has become something of a cliché for me to say so in the introduction to my guides – Ghana really is endowed with some remarkably exciting off-the-beaten-track possibilities. There are, for instance, at least five national parks and reserves ideally suited for equipped independent travellers, yet which currently go months on end without seeing a visitor. It is my hope that, by documenting for the first time the practicalities that surround visiting many of these places, I will encourage adventurous travellers to start realising the enormous potential for exploration that lies beyond Ghana's few relatively well-established tourist trails.

There has been much talk in the last couple of years of an African renaissance and, regardless of what one thinks of such generalisations, it is Ghana along with Uganda that is most frequently cited as being at the forefront of this movement. Trailblazing of this sort is not a new role for Ghana - the former Gold Coast was the first country in Africa to have extended contact with Europeans, one of the first to be formally colonised, and in 1957 it became the first to be granted independence in the post-war era. Less prestigiously, Ghana also became one of the first African countries to slide into post-independence chaos and, while it never plummeted to the depths reached by, say, Liberia or Rwanda, the modern visitor will find it difficult to reconcile accounts of Ghana 15 years ago with the vibrant country they see today.

Ghana is indeed steeped in history and tradition, more tangibly so than most countries I have visited. Yet it is also, emphatically, a country building towards a brighter future – and this paradox, above all, makes it one of Africa's most rewarding and exciting travel destinations. As Ghanaians are so fond of saying, '*Akwaaba!*' – 'Welcome!' Ghana will not disappoint.

Acknowledgements

Many thanks to my wife, Ariadne, for her company in Ghana in 1997/8 and 2000, and for supplying all the photographs used in this guide. Ariadne and I are both deeply indebted to John Awuah of Ghana Airways in South Africa, without whose generous support and assistance this book would never have got off the ground. Also in Ghana, many thanks to John Mason of the NCRC and Paul Symonds of the PADP for regular updates on their projects and other aspects of travel in Ghana; to Yahaya Alhassan for travel tips and guidance in Kumasi; to Holger Tills for valuable insights into Accra's nightlife; and to the management of the Tafi Atome ecotourist project, Golden Beach Hotels, Biriwa Beach Hotel, Labadi Beach Hotel, Shangri-La Hotel, Golden Tulip Hotel, Manet Paradise Hotel, Niagara Hotel, Coconut Grove Hotel, Hans Cottage Botel and Ankobra Beach Resort.

I'm immensely grateful to all the readers of the first edition who wrote to me with updates and comments which have been incorporated into this second edition. A big thanks to you all: Ross Anders, Rosemary Arden, Dan Barthmaier, Andrew Bartram, Caroline Bennett, Paul Berry, Haidy Cameron and Eveline van de Putte, Robert Clark, Ben Clissold, Jane Crittendon, Judith Dekkers, Robert Delien, Stephen Duckworth, Anne and Paul Edwards, Nana Egyir, Jason R Feltz, Mike and Sheelagh Fowler, Inge Frerikson and Peter Heintze, Kevin Froude, Ken and Liz Gambier, Tino Gonzalez-Lacoste, Jane Gossop, Sir Marrack Goulding, Gary Helyer, Monika Hoyer, Roger Jones, Damien Keane and Emily Wallis, Wendy Lubin, Louise Macpherson, Andrew Manos, Leslie Marbury, Barrie McCormick, Katrina Newman, Craig Norman, Maja Pavlic, Mary Payne, Norman Peters, Sasa Pollmann, Billy Register, Christy Reich, Kim Rennie, Leslie Ruyle, Elisabetta Savoldi, Joyce, Joe and George Schlesinger, Julie Sherman, Peter Shimmins, Tom Smith, David Switzer, Chie Takahashi and Giovanni Ganelli, Louis Taussig, John Walker, Christer Willhed, Robert Witter, Gregor and Rahel (no surname given) and Major (no other details supplied).

Finally, thanks to the many travellers and Ghanaians who knowingly or unknowingly helped with my research along the way.

IMPORTANT NOTES ON PRICING

During the year 2000, the Ghanaian cedi devalued by 200% against the US dollar and other hard currencies. Most local prices did not respond to this rapid devaluation, so that while Ghana has long been a relatively inexpensive travel destination, we found it to be ridiculously cheap in hard currency terms when we travelled there to research this second edition in late 2000. Most hotels, for instance, had effectively halved in price in dollar terms, and many cost as little as one-third of what they had cost two years earlier. Only those few upmarket hotels which quote rates in US dollars were unaffected.

In one sense, this was a real pleasure, as we enjoyed our cheapest African trip for many years, and were able to afford minor luxuries that would normally be beyond our means. In terms of researching a new edition of this guide, however, my feelings were rather more ambivalent, as I realised that I might not be updating prices for the new edition so much as gathering artificially low prices. It could well be that by 2002, the prices gathered for the second edition look rather more dated than those quoted in the first edition!

This second edition was researched under what may prove to be freak conditions. For a start, the cost of fuel in Ghana in late 2000 was reportedly the cheapest in the world (around US$0.20 for a litre of petrol). My understanding is that, with an election looming in December 2000, the government intervened to maintain artificially low fuel prices throughout a period when the exchange rate sank dramatically, and international fuel prices rose considerably. Now that election is over, the fuel price must inevitably be adjusted, which will affect the price of everything in Ghana, from tro-tros to food to accommodation.

Even knowing the above, a travel guide is essentially a work of fact, not of prophecy, for which reason I am stuck with quoting prices as they stood when the second edition was researched. As a compromise, however, I have wherever possible quoted the 1998 rate in parenthesis after the current US dollar cost, so that a hotel entry might read 'a double room costs US$8 (1998 US$20)'. This is not the most elegant of solutions, but I can think of no better one, and the important thing is that the two prices quoted should respectively form the lower and upper limit of the price for any given hotel by the time you travel in Ghana.

It does seem reasonable to assume that there will be some consistency in the extent to which cedi prices will catch up with the exchange rate over the next few years. By this I mean that after a few days in the country, a traveller should be able to make a fair guess at what any given hotel room will cost based on the dual rates quoted in this guide. If, for instance, the first hotel you use is quoted as having doubles at US$8 (1998 US$20) and actually costs US$12, and the second is quoted at US$5 (1998 US$13) and actually costs US$8, then you can probably extrapolate that most hotels will charge an actual rate slightly less than halfway between the 2000 and 1998 rate I have quoted.

Two other factors in the accommodation entries are influenced by the rapid devaluation of the cedi. The first is the gap in actual cost between hotels that quote rates in the local currency and those that quote in US dollars. At the end of 1999, the actual cost of a hotel that charged 70,000 cedis for a room and one that charged US$30 was much the same. A year later, the hotel that quoted in cedis (assuming it had not raised its price significantly) worked out to be almost one-third of the price of the one that quoted in dollars. For this reason, hotels that quote dollar rates may seem very overpriced relative to the competition, though it could be that this gap re-closes over the next couple of years. To counter this, I have generally indicated where hotels quote rates in US dollars.

The second difficulty lies in assessing the value for money that any given hotel represents, not so much in relative terms perhaps as in absolute terms. It seems reasonable, for instance, to say that a comfortable but slightly shabby hotel charging US$25 for a room with air-con and en-suite hot shower feels a little run-down at the price. When that price drops to US$8, however, the same hotel starts to look extremely good value – certainly it seems churlish to be critical when in many other West African countries you are routinely asked US$15-plus for a dirty room with neither running water nor reliable electricity. Under present conditions, references to value for money are relative to prices within Ghana.

Were I asked to gaze into my crystal ball, I expect that prices in US dollar terms will climb part of the way back to what they were in 1998. Influenced by whether the cedi holds steady or continues to lose value over the next couple of years, I don't think this will happen overnight, simply because most prices quoted in cedis are geared towards locals – who are unlikely to receive pay rises commensurate with 200% devaluation, and will thus resist inflation every step of the way. I'd wager that when I come to research the third edition of this guide, most prices will remain lower than they were in 1998 in hard currency terms. One thing that could well happen is an increase in the application of the two-tier pricing structure which is commonplace in East Africa, wherein different rates are charged to locals and to foreigners. We will keep tabs on the price situation during the lifespan of this edition, and invite readers to take advantage of our free 'Ghana update newsletter' offer as detailed on page XIV.

It is not just accommodation rates that have been affected by the recent drop in exchange rate; the same syndrome extends to everything from taxis to restaurant meals to curios to entrance fees. For this reason, I do ask readers to display a certain amount of understanding when they note changes in any prices quoted in this edition: please write to keep me informed, but recognise that the future is beyond my control. And price-wise, anything could happen in Ghana over the next couple of years – were the exchange rate to plummet further, it could even be that the prices I quote are too high when this book hits the shops. Readers will have to apply some interpretive skills to all prices quoted in this guide, based on their experience over their first couple of days in the country.

Finally, it is perhaps pertinent to point out that whatever minor frustrations this situation has created for travellers, it has ultimately made a cheap country even cheaper to travel in. For Ghanaians, many of whom already live on or below the breadline, the effect is potentially devastating.

Part One

General Information

2

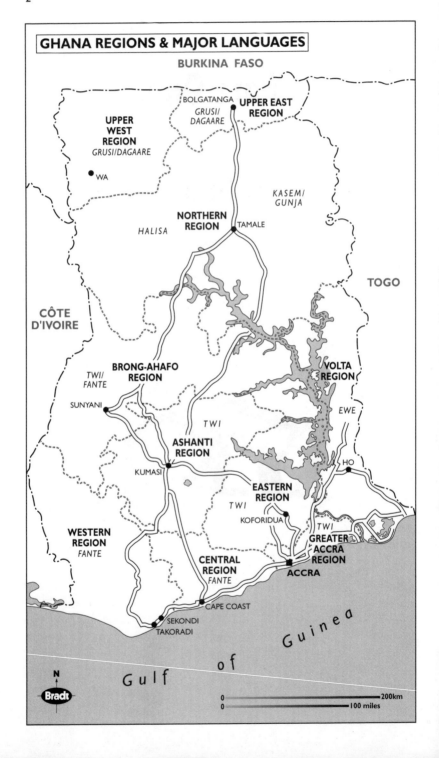

Background Information

FACTS AND FIGURES
Location and size
The Republic of Ghana (formerly the Gold Coast) lies on the Gulf of Guinea on the western coast of tropical Africa. Ghana extends for a maximum of 672km from north to south between latitudes 4.5° north and 11° north, and for 536km east to west between longitudes 3° west and 1° east. It is bordered to the west by Côte d'Ivoire (Ivory Coast), to the north by Burkina Faso, to the west by Togo and to the south by the Atlantic Ocean. With a total land area of 239,460km² (similar to that of Great Britain or the state of Oregon in the USA), Ghana is not a large country by African standards, occupying 30th place between Guinea and Uganda among the 47 countries of mainland Africa.

Capital and other principal cities
The capital of Ghana is Accra, situated on the Atlantic coast about 25km west of the Greenwich Meridian. Population estimates for Accra vary greatly, but the current population certainly exceeds one million and is in all probability far closer to two million. The second largest city in the country is Kumasi, the former capital of the Ashanti Empire and modern capital of the synonymous administrative region, with a population of between half and one million people, depending on which figures you believe.

Various sources quote such wildly different population figures for other large towns in Ghana that it is impossible to rank them by size, at least with any great conviction. However, based on the divergent sources and my own impressions, I would regard the ten largest towns in Ghana, in approximate descending order of population, to be Accra, Kumasi, Tamale, Tema, Takoradi (excluding Sekondi), Cape Coast, Koforidua, Sunyani, Obuasi and Ho. Other towns with a population of around 50,000 or more include Winneba, Bolgatanga, Wa and Bawku.

Administrative regions
Ghana is divided into ten administrative regions, all of which to some degree have borders dating from the earliest days of colonialism. Several of the regions also have names that date from the earliest colonial times in a manner that can create some confusion to new arrivals to the country. The Western, Central and Eastern regions as delineated by the British administration before the annexation of Ashanti in 1902 still go by those names, even though Eastern Region today lies to the west of Volta Region, and Central Region lies nowhere near the centre of modern Ghana but on its southern coast. Likewise, the original Northern Region as delineated by the colonial authorities has

3

since been split in such a manner that Northern Region lies to the south of Upper East and Upper West regions. It is worth being aware of this, because the regions have a high profile in Ghana today, and when most Ghanaians speak of 'eastern', 'central' or 'northern' they mean the administrative region rather than the most easterly, central or northerly part of the country.

The ten modern administrative regions of Ghana are as follows:

	Km²	Population*	Capital	Other large towns
Ashanti	24,390	3,000,000	Kumasi	Obuasi, Tafo, Mampong
Brong-Ahafo	39,557	1,800,000	Sunyani	Techiman, Wenchi, Kintampo
Central	9,826	1,500,000	Cape Coast	Elmina, Winneba, Dunkwa
Eastern	19,223	2,200,000	Koforidua	Akim Oda, Nkawkaw, Akosombo
Greater Accra	3,245	2,500,000	Accra	Tema, Ada, Dodowa, Ashaiman
Northern	70,384	1,800,000	Tamale	Yendi, Bimbilla, Nalerigu
Upper East	8,842	1,100,000	Bolgatanga	Navrongo, Bawku, Zebilla
Upper West	18,476	800,000	Wa	Jiripa, Tumu, Lawra
Volta	20,334	1,800,000	Ho	Hohoe, Aflao, Kpando, Keta
Western	24,000	1,200,000	Sekondi-Takoradi	Tarkwa, Elubo

* Estimated by multiplying the regional population as recorded in the 1984 census by the percentage growth for that region recorded between 1970 and 1984, a calculation which should come close to the 1998 figure assuming the absence of other changing variables.

Time
Bisected by the Greenwich Meridian, Ghana is on GMT, which means that British visitors will remain in the same time zone as at home (except during daylight saving).

Flag
The national flag consists of three horizontal stripes – red, yellow and green from top to bottom – with a black star in the middle of the yellow stripe. The red band represents the blood of the nation's freedom fighters, the yellow its mineral wealth and the green its forest. The black star represents the lodestar of the emancipation of the black man.

Population

The population of Ghana as of July 1990 was estimated at 15 million, but with an annual growth rate of roughly 3.2% it is likely to exceed 18 million today. The majority of the population is concentrated in the southern and central parts of the country, largely for climatic reasons, with Greater Accra Region the most densely populated. The northern three regions, despite covering more than 40% of the national surface area, support only 25% of Ghana's population.

Language

English is the official national language, and it is widely spoken as a result of the country's long links with Britain and an unusually high standard of education from colonial times to the present day. A total of at least 75 African languages and dialects are spoken in Ghana, generally divided into the Akan, Mole-Dagbani, Ewe and Ga language groups. Twi is the main Akan tongue, first language to roughly half the population, including both the Ashanti and Fante, and widely spoken elsewhere in central and southern parts of the country.

Religion

Freedom of religion is a constitutional right in Ghana and, while no official figures seem to be available, it is thought that about 60% of Ghanaians are Christian and at least 25% Muslim. Minority religions include Hinduism, Buddhism, Bahai and various traditional faiths. Although Islam is a minority religion on a national level, it is the predominant faith in the north, having reached West Africa via the trans-Sahara trade routes as early as the 8th century AD. It has been practised in what is now northern Ghana for at least 500 years, probably longer.

Christianity dominates in the southern and central parts of the country. Catholicism was first introduced at the coast by the Portuguese in the late 15th century (the first public mass was said at Elmina in January 1482), but its influence dwindled after the Portuguese withdrew in 1637. Christianity in modern Ghana dates mostly to the latter half of the 19th century. Catholicism, now the most widespread and popular denomination, was reintroduced to the south with the establishment of a French mission at Elmina in 1880 and it arrived in the north in 1906, when the White Fathers opened a mission in Navrongo. The Presbyterian Church reached Ghana in 1828, with the foundation of a Swiss mission at Danish Osu Castle. After initial setbacks as several missionaries were claimed by malaria, Presbyterianism spread into much of what is now Eastern Region in the 1840s. The separate Ewe Presbyterian Church, established by German missionaries in the 1850s, has had its stronghold in what is now Volta Region for almost 150 years. The Methodist Church, formerly the Wesleyan Mission, is almost as widespread as Catholicism – it was established around British castles in the 1830s and spread largely through the pioneering work of the Reverend Thomas Birch Freeman, who served in the Gold Coast and Ashanti from 1838 to 1890. In addition to denominations familiar to most Europeans, a large number of American churches have been established in Ghana, most significantly the AME Zion Church, which spread out of Keta from 1896, as well as more recent ones. Roughly 60% of the present population of Ghana is Christian, though Christian slogans and music are so prevalent that you might easily think that should be 150%!

TRADITIONAL FESTIVALS

A notable feature of Ghanaian society, and one that is of great interest to travellers, is the enormous number of local festivals that take place in various parts of the country throughout the year. Few travellers are likely to deliberately select the dates of their trip to Ghana to coincide with any one particular festival, but it's certainly worth taking note of any festivals that will take place while you are in Ghana and making the effort to be in the right place at the right time, bearing in mind that accommodation may be in relatively short supply in some areas during the most important festivals.

If you are visiting Ghana in early May, do try to get to Winneba for the first weekend of the month in time for the renowned **Aboakyir** deer-hunting festival, one of the most ancient in the country, described in detail in the section on Winneba (page 125).

Most other festivals in coastal parts of Ghana take place during the European autumn. The most important annual festival in Greater Accra region, celebrated in the capital as well as in other Ga towns such as Prampram, is **Homowo**, which literally means 'mocking hunger'. It takes place in August and September, the months that normally yield the largest harvest of fish and grain. A similar festival, called **Damba**, takes place in the Northern Region, centred around Tamale, during the same months.

The most important festival on the Fante calendar is the colourful **Oguaa Fetu Afahye** (the last word literally means 'adorning of new clothes'), on the first Saturday of September, when local chiefs and asafo companies dressed in full traditional regalia lead processions through the streets of Cape Coast.

The main festival in **Anomabu** is the five-day-long Bontungu, in which a variety of drumming and dancing rituals are held to bring God's blessing for the forthcoming year.

In Elmina, the **Bakatue** festival takes place a bit earlier in the year, on the first Tuesday of July, the beginning of a new fishing season. Characterised by a variety of processions and competitions, this festival is said to pre-date the arrival of the Portuguese at Elmina 500 years ago, making it one of the most ancient in Ghana.

Despite Ghana being the most flagrantly Christian country that I've ever visited – exasperatingly so at times, at least for a crusty old rationalist such as myself – various traditional beliefs and customs have also retained an unusually high profile in the country. It's difficult to establish whether this is essentially a case of Christians and traditionalists existing alongside each other, or whether it's simply that a significant number of Ghanaians somehow manage to adhere to what appear to be two contradictory systems of belief. Either way, it makes for an interesting if occasionally bemusing cocktail of faiths to the outsider.

A HISTORICAL BACKGROUND

Before entering any historical discussion, it should be stressed that Ghana, like the other modern states of West Africa, is fundamentally a European creation of the late 19th century. For this reason it would be thoroughly misleading to

In Volta Region, the whole of September is given over to the **Yam Festival**, and two other important festivals take place during November. In Anloga near Keta on the first Saturday of the month, **Hogbetsotso** (pronounced Hobejojo) or the 'Exodus' Festival commemorates the escape of the Ewe people from a tyrannical ruler in what is now Togo. It is marked by processions of traditionally dressed chiefs as well as lively drumming and dancing (note that a similar festival called the **Godigbeza** takes place in nearby Aflao every April). Later in November, the **Agamutsa Waterfall Festival** in Wli traditional area is also characterised by dancing, drumming and colourful costumes.

There is a small festival in Kumasi and other parts of Ashanti twice during each of the nine 42-day cycles or *adae* into which their annual calendar is divided. It is difficult to give dates for these, since they change from year to year (as astute mathematicians will realise, 9 times 42 does not equal 365), but basically the festival days fall on every sixth Sunday and then the 17th day after that, always a Wednesday.

The most important annual festival in Ashanti is **Odwira**, a week-long affair that climaxes on Friday with a procession through town to the palace. The Odwira generally takes place during the ninth *adae* of the calendar, which falls in September. Among the most lively celebrations are those in Kumasi, Akwapim, Akrapong, Akuapem and Akwamu.

Visitors to northern Ghana might want to note the following festival dates:

January 22	Kpini Kyiu Festival	Wa
March 7	Kyiu Sung Festival	Upper East and West Regions
May 14	Don Festival	Wa, Bawku, Bolgatanga
June 11	Dzimbi Festival	Upper East and West Regions
November 1–12	Daa Festival	Tongo
November 9	Sabre Dance Festival	Lawra
November 15	Kobina Festival	Lawra
November 28	Boarim Festival	Tongo
December 1	Fao Festival	Navrongo

write about Ghana as if it were a meaningful entity prior to the colonial era. True, as long ago as AD1700 the coast of modern-day Ghana stood firmly at the epicentre of European maritime trade out of West Africa, while the Ashanti Empire gave political and social cohesion to much of the area between the coastal belt and the Black Volta. But even as recently as 1860, few would have foreseen the eventual existence of a political state with borders approximating to those of present-day Ghana. The modern state of Ghana began to take a recognisable shape only in 1873 as the British Gold Coast colony. Even then, what are now central and northern Ghana were annexed to the colony only in 1902, while the interior to the east of what is now Lake Volta, part of German Togoland before World War I, was formally mandated to Britain by the League of Nations only in 1919.

Bearing the above in mind, I have started this history with a section offering a broad overview of West African history prior to 1500. In the sections that follow this, which focus more specifically on modern-day Ghana, I refer to the coastal belt of what is now Ghana prior to colonisation as the Gold Coast; to the interior south of the Black Volta as Ashanti; and to the interior north of the Black Volta as the northern regions (in colonial times this area was in fact called Northern Region, though it has since been divided into three administrative regions: Northern, Upper East and Upper West). Following this logic, I refer to Ghana in colonial times as the Gold Coast colony, and reserve use of the name Ghana to describe the country after it gained independence in 1957. To preclude confusion between the modern state of Ghana and the ancient state from which its name is taken, the latter is referred to as Ancient Ghana. For the sake of consistency, the term 'Ancient Mali' has been used to refer to another vanished West African empire that was to bequeath its name to a modern state.

West Africa before 1500

The north-western 'bulge' of Africa can be divided into four economic units prior to 1500. The most northerly of these is the Mediterranean coastal belt of North Africa, an area which has had direct links with the other Mediterranean civilisations since ancient times, and which assimilated the influence of Islamic invaders as early as the 8th century AD, barely a century after the religion was founded. To the south of this lies the Sahara Desert, almost as large as Europe, yet devoid of permanent human settlement since time immemorial. South of the Sahara is the Sahel, an ever-expanding belt of dry savannah, thinly populated except where it's crossed by large rivers such as the Niger, Senegal and Volta. And further south still, there is the belt of moister savannah and forest that terminates at the Atlantic coast, the area we normally think of when we refer to West as opposed to North Africa, and the area to which the modern state of Ghana belongs.

Prior to the arrival of the Portuguese on the Gold Coast in the late 15th century, there had existed for centuries a trade relationship between these four regions. Merchant caravans would cross the Sahara from north to south, bringing with them salt, fine cloth and other luxury items which they would trade for goods such as gold, ivory and kola nuts. It is difficult to ascertain exactly when this epoch of trade started, but the available physical evidence would appear to show that a trade route across the Sahara similar to the modern one has existed since before 500BC. It can probably be assumed, too, that the spread of iron-age technology into the Sahel and areas further south before 600BC was influenced by trade routes which, for all we know, may have existed in some form or other for several millennia.

The specifics of this trade and of the societies south of the Sahel are difficult to determine prior to the 8th century AD. Some scholars suggest that there was a substantial increase in trade at around this time, based on the rather unconvincing argument that the first written record of the area south of the Sahel dates to AD773. It is just as likely that the reason no earlier records exist is linked to the rapid increase in written documentation in northwest Africa following the introduction of the Islamic faith in the 8th century AD. What is clear from this first written reference to the Sahel is firstly that its Arabic writer regarded it to be the 'Land of Gold' and secondly that it had long supported a powerful centralised trading empire which effectively acted as the 'middleman' between areas south of the Sahel and north of the Sahara.

This empire was the ancient state of Ghana, which – somewhat confusingly – lay completely to the north of its modern namesake. (Nkrumah's choice of the name Ghana in 1957 was largely symbolic, as the former Gold Coast was the first African colony to gain independence from a European power; contemporary claims by some local historians that many of modern Ghana's main groupings descend from Ancient Ghana have subsequently been discredited.) Ancient Ghana was founded by Mande-speakers at some time between AD300 and AD700; at its peak it spread for roughly 300km from north to south and 500km east to west between the rivers Niger and Senegal. The capital of Ancient Ghana at Kumbi Saleh (now a ruined city in southern Mauritania less than 100km from the Mali border) supported a population of roughly 15,000 and its emperor was able to muster an army numbering 200,000.

In AD992, Ancient Ghana was at the height of its powers, and its leadership decided to cement the hold on the trade routes out of the southern Sahara by capturing the important terminus of Awdaghast, 300km northwest of Kumbi Saleh. In the long term, this proved to be the downfall of the state, as the displaced Berbers of Awdaghast consolidated under a somewhat fanatical religious movement known as the Almoravids (meaning 'the people of the hermitage') and waged a *jihad* culminating in the capture of Kumbi Saleh in the year 1076. The Almoravids held the ancient Ghanaian capital for little more than a decade, but their brief tenure appears to have been the catalyst that caused the vast empire to fissure into several smaller and less powerful states, a situation that evidently persisted throughout the 12th century.

The beginning of the 13th century saw the emergence of a clear successor to Ancient Ghana in the omnipotence stakes, and this was the Ancient Mali empire founded by the Mandinka people of Kangaba. Accounts of the early days of this empire tend to be somewhat vague, but so far as anybody can ascertain the Mandinka had by 1205 taken over large parts of what had formerly been Ancient Ghana. In 1230, the leadership of Mali was assumed by Munsa Sundiata, an inspirational expansionist who had doubled the area of Mali by the time of his death in 1255. In 1240, Sundiata captured Kumbi Saleh, and relocated the capital to the fringe of the Sahara: the exact location selected is a matter of some debate amongst historians, but it evidently proved unsatisfactory, as all later accounts place the capital of Mali at Niani in the vicinity of the Guinea and Côte d'Ivoire border.

You might reasonably wonder what bearing all the above has on modern Ghana. The best answer, in the broadest sense, is simply that it puts paid to the common misconception that this part of Africa was some sort of stagnant backwater prior to the arrival of Europeans. More specifically, the area that lies within the modern state of Ghana played a palpable role in the trade patterns of this era – it was, indeed, the empires of the Sahel that controlled the southern end of the Saharan caravan routes, but it was through a more localised trade system involving the people of the moist savannah and rainforest region that they obtained most of their trade goods. Centuries ago, Ghana was the major supplier of kola nuts to the empires of the Sahel, as well as an important source of ivory. Of more lasting significance, the rainforest belt of modern Ghana was in medieval times, as it would be in the era of coastal trade and remains today, one of the region's richest sources of gold – the gold that not only lay at the heart of the trade route across the Sahara to

Morocco, but would later be one of the factors that caused the Portuguese to set sail in search of a trade route to sub-Saharan Africa.

Another lasting effect of the cross-Sahara trade was the spread of Islam into West Africa. It is not certain when or how deeply Islam first took hold in the region, but the writings of the Arab Al-Bakri in 1067 testify to the presence of a permanent Islamic community situated roughly 10km from Kumbi Saleh. While it is clear from this that the rulers of Ancient Ghana were not converts, the fact that this community boasted 12 mosques suggests it was reasonably significant.

The rulers of Ancient Mali almost certainly *were* Muslim converts right from the empire's earliest days. As early as 1200, Mansa Uli of Ancient Mali undertook a pilgrimage to Mecca. More famous was the pilgrimage of Mansa Musa in 1324–6, when the empire would have been at its economic prime. Contemporary records state that Musa gave away so many gifts of gold that the market for the metal was seriously undermined for some time after. His visit also put Ancient Mali on the world map in the most literal sense; the West African Empire first appeared by name on an Arabic map drawn up in 1339. And it is well documented that Musa returned home with several Islamic scholars who did much to entrench the exotic religion among the common people of Ancient Mali, and were responsible for designing the mud-and-stick style of mosque construction that visitors to modern Ghana will see in places like Larabanga and Wa.

Islam was the state religion of the Songhai Empire, centred to the north of what is now Burkina Faso. One of several small empires that were ruled by the Mansa of Ancient Mali following the collapse of Ancient Ghana, Songhai was revived in the mid-15th century by a leader called Sunni Ali, from his capital at the Niger River port of Gao, and it replaced Ancient Mali as the dominant Sahelian state from roughly 1464. One of the most powerful of Songhai rulers, Askia Mohammed, made the pilgrimage to Mecca in the 1490s, after which Islam was forced on the commoners of the empire. The Songhai Empire collapsed in 1591, following an attack on Gao by an army from Morocco. This event is generally seen as signalling the beginning of what many historians refer to as the West African interior's 'Dark Age', a 300-year period of economic stagnation attributable less to any one single attack than to the reorientation of trade patterns that followed the arrival of Portugal at the Gold Coast in 1471.

Ghana before 1500

On the basis of archaeological evidence, it has been established that modern-day Ghana was inhabited by humans 300,000 years ago, though current knowledge of human movements prior to this would suggest that the country has been occupied for millions of years. The earliest people to inhabit the region were hunter-gatherers, of whom little concrete can be said. It has yet to be determined when agriculture and pastoralism were adopted in the area, but this could have been as early as around 5000BC. Certainly by 2000BC both exotic creatures such as cattle and indigenous ones such as guinea fowl were being raised in domesticity, while archaeological findings near Kintampo demonstrate that substantial villages had been established at this time – a sure indication that hunter-gathering was no longer the predominant lifestyle in what are now Ashanti and Brong-Ahafo Regions. From around AD1000, it appears that an increased trend towards urbanisation was under way, with population centres of more than 2,000 people forming in the central and northern parts of what is now Ghana, presumably as a result of an economy that depended increasingly on trade with the great empires of the Sahel.

Oral tradition suggests that most modern Ghanaian population groups migrated to their present homeland from elsewhere in West Africa. The traditions widely agree that these migrants moved into territory occupied by the Guan, who are still regarded by other Ghanaians to be the true aboriginals of the country, though they are now assimilated into more recently arrived groups, with the exception of a few isolated Guan pockets at places such as Adokrom, Winneba and Efutu. It is difficult to tell whether these migration traditions reflect the influx of an entire group of people who would presumably have gained territory through conquest, or whether they relate to a small group of migrants who formed a ruling class over the existing occupants of an area. What does seem reasonably certain is that the modern country's broad pattern of population had taken a recognisable shape by the late 15th century, when the Portuguese arrived at the coast.

The people of modern Ghana are generally divided into four main regional groupings, each of which shares a similar language and culture. The Mole-Dagbani of the Northern Region were possibly the first to establish their approximate modern territory; tradition has it that they migrated from the Lake Chad region in the 13th century, settling briefly at Pusiga (on the modern border with Togo) before establishing the Mamprusi kingdom at Gambaga. Other northern chieftaincies such as Dagomba, Nanumba and Mossi are traditionally regarded to be offshoots of the Mamprusi, and even today secession disputes in most parts of the region are referred to the Chief of Gambaga (known as the 'Nayiri'), quite possibly the oldest extant chieftaincy in modern Ghana. The only significant exception to the above generalisations regarding the people of the Northern Region is the Gonja Kingdom, which is traditionally said to have been founded by Mande migrants from Ancient Mali in the early 16th century.

As a result of its proximity to the ancient empires of the Sahel, the Northern Region has enjoyed a strong Islamic influence for centuries, though exactly when and how this exotic religion reached the area is a matter of conjecture – some sources place its arrival as early as the 13th century, while others date it to the 17th. This discrepancy in dates might be accounted for by a long delay between the establishment of the first Islamic settlements in the northern regions and a more widespread acceptance of the religion. It has been suggested that the large-scale influx of Islamic ideas into present-day Ghana was blocked for centuries by a powerful anti-Islamic kingdom in what is now Burkina Faso, but this would not have prevented Islamic traders from establishing their own settlements along the main trade routes through the region. The mud-and-stick mosques found in several villages in the northwest of modern Ghana almost certainly pinpoint some of the country's earliest Islamic settlements but, since the antiquity of these mosques is open to debate, it is difficult to draw any firm conclusions about when Islam first reached these villages.

The area to the east of Lake Volta is inhabited by the Ewe, 15th-century migrants from eastern Nigeria. Ewe society is the least centralised of any in modern Ghana; each of the roughly 130 small Ewe chieftaincies is entirely

THE AKAN

The most numerically significant of Ghana's four ethno-linguistic groupings, the Akans of the southern and central part of the country embrace several dozen culturally similar and historically allied peoples, the best known of whom are probably the Ashanti of the Kumasi area and the Fante of the central coast. Most travellers to Ghana will come into regular contact with several Akan cultural institutions, as the country's two main travel circuits pass almost exclusively through Akan territories. Even those who travel further afield – into the Ewe heartland of Volta Region for instance – will soon recognise the Akan influence over the cultural and political organisation of many of their neighbours.

Every Akan village has its chief, whose position is not purely hereditary. Most, although generally of matrilineal aristocratic birth, are selected by a Council of Elders for their perceived capabilities and may be stripped of their powers if they do not perform satisfactorily or indulge in tyrannical behaviour. Practically throughout Ghana the power of the chief is denoted by his possession of the royal stool, which is typically made of wood and blackened after the death of the monarch (notable exceptions being the famous golden stool of Ashanti and the silver stool of Mampong). Akan chiefs are referred to as having been enstooled when they ascend to power and destooled should they lose that position. In many Akan territories, a traditional hierarchy of chiefs is maintained – the King of Ashanti, for instance, is considered paramount to the chiefs of such vassal states as Mampong and Jauben, who in turn preside over several small local chieftaincies. It is customary in Akan societies as well as in other parts of Ghana for visitors to a village to pay their respects to the chief, a custom that is still enforced in villages receiving few foreign visitors.

Most Akan societies show remarkably similar political structures. Every chief is served by a Council of Elders, a body to which he must refer all important matters and which has the power to destool him. Another very important figure is the queen mother, a misleading title since she will not necessarily be the mother of a queen, but serves as spiritual mother to the chief. She will work closely with the Council of Elders in selecting a new chief, will sit in on all council meetings and preside over all births and menstruation rites. Other key figures include the Akyeame, the chief's official spokesman and carrier of a royal staff, and the Adontenhene, the leader of the main military body. Some Akan societies are divided into several *asafo*, military companies that play an important role in defence as well as in the arts (see box *Posuban shrines*, page 132), and is one of the few Akan institutions to follow purely patrilineal lines of inheritance.

The basic unit of traditional Akan society is the extended family, an institution that is maintained along matrilineal lines, evidently on the basis that one can always be certain of the identity of a child's mother. In modern Ghana, patrilineal inheritance lines are now assuming greater importance, and (in urban areas particularly) the nuclear family is valued more highly by many than the extended one. Traditionally, the Akan regard every person to be comprised of three parts: blood, semen and soul. Blood, the most significant, is inherited from the mother as a signifier of family. Semen is the father's contribution, and determines personality and other individual attributes. The soul is believed to be the part of God that enters each child at birth.

Interestingly, the Akan regard a person's soul to be linked to the day of the week on which they were born. For this reason, most Ghanaians' first name is not a given name, but one determined by their day of birth. It is the child's second name that is chosen by the parents eight days after birth, and is normally that of a respected family member, in the belief that the child will have some of the attributes of the person after whom it has been named. Names associated with the day of birth are as follows:

Day	Male	Female
Sunday	Kwasi	Akosua, Asi, Ese
Monday	Kwadwo, Kojo	Adwoa, Ajao
Tuesday	Kwabena, Kobina	Abena, Araba
Wednesday	Kwaku	Akua
Thursday	Yao, Ekow	Yaa
Friday	Kofi	Afua, Afia, Efua
Saturday	Kwame, Kwamena	Ama

The religious beliefs of the Akan are too complex to do justice to here. Briefly, all Akan societies believe in one omnipotent God, but also pay homage to any number of minor local deities (some villages in Ghana have more than 70 local shrines, which may take the form of trees or rocks or any other natural feature) and like most African societies place high emphasis on the veneration of ancestors. Many Akan villages have a totem, often a particular type of animal that may not be killed or eaten by members of that village. Selection of the totem is often bound up in the oral history of that village. The people of Baobeng-Fiema, for instance, believe the sacred monkeys descend from villagers transformed into monkeys by the magical powers of a king who died before he could return them to human form.

At some point visitors are likely to encounter one of the most remarkable aspects of Akan society: its colourful and vibrant funerals. Unusually, Ghanaian societies tend to separate the burial ceremony from the actual funeral – generally by at least three months, but sometimes by as long as two years! At the risk of great oversimplification, burial is generally a quiet and dignified moment, though often preceded by wailing and singing, and is followed by at least nine days of quiet mourning and fasting by close relatives. The funeral itself was traditionally held on a Monday or Thursday several months after the person died, but is now most often held on a Saturday for pragmatic reasons. The general tone is one of celebration rather than mourning, marked by exuberant drumming and dancing, not to say heavy drinking – on attending a Ghanaian funeral, you can't help but feel that it displays an altogether more convincing belief in some sort of afterlife than its sombre Christian equivalent.

For a good overview of Akan culture, I recommend Peter Sarong's book *Ghana in Retrospect* (Ghana Publishing Company, 1974), which is readily available and inexpensive in most Accra bookshops.

autonomous (in other words there is no paramount chief), though the larger Anlo Kingdom based around the port of Keta is something of an exception. The other important grouping of the east is the Ga-Adangbe, which consists of the Ga people of the Accra coastal plain and the Adangbe of Ada and Somanya. The Ga and Adangbe have practically identical languages and they share several customs such as ritual circumcision and a defined order of child-naming, though over the centuries they have adopted a great many customs from the neighbouring Akan. Like the Ewe, the Ga-Adangbe are originally from eastern Nigeria, and it is more than probable that the Ga had settled the Accra area and gelled into a cohesive state by the time the Portuguese arrived.

The most significant population group in modern Ghana, territorially and numerically, is the Akan (see box *The Akan* on pages 12–13). The Akan comprise more than half the country's population and inhabit five of its ten administrative regions: Western, Central, Eastern, Ashanti and Brong-Ahafo. Although every Akan village has its own chief, political centralisation into larger kingdoms has been a recurrent feature of Akan history, from the 14th-century Bono Kingdom of Techiman to more recent entities such as Denkyira, Ashanti and Fante. Superficially, oral traditions relating to the origin of the Akan vary greatly from one society to another, but in essence they tend to run along one of two basic themes: a migration from somewhere further north, or a sudden emergence from the sky or a hole in the ground or somewhere equally improbable. There does, however, appear to be a reasonable degree of consensus among historians that the Akan migrated to modern-day Ghana from the Sahel. Since most traditions claim Bono as the cradle of the Akan, and Bono was firmly established as a gold-mining and trading empire under King Akumfi Ameyaw I (1328–63), any migration must have occurred before the end of the 13th century. On this evidence, it seems reasonable to assume that the Akan migrated to their modern territory as a result of the dissolution of Ancient Ghana. It strikes me that those Akan societies lacking a migration tradition could be older groupings which adopted Akan culture either through long periods of association with or colonisation by one of the larger Akan empires.

The Gold Coast 1471–1665

In 1415, Portugal captured the Moroccan port of Ceuta, one first small step in an era of naval exploration that would result in the circumnavigation of Africa before the end of the 15th century. The motives that lay behind the Portuguese crown backing such a venture were manifold. Portugal believed that by sailing south around Africa they would be able to wrest control of the lucrative eastern spice trade and, although the Portuguese had no idea just how large an obstacle Africa would prove to be, they were ultimately correct in this. Religion, too, was an important factor, in that the Portuguese crown was eager to forge links with the Christian kingdom of Prester John (a legend referred to in many medieval writings, probably based on rumours emanating from Christian Ethiopia) and to spread Christianity to areas lying beyond the Islamic lands north of the Sahara. Finally, through having a foothold in Morocco, Portugal was keenly aware of the quantity of gold being transported across the Sahara, and recognised that finding a sea route to the source of the gold would be a more realistic goal than trying to take direct control of the Arabic caravan routes through the Sahara.

In 1471, the Portuguese arrived at the village which was subsequently named Elmina after the Portuguese *De Costa da el Mina de Ouro* – 'the Coast of Gold Mines' (a phrase which would also give rise to the moniker 'Gold Coast') – and entered into trade with a powerful chief whose name is recorded as Caramansa. Eleven years later, with a written lease from Caramansa, the Portuguese built the castle of St George on a rocky outcrop next to Elmina. Architecturally reminiscent of the castles built by the Crusaders, St George was separated from the village by a dry moat and its strongest bastion faced inland, suggesting that the Portuguese perceived their greatest threat of attack to come not from the sea but from the interior. St George was the first of several forts and lodges established by the Portuguese – in 1515 and 1523 respectively they built forts at Axim and Shama, close to the mouths of the rivers Ankobra and Pra (both of which flowed from parts of the interior rich in gold), and later in the 16th century they constructed a short-lived trading lodge in what is now downtown Accra.

Elmina, however, was to remain the centre of the Portuguese gold trade throughout their 150-year tenure on the Gold Coast. The fact that Portugal found such bountiful gold at Elmina was no mere coincidence. On the contrary, Elmina's importance as a salt-production centre gave Portugal effortless access to a trade route established at least a century before its arrival, connecting Elmina to the Akan gold mines near what are now Tarkwa and Obuasi via the Empire of Eguafo. Gold was far and away the most important export from the West African coast at this time – £100,000 worth annually throughout the 16th century, or roughly 10% of the world supply – but surviving Portuguese ledgers show that there was also a thriving trade in ivory, cotton and animal hides, while major imports included metal pots and bowls, beads, leatherware, alcoholic spirits and guns. Odd as it may seem with hindsight, the Portuguese also imported to Elmina a quantity of slaves, captured or bought in Benin during the period 1486 to 1506, and at São Tomé after 1506.

Some readers may wonder why Ghana (as opposed to, say, Senegal or Liberia) became the centre of European activities in West Africa. First and foremost, this is because Ghana is the only West African country with a coast that lies close to significant gold deposits. But this alone doesn't really explain why all but two of the roughly 60 forts and trading lodges built on the Gulf of Guinea were sited in what is now Ghana – especially as many of these forts were built to service the slave trade rather than the gold trade. Just as important as the presence of gold inland was the physical nature of the Gold Coast. Studded with large rocky outcrops rather than mangrove swamps and sprawling shallow lagoons, Ghana boasts a great many good natural harbours, easily approached by ship, but also easily guarded and protected, with ample local material for constructing fortified buildings.

It is also interesting to note that Portugal's tenure on the Gold Coast was in no respect colonialism as we think of it today. The Portuguese had no jurisdiction beyond their forts, which were built with the permission of the local chiefs on land that was formally leased for the purpose. The Portuguese did make a concerted effort to spread Christianity, but even this was restricted to the immediate vicinity of the forts. They made no serious attempt to venture inland, nor to capture the Akan gold mines, but instead traded with the local chiefs and merchants on an even footing. And, it should be noted, what is true of Portugal is largely true of the European powers that followed. The arrival of the Portuguese ushered in an era of trade that lasted more than three centuries. Only when describing events from the mid-19th century onwards is it valid to talk in terms of colonists.

The level of Portuguese trade out of the Gold Coast had probably peaked as early as 1530, its decline thereafter a result largely of the increasingly widespread Portuguese global 'empire' that spread from Goa, Malindi and Mozambique in the Indian Ocean to South America and the Caribbean. Nevertheless, Portuguese dominance of the Gold Coast was not substantially threatened in the 16th century, although it did not go entirely unchallenged. The first English ships reached the west coast of Africa in roughly 1530, and in 1542 a French ship landed at Dixcove where it purchased 28kg of gold. From the 1550s, non-Portuguese ships were an increasingly common sight off the coast – in 1553, Captain Thomas Wyndham returned with a stash of gold which he sold for £10,000, and a few years later the coast was visited by Francis Drake as part of his successful attempt to circumnavigate the globe. The Dutch, by comparison, were latecomers, and when their first ship did arrive on the Gold Coast, blown off course en route to Brazil in 1593, its captain was imprisoned – though he still managed to return home with a healthy amount of gold.

That the Dutch were the first to seriously challenge Portugal's monopoly on the Gold Coast is often attributed to the tension that already existed between these two countries in Europe. In reality, economics was probably the greater factor. The first Dutch attack on Elmina was an unsuccessful naval bombardment in 1596. From that time on, between 10 and 20 privately owned Dutch ships visited the Gold Coast annually. The Portuguese responded to this influx of new traders first by attacking Dutch ships whenever possible, and secondly by punishing brutally any African caught dealing with a rival European power. The offender's ears would be cut off for a first infringement; a second offence was rewarded with execution. Possibly as a result of this cruel policy, the chief of the Asubu sent two ambassadors to Holland requesting that a fort be erected at his capital 20km east of Elmina at Moree. In 1612, the Dutch did just this, shipping skilled artisans and the requisite materials direct from Holland so that the fort would be built too quickly for the Portuguese to mount an attack during its construction.

With a secure foothold at Moree, the Dutch were positioned to mount a concerted attack on Portugal's Gold Coast possessions, especially after 1621 when the powerfully backed West India Company (WIC) was formed in Amsterdam. By 1622, some 40 Dutch ships were assigned to the Gold Coast trade. Then, in 1630, what was in effect a Dutch navy took to the Atlantic, capturing several Portuguese possessions in the West Indies and Brazil before turning its attention on the West African coast. After an aborted naval attack, Elmina fell in 1637, bombarded from the nearest hill. Shama followed in the same year, and Axim was captured by Dutch boats in 1642, effectively ending Portugal's influence in this part of the world (though Portugal would remain a major player for centuries to come in the Indian Ocean and on the coast of what is now Angola).

The Dutch capture of Portugal's Gold Coast possessions signalled the beginning of a period of intense rivalry for dominance between several European powers, some of which had little lasting impact on what is now

Ghana. The Swedes, for instance, occupied Fort Carolusbourg, which they built at Cape Coast in 1653, for a mere eleven years. The Brandenburgers built Fort Gross Friedrichsburg at Pokesu (Prince's Town) in 1683, only to vacate it in 1717. Even the French, later to become so powerful in West Africa, had little influence on the Gold Coast, never occupying any one place for longer than a decade.

A more important rival to Dutch dominance was Denmark, though on the whole the Dutch tolerated the Danish presence in a tacit alliance against stronger powers. Aside from their rather obscure outpost at Keta, the Danes restricted their activities on the Gold Coast to Osu in modern-day Accra. The Danish castle at Osu grew to be one of the most impressive on the Gold Coast, and the Danes occupied it almost continuously from 1642 to 1850, when it was sold to Britain. The most significant interruption in the Danish occupation of Osu occurred in 1681-3, when the castle was captured and occupied by Portugal; part of a rather desperate last bid at recapturing some of the Gold Coast trade.

The first British 'West Africa Company', formed in 1618, met with little success – its efforts at occupying the Gold Coast climaxed in 1640 with the construction at Cormantin of a small trading lodge that burnt down shortly after it was built, possibly with the assistance of a Dutch saboteur. More successful was the snappily titled 'Company of Royal Adventurers of English Trading to Africa', established in 1660 with a royal charter and the hearty backing of the Duke of York (later King James II, and – take note trivia lovers – rewarded for his efforts in backing the 'Adventurers' by being not only the James of Accra's James Town, but the York of the USA's New York, known as New Amsterdam until it was captured from the Dutch by his charges).

In 1665, the British company launched a concerted attack on Holland's West African possessions, capturing the forts at Takoradi, Shama, Moree and Anomabu, as well as Fort Carolusbourg at Cape Coast, which the Dutch had occupied since 1664. The British company was unable to hold on to all of its newly captured forts, so it concentrated its efforts on ensuring that Fort Carolusbourg was impregnable, converting the modest fort into a castle covering roughly three-quarters of the area it does today. The British company had its foothold on the Gold Coast, one that was strengthened with its transformation to the wealthily backed Royal Africa Company in 1672, and by the end of the century Britain had become, if anything, more economically powerful than its more established rival. The reason for this is perfectly simple: instead of trading in gold, Britain decided to enter an altogether more lucrative arena of trade. The British capture of Cape Coast in 1665 can be seen as the critical point in the process that would, by 1700, cause a Dutch official to bemoan that 'the Gold Coast had changed into a virtual Slave Coast'.

The Slave Coast 1665–1807

However convenient it might be to see the trade in slaves as an abomination introduced to Africa by Europeans, there is no escaping the reality that a slave trade was in existence from the very earliest days of the trans-Sahara caravans, when people captured in the sub-Sahelian region were transported across the desert to be sold into domestic bondage in North Africa and parts of Europe. Nor can it be denied that a slave class has formed a part of practically every centralised African society on record, at least until modern times. And while it is true that in many past African societies slaves have had the opportunity to climb the social ladder, it is also true that in many such societies slaves were treated as sub-human, and cruelly sacrificed to mark special occasions or entreat deities.

None of which makes Africa in any way unusual, since slavery in name or in kind has been a feature of most ancient societies until this century. It is merely worth noting that the slave trade out of the Gold Coast emerged in an environment where not only slavery but also trading in slaves were established practices, just as it should be noted that the Europeans who conducted this trade came from societies where it was customary to hold public executions for crimes as paltry as stock theft, and to burn alive witches and other perceived heretics on a stake. Viewed from the lofty moral heights of the early 21st century, there is a certain uncomfortable irony in the realisation that the very earliest form of slave trade entered into by Europeans on the Gold Coast involved not the export of slaves but their import, as captives bought by Portuguese merchants from African sellers in Benin were sold to African buyers in Elmina.

Nevertheless, the trans-Atlantic slave trade is a singular event in human history, not simply because it operated on an unprecedented scale but also because it was so ruthlessly well-organised, and so shattering and wide-ranging in its effects. Before the arrival of Europeans, slaves were generally incidental captives of inter-tribal war, relatively few in number, and in most cases able to integrate themselves into the society that enslaved them. By the time the trans-Atlantic slave trade hit its peak, it would be an understatement to say that the capture of slaves had been transformed into the *raison d'être* for war; closer to the mark perhaps to say that the entire West African interior had deteriorated into a hunting ground wherein slave raiders with firearms attacked village after comparatively defenceless village, trading their booty at the coastal forts for yet more firepower. It is estimated that between 12 and 20 million Africans were transported across the Atlantic between the late 17th century and early 19th, a five-week trip in conditions so cramped and unhygienic that it was not unusual for a boat to lose half its human cargo in passage. It is impossible to tell how many more people – those who were too young or too old or too weak to be saleable – died in the course of the raids.

Most of us are familiar with the fate of the victims of these raids. Rather less well documented is the devastating affect that the slave trade had on African society. It has been noted, for instance, that many traditional industries were lost to the Gold Coast interior – iron-smelting and gold-mining are good examples – as the product of these industries became increasingly worthless by comparison with slaves, and their practitioners were taken in to bondage. Worse still was the arms race that built up between neighbouring groups, as in the 17th century Britain alone supplied around 100,000 guns annually to West Africa – and it is not difficult to see how this situation forced even the most unwilling of chiefs into finding slaves to trade for the firearms they needed to protect themselves. For two centuries, Africa lost a high proportion of its most able-bodied men and women to the slave trade. In return, it received items that were at best of no lasting value – alcoholic spirits and tobacco – and at worst entirely destructive.

In the 16th and 17th centuries, the Gold Coast was spared the worst of this. Both Portugal and later Holland made it policy not to buy slaves at the Gold Coast – not for any moral reason, but because they believed (correctly as it turned out) that the slave trade would interfere with the gold trade. Instead they concentrated their slaving efforts further south, along the stretch of coast between modern-day Nigeria and Angola. This was to change towards the end of the 17th century, firstly because the recently arrived British had difficulty breaking into the Dutch-controlled gold trade, and secondly as a result of the rise of the Akwamu Empire, which at its peak controlled a 350km stretch of coast east of Accra crossing into what is now Togo, but at no point had access to the gold mines at Akan. The British and to a lesser extent the Danes started trading in slaves from around 1665, a situation that was rapidly exploited by the Akwamu, and the floodgates were opened in 1698 when the RAC forsook its monopoly on British trade, allowing any British boat to trade freely, provided a 10% custom was paid to the company. This policy was a failure in so far as few of the so-called 'ten-percenters' actually paid the required levy, but it did ensure that the market for slaves expanded exponentially from 1698 onwards, with Anomabu in particular becoming a major centre for 'free trade'.

In the late 17th century, two empires dominated the interior immediately north of the coast. These were Akwamu, already mentioned above, and a much older Akan empire called Denkyira, the region's main repository of gold-working skills and the centre of the gold trade to the coast. In 1701, Denkyira was conquered by the recently established Ashanti Empire of Kumasi, creating what was perhaps the most radical power shift in the Ghanaian interior since Portugal had first arrived at the coast. One result of Denkyira's defeat was that the lease papers for Elmina Castle passed into the hands of the Ashanti, who were far more interested in empire-building and trading slaves for guns than they were in such pastoral pursuits as scratching around for gold. Another was that the flow of gold to the coast, already stemmed by the emergent slave trade, dried up to such an extent that in 1703 the governor of Elmina formally requested that Amsterdam allow him to abandon the gold trade in favour of slaves.

The threat posed by the rampant Ashanti, whose king was courted by both the major European powers almost as soon as he conquered Denkyira, appears to have been pivotal in the expansion of the Fante state in the early 18th century. Based in the area around Mankessim and Anomabu, the Fante were in 1700 the most powerful and wealthy of perhaps 20 small Akan kingdoms running along the coast west of Accra, all of which were linked by a common culture and used to having a degree of control over trade with the Dutch and English, both of whose headquarters lay in this part of the country. Between 1707 and 1720, the Fante gradually exerted control over all these groups, including the Oguaa of Cape Coast and Edina of Elmina, using a combination of force and coercion as it became obvious to all that unity was their best weapon against an Ashanti attack. Ashanti, meanwhile, grew in power with almost every passing year, capturing Akwamu in 1730, Brong-Ahafo in 1744–45, and much of what are now Burkina Faso and the northern regions of Ghana in 1745–50. By the end of this period of expansion, Ashanti was probably bigger than Ghana is today, and along with Fante it was by far the most dominant power in what is now Ghana. Unexpectedly, perhaps, the two empires maintained a relatively peaceful co-existence, motivated partly by the recognition that a tacit alliance was the best way to exclude other kingdoms from the lucrative coastal trade, but also enforced to a degree by the British and Dutch, on whom they relied for weapons.

The slave trade out of the Gold Coast continued unabated throughout the 18th century. Roughly 5,000 slaves passed annually through each of the main British trading posts, Cape Coast and Anomabu, and were stored in cold, dark dungeons that are chilling to visit today. The Dutch tried in vain to revive the flagging gold trade in 1702 by building a new fort they named 'Good Hope' at Senya Beraku; ten years later the fort was extended to include slave dungeons. Ashanti prospered, as Kumasi lay at the heart of all three major trade routes to the coast west of Accra; and, although it was forbidden for an Ashanti to enslave another Ashanti, their frequent military expeditions and slave raids ensured the flow of human cargo to the coast never abated.

As the 18th century drew to a close, the anti-slave lobby became an increasingly powerful voice in Europe, a result not only of the strengthening liberal attitudes that emerged following the industrial revolution, but also of a greater public awareness as to how the slave trade actually operated following several publications on the subject. In 1804, Denmark abolished the slave trade, followed by Britain in 1807, the USA in 1808, and Holland, France, Portugal and Spain between 1814 and 1817. Also in 1817, several of the above nations signed a Reciprocal Search Treaty, which in effect allowed Britain to search boats captained by people of other nationalities. The slave trade was subdued by this, but it was by no means halted – it became common practice among slavers to throw all their human cargo overboard at the approach of a British naval patrol. Britain soon recognised that it would take nothing less than the abolition of slavery to end the trade, and it banned slavery throughout its colonies in 1833, followed by France in 1848, the USA in 1865 (after a bloody civil war dominated by the issue) and finally Brazil in 1888.

The build-up to colonialism 1806–1902

By 1800, Britain was the major European trading power on the Gold Coast and, although the Danes were to retain a presence there until 1850 and the Dutch until 1872, developments in the 19th century, in hindsight though perhaps not at the time, show a clear trend towards British colonisation. So far as the interior was concerned, a clear pattern had emerged by 1800 wherein various Fante chieftaincies acted as middlemen between the Ashanti and British traders. This arrangement suited the British, who believed that if Ashanti were to take full control of the interior it would be able to dictate terms of trade to Britain. It suited the Fante too, since without the tacit backing of Britain they would never have had the military prowess to resist an Ashanti invasion. The arrangement was, however, less agreeable to the Ashanti, who lost out substantially by having to deal through the Fante. Nevertheless, a few minor skirmishes aside, Fante and Ashanti had a reasonably healthy relationship in the second half of the 18th century, several times combining forces against upstart states to ensure they retained their joint trade monopoly.

The relationship between the European occupants of the forts and the surrounding chieftaincies changed little in essence between the construction of St George in 1482 and 1820. Theirs was a commercial not a colonial relationship: European control barely extended beyond the forts, and even those chieftaincies closest to the forts remained autonomous political units, though inevitably they were offered a degree of protection by their well-armed European neighbours. This long-standing balance was to waver in the first decade of the 19th century, partly as a result of Britain's wish to curb the slave trade at its Ashanti roots from 1807 onwards, no less because of escalating tension between Fante and Ashanti following a military skirmish between these states in 1806.

There are two main reasons why the Ashanti attacked Fante in 1806. The first is that Fante, always more a federation of disparate states than a cohesive empire, had been weakened by internal disputes such as the wars between Oguaa and Komenda in 1788, Anomabu and Mankessim in 1789, Oguaa and Anomabu in 1802 and Komenda and Shama in 1805. The second was the escalation of a long-standing dispute over trade with Elmina Castle. Ashanti had held the lease to the castle since 1701, for which reason they believed they had the right to trade with its Dutch occupants directly, but the Fante regularly blocked Ashanti access to Elmina in the late 18th century, and even attacked the town on a number of occasions. The above points noted, it was inevitable that sooner or later the vast Ashanti empire would decide to take direct control of the coast, and the remarkable thing is that they waited so long to try.

Between 1806 and 1874, there were nine military clashes between Ashanti and Fante, and three more were averted at the last moment. Up until 1820, these clashes were wholly internal affairs, resulting in one or other of the two dozen or so Fante states being conquered by Ashanti. The Fante, however, refused to recognise Ashanti's traditional rights of conquest, and tension between the two states meant that trade of all forms ground to a virtual halt. In this the Fante were supported by the British, not only because Britain favoured dealing with several small competitive states over an Ashanti monolith, but also because it was eager to end the slave raids in which the Ashanti still indulged. To this end, the British parliament placed all the Gold Coast forts formerly run by its companies under Crown government in 1821. Three years later, Britain for the first time gave military support to the Fante, in a battle at the Adaamso River which ended in an Ashanti victory – one contemporary account claims that the wounded British governor was beheaded by his Ashanti counterpart, and that his head was taken to Kumasi as a trophy. In 1826, Britain and Ashanti clashed again at Akatamanso, to the north of Accra: a battle that ended in a resounding British victory. It would be three decades before another major clash took place between these powers.

By 1828, the British government was prepared to withdraw entirely from the Gold Coast, due to the high cost of maintaining the forts and the massive drop in trade following a decade of instability. In the end, however, it bowed to pressure from British merchants and the beleaguered Fante, selling the forts to a company called the London Committee of Merchants. In 1830, a new governor was installed, Gordon MacLean, who more than any other person would lay the foundation of future British rule. In 1831, MacLean pressed the humbled Ashanti into signing a tripartite treaty which required them to refrain from any further attacks on their southern neighbours. As a sign of good faith, the Ashanti left a large sum of gold with MacLean, to be returned after six years, as well as two Ashanti princes to be educated in Europe. Six years after the treaty was signed, MacLean returned the gold, and in 1841 the princes went back to Kumasi in order to help establish a Methodist mission there, creating a new atmosphere of trust between Ashanti and the British. In addition to his role as peacemaker, Maclean made great efforts to end the slave trade; and he turned around the Gold Coast economy, ushering in a new era of 'legitimate trade' as the value of exports leapt by 275% during the first decade of his governorship, and imports by more than 300%. This remarkably successful administration ended in 1843, when the British government decided to claim back the Gold Coast forts and to install its own governor. Many of Maclean's achievements were formalised with the so-called 'Bond of 1844', a sort of proto-protectorateship over several Fante states, in exchange for which the chiefs had to pledge allegiance to the Queen of England and give up practices regarded to be barbaric, such as human sacrifices and panyarring (the seizure of a debtor's relatives, to be sold into slavery if the debt wasn't met within a specified period). MacLean himself died in 1847, and was buried in the courtyard of Cape Coast Castle. It is said that the chiefs of southern states mourned his passing for months afterwards.

The two decades that followed the MacLean administration were relatively uneventful. In 1850, the year in which the governances of Sierra Leone and the Gold Coast were finally separated, Britain bought the forts at Keta and Osu from Denmark. It is doubtful that the British saw much use for these forts at the time of their purchase, but didn't want them falling into French or Dutch hands, and perhaps hoped to have more success than Denmark in curbing the clandestine slave trade running out of Keta. (As it turned out, Osu Castle would become the seat of government in 1876, a position it has retained to this day.) In 1852, the British authorities introduced a poll tax system which sparked a series of riots and battles (most famously the violent Anglo-Krobo confrontation that took place on Krobo Mountain) without ever raising a great deal of revenue – it was abandoned in 1861.

The year 1863 saw renewed tension between the British and Ashanti, caused by the former's refusal to hand over refugees from Ashanti justice. In 1864, the two armies clashed once again. The battle went the way of the Ashanti, largely because so many British troops died in an outbreak of fever or dysentery brought on by unusually heavy rain. It also signalled the beginning of a rush of events that would conspire to make the period 1867–74 of unparalleled decisiveness in the history of the Gold Coast.

The rush started in 1867, when Britain and Holland arrived at the mutual conclusion that every aspect of their increasingly unprofitable administrations would be improved were Britain to control a continuous strip of coast east of Cape Coast and the Dutch a strip of coast to the west of Elmina. The two countries signed the so-called 'Fort Exchange Treaty', much to the consternation of several Fante states, long allied to a nearby British fort and now suddenly forced to live alongside the Dutch, whom they regarded as foes due to their involvement with the Ashanti who still held the lease to Elmina fort. King Aggrey of Cape Coast led a protest against the treaty, and was arrested by the British and exiled to Sierra Leone. The arrest of Aggrey, along with widespread dissatisfaction with the new status quo, triggered the formation of the Fante Confederation. Founded at Mankessim in 1868, this was the first formal alliance incorporating all the Fante states from Axim to just east of Accra, and although it was to prove short-lived the movement had some success in preventing the Dutch from occupying forts they had traded with Britain. In 1871, Britain arrested the confederation leaders and imprisoned them for a month. In the following year, Holland finally limped away from the Gold Coast, selling its remaining possessions to Britain. In 1873, the Fante Confederation disbanded, having lost direction after the Dutch evacuation of the coast – and in any case riddled with leadership squabbles. By this stage, the British parliament was of the opinion that it would have to take one of two approaches to the governing of the increasingly fractious Gold Coast: in its own words, a 'very evil choice' between following the Dutch and withdrawing completely, or pursuing an active policy of territorial expansion and colonisation. On 24 July 1874, Britain formally declared the Gold Coast a Crown colony.

The withdrawal of Holland from Elmina proved to be the trigger of the notorious Anglo-Ashanti War of 1873–74. Fearing that Britain wouldn't honour the ancient lease, the Ashanti occupied Elmina in 1873. Britain responded with a naval bombardment that flattened the old town to the west of the castle, leaving around 20,000 people without a home. In 1874, British troops entered Ashanti for the first time, defeating its army at Bekwai and – after the Ashanti king refused to accept their initial terms of treaty – burning Kumasi to the ground. The treaty of Fomena, signed in Adanse towards the end of 1874, forced the Ashanti to renounce all claims on territories lying to the south of their core state, most of all Elmina. At the same time, several vassal states to the north (for instance Gonja, Bono and Dagomba) took advantage of the defeat to assert their independence from Ashanti, and so an empire that had once been larger than modern Ghana was reduced to an area similar in size to present-day Ashanti Region.

In its earliest incarnation, the Gold Coast colony was a fraction of the size of modern Ghana, with an identical coastline but barely extending more than 50km inland. So it might have remained were it not for the so-called 'Scramble for Africa', initiated in the late 1870s when Belgium and France entered into a race for control of the Congo. By 1888, most of the modern states of Africa had more or less taken shape, though not Ghana, presumably because its most interesting asset, the Gold Coast, had been British long before the scramble started. By the 1890s, however, both France and Germany were eying the interior of what is now Ghana. As a result of this, Britain extended its borders to cover the whole of the modern Western and Central provinces in 1893, while the northern border was settled with France in 1898 and the eastern border with Germany agreed in 1899 (though the latter was to move further east exactly 20 years later when the League of Nations divided German Togoland between Britain and France).

In the 1890s, Britain's attention turned once again to Ashanti, which it was desperate not to let fall into German or French hands. In 1891, British protectorateship was offered to Ashanti, and soundly rejected by the recently installed King Prempreh I. Britain decided it would have to install a British resident in Kumasi to prevent the French from doing the same, and so it was that in 1896 a British military expedition (whose numbers, incidentally, included the future Lord Baden Powell, just in case you ever wonder why the Scout movement regularly comes up as a topic of small talk with students in this part of the country!) entered Kumasi without firing a shot. Prempreh, along with many other members of the royal family, was arrested and imprisoned in Elmina Castle before being exiled to Sierra Leone and later the Seychelles. Britain then demanded that the remaining Ashanti elders in Kumasi hand over the Golden Stool (not so much the symbol of the king as its embodiment, handed down from generation to generation), a request that had been anticipated to the extent that they had a fake stool ready to hand to Britain (the fake is now on display in the Prempreh II Museum in Kumasi).

In 1900, the Ashanti rose one last time against British colonisation in the war named after its main instigator, Yaa Asantewaa, the Queen Mother of Ejisu. After heavy loss of life on both sides, Ashanti was defeated again in 1901 and yet another contingent of dignitaries, Yaa Asantewaa among them, was imprisoned and exiled to the Seychelles. On 1 January 1902, Ashanti was formally annexed to the British Gold Coast colony, along with the territories that today make up Ghana's three northern regions.

Gold Coast colony 1902–57

The Gold Coast, like most other British colonies in Africa, was run along the system of indirect rule, a sharp contrast to the French and Portuguese systems whereby African colonies were – in theory if not in practice – run as an extension of the so-called 'mother' country. The basic principle underlying indirect rule, as patented by Lord Lugard first in Uganda and later in Nigeria, was that traditional chiefs would continue to rule locally as before, but under the supervision of the colonial administration. The motivations for adopting this system were twofold. Firstly, Britain believed that the Gold Coast would be better served in the long run if it developed a system of government rooted in its own traditions rather than one imposed entirely from outside. More to the point, perhaps, the lack of funding and shortage of European manpower created by Britain's insistence that all colonies should be economically self-sufficient would have made it impossible for most colonial governors to rule in any other manner. Indirect rule was, in the words of the eminent Ghanaian historian Adu Boahen, 'in reality, the most indirect way of ruling directly'. It was also, doubtless, the cheapest.

The core problem with indirect rule as it was administered in the Gold Coast is that it undermined the very institution it was nominally designed to protect. A traditional chief in pre-colonial Ghana was not, as might be supposed, a hereditarily determined autocrat, but an appointee of the council of elders. And the elders who appointed a chief had not only a right to veto any ruling he made, but the customary right to remove him from the stool. Prior to the colonial era, then, the authority of the chief was rooted in the council of elders over whom he presided. Under Britain, the authority of the chief came from the colonial administration, a situation that was bound to become a problem the moment that the administration tried to enforce an unpopular ruling through the chief.

The first steps towards indirect rule took place in 1883, when all chiefs in the Gold Coast (then only a fraction of what is now Ghana) were required to apply for recognition by the colonial administration. The policy took a more formal shape with the formation of so-called 'Native Authorities', comprising a paramount chief and his main sub-chiefs; an institution which, to its credit, paved the way for the modern regional and district councils of Ghana. In reality, Britain often tried to appoint a chief who was wholly unacceptable to his subjects. The clearest example of this occurred in Ashanti, where King Prempreh I and many other important chiefs were held in exile from 1896 until 1924, while the British authorities attempted to gain recognition for a dummy king of their choosing. Even when Prempreh I was returned to the stool in 1926, it was as King of Kumasi rather than King of Ashanti. Only in 1935 did Britain come full circle and restore the Ashanti Confederacy Council which it had abolished following the Yaa Asantewaa War in 1901, at the same time allowing the recently enstooled King Prempreh II to assume his full traditional role.

Resistance to colonial rule emerged as early as 1897, when the Aboriginal Rights Protection Society successfully blocked a bill that would have made all physically unoccupied territory in the colony the property of the colonial administration. It appeared in a more orchestrated form in the wake of World War I with the formation of the National Congress of British West Africa (NCBWA) by the Gold Coast barrister, Casely Hayford. The formation of the NCBWA is widely seen as the beginning of a formal split between educated nationalists, who were excluded from government under the system of indirect rule, and the uneducated and generally conservative traditional chiefs who gained from it. The inaugural meeting of the NCBWA took place in Accra in 1920, bringing together a total of 20 nationalist delegates from the Gambia, Nigeria, Sierra Leone and of course the Gold Coast. The delegates drew up a list of demands; notably that the government should provide equal job opportunities for Africans and Europeans with equivalent qualifications, that at least half of the legislative council in all countries should be freely elected, and that the colonial administration should cease interfering in the selection and removal of traditional chiefs. An NCBWA delegation was sent to London to present these demands to the Colonial Secretary, but was refused an appointment. Nevertheless, a great many changes along the lines suggested by the organisation had been set in place by the time of Casely Hayford's death in 1930, by which time the organisation was close to disintegration.

It was World War II, however, that proved decisive in ending the colonial era in the Gold Coast as elsewhere in Africa. In the Gold Coast specifically, at least 65,000 African volunteers were shipped to fight in the European war (mostly in East Africa and Burma), where they were exposed on a daily basis to the democratic and anti-imperialistic ideals of the Allied Forces. The Atlantic Charter signed by Roosevelt and Churchill stated categorically that the signatories would 'respect the right of all peoples to choose the form of government under which they will live'. Churchill would later retract the statement insofar as colonies were concerned, but the American government affirmed that by all people they meant *all* people. When these African servicemen returned home after the war, they had high hopes of benefiting from the democratic ideals for which they had been obliged to fight. Instead, in at least 50,000 cases in the Gold Coast alone, the ex-servicemen returned home to unemployment, not to say a capital city whose population had increased threefold as a result of short-lived employment opportunities created by the European war.

In the Gold Coast more than any other British colony, the immediate post-war period saw events move with remarkable speed and purpose. In 1946, Governor Burns responded to the mood of the time with a new constitution that allowed 18 of the 30 seats in the colony's Legislative Council to be elected, 13 by the Provincial Council of Chiefs of the southern Regions and Ashanti, and five by the small number of registered African voters in Accra, Cape Coast and Sekondi. In 1947, the United Gold Coast Convention (UGCC), formed by Dr Danquah, demanded 'self-government within the shortest possible time' and objected to the new constitution on the valid grounds that the Provisional Council of Chiefs was seen as a stooge organisation by most commoners, that the electoral roll in the above mentioned cities was laughably unrepresentative, and that the Northern Region had no vote at all. November 1947 saw the return from 12 years in the USA and UK of the nationalist and pan-Africanist Dr Kwame Nkrumah, invited home by Danquah to act as Secretary General to the UGCC.

On February 28 1948, colonial officers opened fire on a peaceful march organised by ex-servicemen to deliver a petition to the governor. Three marchers were killed, including the leader of the ex-servicemen, and another 12 died in the rioting that followed. This event proved decisive in the history of modern Africa. The Gold Coast was Britain's 'model colony', the most prosperous, educated and organised of them all, and the administration reasoned that if this could happen in the Gold Coast, then colonialism in Africa was surely doomed. Even before 28 February 1948, Britain had generally seen self-government as the end goal for its colonies, but it had been thinking ahead to a time decades, perhaps even centuries away. After 28 February, that time span changed to one of years.

In the short term, however, the colonial administration put the UGCC leadership in jail, hoping that would help quieten things down. On his release in July 1949, Nkrumah formed the new and more radical Convention People's Party (CPP) – motto 'self government now'! – and set about organising a series of strikes and boycotts that peaked in January 1950, with the aim of making the colony ungovernable. Nkrumah was once again thrown in jail, but the colonial administration backed down by installing a new constitution that allowed 36 seats in the government to be elected by the African population. In the 1951 election, the CPP won 33 of the seats, and Nkrumah was released to enter government. In March 1952, Nkrumah became the Gold Coast's first African prime minister. He then set about writing a new constitution which gave the Gold Coast virtual self-government after the 1954 election in which the CPP won 79 out of 104 seats. Nkrumah then lobbied for full independence from Britain, but this was held up while the UN resolved the so-called 'Ewe Question' (a legacy of the split of the Ewe homeland when the former German Togoland was divided between Britain and France by the League of Nations in 1919) with a referendum that went in favour of the British section becoming part of independent Ghana. In the election of July 1956, the CPP won 74 out of 104 seats on a pro-Independence ticket. Britain had no choice but to acquiesce to popular demand, and so on 6 March 1957 the former Gold Coast colony became independent Ghana. It was the first African colony to be granted independence in the post-war era, and its name was adopted from the most ancient of West African empires; in the words of Nkrumah, 'as an inspiration for the future'.

Ghana (1957–1981)

Ghana's pioneering status as the first independent former colony in Africa is pivotal to understanding much of what occurred in the country under Nkrumah, who evidently perceived himself as a spokesman not merely for his country, but for the far broader goal of liberating Africa from colonial rule. It is for this reason that the grassroots development of agriculture and the mining era were often ignored in favour of frittering away the country's financial reserves on a variety of grand schemes and empty gestures. Nkrumah's role as an African statesman cannot be denied – he was, for instance, the prime mover behind the formation of the Organisation of African Unity (OAU) in 1963, and he frequently gave generous financial support to other newly independent countries. But nor can one ignore a level of economic mismanagement and wastefulness that resulted in Ghana having accumulated a foreign debt of US$1 billion by 1966, despite having had foreign reserves ten times greater than its foreign debt at the time of independence. Characteristic of the Nkrumah era was the construction of an enormously expensive OAU Headquarters in Accra, one that was never to be used after the OAU decided to base itself in Ethiopia instead.

The Nkrumah government did have several far-reaching successes, for instance the vast improvement in the country's transport network between 1957 and 1966 – notably the laying of the 'new' Kumasi–Tamale road and surfacing of several other major trunk routes, and the construction of Akosombo Dam and a deepwater harbour at Tema. Another success was the expansion of an education system that already ranked among the best in Africa, resulting in a fivefold to twentyfold increase in enrolment at every level from primary school to university. And if Nkrumah's biggest failings were in the development of the crucial agricultural sector, then the 60% drop in the externally determined cocoa price during his rule must be cited as an important mitigating factor. It is also the case that post-independence Ghana was something of a victim of the cold war mentality – Nkrumah's espoused policy of African socialism, not to say his strong diplomatic ties with the Eastern Bloc, made him an increasingly unpopular figure in the West, so that many Western governments were unwilling to provide Ghana with the support they might otherwise have given.

On the political front, the Nkrumah regime followed a path which, in hindsight, feels naggingly familiar. In July 1958, the Preventative Detention Act was passed in response to the formation of the opposition United Party under the leadership of Dr Kofi Busia, allowing for the detention without trial of perceived political opponents for a period of up to five years. In July 1960, following a national referendum, Ghana was decreed a republic with Nkrumah elected as executive president. Shortly after the presidential election, Nkrumah's main opponent for the presidency, J B Danquah, was placed in detention, where he would eventually die, as would another former ally of Nkrumah's, Obetsebi Lamptey. It is estimated that by this time the jails of Ghana held some 3,000 political detainees, a number that would increase dramatically following the attempted assassination of the president in 1962. It was this harsh repression of criticism, combined with the elevated status given to the Presidential Guard of the normal military, that would result in Nkrumah's downfall. On February 24 1966, while the president was away in Hanoi, control of the country was assumed by the military. Nkrumah never returned home, and he died of cancer in exile in 1972.

Between 1966 and 1969, Ghana was ruled by the military National Liberation Council under the leadership first of Lieutenant General Joseph Ankra, and later (and more briefly) Brigadier Akwasi Afrifa. This regime did much to restore democracy by releasing all political detainees and allowing a reasonable degree of free speech and a free press. It also restored Ghana's credibility in the West by breaking ties with the Eastern Bloc and initiating a widespread policy of privatisation. In May 1969, in line with a freshly drawn-up Bill of Rights, political parties were legalised. The election held a few months later was won by the Progress Party (PP) under Dr Kofi Busia, recently returned to the country after having fled to exile in 1959.

Busia's most notable contribution to the country was a remarkable drive towards rural improvement, for instance by building several new clinics and hospitals, drilling boreholes, and installing electricity in many places. By and large, the Busia regime maintained a policy of free speech and a free press, but these democratic ideals were undermined somewhat by their inconsistent application – at one point, for instance, Busia made it a criminal offence to mention Nkrumah by name, a response to the increasing lionisation of the former president. Busia's biggest failings were on the economic front and, although much of this can be blamed on a legacy of mismanagement left by former regimes, it would be an economic decision – the devaluation of the cedi by 44% – that triggered the coup which removed him from power on 13 January 1972.

The six-year presidency of General Ignatius Acheampong started out well enough, but all the initial grand talk of economic self-reliance and democracy soon deteriorated into a more familiar scenario. Acheampong's gross economic mismanagement and stubborn refusal to take advice regarding the freeing of the exchange rate resulted in an annual inflation rate of 130%, prompting an economic collapse that was exacerbated by two severe droughts during the early years of the regime. The repression of political activity continued with the mass detention of perceived political opponents. Meanwhile, the national coffers were drained by the regime, nepotism was rampant, and the level of corruption soared so high it caused one prominent Ghanaian to coin the term kleptocracy – rule by thieves. Amid an increasing level of civil unrest and widespread cries for a return to civilian rule, the military sacked Acheampong in 1978, and installed in his place Lieutenant General Akuffo. The ensuing months saw the unveiling of a new constitution, as well as a lift on the six-year-old ban on political parties, and an election date was set for 1979.

On June 4 1979, exactly two weeks before the scheduled election date, power was seized in a coup led by Flight Lieutenant Jerry Rawlings, a 32-year-old Ghanaian of mixed Scottish descent. Rawlings vowed that the election would go ahead, but that before power was transferred to the victor it was essential to purge corruption from the military and civil service. In the bout of bloodletting that followed, a great many civil servants were removed from office, tax offenders were forced to pay their debts, and several high ranking members of the military were executed publicly by firing squad, among them three former heads of state: Afrifa, Acheampong and Akuffo. Remarkably, on September 24, a week ahead of schedule, civilian rule was restored when Rawlings handed power to the newly elected People's National Party under President Hilla Limann. The initial popularity of this government, however, was soon offset by the country's continued economic slide, and within a year the new government had become as corrupt as any before it.

Ghana: The Rawlings Years and beyond (1982–2001)

On December 31 1981, Ghana suffered its fourth coup in 15 years, as power was seized once again by the popular figure of Jerry Rawlings. The constitution was abolished, parliament was dissolved, political parties were banned, and a number of prominent figures were jailed, President Limann among them. Rawlings installed a Provisional National Defence Council comprising three civilians and four military men, and at a local level he replaced councils with People's Defence Committees (later called Committees for the Defence of the Revolution). The next few years were marked by two clear trends. The first was unprecedented economic growth (a result of Rawlings' massive devaluation of the cedi), large-scale paring down of the civil service, privatisation of several state assets, and improved payments at the grassroots of the crucial cocoa industry. The second trend was one of repeated political instability, including several attempted coups and the unravelling of alleged assassination conspiracies against Rawlings, as well as a great many strikes and protests.

Things came to a head in 1989, when universities nationwide were closed for four months after protests and rioting, and Rawlings had introduced severe press restrictions. An attempted coup against the government was foiled in September, and a few months later one of its instigators was found hanged in his cell, prompting an international outcry led by Amnesty International as well as providing a rallying point for the many Ghanaians who wanted a return to civilian rule. In December 1990, Rawlings announced that a new constitution would be put in place within a year – it would in fact be enacted in April 1991 following a 92% approval among the 44% of the population who turned out for the national referendum. In May 1991, Rawlings endorsed the implementation of a multi-party system; the next month he passed amnesty on all political detainees, and six opposition groups were granted legal status. The most important of these were Dr Limann's People's National Convention (PNC) and Dr Boahen's New Patriotic Party (NPP), while Rawlings announced that he would retire from the military as per the new constitution and stood as president for the National Democratic Congress (NDC).

The election was held in two phases. The presidential elections in November 1992 saw Rawlings poll a clear majority of 58%, almost twice as many votes as his closest rival Boahen, who polled 30%. The election was declared substantially free and fair, but this was contested by the NPP and PNC who decided to boycott the constituent elections held on 29 December 1992 in protest. As a result, the NDC took 189 out of a possible 200 seats, with only a 29% poll recorded.

Rawlings' years as an elected president saw many positive developments on the economic front, as well as an increased level of political freedom with the release of political detainees and the re-emergence of a free press. The government managed to weather two major storms during Rawlings' first term. The first of the crises to beset Ghana in recent years was an outbreak of ethnic violence in the northern regions, which originated from a land dispute between the Konkomba and Nunumba of the Bimbilla district in February 1994. Within months, the violence had spread to many parts of the north, leaving as many as 6,000 people dead and a further 100,000 displaced as 200 villages were razed. The second was an attempt to replace the existing sales tax with a new VAT system in February 1995, an unpopular decision which resulted in widespread rioting, the death of five people in Accra, and – eventually – the reinstatement of the familiar sales tax system. The above events notwithstanding, Rawlings was voted back into power in December 1996, defeating John Kufuor's New Patriotic Party (NPP) with a diminished but still comfortable majority of 133 seats.

Most observers agree that Ghana's days of coup and countercoup are long since gone, a view supported by the momentous election of December 2000,

MUSIC

West Africa is well-known for its vibrant and largely self-contained music scene, and for many years Ghana was perhaps the leading innovator when it came to styles that combined traditional African sounds with foreign influences. More recently, Ghana has by and large relinquished its status as innovator to its francophone neighbours; nevertheless, a practically incessant backdrop of music remains a notable feature of travelling in urban parts of the country, and visitors will find themselves exposed to a rich variety of unfamiliar sounds.

The most popular music to have emerged out of Ghana is highlife, a term that covers a broad spectrum of homegrown styles fusing traditional percussive beats with various European, American and even Caribbean influences. Highlife, developed in the 1920s along the ports of what was then the Gold Coast, was first recorded in the late 1930s, reaching a popular peak in the period 1950–70. Its leading practitioners included E T Mensah, the African Brothers International Band, and more recently Alex Konadu and Koo Mino's Adadam Band.

Less easy to hear are the myriad traditional musical styles that hark from all around the country, generally drum-based in the south, more reliant on fiddles and other string instruments in the far north. It is in the north, though, that you are most likely to hear the peculiar 'talking drum', an instrument associated with the Sahel, as well as colourfully robed ensembles of Dagomba drummers (one of which we encountered by chance at a funeral in Bolgatanga).

Within Ghana, locally recorded music is largely drowned out by a plethora of exotica, not only the familiar contemporary Western hits, but

which ushered in the first transfer of power from one elected leader to another in Ghanaian history. It also marked the end of an era, as Rawlings stepped down after 18 years in power, having served his maximum of two presidential terms as stipulated in the 1991 constitution. In the first round of Ghana's Election 2000, neither of the two main parties seized enough seats to assume outright power, but in run-off elections that followed a few days later John Kufuor, the leader of the former opposition NPP, defeated Rawlings' handpicked successor, Vice President John Atta Mills, by a substantial margin. Despite some fears to the contrary, the election took place in a peaceful atmosphere; both the result and the process by which it was obtained drew widespread international praise. The NDC now has 92 seats against 100 for the NPP. Kufuor and Rawlings appeared together on television shortly after the election, to demonstrate their mutual commitment to smooth transition. 'We need to co-operate to find solutions to the economic problems that are going to beset this country for the next years to come,' Rawlings said generously. Kufuor's response was: 'We welcome very much your constructive criticism, because that is the essence of multi-party democracy.'

Ghana does indeed face severe economic problems as its new president assumes power. Despite boasting one of the highest growth rates in Africa throughout the 1990s, the country is in the midst of a currency crisis which saw the sudden but rapid devaluation of the cedi to the order of 200% against the also vibrant guitar music from the Congo and other parts of francophone Africa, as well as reggae – the South African reggae singer Lucky Dube is quite possibly the most popular recording artist in the country. Traditional Ghanaian music is most likely to be encountered by chance, at a street funeral or similar public festival, though in the north you could ask whether there is a specific day when music will be performed for the chief. The Academy of African Music and Arts on Kokrobite Beach near Accra is regarded to be one of the best places in West Africa to hear and learn about traditional and contemporary Ghanaian music.

Cassettes of popular Ghanaian recording artists – admittedly not always of the highest quality sound-wise – can be bought for next to nothing in lorry parks and markets in most substantial towns. The selection can be daunting; perhaps the simplest way to go about choosing a few cassettes as mementos of your trip is to make a habit, when you hear something you like in a bar or on a tro-tro, of asking somebody what's playing.

The most useful practical handbook to exploring Ghanaian and other contemporary and traditional African music forms is the Rough Guide's comprehensive tome *World Music*. In London, Stern's African Record Centre in Covent Garden (tel: 020 7387 5550) boasts an extensive catalogue of African recordings. Good starting points include E T Mensah's *All for You*, effectively a 'greatest hits' package, and various artists' compilations (*Akomko*, *Giants of Dance Band Highlife*, *I've Found my Love* and *The Guitar and the Gun*), several of which are available on CD. For a broader overview of contemporary African music try Stern's *Guide to Contemporary African Music*, or the informatively packaged three-CD compilation *Africa Never Stands Still*, also available through Stern's.

US dollar during 2000. Although experts tie this crisis to a drop in international gold and cocoa prices, as well as the rise in international fuel prices, the reasons for the scale of devaluation are difficult to identify. Nor, at the time of writing, has the full effect of the currency crisis been absorbed into the local economy, or by the man in the street: the NDC maintained an artificially low fuel price throughout 2000, one that ensured that inflation rates – while still high – were not anything like proportional to the devaluation of the currency. One does not envy Kufuor the task that lies ahead, and it may well be that in time he becomes the popular scapegoat for events that were initiated before he assumed power. All the same, Ghana remains strikingly economically vibrant by comparison to most parts of Africa, and a weak currency can often create economic opportunities in areas such as tourism and exports. With the co-operation of his predecessor, and in the sustained atmosphere of political freedom, stability and economic growth that has characterised Ghana in recent years, Kufuor has inherited the presidency of a country whose outlook is as bright as it has been at any time since independence.

ECONOMY AND INFRASTRUCTURE

Ghana is a country of great mineral and natural wealth, for which reason it has been an important centre of trade since prehistoric times. Skipping briefly through subjects covered more fully in the above history section, Ghana is thought to have been the main West African producer of kola nuts (sharp tasting and mildly narcotic, favoured by Muslims who are forbidden from drinking alcohol, and available in any Ghanaian market today) prior to the 15th century, at which time it also supplied amounts of gold and salt to Islamic traders in the Sahelian region to its north. From 1471 until the late 17th century, the Gold Coast supplied roughly 10% of the world's gold, as the empires of the south entered into a maritime trade with Portuguese and later Dutch traders. From the late 17th until the early 19th century, this trade in gold and other natural assets was swamped by the nefarious trans-Atlantic slave trade, operated by British and Dutch traders out of the Gold Coast and by several other European powers elsewhere off the west coast of Africa.

The roots of the modern Ghanaian economy can be traced to Britain's attempts to re-establish what they termed 'legitimate trade' after the slave trade was legally abolished in 1807. The main problem facing Britain in this regard was that many traditional trade-related skills such as gold-mining were lost during the era when slaves were the main item in demand by European merchants. In any case, the powerful Ashanti empire of the interior had been built largely on the slave trade, so that it was in both their interest and that of many European merchants to continue operating a clandestine trade in slaves, one that continued out of the Gold Coast at least until Britain's first defeat of Ashanti in 1826.

The first important item of legitimate trade to emerge in the 19th century was palm oil, used for cooking and in the manufacture of detergents, and exported from the Gold Coast as of 1820. This was of necessity a small-scale trade harvested from wild palms (the oil palm still cannot be properly cultivated), but plantations were slowly established in many areas, notably in what is now the interior of Eastern Region, and the emergent industry had the important effect of restoring respectability to agriculture after a century in which cultivation had been seen by many Africans as work fit only for slaves. By 1850, palm oil was the principal export from the Gold Coast, and by the 1880s it accounted for almost 75% of export revenue raised by the recently established Gold Coast colony. At the peak of the palm-oil era in 1884, some 20,000 tonnes of pure oil and twice that of palm kernels were exported, mostly to Germany.

Two other relatively important crops that took hold in the 19th century were cotton and rubber. The former never became an export crop due to infestations of disease and insects, but the crop was generally adequate to supply local needs, sometimes with a bit to spare for export. Rubber trees, by contrast, had been grown and tapped in the forest zone since the 17th century, but it was only in the 1870s that rubber was cultivated on a large scale, when its global importance soared as a result of the invention of the pneumatic tyre. In 1880, the Gold Coast exported a mere 0.05 tonnes of rubber. By 1886 that figure had increased to 692 tonnes, and by the early 1890s rubber was a bigger earner than palm oil, and the Gold Coast had become the world's third largest supplier. In the early 1900s, however, the bottom fell out of the rubber market; prices slid; and the industry in the Gold Coast collapsed, never to recover.

Perhaps the pivotal moment in Ghana's future economic development came in 1879, when Tetteh Quarshie returned home to the Gold Coast from Fernando Po with a few cocoa seedlings which he planted in his garden in Mampong. The climate and soil of the Gold Coast proved ideal for growing cocoa, and the crop was exported from 1891. By the turn of the century, cocoa had replaced rubber as the colony's biggest earner of foreign revenue, and by 1935 the Gold Coast was supplying half the world's cocoa. Cocoa remains to this day Ghana's most important agricultural earner (though it lies second on the production table after neighbouring Côte d'Ivoire), and the failure of the annual crop due to disease has, along with the rise and drop of the internationally determined cocoa price, often had a major influence on the country's politics. This is largely because the cocoa industry still favoured the small-scale farmer – it has been estimated that in 1951 roughly 500,000 people were employed by the cocoa industry or earned their primary income from cocoa production.

Much of Ghana's modern transport infrastructure dates to the colonial era, and there is little doubt that in this regard, if no other, Ghana was reasonably well served by its colonists, particularly by Gordon Guggisberg, the governor from 1919 to 1927. By the end of World War II, the Gold Coast had some 10,000km of roads (about one-third of the present road network) and all its present rail systems had been constructed – the Tarkwa–Sekondi line was completed as early as 1901 and extended to Kumasi in 1903, while the Accra–Kumasi line was finished in 1927. Under Guggisberg, the colonial administration provided a solution to the country's lack of a natural deepwater harbour with the construction of an artificial one at Takoradi in 1928. It was extended in 1956 as the colonial era drew to a close and is still the most important harbour in the country.

Two major engineering projects that were first mooted in the colonial era, but only brought to fruition later, largely at the instigation of Nkrumah, were the development of Tema as a deepwater harbour close to Accra, and the linked construction of a dam on the Volta at Akosombo, the latter not only important to the transport network of the north and east, but also capable of producing enough electricity for the whole country, as well as for export to neighbouring countries.

Just as important to economic development as a healthy transport infrastructure is good education, and here again the colonial administration was unusually forward-looking, with primary school attendance reaching 300,000 by 1951 and secondary school attendance 7,700. By the time of independence, the Gold Coast had 29 teacher-training colleges as well as a highly regarded university and a number of trade colleges. The adult literacy rate at this time stood at roughly 25% – nothing to shout about by Western standards, perhaps, but remarkable by comparison with many other African countries at the end of the colonial era.

It is difficult to be so positive about the colonial administration's development of the mining industry – not because the colony's great mineral wealth was left unexploited, but because the industry was structured in such a manner that very little of the significant profit it raised would stay in the colony. Formal gold mining in the Gold Coast started at Tarkwa in 1877 and at Obuasi two years later, and it was also soon discovered that the colony had significant deposits of several other minerals, notably diamonds and manganese. By 1951, the year in which Nkrumah's CPP entered government, annual gold exports exceeded £8 million annually, with manganese and diamonds close behind at around £7 million and £6 million respectively. For the sake of comparison, the value of cocoa exports in this year was a massive £60 million and timber, the second most important agricultural export, stood at £5 million.

At the time of independence in 1957, Ghana had one of the strongest economies in Africa, with foreign revenue reserves ten times greater than the foreign debt. By 1966, the situation had practically reversed, with foreign debt in the region of US$1 billion. The reasons for Ghana's economic decline in the decades immediately following independence, and particularly between 1966 and 1981, are clearly linked to the political instability of that era, though exacerbated by external factors such as the 60% drop in the cocoa price during the Nkrumah era. More important here and now is that Ghana has undergone more than a decade of substantial economic growth since productivity reached a post-independence nadir in the early 1980s. Many people – not just Ghanaians – regard the country to be the most promising economic prospect in Africa at the moment. Real gross domestic product (GDP) growth since 1984 has typically hovered at around 5%, and an ambitious plan for the next 25 years has set a goal of roughly 8% per annum.

Despite a marked increase in industrialisation in recent times, agriculture remains at the heart of the economy, contributing almost 50% of GDP and directly or indirectly supporting 80% of the population. Cocoa remains the most important crop in export terms and, although output dropped from over 500,000 tonnes annually in the early 1960s to 158,000 tonnes in 1983, it has recently risen back above the 300,000 tonne mark. Other important crops include cassava, plantains, coco yams, yams, maize, groundnuts, millet, rice, sorghum and sugar cane.

In recent years, mining has become the most important source of foreign revenue: renewed development in the goldfields of the south means Ghana is now Africa's largest gold exporter after South Africa, with production rising from 17,000kg in 1990 to more than 35,000kg in recent years, while diamond exports have topped 700,000 carats annually since 1991. After gold and cocoa, tourism has recently risen to become the country's third largest earner of foreign revenue, generating an income of US$233 million in 1995 by comparison with US$19 million ten years earlier – an increase of greater than 1,000% in one decade!

THE NATURAL WORLD
Geography
Ghana is in essence flat and low-lying. Almost half of the country lies at an altitude of below 150m and nowhere does it top an altitude of 1,000m. The far south of the country is dominated by the low-lying coastal plain which runs between 100km and 150km inland of the Atlantic coastline, except near Accra where the Akwapim Mountains around Aburi rise from the coastal plain only 20km inland. At the heart of the country is the low-lying Volta Basin, Ghana's most important drainage system, stretching from around Tamale in the north to the Volta mouth at Ada. Much of it is now submerged in the 8,500km² Lake Volta, the world's largest artificial body of water.

The Volta Basin is flanked by mountains to the east and west. The eastern highlands, part of the Togo-Atakora range that stretches through to Benin, reach altitudes in excess of 900m near the Togolese border. The county's highest peak, Mount Afadjayo, is part of this range. The highlands to the east and west of the Volta Basin are characterised by a high number of waterfalls, most famously the Wli Falls near Hohoe, reputedly the highest waterfall in West Africa.

Climate

The combination of low altitude and proximity to the Equator gives Ghana a typical tropical climate. Daytime temperatures are high throughout the country, approaching or topping 30°C on most days. Temperatures do drop at night, more noticeably in the relatively dry north than the humid south, but visitors from cooler climes will generally consider most parts of Ghana to be hot both day and night. The only really temperate parts of the country are the highlands flanking the Volta Basin, where temperatures can be genuinely cool after dusk.

Owing to its equatorial location, Ghana does not experience the strong seasonal changes to which most Europeans and North Americans are accustomed. Temperatures are reasonably consistent throughout the year, and in many parts of the country the average temperature for the northern hemisphere winter months is actually higher than for the summer months – Accra, for instance, experiences its hottest temperatures from November to January, despite lying in the same hemisphere as Europe. The main seasonal factor to be aware of is rain, which falls almost exclusively during the European summer months of April to September, peaking in May and June. Rainfall figures are highest in the forested southwest, where some areas regularly experience in excess of 2,000mm per annum, and are lowest in the north and the plains immediately around Accra, where it is very unusual for as much as 1,000mm of rain to fall in a calendar year.

A noteworthy phenomenon in this part of the world is the Harmattan winds which blow from the northeast during the dry season, bringing dust from the Sahara and reducing visibility to as little as 1km. Generally the winds come in late November or early December and continue until some time in March. The Harmattan will have little effect on most tourists, but it is a nightmare for photographers and will cause disappointment to those who've come to admire the scenery in mountainous areas.

Vegetation

Most of southern Ghana for about 250km inland of the Atlantic is naturally covered in rainforest and, while clearing for cultivation and logging activities have left few areas of true rainforest intact outside of designated reserves, southern Ghana remains very lushly vegetated. For most visitors to Ghana, exposure to the rainforest is limited to a day trip to Kakum National Park, noted for its unique and spectacular canopy walkway, but there are countless other opportunities for more adventurous travellers to explore Ghana's forests, ranging from a number of relatively accessible reserves close to Kumasi to a handful of obscure national parks suited to self-sufficient hikers.

The central and northern parts of the country support savannah habitats, gradually becoming drier and more sparsely vegetated as you head further north. In conservation terms, Ghana's most important savannah habitat is Mole National Park, easily visited as an overnight trip from Tamale.

Wildlife

Like other West African countries, Ghana lacks the vast conservation areas and huge herds of wildlife still to be found in most countries in eastern and southern Africa. Several large mammals typically associated with Africa do not occur in West Africa, for instance rhino, zebra, wildebeest and gorilla; while many other large mammal species have been driven to extinction in Ghana in historical times, notably giraffe, cheetah and probably African hunting dog. Within Ghana, the status of several other large mammal species, including lion, is highly vulnerable.

For all that, Ghana still offers some great opportunities for game viewing, with a wide variety of large mammals present and monkeys in particular well represented and easily observed. The following overview of the more interesting mammals to be found in Ghana is designed to help readers who are not carrying a field guide of any sort, but it should also be useful to those carrying a continental guide and seeking more specific information about the distribution and status of various mammal species within Ghana.

It is worth noting that while large mammals understandably draw the attention of most visitors to the game reserves and forests, Ghana does support a tremendous variety of other animals. Several of its forests boast in excess of 400 varieties of butterfly and, while the average visitor is unlikely to see even a fraction of these species, it is quite normal to see ten to 20 visibly different types of butterfly in the course of a walk, many of them quite exquisitely coloured.

Birdwatchers will find Ghana a highly rewarding country and, even if the avian variety doesn't quite match that of East Africa's finest birding countries, there are still plenty of places in Ghana where a reasonably experienced birder could expect to notch up 100 species in a day. For savannah birds, the best spot in the country is undoubtedly Mole National Park, where you can expect to see several varieties of colourful bee-eater, barbet and kingfisher, as well as larger birds such as various storks, herons, eagles, vultures and guinea fowl – enough to arouse the interest even of those with no particular interest in birds. Any forest will offer good birding too, with a greater chance of seeing some genuine rarities, but novices should be warned that the dense vegetation can make birding in the rainforest a frustrating and somewhat tiresome experience by comparison with the same activity in a more open environment. Sadly for birders, relatively little useful literature is available regarding Ghana's birds, and although I've included relevant comments based on our experience wherever possible in the guide, a lack of accessible source material means that coverage is less detailed than I would like.

Predators

The **lion**, *Panthera leo*, is Africa's largest predator, and the animal everybody hopes to see on safari. It is a sociable creature, living in prides of five to ten animals and defending a territory of between 20 and 200km². Lions hunt at night, and their favoured prey is large or medium-sized antelope. Most of the hunting is done by females, but dominant males normally feed first after a kill. When not feeding, lions are remarkably indolent – they spend up to 23 hours of any given day at rest – so the anticipation of a lion sighting is often more exciting than the real thing. Lions naturally occur in any habitat but desert and rainforest, and they once ranged across much of the Old World; these days they are all but restricted to large conservation areas in sub-Saharan Africa (one remnant population exists in India). In Ghana, a small population of lions remains in Mole National Park, though few tourists see them. There may also be lions present in some other relatively unexplored conservation areas.

The powerful **leopard**, *Panthera pardus*, is the most solitary and secretive of Africa's large cats. It hunts using stealth and power, often getting to within 5m of its intended prey before pouncing, and it habitually stores its kill in a tree to keep it from hyenas and lions. Where the two co-

Leopard

Leopard

Leopard

Cheetah

exist, the leopard can be distinguished from the superficially similar cheetah by its rosette-like spots, lack of black 'tear marks' and more compact, powerful build (though current information suggests that cheetahs are extinct in Ghana). Leopards occur in all habitats, favouring areas with plenty of cover such as riverine woodland and rocky slopes, and there are many records of individuals living for years undetected in close proximity to humans. The leopard is the most common large feline, occurring in many forests, but you'd be extremely fortunate to see one.

Of the smaller cats, the **serval**, *Felis serval*, built rather like a miniature cheetah, with black-on-gold spots giving way to streaking near the head, is seldom seen but widespread and quite common in moist grassland, reed beds and riverine habitats. The **caracal**, *Felis caracal*, closely resembles the European lynx with its uniform tan coat and tufted ears, and it favours relatively arid savannah habitats. The not dissimilar **golden cat**, *Felis aurata*, lives in forested areas, lacks ear tufts and has a spotted underbelly. The markedly smaller **African wild cat**, *Felis sylvestris*, ranges from the Mediterranean to the Cape of Good Hope, and is similar in appearance to the domestic tabby cat.

Caracal

The **African hunting dog**, *Lycaon pictus*, distinguished by cryptic black, brown and cream coat, was known to occur in Mole National Park until recent times, but is probably now extinct in Ghana. The **black-backed jackal**, *Canis mesomelas*, and **side-striped jackal**, *Canis adustus*, both occur sparsely in northern Ghana and are listed for Mole National Park. The first species can be identified by its prominent black saddle flecked with a varying amount of white or gold, while the second has an indistinct pale, vertical stripe on each flank and a white-tipped tail.

African hunting dog

Black-backed jackal

Spotted hyena

The **spotted hyena**, *Crocuta crocuta*, probably the most common large predator in Ghana, has a bulky build, sloping back, brown-spotted coat, powerful jaws and dog-like expression. Contrary to popular myth, hyenas are not exclusively scavengers: the spotted hyena in particular is an adept hunter capable of killing a large antelope. Nor are they hermaphroditic, an ancient belief that stems from the false scrotum and penis covering the female hyena's vagina. Sociable animals, and fascinating to observe, hyenas live in loosely structured clans of about ten animals, led by females who are stronger and larger than males. The North African **striped hyena**, *Hyaena hyaena*, pale brown with several dark vertical streaks and a blackish mane, may occur in the very far north of Ghana.

A great many small nocturnal predators occur in Ghana. The **African civet**, *Civettictus civetta*, is a bulky, long-haired creature with a rather feline appearance, primarily carnivorous but also partial to fruit, and widespread and common in many habitats but very rarely seen. The smaller, more slender **tree** or **(two-spotted) palm civet**, *Nandinia binotata*, is an arboreal forest

African civet

animal with a dark-brown coat marked with black spots. The **small-spotted genet**, *Genetta genetta*, **large-spotted** or **blotched genet**, *Genetta tigrina*, and **panther** or **pardine genet**, *Genetta pardina*, are Ghanaian representatives of a taxonomically confusing genus comprising perhaps ten species, all very slender and rather feline in appearance, with a grey to gold-brown coat marked with black spots and a long ringed tail.

The **ratel** or **honey badger**, *Mellivora capensis*, black with a puppyish face and grey-white back, is an opportunistic feeder best known for its symbiotic relationship with a bird called the honeyguide which leads it to a bee hive, waits for it to tear open the hive, then feeds on the scraps. The **Cape clawless otter**, *Aonyx capensis*, is a brown freshwater mustelid with a white collar, while the smaller **spotted-necked otter**, *Lutra maculicollis*, is darker with light, white spots on its throat.

Six mongoose species occur in Ghana, most of them diurnal, terrestrial and reasonably common – all six have, for instance, been recorded in Mole National Park. The **marsh mongoose**, *Atilax paludinosus*, is large, normally solitary, with a very scruffy brown coat, often seen in the vicinity of water. The **Egyptian** or **large grey mongoose**, *Herpestes ichneumon*, is also large, and often associated with water, but its grey coat is grizzled in appearance and it is most often seen in pairs or family groups. Restricted to rainforest habitats, where it is often quite common, the **cusimanse**, *Crossarchus obscuras*, is a small, sociable mongoose with a shaggy brown coat, almost always seen in family groups.

The **white-tailed mongoose**, *Ichneumia albicauda*, is a large, solitary brown mongoose, generally found in savannah country, and easily identified by its bushy, white tail. The **slender** or **pygmy mongoose**, *Galerella sanguinea*, is another solitary inhabitant of the savannah, but very much smaller and with a uniform brown coat and blackish tail tip. The **Gambian mongoose**, *Mungos gambianus*, dark brown with the distinctive combination of pale throat and black cheek stripe, is the most sociable

Gambian mongoose

mongoose found in savannah country, occurring in groups of up to 30 animals.

Primates

The **common chimpanzee**, *Pan troglodytes*, still occurs in
reasonable numbers in the rainforest of southern Ghana.
Along with the bonobo, *Pan paniscus*, of the southern
Congo, it is more closely related to man than to any other
living creature. The chimpanzee lives in large troops
based around a core of related males dominated by an
alpha male. Females aren't firmly bonded to their core
group, so emigration between communities is normal.
Primarily frugivorous, chimpanzees eat meat on occasion
and, though most kills are opportunistic, stalking of prey is
not unusual. The first recorded instance of a chimp using

Chimpanzee

a tool was at Gombe Stream in Tanzania, where modified sticks
were used to 'fish' in termite mounds. In West Africa, chimps have been
observed cracking open nuts with a stone and anvil. In the USA, captive chimps
have successfully been taught Sign Language and have created compound words
such as 'rock-berry' to describe a nut. A widespread and common rainforest
resident, the chimpanzee is thought to number 200,000 in the wild. In Ghana,
there are no habituated chimps, and they are unlikely to be seen by tourists.

The **anubis** or **olive baboon**, *Papio (cynocaphalus) anubis*, a powerful
terrestrial primate, and distinguished from any monkey by its much larger size,
inverted 'U'-shaped tail and distinctive dog-like head, is fascinating to watch
from a behavioural perspective. It lives in large troops which boast a complex,
rigid social structure characterised by matriarchal lineages and plenty of intra-
troop movement by males seeking social dominance. Omnivorous and at
home in almost any habitat, the baboon is the most widespread primate in
Africa. It is quite frequently seen in Ghana, especially in Mole National Park
and the Shai Hills.

The **green monkey**, *Cercopithecus (aethiops) sabaeus* is a type of vervet
monkey, probably the world's most common monkey super-
species, and the most widespread representative of the
Cercopithecus guenons, a taxonomically controversial genus
associated with African forests. The vervets are atypical
guenons, in that they inhabit savannah and woodland rather
than true forest, spending a high proportion of their
time on the ground. For this reason, vervets are more
likely to be confused with the much larger and
heavier baboon. However, the green monkey's light-
grey coat and white forehead band should be

Vervet monkey

diagnostic – as should the male's garish blue genitals. The green
monkey is common in most Ghanaian reserves.

The terrestrial **patas** or **red monkey**, *Erythrocebus
patas*, larger and more spindly than the vervet, has
an orange-tinged coat and black forehead stripe.
Essentially a monkey of dry savannah, the patas
occurs in northern Ghana, and can quite easily be
seen alongside the green monkey in Mole
National Park.

Probably the easiest to see of Ghana's true
forest monkeys is the **mona monkey**,

Patas monkey

Mona monkey

Cercopithecus mona, of which six long-recognised races are now regarded by some authorities to be distinct species on the basis of recent chromosome studies. The most widespread mona in Ghana is **Lowe's monkey** *Cercopithecus (m.) loweii*, a pretty and cryptically coloured grey, white and black guenon distinguished by the pale stripe over its eye. Lowe's mona is the common monkey at Baobeng-Fiema monkey sanctuary, and it occurs in most Ghanaian rainforests, where it is offered some protection against hunting. It is replaced in Tafi Atome in the east by the **true mona** *Cercopithecus (m.) mona*, which is similar in overall appearance but can be distinguished by the prominent white discs on its hips, easily seen when it moves away from the observer.

Two other distinctive species of forest guenon occur in Ghana. The **lesser spot-nosed monkey** *Cercopithecus petaurista* is a small guenon easily distinguished by its prominent white nose. Though widespread in Ghana's forests, the lesser spot-nosed monkey is most likely to be seen on Monkey Hill in Takoradi, where a small and relatively habituated troop survives within a few hundred metres of the city centre. Much rarer is the beautiful, white-bearded, orange-rumped **Roloway's Diana monkey**, *Cercopithecus diana roloway*, which may now be locally extinct in Kakum, but survives in the Ankasa and Bia Resource Reserves near the Ivorian border, where it is rarely seen.

The **western** or **Geoffrey's black-and-white colobus**, *Colobus vellerosus*, is a beautiful jet-black monkey with bold, white facial markings and a long, white tail, widespread where it hasn't been hunted to extinction and easily seen at Baobeng-Fiema Monkey Sanctuary. Almost exclusively arboreal, it is capable of leaping distances of up to 30m, a spectacular sight with its white tail streaming behind. The Miss Waldron's bay race of **western red colobus**, *Procolobus badius waldroni*, is a distinctly red, long-limbed forest monkey

Black and white colobus

formerly restricted to a few forests in southwestern Ghana. It is now officially regarded to be extinct in Ghana, though recent reports suggest a relic population survived in the remote Krokosua Hills Forest Reserve near the Bia Resource Reserve. The smaller and duller **olive colobus**, *Procolobus verus*, an olive-grey monkey distinguished by two light grey patches on its forehead, occurs in several forests in southern Ghana, including Kakum National Park, but is most likely to be seen on Monkey Hill in Takoradi.

The one other forest monkey to occur in Ghana, the **sooty mangabey**, *Cercocebus atys*, is the only West African representative of a genus that's more widely represented in the central African rainforest. It is the only uniform dark-grey monkey to occur in Ghana, where it is confined to western forests such as Bia and Ankasa. The race found in Ghana *Cercocebus a. lunulatus* has a small white collar, and is sometimes referred to as the white-naped or white-checked mangabey.

Also present in Ghana are several species of nocturnal **bushbaby**, *Galago spp*, often quite easy to locate if you know where to find them and have a good spotlight. The **potto**, *Perodicticus potto*, is a sloth-like nocturnal primate of rainforest interiors, also most easily located with the aid of a spotlight.

Antelope

The **roan antelope**, *Hippotragus equinus*, is the largest plains antelope found in Ghana, with a shoulder height of 120–150cm. It is a handsome horse-like creature, uniform fawn-grey with a pale belly, short decurved horns and a light mane. It occurs in several savannah reserves, and is the common antelope of Gbele Resource Area near Tumu in the north. The roan is quite likely to be seen by visitors spending a few days in Mole National Park.

Roan antelope

The **Defassa waterbuck**, *Kobus (ellipsiprymnus) defassa*, is another very large antelope, easily recognised by its shaggy brown coat, white rump and the male's large, lyre-shaped horns. It is normally seen in small family groups grazing near water, and is almost certain to be seen in the vicinity of the hotel at Mole National Park. The closely related **kob**, *Kobus kob*, is a beautiful, red-gold antelope with a white throat, but otherwise few distinguishing features. It is probably the most common large antelope in Ghana, and family herds are almost certain to be seen by visitors to Mole National Park and Shai Hills.

Defassa waterbuck

Kob

The **western hartebeest**, *Alcelaphus buselaphus*, is a large, ungainly antelope readily identified by the combination of large shoulders, sloping back, red-brown or yellow-brown coat and smallish horns in both sexes. It is resident in several savannah reserves in Ghana, but quite rare everywhere.

Hartebeest

Secretive and scarce, the **bongo**, *Tragelaphus euryceros*, is a very large, stocky and clearly striped rainforest species, isolated populations of which occur in several Ghanaian reserves, including Kakum National Park. It is highly unlikely to be seen by a casual visitor. A far more common and widespread resident of forest and thick woodland, though also quite secretive, the **bushbuck**, *Tragelaphus scriptus*, is an attractive, medium-sized antelope. The male is dark brown or chestnut, while the much smaller female is generally a pale reddish brown. The male has relatively small, straight horns. It can be seen in just about any Ghanaian forest or game reserve, and is quite frequently observed in Shai Hills and Mole National Park.

Bushbuck

Less common, the **Bohor reedbuck**, *Redunca redunca*, is a plain, light fawn, medium-sized antelope generally seen in pairs in open country near

Reedbuck

water. The **oribi**, *Ourebia ourebi*, is rather like a miniature reedbuck, uncommon in grassland habitats. Even smaller, the **common** or **grey duiker**, *Sylvicapra grimmia*, is an anomalous member of the duiker family in that it occurs in savannah and woodland rather than true forest. Distinguished by the black tuft of hair between its small horns, it is the only small, grey antelope likely to be seen in non-forested habitats in Ghana.

Common duiker

The forest duikers are a taxonomically confusing group of 12 to 20 species restricted to the rainforests of Africa. Six species occur in Ghana, all of them widespread (all but the red-flanked, for instance, occur in Kakum National Park), but secretive and rather unlikely to be seen in the wild by tourists. The largest of these is the nocturnal **yellow-backed duiker**, *Cephalophus leucogaster*, a bushbuck-sized antelope with a blackish coat and yellow patch on its back which occurs sparsely in most true rainforests, including Kakum National Park.

Three of Ghana's remaining duiker species are also rather large by the standards of the family, with a shoulder height of up to 55cm. The most distinctive of these, the **black duiker**, *Cephalophus niger*, with a thick off-black coat and red forehead and throat, is realistically only likely to be seen clearly at Owabi Wildlife Sanctuary outside Kumasi. More widespread, the **bay duiker**, *Cephalophus dorcas*, red-brown with a wide, black dorsal stripe, would be difficult to tell apart at a glance from **Ogilby's duiker**, *Cephalophus ogilbyi*, which is similar but has a narrower dorsal stripe.

The most common forest antelope in Ghana, **Maxwell's duiker**, *Cephalophus maxwelli*, is a small, grey duiker with a distinctive, pale eye stripe, likely to be seen in any forest in southern Ghana. Similar in size to Maxwell's, but with colouring closer to the bay duiker, the **red-flanked duiker**, *Cephalophus rufilatus*, is best distinguished from members of its genus by habitat and distribution, since it is essentially a species of forest fringe and woodland which differs from *all* other forest duikers in that it occurs only in the northern half of Ghana.

Also occurring in the Ghanaian rainforest, the **royal antelope**, *Neotragus pygmaeus*, is a common, but infrequently observed, brown antelope with a red throat collar, which with a shoulder height of up to 28cm is regarded to be the world's smallest horned ungulate. More closely related to European deer than any antelope, the **water chevrotain**, *Hyemoschus aquaticus*, is an odd, hare-sized nocturnal creature with a brown coat and white stripes and spots, generally associated with wet habitats within rainforests.

Other mammals

The **African elephant**, *Loxodonta africana*, is the world's largest land animal, and both the savannah and smaller forest species occur in Ghana. It is an intelligent, social animal, and often very entertaining to watch. Female elephants live in closely knit clans in which the eldest female plays matriarch over her sisters, daughters and granddaughters. Mother-daughter bonds are strong and may last for up to 50 years. Males generally leave the family group at around 12 years to roam singly or form bachelor herds. Under normal circumstances, elephants range widely in search of food and water, but when concentrated populations are forced to live in conservation areas, their habit of uprooting trees can cause serious environmental damage. Elephants are widespread and common in habitats ranging from desert to rainforest, and despite heavy poaching they are still present in several national parks and reserves. Mole National Park, with a population of between 500 and 800 elephants, is the best place to see them.

Characteristic of Africa's large rivers and lakes, the **hippopotamus**, *Hippopotamus amphibius*, is a large, lumbering animal that spends most of the day submerged, but emerges at night to graze. Strongly territorial, herds of ten or more animals are presided over by a dominant male who will readily defend his patriarchy to the death. Hippos are present in Mole National Park, but not within day-walk distance of Mole Motel, and they are very common in the part of the Volta River protected by Bua National Park.

The **West African manatee**, *Trichechus senegalensis*, is an unmistakable large, grey, hairless mammal, related to the marine dugong but entirely restricted to freshwater habitats. Increasingly very rare, manatees are still seen from time to time on Lake Volta and the Volta estuary area near Ada.

The **African buffalo**, *Syncerus caffer*, frequently but erroneously referred to

African buffalo

as a water buffalo (an Asian species), is a distinctive ox-like animal which lives in large herds on the savannah and occurs in smaller herds in forested areas. It is common and widespread in sub-Saharan Africa, and historically both the black savannah race and the smaller, redder forest race occur in Ghana, though the latter is now very rare and possibly extinct. The country's largest buffalo population of roughly 1,000 animals is found in Mole, but buffalo also occur in some forest reserves and in Kalapka Resource Reserve near Ho.

The rather endearing **warthog**, *Phacochoreus africanus*, is grey in colour with a thin covering of hairs, wart-like bumps on its face, and rather large upward-curving tusks. Africa's only diurnal swine, the warthog is often seen in family groups, trotting off briskly with its tail raised stiffly (a diagnostic trait) in a determinedly nonchalant air. In Ghana it occurs in most savannah reserves, though is only likely to be seen in Mole National Park, where it is common. The **red river hog**, *Potamoccoerus porcus*, is a larger forest swine, common but primarily nocturnal, and regarded by some authorities to be a race of the East Africa bushpig, from which it is readily distinguished by a decidedly red coat and clear, white stripe along its back.

Warthog

Larger still, the **giant forest hog**, *Hylochoerus meinertzhageni*, a very hairy, dark-brown swine that weighs up to 250kg, is a fairly common but difficult-to-observe nocturnal resident of most rainforests in Ghana.

The **aardvark**, *Orycteropus afer*, is a singularly bizarre insectivore, quite common in dry savannah country, and unmistakable with its long snout and huge ears, but rarely seen due to its nocturnal habits. Equally distinctive, **pangolins** are rare nocturnal insectivores with armour-plating and a tendency to roll up in a ball when disturbed. Spiky rather than armoured, several **hedgehog** and **porcupine** species occur in the region, the former generally no larger than a guinea pig, the latter generally 60–100cm long.

One small mammal species that you're quite likely to encounter in the right habitat is the **rock hyrax**, *Procavia capensis*, a rodent-like creature more closely related to elephants and often seen sunning itself in rocky habitats. Probably more numerous in Ghana, but less easily seen, the similar looking **tree hyrax**, *Dendrohyrax dorsalis*, is a nocturnal forest creature which announces its presence with an unforgettable shrieking call.

Rock hyrax

Of the great many squirrel species present in Ghana, all but one are essentially restricted to forest and woodland. The exception, a widespread inhabitant of the northern savannah, is the **unstriped ground squirrel**, *Xerus inauris*, a terrestrial animal with a white eye ring, silver-black tail, and the characteristic squirrel mannerism of holding food in its forepaws while standing on its hind legs.

Ground squirrel

Planning and Preparation

WHEN TO GO

In most respects, the best time to visit Ghana is during the northern hemisphere winter. The months of October through to April are not significantly hotter or cooler than other times of the year, but they are a great deal more comfortable since humidity levels are lower. More importantly, these months form the dry season, which means there are fewer mosquitoes (and correspondingly there's a lower risk of contracting malaria), dirt roads are in better condition, and there is less likelihood of you or your luggage being drenched in an unexpected storm. The dry season is particularly suitable for those with a strong interest in natural history, since game viewing is best when the grass is low and resident bird populations are supplemented by all sorts of Palaearctic migrants.

The main disadvantage of the dry season, particularly from December through to February, is that visibility is seriously impeded by sands blown from the Sahara by the Harmattan winds. This won't greatly affect most travellers, but the beaches lose much of their beauty, people who plan on doing a lot of hiking will miss the best of the mountain scenery, and serious photographers will find the dull ambient light and grey skies not at all conducive to getting decent pictures.

PAPERWORK

Check well in advance that your **passport** hasn't expired and will not do so for a while, since you may be refused entry on a passport that's due to expire within six months of your intended departure date.

Visitors of practically all nationalities require a **visa** to enter Ghana. This takes up to three days to issue at any Ghanaian Embassy or High Commission, and you will generally have to produce three passport-sized photos and pay a fee of around US$20 or upward for a single-entry visa valid for a stay of up to 60 days. If you plan on spending longer in Ghana, you are likely to be told that you must buy a 90-day multiple-entry visa, at three times the cost of an ordinary visa. This is pure fabrication on the part of some embassies: the purpose of a multiple-entry visa is quite simply that you can enter and exit the country any number of times while it is valid. Upon entering the country with a valid visa, you will be stamped for a maximum of 60 days regardless of what type of visa it is. And if you want to stay on for longer than 60 days, you will have to apply for a visa extension once you are in the country and to pay an additional US$10 for every extra 30 days, regardless of whether you have paid for a single or multiple-entry visa. The good news is that visa extensions can be organised at any time in your trip (we extended ours to three months after a week in the country) and the process seems very straightforward. It's worth knowing that a visa extension in Accra might take two weeks to process, whereas it shouldn't take more than 48 hours at any other regional capital. Obviously, if you expect to leave and re-enter Ghana, then you most definitely do want a multiple-entry visa.

The Ghana High Commission in the UK is at 104 Highgate Hill, London N6 5HE; tel: 020 8342 8686 or 7586. It takes about ten days for them to issue a visa by post; they require four passport-sized photographs and charge £15 for a single-entry visa. The visa application form can be obtained from their website at www.ghana-com.co.uk.

It is, in theory, compulsory to have a valid **yellow fever vaccination** to enter Ghana, though we've never been asked for one in the past, and cannot say what would happen were you to be asked to produce a certificate you don't have.

Should there be any possibility you'll want to drive or hire a vehicle while you're in the country, do organise an **international driving licence** (any AA office in a country in which you're licensed to drive will do this for a nominal fee).

For security reasons, it's advisable to detail all your important information on one sheet of paper, photocopy it, and distribute a few copies in your luggage, your money-belt, and amongst relatives or friends at home. The sort of things you want to include on this are your travellers' cheque numbers and refund information, travel insurance policy details and 24-hour emergency contact number, passport number, details of relatives or friends to be contacted in an emergency, bank and credit card details, camera and lens serial numbers etc.

Should your passport be lost or stolen, it will generally be easier to get a replacement if you have a photocopy of the important pages.

Something that you no longer need to be concerned about, at least in our experience, is having policemen ask you to produce your passport on a whim.

GETTING THERE
By air
The national carrier Ghana Airways is a reputable airline that flies between Accra and London, Dusseldorf and Rome in Europe, New York in the USA, Harare and Johannesburg in Southern Africa, and eight West African capital cities. Other airlines with scheduled flights to Accra include Air Afrique, Alitalia, British Airways, Egypt Air, Ethiopian Airlines, KLM, Lufthansa and Swissair. Bearing in mind that a Virgin Airways flight from some parts of the USA to London costs as little as US$250, North Americans with more time than money may find it advantageous to fly to London and organise a ticket to Africa from there.

There are dozens upon dozens of travel agents in London offering cheap flights to Africa, and it's worth checking out the ads in magazines like *Time Out* and *TNT* and phoning around before you book anything. The following include Ghana specialists:

Africa Travel Centre 4 Medway Court, Leigh St, London WC1H 9OX; tel: 020 7387 1211; fax: 020 7383 7512; email: info@africatravel.co.uk.
Alpha Holidays Suite 406, 71 Bondway, Vauxhall, London SW8 1SQ; tel: 020 7793 1667; fax: 020 7793 1985; email: alphaholidays@clara.co.uk
Interchange 27 Stafford Rd, Croydon, Surrey CR4 4NG; tel: 020 8681 3612; fax: 020 8760 0031; email: interchange@interchange.uk.com; web: www.interchange.uk.com

Nomadic Expeditions 22B Barkham Ride, Finchampstead, Berks RG40 4EU; tel: 0870 2201718; fax: 0870 2201719; email: info@nomadic.co.uk; web: www.nomadic.co.uk

Southern Africa Travel Tel: 01904 692469; fax: 01904 691340. Features tours to Ghana and can organise tailor-made trips.

STA 117 Euston Rd, London NW1 2SX; tel: 020 7361 6262; fax: 020 7937 9570. There are 40 STA branches in the UK specialising in cheap round-the-world-type tickets.

Trailfinders 42–48 Earls Court Rd, London W8 6EJ; tel: 020 7938 3366; fax: 020 7937 9294. Also specialise in cheap round-the-world tickets.

Travel Ghana Berkeley House, 73 Upper Richmond Rd, Putney, London SW15 2SZ; tel: 020 8877 9262; fax: 020 8877 9690; email: travelghana@lineone.net

Unless it's absolutely unavoidable, don't even think about flying to Ghana on a one-way ticket and organising your ticket out once you are there. For starters, you may hit serious problems with airport immigration officials if you don't arrive on a return ticket, and secondly, flights out of Accra are very expensive, so you'll almost certainly end up paying double what you would for a cheap return.

Overland from Europe

There are two overland routes between Europe and Ghana. Both start in Morocco and involve crossing the Sahara, one via Algeria and the other via Mauritania, then continue through Mali and Burkina Faso. The Algeria option has been impassable for some years now, but the situation with either route is highly changeable and you should seek current advice. For readers based in the UK, the best way to gauge the situation would be to get in touch with the many overland truck companies that advertise in magazines such as *TNT* and *Time Out*. And, frankly, unless you've a reliable 4x4, joining an overland truck trip is almost certainly the best way of doing this difficult route, especially if you have thoughts of continuing through the Democratic Republic of the Congo (formerly Zaire) to East Africa. Operators who offer overland trips by truck in and through Ghana include:

Dragoman Tel: 01728 861133; email: info@dragoman.co.uk

Explore Worldwide Tel: 01252 319448; email: info@exploreworldwide.com. offer overland trips by truck in and through Ghana.

Guerba Expeditions Tel: 01373 826611; fax: 01373 858351; email: info@guerba.co.uk.

Travellers visiting Ghana overland from Europe will presumably want to carry a regional or continental guide. If you are taking your own vehicle, then the *Sahara Handbook* by Chris Scott (Trailblazer, 2001) is the essential companion, while *Africa by Road* by Charlie Shackell and Illya Bracht (Bradt Travel Guides, 2001) is very useful when it comes to general planning. It might also be worth investing in a regional guide to West Africa (see *Further Reading,* page 341), or even a more general guide to Africa; but bear in mind that the wider the scope of the guide, the skimpier it is on individual detail.

WHAT TO TAKE

There are two simple rules to bear in mind when you decide what to take with you to Ghana. The first is to bring with you *everything* that you could possibly need and that might not be readily available when you need it. The second is to carry as little as possible. Somewhat contradictory rules, you might think, and you'd be right – so the key is finding the right balance, something that probably depends on personal experience as much as anything. Worth stressing is that most genuine necessities are surprisingly easy to get hold of in Ghana, and that most of the ingenious gadgets you can buy in camping shops are unlikely to amount to much more than deadweight on the road. If it came to it, you could easily travel in Ghana with little more than a change of clothes, a few basic toiletries and a medical kit.

Carrying luggage

Assuming that you'll be using public transport, you'll want to carry your luggage on your back, either in a backpack or in a suitcase that converts into one, since you'll tend to spend a lot of time walking between bus stations and hotels. Which of these you choose depends mainly on your style of travel. If you intend doing a lot of hiking you definitely want a proper backpack. On the other hand, if you'll be doing things where it might be a good idea to shake off the sometimes negative image attached to backpackers, then there would be obvious advantages in being able to convert your backpack into a conventional suitcase.

My preference, before travelling with a photographer made it impractical, was a robust 35cl day pack. The advantages of keeping luggage as light and compact as possible are manifold. For starters, you can rest it on your lap on bus trips, avoiding complications such as extra charges for luggage, arguments about where your bag should be stored, and the slight but real risk of theft if your luggage ends up on the roof. A compact bag also makes for greater mobility, whether you're hiking or looking for a hotel in town. The sacrifice? Leave behind camping equipment and a sleeping bag. Do this, and it's quite possible to fit everything you truly need into a day pack, and possibly even a few luxuries – I've always travelled with binoculars, a bird field guide and at least five novels – and still keep the weight down to around 8kg. Frankly, it puzzles me what the many backpackers who wander around with an enormous pack and absolutely no camping equipment actually carry!

If your luggage won't squeeze into a day pack, a sensible compromise is to carry a large day pack in your rucksack. That way, you can carry a tent and other camping equipment when you need it, but at other times reduce your luggage to fit into a day pack and leave what you're not using in storage.

Travellers carrying a lot of valuable items should look for a pack that can easily be padlocked. A locked bag can, of course, be slashed open, but in Ghana you are still most likely to encounter casual theft of the sort to which a lock would be a real deterrent.

Clothes

Take the minimum, bearing in mind that you can easily and cheaply replace worn items in Ghana. In my opinion, what you need is one or possibly two pairs of trousers and/or skirts, one pair of shorts, three shirts or T-shirts, one light sweater, maybe a light waterproof windbreaker during the rainy season, enough socks and underwear to last five to seven days, one solid pair of shoes or boots for walking, and one pair of sandals, thongs or other light shoes.

When you select your clothes, remember that jeans are heavy to carry, hot to wear, and slow to dry. Far better to bring light cotton trousers and, if you intend spending a while in montane regions, tracksuit bottoms which will provide extra cover on chilly nights. Skirts are best made of a light natural fabric such as cotton. For reasons of protocol, women may prefer to wear a skirt that goes below the knees in the Muslim north – it's by no means necessary, since Ghanaians are relatively relaxed about dress codes, but single women in particular might find that a dress draws much less attention than skimpier attire.

T-shirts are lighter and less bulky than proper shirts, though the top pocket of a shirt (particularly if it buttons up) is a good place to carry spending money in markets and bus stations, since it's easier to keep an eye on than trouser pockets. One sweater or sweatshirt will be adequate, since no part of Ghana lies at an altitude above 1,000m, so night-time temperatures are almost invariably comfortable to sweaty. There is a massive used-clothing industry in Ghana, and at most markets you'll find stalls selling jumpers of dubious aesthetic but impeccable functional value for next to nothing – you might consider buying such clothing on the spot and giving it away afterwards.

Socks and underwear must be made from natural fabrics. Bear in mind that re-using sweaty undergarments will encourage fungal infections such as athlete's foot, as well as prickly heat in the groin region. Socks and underpants are light and compact enough that it's worth bringing a week's supply. As for footwear, genuine hiking boots are worth considering only if you're a serious off-road hiker, since they are very heavy whether on your feet or in your pack. A good pair of walking shoes, preferably made of leather and with good ankle support, is a good compromise. It's also useful to carry sandals, thongs or other light shoes.

Getting clothes made from local fabrics is also quick and relatively inexpensive. The markets sell all sorts of cotton-based cloth by the yard (slightly shorter than a metre) and the vendors will be able to take you to reliable local seamstresses.

Camping equipment

The case for bringing camping equipment to Ghana is compelling only if you intend hiking or visiting some of the more obscure reserves, where there is no other accommodation. In most other situations, rooms are cheap and campsites few and far between, so this isn't a country where camping will save huge sums of cash. The main argument against carrying camping equipment is that it will increase the weight and bulk of your luggage by up to 5kg, all of which is deadweight except for when you camp.

If you decide to carry camping equipment, the key is to look for the lightest available gear. It is now possible to buy a lightweight tent weighing little more than 2kg, but make sure that the one you buy is mosquito proof. Other essentials for camping include a sleeping bag and a roll-mat, which will serve as both insulation and padding. You might want to carry a stove for occasions when no firewood is available, as is the case in many montane national parks where the collection of firewood is forbidden, or for cooking in a tropical storm. If you do carry a stove, it's worth knowing that Camping Gaz cylinders are readily available only in southern Ghana (which is where you're most likely to do most of your camping and open-air catering). A box of firelighter blocks will get a fire going in the most unpromising conditions. It would also be advisable to carry a pot, plate, cup and cutlery.

Other useful items

Most backpackers, even those with no intention of camping, carry a **sleeping bag**. A lightweight sleeping bag will be more than adequate in Ghana; better still in this climate would be to carry a sheet sleeping bag, something you can easily make yourself. You might meet travellers who, when they stay in local lodgings, habitually place their own sleeping bag on top of the bedding provided. Nutters, in my opinion, and I'd imagine that a sleeping bag would be less likely to protect against fleas than to be infested by the things.

I wouldn't leave home without **binoculars**, which some might say makes me the nutter. Seriously, though, if you're interested in natural history, it's difficult to imagine anything that will give you such value-for-weight entertainment as a pair of light compact binoculars, which these days needn't be much heavier or bulkier than a pack of cards. Binoculars are essential if you want to get a good look at birds (Africa boasts a remarkably colourful avifauna even if you've no desire to put a name to everything that flaps) or to watch distant mammals in game reserves. For most purposes, 7x21 compact binoculars will be fine, though some might prefer 7x35 traditional binoculars for their larger field of vision. Serious birdwatchers will find a 10x magnification more useful.

Some travellers like to carry their own **padlock**, though in Ghana there are few circumstances where you are likely to need one, unless you have a pack that is lockable. A combination lock might be the best idea, since potential thieves in Ghana are far more likely to have experience of picking locks with keys.

Your **toilet bag** should at the very minimum include soap (secured in a plastic bag or soap holder unless you enjoy a soapy toothbrush!), shampoo, toothbrush and toothpaste. This sort of stuff is easy to replace as you go along, so there's no need to bring family-sized packs. Men will probably want a **razor**. Women should carry enough **tampons** and/or **sanitary pads** to see them through, since these items may not always be immediately available. If you wear **contact lenses**, be aware that the various cleansing and storing fluids are not readily available in Ghana and, since many people find the intense sun and dry climate irritates their eyes, you might consider reverting to glasses. Nobody should forget to bring a **towel**, or to keep handy a roll of **loo paper**, which although widely available at shops and kiosks cannot always be relied upon to be present where it's most urgently needed.

Other essentials include a **torch**, a **penknife** and a compact **alarm clock** for those early morning starts. If you're interested in what's happening in the world, you might also think about carrying a **short-wave radio**. Some travellers carry **games** – most commonly a pack of cards, less often chess or draughts or travel Scrabble. A light plastic **orange-squeezing device** gives you fresh orange juice as an alternative to fizzy drinks and water.

You should carry a small **medical kit,** the contents of which are discussed in *Chapter 4*, as are **mosquito nets**. Two items of tropical toiletry that are surprisingly difficult to get hold of in Ghana are mosquito repellent of a type suitable for skin application, and high-factor sunblock. In both cases, you are advised to bring all you need with you. One could spend a day in Accra unsuccessfully trying to get hold of mosquito repellent, though aerial repellents and mosquito coils can be bought almost anywhere. Only a few pharmacies in Accra stock sunblock (eg: the Pillbox Pharmacy off

Cantonments Road), and finding anything stronger than Factor 6 is nigh impossible.

MONEY
Organising your finances

There are three ways of carrying money: hard currency cash, travellers' cheques, or a credit card. My advice is to bring at least as much as you think you'll need in a combination of cash and travellers' cheques, but if possible to also carry a credit card to draw on in an emergency. I would strongly urge any but the most denominationally diehard of backpackers to bring their cash and travellers' cheques in the form of US dollars, and to learn to think and budget in this currency.

From the point of view of security, it's advisable to bring the bulk of your money in the form of travellers' cheques, which can be refunded if they are lost or stolen. It is best to use a widely recognised type such as American Express and Thomas Cook, and to keep the proof of purchase separate from the cheques, as well as noting which cheques you have used, in order to facilitate a swift refund should you require one. Buy your travellers' cheques in a healthy mix of denominations, since you may sometimes need to change a small sum only, for instance when you're about to cross into another country. On the other hand, you don't want an impossibly thick wad of cheques. For a trip to one country, I'd take five US$20 cheques and the remainder of my money in US$100 cheques. Whatever your bank at home might say, currency regulations and other complications make it practically impossible to break down a large denomination travellers' cheque into smaller ones in most African countries, so don't take denominations larger than US$100.

In addition to travellers' cheques, you should definitely bring a proportion of your money in hard currency cash, say around US$200–300, since you are bound to hit situations where travellers' cheques won't be accepted. Also cash gets a better exchange rate, especially large denomination bills – which isn't much consolation if all your money is stolen, so I'd strongly advise against bringing cash only, but would suggest that you save what cash you do bring for situations where it will buy you a real advantage.

Carry your hard currency and travellers' cheques, as well as your passport and other important documentation, in a money belt – one that can be hidden beneath your clothing rather than the sort of fashionable externally-worn type which in some circumstances will serve as a beacon rather than protection. Your money belt should be made of cotton or another natural fabric, and everything inside the belt should be wrapped in plastic to protect it against sweat.

Credit cards are not widely accepted, though they are of limited use in Accra. You can normally draw up to US$200 daily in local currency with a Visa card at autotellers outside any main branch of Barclays or Standard Chartered Bank. This facility is now available not only in Accra, but also in Kumasi, Cape Coast, Takoradi and many other large towns. Note, however, that every time I've travelled in Africa recently I've bumped into at least one person who's strayed a bit too far off the beaten track with only a credit card for support, so be conservative in your assumptions about where you'll be able to draw money against it. No matter how long you are travelling, do make sure that you won't need to have money transferred or drafted across to West Africa.

An airport departure tax of US$50 is levied on international flights out of Accra, a swingeing increase from US$20 that was imposed in April 2001. Before you pay it, check whether it has already been included in the price of your ticket.

In theory, any excess local currency can be changed back into dollars when you leave Ghana, provided you can provide proof of purchase from a bank or other licensed foreign exchange bureau. In practice, the banks at the airport will often refuse to offer this service, which leaves you stuck with spending your leftover cedis in unexciting duty-free shops which tend to charge high dollar rates and to offer a poor rate of exchange when spending local currency!

Costs and budgeting

Ghana is not an expensive country in which to travel. So far as travel basics go, at pre-2000 exchange rates accommodation for one or two people will probably average out at around US$5 per day for the cheapest room, US$8 per day for a self-contained room, and from US$20 per day for air-conditioned comfort. For food, expect to spend around US$2 per day per head if you eat street food only, and around US$5 if you eat once daily in a restaurant. Depending on how often and how far you travel, public transport shouldn't come to more than US$2 per day per head, while a charter taxi ride in most towns costs no more than US$1. The main thing you need to add to the above on a daily basis is liquid. Unless you drink tap water only, which is not advisable, you'll spend a lot of money just keeping your thirst quenched in Ghana's hot climate – say US$2 per head daily if you stick to mineral water and soft drinks, perhaps US$4 daily if you add on a couple of beers. Most of these prices had effectively halved at the end of 2000, as a result of the collapse in the exchange rate, but the likelihood is that this imbalance will not persist indefinitely.

Put this together, and you're looking at a rock-bottom budget of US$10/15 daily for one/two people (considerably more for any nights you spend at Mole National Park, unless you camp there). To travel in reasonable comfort, eat and drink what you feel like within reason and take the odd taxi, a budget of around US$20/30 for one/two people would be about right. If you want air-conditioning, two solid meals and the rest, I'd budget on US$40/50 for one/two people.

The above reckoning excludes one-off expenses such as entrance fees to museums or guiding fees in parks, factors that tend to create the occasional expensive day, markedly so for those on a tight budget. In countries such as Tanzania where national park fees and safari costs are very high, I've sometimes found it a useful budgeting device to separate one-off expenses from the more predictable day-to-day costs. As a rule, you'll have relatively few major one-off expenses in Ghana, though tips and guide fees, etc can start to add up in some places. If you are very tight for cash, rather than allocating yourself a budget of, say, US$15 per day, it might work better to aim for a daily budget of US$10 and set aside the rest for one-offs.

Travelling in Ghana

TOURIST INFORMATION AND SERVICES

There is a regional office of the Ghana Tourist Board in each of the country's ten regional capitals. On the whole, these offices should be worth visiting if you want to check up on new developments in the region, though our experience was that the staff are often surprisingly ignorant about even the most important local attractions. The most proactive tourist office in Ghana is undoubtedly the one for Volta Region, in the town of Ho – if you plan to explore this eastern part of Ghana then do pop in there.

All in all, however, your best source of current practical information will be travellers who have already been to the places where you are heading. Good places to connect with the travellers' grapevine include the Hotel de California in Accra, the Presbyterian Guesthouse in Kumasi, the motel in Mole National Park, Cape Coast, Busua on the west coast, and (as soon as it becomes better known) the Estuary Beach Camp near Ada on the east coast.

Contact addresses for regional tourist offices are as follows:

Accra Regional Admin Office, Barnes Rd, PO Box 3106, Accra; tel: 021 23 1817.
Bolgatanga (Upper East) Information Services Dept, PO Box 395, Bolgatanga; tel: 072 3416.
Cape Coast (Central) Jackson Road, PO Box 847, Cape Coast; tel: 042 32062.
Ho (Volta) SIC Building, PO Box 568, Ho; tel: 0756 22431.
Koforidua (Eastern) SIC Building, PO Box 771; tel: 081 23209/32128.
Kumasi (Ashanti) National Cultural Centre, PO Box 3065, Kumasi; tel: 051 26242/22421.
Sekondi-Takoradi (Western) Third Floor, SIC Building, PO Box 781, Takoradi; tel: 22357)
Sunyani (Brong Ahafo) Regional Admin Office, PO Box 802, Sunyani; tel: 061 7108.
Tamale (Northern) Regional Admin Office, PO Box 1053, Tamale; tel: 071 22212.
Wa (Upper West) Ministry of Trade and Industry, PO Box 289, Wa; tel: 0756 22431.

PUBLIC HOLIDAYS

Although several public holidays are recognised in Ghana, the only major impact they will have on tourists is that banks and government offices are closed and the volume of public transport decreases to a level you'd expect on a Sunday. There are five variable-date public holidays: the Christian Good Friday and Easter Monday, the Muslim Eid il Fitr and Eid il Adel, and Farmers' Day (first Friday in December). In addition, the following fixed- date public holidays are recognised:

January 1	New Year's Day	July 1	Republic Day
March 6	Independence Day	December 25	Christmas Day
May 1	May Day	December 26	Boxing Day
June 4	June 4 Anniversary		

MONEY

The unit of currency is the cedi (pronounced 'seedy'), formerly divided into 100 pesewas, but now so heavily devalued that any further subdivision would be meaningless. The value of the cedi has been in steady decline for some years. During the early 1990s, it devalued by roughly 100%, but then held reasonably steady at between 2,000 and 2,500 cedis to the US dollar until late 1999, since when it has devalued a further 200% to approach 7,000 to the dollar (10,000 to the UK£) in May 2001. It is impossible to predict what the exchange rate will be by the time readers of this guide visit the country.

Foreign exchange

The most widely recognised foreign currency is the US dollar. US dollars in cash can be exchanged for local currency in practically any town or border post, often at a bank or a private bureau de change (forex bureau). In Accra, Kumasi and to a lesser degree the other regional capitals, there's generally a large number of places where you can exchange US dollars cash and the rate may vary by as much as 10%, so it's worth shopping around. In smaller towns your options will probably be limited to one bank or forex bureau, so you'll have to take whatever rate you're offered. In towns where there are no banks, or if you want to exchange money outside the normal banking hours of 08.30 to 14.00, you'll rarely have a problem finding a private individual to exchange your US dollars. There is always a danger of being conned in such a situation, however, particularly when you deal with 'professional' money-changers at borders, so I would advise against changing significantly more money than you need to get to the next town with banking facilities.

The situation is less straightforward with more obscure currencies and with travellers' cheques. With other currencies, even major ones like the British pound or the German mark, you can forget about exchanging money with private individuals, and should plan ahead to ensure that you don't run out of money in a town without a bank or forex bureau. The same goes for travellers' cheques, with the added complication that practically no forex bureau will accept them, and that even the larger banks outside Accra have to get rates on a daily basis from the capital, a procedure that becomes less reliable the further north you go. If you are carrying mostly travellers' cheques, you should probably rely on being able to exchange money only in the regional capitals. North of Kumasi, you may be held up a day or two waiting for the rates to be faxed up. The simple solution to all this is to carry enough US dollars in the form of cash.

The three main banks with foreign exchange facilities are the Commercial Bank of Ghana, Barclays and the Standard Chartered. In general, they offer a lower rate of exchange for cash than the private forex bureaux. When we were in the country, the best exchange rate for travellers' cheques was invariably at the Standard Chartered Bank, which normally charges no commission.

If you are changing a large sum of money, do check that the bank or forex bureau can give you the bulk of your local currency in 5,000 cedi notes! It's also worth thinking about how and where you will carry your newly acquired pile of bank notes after a major transaction. You don't want to be walking around the streets of Accra with a few hundred US dollars worth of cedis and nowhere to conceal them.

Small change
The largest bill available is the 5,000 cedi note, which is worth less than US$1, yet finding small change (or as locals call it, 'balance') is an ongoing problem for Ghanaian traders – not to say for travellers. It's not at all unusual to be unable to make a purchase for, say, 100 cedis because nobody can find change for a 500 or 1,000 cedi note! The simple solution to this is to try to keep a reasonable balance of small bills and coins on you at all times. Bear in mind that tro-tro conductors and taxi drivers *always* seem to be able to find change, so never use your last 2,000 cedi bill on a taxi or tro-tro ride, but rather give them a big bill and get change from them. And if you are in a hurry and don't have the right amount when you buy something like a Coke, then pay before you start drinking so the vendor has time to find change.

Prices
With few exceptions (basically a handful of upmarket hotels in Accra), pretty much everything in Ghana can be paid for in the local currency. In many situations, attempting to pay for something in anything but cedis would create complete confusion. Nevertheless, when I first wrote this guide in 1998, I chose to quote prices in US dollars, partly to create a more useful impression of costs at the planning stage of a trip, but mostly because the high rate of inflation in Ghana and ongoing devaluation of the cedi threatened to make any price quoted in local currency look meaningless a few years on – and indeed the cedi devalued by more than 200% during the lifespan of the first edition.

The prices quoted in this second edition were collected over the last two months of 2000 and have been converted to US dollars at a rough rate of 7,000:1. This means that a hotel room which cost 21,000 cedis in late 2000 is quoted at US$3. Many hotels had barely increased their rates over 2000, despite the devaluation of the cedi, so that the same room might well have cost US$10 at the beginning of the same year. For this reason, I have, wherever possible, included the 1998 price of any given hotel as well as the current price – should it be the case that local prices do start to catch up with the drop in the exchange rates, it might well be that the older prices are a more reliable guide to what you'll be paying for a room come mid-2001 than the newer prices. Do note that all prices are approximate, since exchange rates vary widely, depending on where you change your hard currency and whether it is in the form of travellers' cheques or cash, and are generally rounded up or down to the nearest US$0.50.

A government levy of 15% is charged on all accommodation and restaurant meals in Ghana. At the lower end of the price range, hotels and restaurants generally include the levy in any advertised price, hence the frequency with which one comes across a room rate such as 16,900 or 18,050 cedis, seemingly designed to do nothing but waste time in a country where finding small change is a constant precipitator of mini-crises. By contrast, most upmarket hotels and restaurants quote prices exclusive of the levy, so that a room quoted at US$40 will actually cost you US$46. Where I am aware of the latter situation, I've raised figures accordingly to reflect what the room will actually cost.

GETTING AROUND
Car rental and driving
Of the established international companies, Hertz & Europcar have desks in some of the hotels in Accra (eg: Novotel, Golden Tulip, Labadi Beach). The head office for Hertz is on Nima Maamobi Highway (PO Box 15119, Accra North; tel: 021 223389/220510/776499; fax: 012 775009). They normally offer the car with driver (you pay his expenses) or you can ask for what they call 'self drive', where you pay quite heavy full cover insurance charges. Either way it is more expensive than Europe due to the lack of competition, and there are no small cars.

For a better price, contact the Niagara Hotel in Accra (see page 99), which can arrange sensibly priced car hire with a driver. They currently offer an excellent deal, particularly suitable for people who want to explore the Greater Accra area from the capital, which includes a 4x4 vehicle with driver plus a double room at the hotel for US$110 per day

An affordable alternative to renting a vehicle formally is to charter a taxi driver for one or more days. The rate for this sort of service is highly negotiable, and it will depend on the distance you want to travel, the number of days, and whether fuel and the driver's meals and room is included, but at worst you should be looking at around US$15–20 daily exclusive of extras such as fuel – a lot cheaper than car rental.

Petrol stations are plentiful (even if it's just a man with a few barrels by the roadside) and fuel is very cheap by any standards. There are tolls on most major routes, often at bridges, charging nominal fees. Official road signs exist, usually at junctions, and have white text on a green background. Otherwise, there is little indication of distances, or route confirmation on the roads.

Unusually for a former British colony, Ghana drives on the right-hand side of the road. Ten years ago, the state of Ghana's roads was appalling. In recent times, however, there has been large-scale upgrading of all the main routes, most of which are now surfaced. You could easily drive the entire coastal road from Aflao to Elubo in a saloon car, as you could the main north–south road from Accra to Paga via Kumasi and Tamale. In fact, there are now very few parts of the country which aren't accessible to practically any carefully driven vehicle – as evidenced by the ancient Peugeot taxis that cover the most unlikely of routes throughout Ghana. All the same, it would be prudent to seek local advice repeatedly as you move around the country, particularly if you visit more remote areas during the rainy season.

If you've never driven in Africa before, be aware that the general approach to driving is quite different to that in more developed countries. Ghanaians tend to be complete maniacs on the road, and visitors should be very cautious, particularly if they are also adapting to driving on the right-hand side of the road. In addition to a heart-stopping approach to overtaking, you will have to contend with potholes, pedestrians and domestic animals on the road. And be acutely aware that it's customary not to slow down on a blind curve but to race around it hooting wildly – if you don't hoot back, it will be assumed that no vehicle is coming! Driving at night is inadvisable, not so much for security reasons, but because the general chaos on the road is exacerbated by a lack of street lights and many vehicles without headlights.

Foreigners may drive for up to 12 months in Ghana on an international or foreign driving licence.

Public transport
Rail
What is effectively a triangle of railway lines connects Accra, Kumasi and Takoradi. The most popular rail service in the country is the one between Kumasi and Takoradi, largely because the equivalent road is in relatively poor condition. Details of this service are in the *Getting there and away* section under Kumasi.

Road
All major roads through Ghana are covered by a variety of public transport, divisible into three broad categories: buses, tro-tros and taxis. By comparison with many African countries, getting around Ghana's roads is very straightforward and comfortable, though the standard of driving leaves a great deal to be desired on the safety front.

In small towns and villages, there is generally one place from where all public transport leaves, referred to by Ghanaians as the 'station' or 'lorry station'. In larger towns, there will often be several different stations, each serving a set of destinations in one direction. STC, OSA and City Express buses may well leave from a different station to the one used by private tro-tros. This can become very confusing and, while I've tried to indicate the most important stations in most large towns, I'd advise readers to do things the easy way. Cough up a taxi fare (often as little as 50 cents) and ask the driver to take you to the right place. The convention is to ask for the 'station' for the destination you want – in other words, should you be looking for transport to Mampong, then ask to be taken to Mampong Station.

Most buses and tro-tros charge an extra fee for large luggage such as a backpack. On STC buses, you are charged formally according to the weight of the luggage going in the hold, a two-phase procedure which entails having your luggage weighed and being issued with a baggage tag, then going to a separate kiosk to pay the fee – which for a normal rucksack should be less than US$0.50. On other services, the charge is negotiable, and there are no hard and fast rules about how to handle it. In most cases, the fee is legitimate, and is also charged to local people, but travellers might well be overcharged sometimes, and may occasionally be asked for a luggage fee when a local wouldn't be. I was more inclined to accept the legitimacy of the fee when I was asked for it upfront rather than at the end of the trip, and when the sum seemed proportionate.

Buses
As a rule the safest and most efficient way of travelling is by bus. This is particularly the case when you travel directly between two major centres, for instance from Accra to Kumasi or Accra to Takoradi, since the government State Transport Company (STC) runs regular, reliable direct bus services along most major surfaced routes. STC buses typically cover around 80km/hour with one scheduled 15-minute meal break. Most STC buses will drop off passengers along the way, provided that they are prepared to pay full fare – in other words, the Accra–Kumasi bus will drop you at, say, Nkawkaw, but you must pay the same fare as you would to get to Kumasi. STC buses run to fixed departure times. On regular routes such as between Accra and Kumasi or Accra and Takoradi (buses virtually every hour throughout the day), we've

never had a problem just pitching up at the STC bus station, and buying a ticket for the next bus to leave. Some travellers have, however, reported not being able to buy tickets on the day, so if you want to play safe – particularly on minor routes or over holiday periods – I suggest you book your ticket the day before you want to travel.

On practically every major route in the country, even those where there is no STC bus, a cheaper service is provided by the OSA and/or City Express lines. Also run by the government, these lines are just as safe as the STC, but they are generally slower, partly because they stop for passengers more often and partly because the buses are older. OSA and City Express buses generally pick up and drop passengers as required, and fares are charged accordingly.

Bus fares in Ghana are very reasonable. A ticket for the STC bus between Accra and Kumasi, for instance, costs US$3.50 for a 250km ride that takes four to five hours. OSA and City Express buses are slightly cheaper for comparable distances.

Tro-tros

If anybody is aware of a more precise definition of a tro-tro than 'pretty much any passenger vehicle that isn't a bus or a taxi', then they are welcome to let me know about it. Tro-tros cover the length and breadth of Ghana's roads, ranging from comfortable and only slightly crowded minibuses to customised, covered trucks with densely packed seating, a pervasive aura of sweat, no view, and not much more chance of finding an escape route should you be involved in an accident. You will have little choice but to depend on tro-tros when you travel between smaller towns, but I would advise you to use buses wherever possible, not so much because tro-tros are slower or less comfortable than buses (though generally they are both) but because the risk of being involved in a fatal accident is so much greater.

Most tro-tros leave when they are full, and on all main roads you'll rarely wait more than 30 minutes for a vehicle heading in your direction. Be warned that many of the touts whose task it is to fill up tro-tros have a quite neurotic need to physically 'see' bums on seats. It can take all your powers of persuasion to convince them that if they could only use their imagination and pretend you are sitting in your seat, then you could stand outside while you wait for the vehicle to fill up rather than having to practise being uncomfortable in a sweaty, cramped, motionless vehicle for half an hour. And even when you think that you've had an incandescent moment of cross-cultural communication, as the tout appears to light up with recognition of the good sense of your position, he'll be edging up to you two minutes later hissing 'you sit, white man, you sit!'

Only on routes where there is very little transport do you need to think in terms of set departure times, and in such circumstances you should definitely check the situation the day before – it may, for instance, be the case that all the transport leaves before 06.00. It is also worth being aware that many tro-tros don't run on Sundays, particularly in Christian parts of the country, which means you'll generally wait longer for something to leave along main roads and may be delayed for hours or find that nothing is going at all along minor routes. Where possible, I would avoid travelling on a Sunday, though we frequently did and usually got where we wanted to in the end.

Fares on tro-tros are cheaper than on buses. I've not quoted fares in this guide, because they are subject to inflation and generally pretty predictable once you've been in the country for a few days. Typically, you can expect to pay around US$1 per 100km on a good road, and a little more on an inferior road because the journey takes longer. In many places, you have to buy a ticket at the booth of the Private Transport Union (or the GRPTU of TUC to give its full set of initials) for that specific route, and even when you just pay the conductor on the road, fares are fixed and overcharging is not a significant concern. As with buses, some tro-tros will charge the full fare to passengers dropping along the way.

Some Ghanaians refer to both buses and tro-tros as 'lorries'.

Taxis

I've never seen a country with so many taxis as Ghana, and I'd not be surprised to be told that they account for more than 80% of the vehicles on the road. Typically battered old Peugeots with orange wings, Ghanaian taxis can be split into two systems of operating: dropping and passenger taxis. The dropping system is essentially the one we are familiar with, where you charter a taxi privately, with the major difference being that Ghanaian taxis are not metered, so a price must be agreed in advance. The passenger system is where a taxi plies a specific route at a fixed fare, either picking up passengers along the way or else filling the vehicle at a recognised terminal.

Whichever system you use, taxis in Ghana are quite incredibly inexpensive, and it is well worth making use of them. In most parts of the country a dropping taxi will charge between US$0.50 and US$1 for a ride within a town (the price is a little higher in Accra) and a fare on a passenger taxi within any given town may be less than US$0.10 and will rarely be more than US$0.20.

Passenger taxis are often the main form of transport between two nearby towns, notably in the part of Ashanti northeast of Kumasi. They also often cover short roads between a junction and a nearby town, especially along the coast, where many towns and villages lie a few kilometres south of the main road. Generally these taxis take six passengers, two in the front and four in the back, but on some routes the convention is five or four passengers – don't ask me why! It will often be assumed by taxi drivers that any foreigner prefers a private taxi, so always specify when you want a 'passenger' not a 'dropping' vehicle. In most towns, you can normally assume that any empty taxi that stops for you will be offering you a 'dropping' service to wherever you like at a negotiable fare, whereas a vehicle that already has passengers will be offering you a lift in a specific direction at a fixed fare.

There may often be circumstances where you do want to use a private taxi. In Accra, for instance, it's barely worth figuring out the passenger taxi routes if you're only spending a night or two there. When you arrive in a town with luggage, it is often pleasant to catch a taxi to a hotel. Likewise, you may consider it a waste of time to wait an hour for a passenger taxi to fill up when, for instance, it is covering an 8km road at a cost of 500 cedis (US$0.07) per person, and you could charter the whole thing for 3,000 cedis (US$0.45). And note that in such circumstances it would be perfectly acceptable to pay the difference where the taxi is partially full – using the example above, if two passengers each paying 500 cedis were already sitting in the taxi when you arrived, you could offer to pay 2,000 cedis to make up the full fare of 3,000.

It should be understood by travellers that while passenger taxi fares are seen by Ghanaians to be fixed, dropping fares are perceived to be negotiable. You might ask a cab driver how much a passenger fare is and he'll tell you it's 500 cedis, then when you ask how much to charter the same taxi on the same route he'll say 5,000 cedis. It's very difficult to come up with a rule of thumb for determining the right dropping fare – you might ask two different taxi drivers for the same route and one will ask half what the other does – but you'll quickly get a feel for what seems reasonable, and should bear in mind that the dropping fare between two spots should work out at between four and six times the passenger fare.

Boat
The only ferry service in Ghana is the weekly Lake Volta ferry between Akosombo and Yeji, details of which are under *Akosombo* on page 218.

SLEEPING, EATING AND DRINKING
Accommodation
Accra, Kumasi and the major coastal resorts boast a selection of hotels suitable to most tastes and budgets, ranging from international-class skyscrapers to simple local resthouses and church-run establishments. Elsewhere in the country, the majority of hotels are simple and unpretentious places, geared primarily to the local market, and generally very good value for money, especially in late 2000 when the collapse of the exchange rate reduced most prices by 50% in hard currency terms (for which reason, we have in this edition followed current prices with 1998 prices in parenthesis, see note on page 55). For the most budget-conscious travellers, rooms typically start at around US$2–3 (1998 US$3–4) in smaller towns and in the north, and US$3–4 (1998 US$5–6) in larger towns and along the coast. Even at the bottom end of the price range, you'll rarely have to stay in real dumps of the sort you find in many other parts of Africa – the cheapest hotels generally have fans in the rooms, electricity in towns where there is a supply, and acceptable washing facilities. In most towns US$5–8 (1998 US$8–12) will get you a self-contained room with a fan, while for US$8–12 (1998 US$15–20) you can expect to find a room with air-conditioning and possibly television, running hot water and a fridge. Note that in Ghana, rooms with en-suite toilet and bath are generally referred to as self-contained, denoted in this guide as s/c.

One quirk to watch out for, particularly if you are travelling as a couple, is that a single room in Ghana is often a room with a double bed, while a double room is actually a twin (ie: with two beds). Sometimes, you'll also find that by single room the hotel actually means a double room sharing toilet and shower facilities, while a double room has exactly the same bed, but is self-contained. Generally, a couple will first be shown a room with two beds, presumably because it's normally the most expensive option, so if your preference is to share a bed, then ask to look at a single room first. If you're having trouble making your meaning clear, Ghanaians often talk about big and small beds – you're less likely to be misunderstood if you ask for a room with one big bed as opposed to asking for a double room. Single travellers might also take note that when I went out looking at hotels on my own, my request to see a room at a hotel where no prices were advertised almost invariably resulted in my being shown the most expensive option, often one with two large double beds

– quite what the receptionist imagined I would want to do with this prairie-like expanse of soft mattress, I don't know!

It is customary in Ghana for hotels to supply guests with an under-sheet only. Many hotels will supply you with a sheet to sleep under upon request, but many won't. Most of the time in Ghana you don't really need a top-sheet to keep you warm, but it can be pleasant to have something to break the direct effect of a fan and to help keep off mosquitoes. And then there are some people who just hate sleeping without some sort of cover. Ariadne says: if you're in that category, bring a sheet or similar with you.

There are relatively few opportunities for camping in Ghana and, accommodation being as cheap as it is, I think that for most people the hassle of carrying a tent and other camping equipment will outweigh the advantages. The major exception is if you expect to spend a lot of time visiting remote wildlife reserves and national parks, many of which are only realistically accessible to people with camping equipment.

Accommodation entries for the second edition of this guide have been categorised under four headings: upmarket, moderate, budget and shoestring. This categorisation is not rigid, but should nevertheless help travellers isolate the range of hotels in any given town that best suits their budget and taste. Broadly, upmarket hotels are three- to five-star affairs which meet international standards and typically quote rates in US dollars. Moderate hotels are typically one or two-star lodgings which approach but don't quite meet international standards, and are still comfortable enough for most tourists, offering a range of good facilities such as air-conditioning, satellite television, en-suite hot showers and toilet. Budget accommodation mostly consists of ungraded hotels which are aimed largely at the local market and definitely don't approach international standards, but are still reasonably comfortable and in many cases have air-conditioning and en-suite facilities. Shoestring accommodation consists of the cheapest rooms around, usually unpretentious local guesthouses or church-affiliated hostels. The categorisation has been decided on the feel of the hotel as much as the price; it is often relative to the other options in that town, and there are many hotels which were borderline cases. All the same, shoestring accommodation usually works out at comfortably under US$5 per double at 2000 exchange rates, budget at less than US$10, and moderate at under US$30 (except in Accra where it is more expensive). Most hotels in the lower three brackets quote room rates in local currency, which means that they were a lot cheaper in late 2000 than they would have been a year earlier.

Food

We found the food in Ghana to be refreshingly tasty, or perhaps that should more accurately be distinctly spicy, since it is the ubiquitous and liberal use of a hot, red type of powdered pepper that distinguishes Ghanaian cuisine from the bland local food served in most parts of eastern and southern Africa.

Among the great many starch-based staples you're likely to encounter in Ghana, the most popular are *fufu, kenkey, banku, tuo zafi* (TZ), *omo tua* (rice balls), boiled rice, and fried yam or plantain. Particularly popular in the south, *fufu* is made of cassava, plantain or yam, mashed to a pulp then cooked with no water to form a very gooey ball that's normally served submerged either in a light soup, or with palm oil or groundnut sauce. Almost identical to each other in taste and texture, and found throughout Ghana, *kenkey* and *banku* are made of fermented maize meal, the former boiled in a removable wrapping of plantain leaves, and normally eaten with a very spicy tomato relish. Largely restricted to the north, *tuo zafi* is a millet or maize-based porridge. Fried yam, often sold at markets, is not dissimilar in taste and texture to potato chips, though when bought on the street it often has a lingering, petroleum-like taste, presumably a result of using the same oil for too long. Most travellers find Ghanaian staples to be an acquired taste, and it's probably fair to say that while you wouldn't want to travel in Ghana without trying *fufu* or *kenkey*, you're unlikely to miss them when you return home.

Local food can be eaten in small restaurants known as 'chop bars', where you will generally be served with a plate of *fufu* or *kenkey* or rice along with a portion of meat or vegetable stew. Another typical chop bar dish is *jollof rice* – rice with chicken or meat cooked into it. A more interesting way of eating local food, and dirt cheap, is on the street. Most towns have at least one place where vendors sell a huge variety of dishes from informal stalls, often near the lorry station or the market. One advantage of eating on the street is you can try a bit of this or that, rather than be confronted with one specific dish. In addition to the usual staples, street vendors often sell grilled poultry (chicken, or in the north guinea fowl), spicy beef or goat kebabs, delicious sweet fried plantain with pepper seasoning, smoked fish, and deep-fried doughnut-like balls called *bo froot*.

Fresh fruit and vegetables are widely available, with a degree of regional and seasonal variety. The most characteristic fruits are probably pineapples, coconuts and oranges, the latter skinned in a way that makes it easy to suck the liquid out without getting sticky fingers. Another unexpected pleasure for the sweet of tooth is the locally manufactured chocolate – not a complete surprise when you consider that Ghana is one of the world's major cocoa producers, but unexpectedly good all the same. As for vegetables, tomatoes, onions and yams are available practically everywhere, but most others are mainly restricted to the south and the larger towns of the north.

When it comes to breakfast, you'll pay a small fortune for an egg, bread and tea in your hotel, so head rather for one of the tea stalls that are to be found in most markets and lorry stations. These places serve fresh, tasty tomato and onion omelettes, as well as bread and hot drinks. Note, however, that in Ghana tea seems to be a blanket term covering all hot drinks, so instead of asking for tea or coffee you should ask by brand name for Lipton (tea), Nescafé (coffee) or Milo (a chocolate malt drink). Bread, meanwhile, comes in three forms. The ordinary loaves, squarish but often with a pattern baked in, are known simply as 'bread' and are generally stale and unpleasantly sweet. What you want is tea bread, a crustier loaf that's often not much bigger than a large roll. You'll normally be able to find fresh tea bread somewhere around the market or lorry station, though you may want to resist any offer to have it smothered in margarine, since this is most often rancid. Butter bread is light and soft, and frequently easier to find than tea bread.

Finally, most towns of substance have at least one restaurant serving exotic dishes, most often straight Western chicken or steak with chips or rice. Quite why, I don't know, but there are a large number of Chinese restaurants in Ghana, and many of the more Westernised places and superior chop houses serve Chinese-style fried rice and spring rolls. A meal in a proper restaurant generally costs around US$4–6 per head excluding drinks, so it is a lot more expensive than eating on the street or in chop bars. If you are not carrying a lot of cash on you, remember to check the small print of the menu before you order, since many restaurants quote prices exclusive of the government levy and service charge – so that you actually pay around 15% more than the stated price.

Drinks

Starting with the familiar, all the usual brand name sodas are widely available in Ghana's fridges, particularly Coca-Cola, Fanta, Sprite and Schweppes soda water and tonic water. Locally bottled minerals are very cheap by any standards, though as a tourist you may sometimes be urged to waste your money on imported tins of the same drinks for twice the price. In addition to the international brands, there are a few uniquely Ghanaian minerals available. Now, it's not very nice to take the Mickey out of other people's names, but there is such a thing as asking for it. And ask for it, I'm afraid, is exactly what Mr Pee did when he started up a soft-drink factory and decided to name the product after himself – Pee Cola, indeed.

They say that the sound of the African bush is the piercing cry of the fish eagle. Well then, the sound of the Ghanaian bus station is indisputably the banshee wail of *Aaaaiiiiiiiiswuhtuh* emitted in best announcement voice by hordes of generally pre-pubescent girls. What they are selling is ice water: sealed plastic bags that contain chilled clear water and cost next to nothing. Two types of ice water are available. The more ubiquitous, often available even in small villages, comes in an unmarked bag and holds water from an undetermined source. The other type, slightly more expensive, and often referred to as 'pure water', is labelled, factory-sealed, and contains genuine mineral water. We drank both varieties without ill effect, which could well have been a triumph of luck over judgement. More sensible readers will probably prefer to stick to the labelled 'pure water' – or the more expensive 1.5-litre bottles of still mineral water that are widely available, though rarely chilled.

At most bus stations, you'll also see men trundling around with a selection of Fan Ice products, which include great frozen yoghurts in sachets, and a refreshing citrus-based drink called Tampico. Bottled pure orange and pineapple juice from Accra is also widely available at bars and restaurants catering to tourists. Also worth trying are the surprisingly good, sweetened Refresh fruit juices that come in 250ml packs. I never acquired much of a taste for Bruna, a fizzy, locally bottled fruit punch, but we both liked its Togolese equivalent, called Cocktail de Fruits, which is widely available in 750ml bottles in the Togolese border area. A cheap, refreshing and highly nutritious drink is fresh coconut juice. You'll often see street vendors selling piles of coconuts, particularly along the coast – just ask them to chop one open and you can slurp down the liquid.

The most widespread alcoholic drink is lager beer, which is brewed locally and generally pretty good. A 750ml bottle costs around US$1, depending on where you drink. Four brands of bottled beer are available: we settled on a preference order of Gulder, ABC, Star and finally Club. In the south, draught beer or Bubra is widely available and can go for as little as US$0.50 per pint. Also widely available are litre boxes of Spanish red and white wine, which sell for around US$1 per carton and are very drinkable at the price. Local bars in

Ghana are also called 'spots', and they can generally be distinguished a mile away by the blue-and-white picket fences that customarily enclose bars.

If you're interested in trying local tipples, several are available, all very cheap and generally rather potent. *Pito* is a type of millet beer, similar to the local beer brewed in villages in many parts of Africa, and most easily located in the *pito* bars that can be found in most towns, especially in the north. Palm wine, easily located on the coast, is called *ntunkum* in its mildest form and *doka* when it is older and stronger. *Akpeteshie* is a fiery spirit distilled from palm wine. It's frequently offered to visitors when they visit a village chief – the correct protocol is to spill a few drops on the ground in honour of the ancestors before you swig it down. Another popular drink is the locally bottled Schnapps, which many chiefs prefer as a libation to money!

INTERACTING WITH GHANAIANS

Ghana has a reputation as the friendliest country in West Africa, a title that is patently absurd but certainly not unjustified. Taken as a whole, Ghanaians do seem to be remarkably affable and friendly both among themselves and in their dealings with tourists, and I find it difficult to think of any other African country where I felt so safe or unhassled. First-time visitors to Africa, or at least those with a white skin, may be surprised at the amount of attention they draw by virtue of their conspicuous foreignness – symptoms of which range from having every passing taxi in Accra blare its horn at you to being greeted by mobs of exuberant children chanting *obruni* as you walk past. At times, this can be exhausting, but I cannot recall an incident of this type that was underscored by anything approaching malice. Put simply, Ghana is an amazingly welcoming country and, although you'll sometimes encounter people who treat all Westerners like a walking ATM, they are the exception, not the rule. You'd have to be extraordinarily unlucky to experience anything that could be described as seriously threatening or unpleasant.

Etiquette

Ghana, like any country, has its rules of etiquette, and, while allowances will normally be made for tourists, there is some value in ensuring they don't have to be made too frequently!

Perhaps the most important single point of etiquette for visitors to bear in mind is that it is considered highly insulting to use your left hand to pass or receive something or when shaking hands – a common custom in Muslim countries, and practised throughout Ghana. If you eat with your fingers, it is also customary to use the right hand only. Even those of us who are naturally right-handed will occasionally need to remind ourselves of this custom (it may happen, for instance, that you are carrying something in your right hand and so hand money to a shopkeeper with your left) and for those who are left-handed it will require constant effort.

Greeting procedures tend to be more formalised in Ghana than in modern Western societies, especially in small towns and villages, and elderly people in particular should be treated with special respect. If you need to ask somebody directions, or anything else for that matter, it is considered very rude to blunder straight into interrogative mode without first exchanging greetings – even when shopping! At village level, it is polite for strangers to nod to anybody they pass along the way.

It is customary to visit the chief of any village where you intend to stay overnight or to do any local sightseeing. In practice, this is no longer necessary in many villages, and where the custom has been continued in places that regularly receive tourists it tends to feel a bit showy. Only when you travel in really out-of-the-way areas is a visit to the chief likely to feel like a matter of etiquette over commerce, and here you should be especially careful to observe protocol. You will be expected to pay tribute in the form of kola nuts, a bottle of Schnapps, or money (the equivalent of about US$1 is normally fine). In return you may receive a glass of *Akpeteshie* (local gin), and it would be rude to refuse unless you use the excuse that you don't touch alcohol. Before drinking the gin, pour a few drops on the ground as a tribute to the forefathers. You should always take off your hat or cap in the presence of a chief (or any old person), and should never sit with your legs crossed in his presence.

Guides and tipping

One aspect of travel in Ghana that can become mildly enervating is the constant stream of guides and wannabe guides that tend to attach themselves to travellers. This is not something that's unique to Ghana, I grant you, but it is certainly more prevalent in Ghana than in many other African countries, so it is worth thinking through your attitude to this in advance. There is no doubt in my mind that using guides is in principle a good thing, since it ensures that tourism provides an income to local people, but there is also a line to be drawn; basically that the guide should in some way contribute to your experience.

Starting positively, there are many situations where a guide is an unambiguously worthwhile investment, for instance when visiting game reserves (where it is not permitted to walk without an armed guide) or at many historical sites (where knowledgeable guides are generally provided by request only). In such clear-cut circumstances – basically, where you are allocated a guide by an institution – you *will* normally pay a fee, but since this will not go directly to the guide (who in all probability is poorly paid) it is proper and customary to tip. It's difficult to give an exact guideline for tipping, since this depends on group size and the quality of service, but at current exchange rates a figure of around 2,000 cedis (US$0.30) per group member per hour feels about right. Another way of looking at it would be to tip around half of what you paid as an actual fee, bearing in mind the guide fees in Ghana are generally very reasonable.

The guide situation becomes more ambiguous when it isn't institutionalised. Even here, though, there are some reasonably straightforward scenarios. At places such as Bonwire or Tongo, for instance, visitors are normally approached by a cluster of prospective guides on arrival. There is no reason why you should take one on in such circumstances but, once you've selected somebody who seems a good bet and you've agreed a fee, you'll be left in peace by the other guides, and the one you've chosen will generally be able to add a great deal of insight to what you see. One cautionary note in this sort of situation is that guides will often agree to a fee, but then when you pay them this amount they go on a major sulk because you haven't tipped them. Personally, I don't see any valid reason why an additional tip should be given to a private individual with whom you've already agreed a fee, and nine times out of ten, when people sulk, they are simply chancing it.

The right approach to this sort of situation is to talk through costs at the negotiation stage. Stress to the guide that whatever fee is agreed is final and inclusive of a tip. Check, too, what other fees must be paid – it's not unusual to agree to a guide fee thinking that it covers the full excursion, only to find that the village chief also wants his fee, the caretaker his fee, the guy who thrusts himself unbidden into the middle of your photo his modelling fee, etc. This may feel like nit-picking to our Western mentalities, but Africans are accustomed to negotiation and will not be offended if it is conducted in good humour. The reality is that most of us in most situations are more comfortable when we get a full quote than when there are hidden extras (think of taking your car to a garage!). The overwhelming argument in favour of clarifying things at the outset is that it will decrease the likelihood of bad feeling later.

Now for the difficult bit, difficult because it is so riddled with ambiguity. This might aptly be described as people who are under the illusion (or think that you are under the illusion) that they are a guide. One type is the person who, for instance, greets you at the bus station, asks you where you are going, follows you there, then demands a fee for being your guide. Then there are those who attach themselves to you in a manner that is nothing short of intrusive, butting into your conversation and prattling on about themselves in a way that can only be described as self-absorbed, and then expect you to give them a guide fee or a tip when finally you part ways – penance, presumably, for having been too polite to have told them to bugger off and annoy somebody else in the first place. It's pretty easy to refuse in this sort of situation, but there is a whole hazy area in between. For instance you meet a perfectly likeable guy, get chatting, wander around together for a while, then suddenly find that he is dropping broader and broader hints in the direction of payment for an imagined service. It is easy enough to explain and understand this behaviour, and I don't see any point in reiterating the obvious here. The point is whether tourists should allow guilt or whatever else to make them feel obliged to pay somebody for no other reason than that they have been asked, and the person who asked is poorer than they are. Be generous with genuine beggars. Be generous when tipping genuine guides. By all means, slip a small note to the person who cleans your room, and shrug your shoulders over 100 cedis change. But before you give money to a random individual who in all probability befriended you for the express purpose of financial gain, think – if not about those travellers who will follow in your wake, then certainly about the type of relationship you would like to see develop between the people of Ghana and the tourists who, collectively, are already the country's third biggest source of foreign revenue.

On a less ardent note, it is not customary to tip for service in local bars and chop bars, though you may sometimes want to leave a tip (in fact, given the difficulty of finding change in Ghana, you may practically be forced to do this in some circumstances), in which case 5% would be very acceptable and 10% generous. Most restaurants catering to Western palates automatically add a 5% or 10% service charge to the bill, and this (in theory) goes to the waiter, but it can do no harm to give a cash tip if you feel the service was good.

Bargaining and overcharging

Tourists to Ghana do sometimes need to bargain over prices, particularly in Accra, but generally only in reasonably predictable circumstances, such as when chartering private taxis, organising guides, or buying curios and to a lesser extent other market produce. Prices in hotels, restaurants, shops and public transport are generally fixed, and overcharging in such places is too unusual for it to be worth challenging a price unless it is blatantly ridiculous.

You're bound to be overcharged at some point in Ghana, but it is important to keep this in perspective. Some travellers, after a couple of bad experiences, start to haggle with everyone from hotel owners to old women selling fruit by the side of the road, often accompanying their negotiations with aggressive accusations of dishonesty. Unfortunately, it is sometimes necessary to fall back on aggressive posturing in order to determine a fair price, but such behaviour is also very unfair on those people who are forthright and honest in their dealings with tourists. It's a question of finding the right balance, or better still looking for other ways of dealing with the problem.

The main instance where bargaining is essential is when buying curios. What should be understood, however, is that the fact a curio seller is open to negotiation does not mean that you were initially being overcharged or ripped off. Curio sellers will generally quote a price knowing full well that you are going to bargain it down (they'd probably be startled if you didn't) and it is not necessary to respond aggressively or in an accusatory manner. It is impossible to say by how much you should bargain the initial price down. Some people say that you should offer half the asking price and be prepared to settle at around two-thirds, but my experience is that curio sellers are far more whimsical than such advice allows for. The sensible approach, if you want to get a feel for prices, is to ask the price of similar items at a few different stalls before you actually contemplate buying anything.

In fruit and vegetable markets and stalls, bargaining is often the norm, even between locals, and the most healthy approach to this sort of haggling is to view it as an enjoyable part of the African experience. There will normally be an accepted price band for any particular commodity. To find out what it is, listen to what other people pay and try a few stalls. A ludicrously inflated price will always drop the moment you walk away. When buying fruit and vegetables, a good way to get a feel for the situation is to ask for a bulk discount or a few extra items thrown in. And bear in mind that when somebody is reluctant to bargain, it may be because they asked a fair price in the first place.

Above all, don't lose your sense of proportion. No matter how poor you may feel, it is your choice to travel on a tight budget. Most Ghanaians are much poorer than you will ever be, and they do not have the luxury of choosing to travel. If you find yourself quibbling with an old lady selling a few piles of fruit by the roadside, stand back and look at the bigger picture. There is nothing wrong with occasionally erring on the side of generosity.

Theft

The level of crime against tourists is remarkably low in Ghana, and it is difficult to think of a safer African capital than Accra. In our entire time in the country, we heard one third-hand report of a tourist being robbed. Tellingly, even upmarket hotel managers seem to feel that walking around Accra is safe at any time of day or night, and one said that he doesn't bother locking his car when he parks it in the city centre. Of the 50-plus emails and letters I received in response to the first edition of this guide, only a couple mentioned first- or second-hand problems with crime, none of which was life-threatening

(Kokrobite Beach is evidently the one place in Ghana where there is a regular problem with tourists being robbed). While hugely reassuring, this should not be cause for complacency. Firstly, things can change – Malawi was just as safe as Ghana is now when I spent three months there in 1995, yet these days every letter I receive from readers of my Malawi guide stresses that several people they met in the country had been mugged or robbed. And even in a relatively safe African country, tourists are easy game for whatever criminal element exists. As things stand, it would be wholly inappropriate to be anything but relaxed and open in your dealings with Ghanaians; you certainly oughtn't to be ruled by fear. Nevertheless, the risk of being pickpocketed or mugged does exist, and the basic common-sense precautions appropriate to travelling in any African country are worth repeating here:

- Most casual thieves operate in busy markets and bus stations. Keep a close watch on your possessions in such places, and avoid having valuables or large amounts of money loose in your day pack or pockets.
- Keep all your valuables and the bulk of your money in a hidden money belt. Never show this money belt in public. Keep any spare cash you need elsewhere on your person.
- I feel that a button-up pocket on the front of the shirt is the most secure place for money, as it cannot be snatched without the thief coming into your view. It is also advisable to keep a small amount of hard currency (ideally cash) hidden away in your luggage so that, should you lose your money belt, you have something to fall back on.
- Where the choice exists between carrying valuables on your person or leaving them in a locked room I would tend to favour the latter option (only one of the hundreds of thefts I've heard about in Africa happened from a locked hotel room, and that was in Nairobi where just about anything is possible). Obviously you should use your judgement on this and be sure the room is absolutely secure. A factor to be considered is that some travellers' cheque companies will not refund cheques which are stolen from a room.
- Leave any jewellery of financial or sentimental value at home.

Women travellers

It's difficult to imagine a country where women have less to fear on a gender-specific level. We met several women travelling alone in Ghana, and none of them had any serious problems in their interactions with locals. An element of flirtation is about the sum of it, perhaps the odd direct proposition, but nothing that cannot be defused by a firm 'no'. And nothing, for that matter, that you wouldn't expect in any Western country, or – probably with a far greater degree of persistence – from many male travellers. It may, however, sometimes help to pretend you have a husband at home.

It would be prudent to pay some attention to how you dress in Ghana, particularly in the more conservative Muslim north. It's not that Ghanaians would be deeply offended by women travellers wearing shorts or other outfits that might be seen to be provocative, but it pays to allow for local sensibilities, and under certain circumstances revealing clothes may be perceived to make a statement that you don't intend.

More mundanely, tampons are not readily available in smaller towns, though you can easily locate them in Accra and Kumasi. If you're travelling in out-of-the-way places, it's advisable to carry enough to see you through to the next time you'll be in a large city, bearing in mind that travelling in the tropics can sometimes cause women to have heavier or more regular periods than they would at home. Sanitary pads are available in most towns of any size.

Ariadne and I travelled as a couple, and were thus shielded from hassles facing single travellers (male or female), so by way of reassurance let me quote a letter from Louise Macpherson, a reader of the first edition: 'I was a single white female travelling alone and I have never felt so safe.'

Public toilets

For those unused to travel in the developing world, it should be noted that public toilets in Ghana, as in most other parts of Africa, leave much to be desired by Western standards. Often, few such facilities are available – in many rural areas specific stretches of beach or patches of wasteland serve as communal dumping grounds – and where they do exist they tend to be dirty and may not have running water. Restaurants, hotels and bars are your best bet if you are caught short, though smaller chop shops and drinking spots won't normally have a toilet. Many bus stations have public toilets which are kept clean by virtue of charging a small fee for use. It's a good idea always to carry some toilet paper around with you, as not all toilets will have it.

Among Ghanaians, it seems to be perfectly acceptable to urinate publicly – men pretty much anywhere, women more generally in rural areas than in towns – a solution more likely perhaps to appeal to male travellers than females. To be sure of not offending anybody, it's a good idea to ask a local person of the same gender where you can urinate. Nobody will find this strange – in my experience, Ghanaians are not at all coy about this sort of thing (I've often asked for a toilet in a bar and been asked bluntly – sometimes with graphic miming gestures – whether I need to urinate or the other thing). What will create total confusion is if you resort to euphemisms or more informal, slangy terms – most Ghanaians will not know what is meant by a rest room or a piss!

Bribery and bureaucracy

For all that you read about the subject, bribery is not the problem it is often made out to be, and I've heard of no specific incident where a traveller to Ghana was asked for a bribe. Don't worry about it!

As for the tendency to portray African bureaucrats as difficult and inefficient in their dealings with tourists, this says a great deal more about Western prejudices that it does about Ghana. Sure, you come across the odd unhelpful official, but then such is the nature of the beast everywhere in the world. In Ghana, we encountered nothing but friendliness from almost every government official we had dealings with. This, I can assure you, is far more than most African visitors to Europe will experience from officialdom.

A factor in determining the response you receive from African officials will be your own attitude. If you walk into every official encounter with an aggressive, paranoid approach, you are quite likely to kindle the feeling held by many Africans that Europeans are arrogant and offhand in their dealings with other races. Instead, try to be friendly and patient, and accept that the person to whom you are talking may not speak English as fluently as you, or may struggle to follow your accent. Treat people with respect rather than disdain, and they'll tend to treat you in the same way.

Asking directions

There is no polite way of saying it: most Ghanaians are utterly clueless when it comes to estimating distance or time in any measure more objective than 'far' and 'not far'. Travellers, particularly those needing directions off the beaten track, will have to allow for this.

One regular and reasonably straightforward area of confusion is the difference between miles and kilometres, measurements which many Ghanaians seem to see as interchangeable. It's always better to ask for a distance in miles, the measure still used by most people, even though signposts generally show distances in kilometres. If you're not familiar with one or other system of measurement, you can convert distances using the equation that five miles is roughly equivalent to eight kilometres, while three feet (or a yard) is basically the same as one metre – imprecise equations, I grant you, but more than adequate for practical travel purposes. Another way of verifying distances is to ask both the distance and the time – in reasonably flat conditions, a reasonably fit walker will cover 5km (3 miles) in one hour.

That said, it's difficult to figure out how a bar worker who not only speaks good English, but also has the capacity to make drawing a pint of draught look as exhausting as running a marathon, can say that a hotel 2km distant is three minutes' walk away. Or how people living at Larabanga and Mole, not to say various books, can come up with estimates as divergent as 3km and 10km for the road between Larabanga and Mole Motel. Or how a signpost at Vame reads 'Amedzofe 5km' when the two towns are less than 3km apart by road. We hit this sort of problem on a daily basis, and found it difficult to escape the conclusion that a lot of Ghanaians simply say whatever figure first comes into their head – not with the deliberate intent of misleading visitors, but because the measurements that are so important to us mean very little to somebody who has lived in a small town all their life and 'knows' how far one place is from another without ever having had reason to translate that knowledge into hours or kilometres.

It goes without saying that a great deal more interrogation about distances is required when you're researching a travel guide than when you are using one. Still, two points ought to be passed on to readers. The first, particularly if you are hiking, is to ask at least three or four people how far away somewhere is, to use some judgement in interpreting the answers, and to accept that you'll probably never know for sure until you walk there yourself. The second is that I've had to guestimate a great many walking distances in this guide, but they are informed and generally based on first-hand experience and, unlike many of the short distances that are quoted so emphatically by other books, by people you meet, and even on some maps, they will not be wildly out!

Photographic etiquette

The unwritten law of photography in Africa is that anybody you actually want to photograph will refuse permission, while it is often practically impossible to take a photo of a static subject without having 20 snotty brats leaping uninvited into the frame. Seriously, though, the question of photographing people is a sticky one, especially in Muslim parts of the country, and the first rule at all times is to ask permission and accept gracefully if it is refused, no matter how much it hurts (and if, like Ariadne, photography is the main purpose of your trip to Ghana, then it can be really depressing to miss wonderful photograph after wonderful photograph through the potential subject's refusal to co-operate). It is not customary in most parts of Ghana to pay to take a photograph, and I must admit that I'd be sad to see such a custom develop. That said, there are a few instances (the *kente* weavers at Bonwire leap to mind) where you will be expected to pay to photograph a particular subject.

When somebody does agree to let you photograph them, your next question will often be how to go about it without every nearby child leaping into the frame. If you have a point-and-shoot, the answer is to take the picture as quickly as you can. On the other hand, if you have a camera that requires a certain amount of fiddling around, then you may have to compromise by first taking a group photo, and then trying to clear the frame of extraneous kids, bearing in mind that if they then decide to line up behind you, there's a good chance that the photograph will be spoiled by their shadows. Another thing to bear in mind is that people often pose very stiffly when you point a camera at them and relax only when the flash goes off, so it may help to take two shots in quick succession, hoping that the second one will capture a more natural pose. As a rule, you can forget about taking good photos of Africans without fill-in flash, since their skin is very dark by comparison with the bright light.

You should be conscious that until recently there were strict photographic restrictions in Ghana, and that even now you could get in trouble by pointing a camera at any sensitive subject, such as a bridge, dam wall, prison (which includes several of the old coastal forts) or military installation. In general, however, you can photograph what you like, though you may sometimes encounter individuals who will feel a need to interfere in what you're doing. Mostly they're just playing to the crowd, but that doesn't mean you shouldn't recognise when you'd be better off standing down. One way to counter this type of thing is always to ask somebody standing around whether it's OK to 'snap' (as they say locally) whatever subject takes your fancy – once somebody has given you the nod, they will generally back you up should somebody else make a problem, though here again you should be sensitive to not letting anything ugly develop.

One last thought, if you're not particularly keen on photography, is this: why not leave your camera at home and buy a few postcards before you leave? Ultimately, cameras are heavily intrusive, and trying to get good photos of people will often create more frustration than pleasure.

For more technical tips about photography, see the photography box on page 72.

Please give me ...

... are the opening three words of many a one-line interaction with children in Ghana (and elsewhere in Africa). Usually the sentence finishes with a request for one of three things: money, a pen, or an address. In general, I suggest you answer the first two in the negative. Children who ask for money are not necessarily especially needy, more likely just chancing it, and every tourist who accedes to such a request with a pittance is guilty of reinforcing behaviour that has a far greater effect on people's dignity than on their well-being – it is notable that swarms of children asking for money is a

PHOTOGRAPHY
Ariadne Van Zandbergen
Equipment

Although with some thought and an eye for composition you can make nice photos with a 'point and shoot' camera, you need an SLR camera with one or more lenses if you are at all serious about photography. If you carry only one lens in Ghana, a 28-70mm or similar zoom should be ideal. For a second lens, a 80-200mm or 70-300mm or similar will be excellent for candid shots, for wildlife, and for varying your composition.

Film

Print film is the preference of most casual photographers, slide film of professionals and some dedicated amateurs. Slide film is more expensive than print film, but this is broadly compensated for by cheaper development costs. Most photographers working outdoors in Africa favour Fujichrome slide film, in particular Sensia 100, Provia 100 (the professional equivalent to Sensia) or Velvia 50. Slow films (ie: those with a low ASA (ISO) rating) produce less grainy and sharper images than fast films, but can be tricky without a tripod in low light. Velvia 50 is extremely fine-grained and shows stunning colour saturation; it is the film I normally use in soft, even light or overcast weather. Sensia or Provia may be preferable in low light, since 100 ASA allows you to work at a faster shutter speed than 50 ASA. Because 100 ASA is more tolerant of contrast, it is also preferable in harsh light.

For print photography, a combination of 100 or 200 ASA film should be ideal. For the best results it is advisable to stick to recognised brands. Fujicolor produces excellent print films, with the Superia 100 and 200 recommended.

Some basics

The automatic programmes provided with many cameras are limited in the sense that the camera cannot think, but only make calculations. A better investment than any amount of electronic wizardry would be to read a photographic manual for beginners and get to grips with such basics as the relationship between aperture and shutter speed.

Beginners should also note that a low shutter speed can result in camera shake and therefore a blurred image. For hand-held photographs of static subjects using a low magnification lens (eg: 28-70), select a shutter speed of at least 1/60th of a second. For lenses of higher magnification, the rule of thumb is that the shutter speed should be at least the inverse of the magnification (for instance, a speed of 1/300 or faster on a 300 magnification lens). You can use lower shutter speeds with a tripod.

Most modern cameras include a built-in light meter, and give users the choice of three types of metering: matrix, centre weighted or spot metering. You will need to understand how these different systems work to make proper use of them. Built-in light meters are reliable in most circumstances, but in uneven light, or where there is a lot of sky, you may want to take your metering selectively, for instance by taking a spot reading on the main subject. The meter will tend to under- or overexpose when pointed at an almost white or black subject. This can be countered by taking a reading against an 18% grey card, or a substitute such as grass or light grey rocks - basically anything that isn't almost black, almost white or highly reflective.

Dust and heat

Dust and heat are often a problem in Africa. Keep your equipment in a sealed bag, stow films in an airtight container (such as a small cooler bag), leave used films in your hotel room, and avoid changing film in dusty conditions. On rough roads, I always carry my camera equipment on my lap to protect against vibration and bumps. Never stow camera equipment or film in a car boot (it will bake), or let it stand in direct sunlight.

Light

The light in Africa is much harsher than in Europe or North America, for which reason the most striking outdoor photographs are often taken during the hour or two of 'golden light' after dawn and before sunset. Shooting in low light may enforce the use of very low shutter speeds, in which case a tripod (ideally) or monopod (lighter) will be required to avoid camera shake. Be alert to the long shadows cast by a low sun; these show up more on photographs than to the naked eye.

With careful handling, side lighting and backlighting can produce stunning effects, especially in soft light and at sunrise or sunset. Generally, however, it is best to shoot with the sun behind you. Because of this, most buildings and landscapes are essentially a 'morning shot' or 'afternoon shot', depending on the direction in which they face. When you spend a couple of nights in one place, you'll improve your results by planning the best time to take pictures of static subjects (a compass can come in handy).

When photographing people or animals in the harsh midday sun, images taken in light but even shade are likely to look nicer than those taken in direct sunlight or patchy shade, since the latter conditions create too much contrast. Fill-in flash is almost essential if you want to capture facial detail of dark-skinned people in harsh or contrasty light.

Serious photographers should avoid travelling during the Harmattan, since the sky is perpetually grey and ugly during this period (see page xx).

Protocol

Except in general street or market scenes, it is unacceptable to photograph people without permission. Expect some people to refuse or to ask for a donation. Even the most willing subject will often pose stiffly when a camera is pointed at them; relax them by making a joke, and take a few shots in quick succession to improve the odds of capturing a natural pose.

EDUCATION AND THE 'TREE' SCHOOL

Tricia Hayne

Near the fishing village of Nyanyano, west of Accra, there is a school which today has over 500 pupils. Not so extraordinary, except that this school was the inspiration of just one man. Seven years ago, Dave Mustill came across a group of children sitting under a tree, singing. It was an ordinary school day, but during the heavy rains, school was cancelled. Struck by the unfairness of the situation, Dave set about giving these children a roof over their heads – and so was born 'The Lord is My Shepherd Educational Centre'.

Although the government aims to make primary school compulsory, the reality is that only 60% of children receive any formal education. The children here are among the lucky ones. Their fees of around US$1.50 a week, the norm in Ghana, include their tuition, meals and transport – it takes two buses an hour and a half to bus all the children to and from school! As well as a hall, modern classrooms and a library, there is a science room, and workshops where older children are trained in dressmaking and carpentry, giving them a viable trade and raising money from the sale of their work to boost funds. The more academic sit the West Africa exams to go on to senior school. But, most important of all, school doesn't stop when it rains.

For further information contact Dave Mustill, 61 Malden Hill Gardens, New Malden KT3 4HX, England; tel: 020 8949 2864. Cheques should be made out to 'Ghana School Project'.

phenomenon associated with areas where you find the greatest numbers of tourists, not the worst levels of poverty. And be aware that children who ask tourists for pens are no more worthy than their money-grabbing peers, just a great deal more sophisticated – they know that the average liberal Westerner is more likely to part with a pen than with cash. Finally, there's no need to be rude when fobbing off what are basically light requests; far better to do something that makes the children laugh, like pulling a silly face or something else unexpected.

The address business – a request you can expect at least a dozen times a day – is an odd one. For years I mostly handed out fake addresses when I travelled in Africa, simply because it became too complicated to explain that I'd never get around to writing to the hundreds of people who asked for my address on every trip. Recently, however, it occurred to me that even though I'd also often given out my genuine address, mainly to people with whom I'd actually become friendly, I have only once ever had a response (and this, bizarrely, five years after the event from a person who described a meeting I couldn't recall in a place I'd never visited!). In Ghana, as an experiment, I gave my genuine address to hundreds of people. I've yet to have one response. My only explanation is that we're dealing with the African equivalent of autograph hunting – it is the address itself, not the writing, that is the point of the exercise. One reader responded to these comments in the first edition by saying they had handed out their address regularly and received a huge volume of mail, so perhaps we've been lucky.

I should probably clarify, just in case anybody thinks I'm being a monster, that the above comments about giving money and pens apply only to children (or occasionally adults) who ask for things purely because you are a Westerner. I see no harm whatsoever in giving money to a genuine beggar (in other words somebody who was begging before you came on the scene) and would actively encourage generosity towards those who obviously have no other means of sustaining themselves – I was struck by the ease with which salaried Ghanaians give to beggars, and would suggest that if they can do it, then so can we.

MEDIA AND COMMUNICATIONS
Newspapers
Several English-language newspapers are printed in Ghana, of which the well established *Daily Graphic* is probably the best. The weekly *Graphic Sport* is of great interest to ardent followers of African football, but coverage of other sports is at best cursory. In Accra you can buy imported newspapers at a highly inflated price – far better to spend a cosy hour catching up on international news in the air-conditioned confines of the British Council in Accra or Kumasi, both of which have a pile of English newspapers from three to four days old.

Telephone
Ghana's telephone system is reasonably efficient. From overseas, it's one of the easiest African countries to get through to first time. The ringing tone is a single short tone followed by a longer pause, and the engaged tone is equal lengths on and off. International calls out of Ghana can be made at official telecommunication centres, and a bit more expensively (but with less queuing) at many upmarket hotels and at private telecommunication centres offering IDD (International Direct Dialling) – the latter are usually available even in small towns. Cheapest and most efficient of all, at least where the facility is available, is to use a phone booth that takes phonecards. When dialling overseas, the country code should be preceded by 00.

Dialling into Ghana, the international code is +233. Major area codes are as follows:

Accra	021	Ho	091	Takoradi	031
Ada	0968	Hohoe	0935	Tamale	071
Akosombo	0251	Keta	0966	Tema	0221
Axim	0342	Koforidua	081	Wa	0712
Bolgatanga	072	Kumasi	051	Winneba	041
Cape Coast	042	Navrongo	072		
Dunkwa	0372	Sunyani	061		

Post
Post from Ghana is cheap and reasonably reliable, but often very slow. Poste Restante letters can be collected in most large towns, and they should be addressed as in the following example:

Philip Briggs
Poste Restante
Accra
Ghana

Electric devices

Electricity is 220V AC at 50 cycles. Stabilisers are required for sensitive devices and adaptors for appliances using 110V. Batteries are useful during power cuts, though such events are increasingly rare.

Radio and television

The Ghana Broadcasting Corporation produces a reasonable television service by African standards, though it's nothing to shout about by any other. The state-owned radio service, by contrast, is quite exceptional, with some good news and issue coverage and an eclectic mix of music – except on Sundays when it's hijacked by God. You can pick it up on 95.7 FM. Travellers with short-wave radios can pick up BBC World Service on 15400 KHz throughout most of the day and 17830 KHz between 08.30 and 23.30 – programme details are available from the British Council in Accra. Voice of America broadcasts from 03.00 to 22.30, but the frequency changes regularly throughout the day.

An increasing number of hotels in the middle to upper price range, as well as many bars catering to expats and tourists, subscribe to a South African satellite multi-channel pay service called DSTV. The package varies from one hotel to the next, but it generally includes M-Net, which shows reasonably current movies and serials, as well as Movie Magic (mostly one- to two-year old movies), BBC World, CNN and Supersport, the latter showing a good selection of current sporting events, with an inevitable bias to sports popular in South Africa (football, cricket, rugby) and events involving South African teams.

Internet and email

The internet has caught on in Ghana in a big way, making communication with home far easier and cheaper than it was even a couple of years ago. There must be dozens of internet cafés in Accra, concentrated in Osu and to a lesser extent Adabraka, the two suburbs where most travellers stay, and there are private internet cafés in most other substantial towns, including Kumasi, Tamale, Cape Coast, Takoradi, Ho and Hohoe. In smaller towns, the post office or telecommunication centre may have internet facilities. Rates are very reasonable, though cheaper in Accra than elsewhere, but do note that servers are generally rather slow by comparison to Europe or North America.

Business

The first port of call for anybody thinking of establishing a business in Ghana should be the Ghana Promotion Investment Centre, PO Box M193 Accra; tel: 021 665125/6/7/8/9; fax: 021 663801.

Health and Safety

Written in collaboration with Dr Jane Wilson-Howarth and Dr Felicity Nicholson

This is the chapter which always gives me the creeps when I read a travel guide, and I'm quite sure that some readers will question the sanity of travelling to Ghana by the time they finish it. Don't let it get to you – with the right vaccinations and a sensible attitude to malaria prevention the chances of serious mishap are small. It may help put things in perspective to point out that, after malaria, your greatest concern in Ghana should not be the combined exotica of venomous snakes, stampeding elephants, gun-happy soldiers and the Ebola virus, but something altogether more mundane: a road accident.

HEALTH
Preparations
In addition to considering the points made directly below, do read this entire section before you leave, since subjects such as malaria prevention are discussed under a separate heading.

Travel insurance
Don't think about travelling without a comprehensive medical travel insurance policy, one that will fly you home in an emergency. The ISIS policy, available in Britain through STA (tel: 020 7361 6160), is inexpensive and has a good reputation. Pack a good insect repellent, at least one long-sleeved cotton shirt and one pair of long trousers, a hat and sunscreen; these are important insurance measures.

Immunisations
You must have a yellow fever immunisation, and you may be required to show an international immunisation certificate as proof of this upon entering the country. Yellow fever immunisation is not valid until ten days after your vaccination and lasts ten years. It is also wise to be up to date on tetanus (ten-yearly), polio (ten-yearly), diphtheria (ten-yearly), hepatitis A and typhoid. Immunisations against meningococcus, tuberculosis and rabies are also worth considering. The majority of travellers are advised to have immunisation against hepatitis A with hepatitis A vaccine (eg: Havrix Monodose, Avaxim). One dose of vaccine lasts for one year and can be boosted to give protection for up to ten years. The course of two injections costs about £100. The newer typhoid vaccines last for three years, are about 85% effective and should be encouraged unless you are leaving within a few days for a trip of a week or less when the vaccine would not be effective in time. Immunisation against cholera is currently ineffective. Hepatitis B vaccination should be considered for longer trips or for those working in situations where contact with blood is

increased. Three injections are ideal, given over a period of 4-8 weeks before travel. If you need several immunisations, it's best to go to a travel clinic a month or two before departure.

Travel clinics
UK
British Airways Travel Clinic and Immunisation Service 156 Regent St, London W1; tel: 020 7439 9584. This place also sells travellers' supplies and has a branch of Stanford's travel book and map shop. There are now BA clinics all around Britain and three in South Africa. To find your nearest one, phone 01276 685040.
Fleet Street Travel Clinic 29 Fleet St, London EC4Y 1AA; tel: 020 7353 5678
MASTA (Medical Advisory Service for Travellers Abroad) Keppel St, London WC1 7HT; tel: 09068 224100. This is a premium-line number, charged at 50p per minute.
NHS travel website, web: www.fitfortravel.scot.nhs.uk, provides country-by-country advice on immunisation and malaria, plus details of recent developments, and ·a list of relevant health organisations.
Nomad Travel Pharmacy and Vaccination Centre 3-4 Wellington Terrace, Turnpike Lane, London N8 0PX; tel: 020 8889 7014.
Thames Medical 157 Waterloo Rd, London SE1 8US; tel: 020 7902 9000. Competitively priced, one-stop travel health service. All profits go to its affiliated company InterHealth which provides healthcare for overseas workers on Christian projects.
Trailfinders Immunisation Clinic 194 Kensington High St, London W8 7RG; tel: 020 7938 3999. Non-profit-making private clinic with a one-stop shop for health advice, vaccines and travel goods, visas and passport services and foreign exchange.

Irish Republic
Tropical Medical Bureau Grafton Street Medical Centre, Grafton Buildings, 34 Grafton St, Dublin 2; tel: (353-1) 671 9200. This organisation has a useful website specific to tropical destinations: http://www.tmb.ie.

USA
Centers for Disease Control 1600 Clifton Rd, Atlanta, GA 30333; tel: 877 FYI TRIP; 800 311 3435; web: www.cdc.gov/travel. This organisation is the central source of travel information in the USA. Each summer they publish the invaluable *Health Information for International Travel* which is available from the Division of Quarantine at the above address.
Connaught Laboratories PO Box 187, Swiftwater, PA 18370; tel: 800 822 2463. They will send a free list of specialist tropical-medicine physicians in your state.
IAMAT (International Association for Medical Assistance to Travelers) 736 Center St, Lewiston, NY 14092. A non-profit organisation which provides lists of English-speaking doctors abroad.

Canada
IAMAT (International Association for Medical Assistance to Travellers) Suite 1, 1287 St Clair Av West, Toronto, Ontario M6E 1B8; tel: (416) 652 0137.
TMVC (Travel Doctors Group) Sulphur Springs Rd, Ancaster, Ontario; tel: (905) 648 1112; web: www.tmvc.com.au.

Australia and New Zealand
TMVC Tel: 1300 65 88 44; website: www.tmvc.com.au. TMVC has 20 clinics in Australia, New Zealand and Thailand, including: *Auckland* Canterbury Arcade, 170 Queen St, Auckland City; tel: 373 3531; *Brisbane* Dr Deborah Mills, Qantas Domestic Building, 6th floor, 247 Adelaide St, Brisbane, QLD 4000; tel: 7 3221 9066; fax: 7 3321 7076; *Melbourne* Dr Sonny Lau, 393 Little Bourke St, 2nd floor, Melbourne, VIC 3000; tel: 3 9602 5788; fax: 3 9670 8394; *Sydney* Dr Mandy Hu, Dymocks Building, 7th floor, 428 George St, Sydney, NSW 2000; tel: 2 221 7133; fax: 2 221 8401.

South Africa
There are six **British Airways travel clinics** in South Africa: *Johannesburg*, tel: (011) 807 3132; *Cape Town*, tel: (021) 419 3172; *Durban*, tel: (031) 303 2423; *Knysna*, tel: (044) 382 6366; *East London*, tel: (043) 743 7471; *Port Elizabeth*, tel: (041) 374 7471.
TMVC (Travel Doctor Group) 113 DF Malan Drive, Roosevelt Park, Johannesburg; tel: +27 (011) 888 7488. Consult website www.tmvc.com.au for addresses of other clinics in South Africa.

Switzerland
IAMAT (International Association for Medical Assistance to Travellers) 57 Voirets, 1212 Grand Lancy, Geneva; web: www.sentex.net/~iamat.

Medical kit
Take a small medical kit. This should contain malaria prophylactics, as well as a cure for malaria and a thermometer (the latter is crucial should you need to diagnose yourself), soluble aspirin or paracetamol (good for gargling when you have a sore throat and for reducing fever and pains), plasters (Band-aids), potassium permanganate crystals or another favoured antiseptic, iodine for sterilising water and cleaning wounds, sunblock, and condoms or femidoms. Some travel clinics in Britain will try to persuade you to buy a variety of antibiotics as a precaution. This is not necessary: most antibiotics are widely available in Ghana, and you should be hesitant about taking them without medical advice. Restaurant meals in Ghana tend to be based around meat and carbohydrate, so you might like to carry vitamin pills.

Further reading
Self-prescribing has its hazards so if you are going anywhere very remote consider taking a health book. For adults there is *Bugs Bites & Bowels,* the Cadogan guide to healthy travel by Dr Jane Wilson-Howarth, and if travelling with children look at *Your Child's Health Abroad: A manual for travelling parents* by Dr Jane Wilson-Howarth and Dr Matthew Ellis, published by Bradt.

Medical facilities
There are private clinics, hospitals and pharmacies in most large towns, and doctors generally speak fluent English. Consultation fees and laboratory tests are remarkably inexpensive when compared to most Western countries, so if you do fall sick it would be absurd to let financial considerations dissuade you from seeking medical help. Commonly required medicines such as broad-spectrum antibiotics and Flagyl are widely available and cheap throughout the region, as are malaria cures and prophylactics. Fansidar and quinine tablets are best bought in advance – in fact it's advisable to carry all malaria-related tablets

with you, and only rely on their availability locally if you need to restock your supplies.

If you are on any medication prior to departure, or you have specific needs relating to a known medical condition (for instance if you are allergic to bee stings or you are prone to attacks of asthma, which may be exacerbated by the high dust levels), then you are strongly advised to bring any related drugs and devices with you.

Travellers' diarrhoea

Most travellers to the tropics suffer a bout of travellers' diarrhoea during their trip. The newer you are to tropical travel, the more likely you are to suffer. Travellers' diarrhoea is caused by getting other people's faeces in your mouth, which most often results from cooks not washing their hands after a trip to the toilet, but even if the restaurant cook does not understand basic hygiene, you will be safe if your food has been properly cooked and arrives piping hot. As for what food is safe to eat, any fruit or vegetable that you've washed and peeled yourself should be fine, as should hot cooked food. Raw food and salads are risky, as is cooked food that has gone cold or been kept lukewarm in a hotel buffet. Avoid ice-cream, often not kept adequately frozen due to power cuts. Ice may have been made with unboiled water or deposited by the road on its journey from the ice factory.

It is less common to get sick from drinking contaminated water, but it can happen. To be absolutely safe, you should avoid drinking tap water wherever possible (mineral water is relatively cheap and widely available). Any dodgy water should be brought to the boil, filtered through a good bacteriological filter or purified with iodine. Chlorine tablets (eg: Puritabs) are slightly less effective and taste nastier.

By taking precautions against travellers' diarrhoea you will also avoid typhoid, cholera, hepatitis, dysentery, worms, etc.

Treatment

Dehydration is the reason you feel awful during a bout of diarrhoea, so the most important part of treatment is to imbibe lots of clear fluids. Sachets of oral rehydration salts (eg: Electrolade) give the perfect biochemical mix, but any dilute mixture of sugar and salt in water will do you good. Try a solution of a four-finger scoop of sugar with a three-finger pinch of salt in a glass of water, with a squeeze of lemon or orange juice to improve the taste. If no safe drinking water is available, then Coke or similar with a three-finger pinch of salt added to each glass will do the trick. Drink two large glasses after every bowel action, more if you are thirsty – if you are not eating you need to drink three litres a day *plus* the equivalent of whatever is coming out the other end.

With most diarrhoea attacks, medication will be less effective than simply resting up and forsaking greasy foods and alcohol. If you have bad stomach cramps avoid solids completely for a day or so or stick to dry biscuits, boiled potatoes or rice. The bacterium responsible for diarrhoea and related symptoms normally dies after 36 hours. Avoid taking blockers such as Imodium, Lomotil and codeine phosphate unless you have no access to sanitation, for instance if you have to travel by bus, since they keep the poisons in your system and make you feel bad for longer. It is dangerous to take blockers with dysentery (evidenced by blood, slime or fever with the diarrhoea). Should diarrhoea or related symptoms persist beyond 36 hours, or you are passing blood or slime or have a fever, then consult a doctor or pharmacist. Chances are you have nothing serious, but you may have something treatable, for instance giardia (indicated by severe flatulence, abdominal distension, stomach cramps and sulphurous belching), which is cured by taking a single 2g of tinidazole with another dose one week later if symptoms persist. If this is unavailable then metronidazole 2g daily for three days can be used. Do not drink alcohol with either of these. If you can't get to a doctor, a three-day course of an antibiotic such as ciprofloxacin (500mg twice daily), is effective against dysentery and severe diarrhoea.

Malaria

Malaria kills a million Africans annually, and (after accidents) it poses the single biggest serious threat to the health of travellers to tropical Africa, where it should be assumed to be present at altitudes of below 1,800m, a category that includes *all* of Ghana. The *anopheles* mosquito which transmits the malaria parasite is most abundant near the marshes and still water in which it breeds. As a rule the danger of contracting the disease is greatest during the hotter, wetter months. This mosquito comes out from dusk till dawn and flies low to the ground.

It is unwise to travel in malarious parts of Africa whilst pregnant or with children: the risk of malaria in many parts is considerable and such travellers are likely to succumb rapidly to the disease.

Prophylactic drugs

There is no vaccine against malaria, but various prophylactic drugs offer a level of protection against the disease. Just as important as taking malaria pills is avoiding mosquitoes bites between dusk and dawn – see *Insects*, page 84. Travellers to Africa cannot acquire any effective resistance to malaria, and those who don't make use of prophylactic drugs risk their life. Mefloquine (Lariam) is the most effective prophylactic agent for Ghana, but is not suitable for everyone, so should only be taken on a doctor's recommendation. If this drug is suggested, then start two and a half weeks before departure to check it suits you.

Doxycycline (100mg daily) is a good alternative if Lariam is unsuitable and need only be started one day before arrival in a malarial region. It can only be obtained from a doctor. There is a possibility of allergic skin reactions developing in sunlight in approximately 5% of people. If this happens the drug should be stopped. Women using the oral contraceptive should use additional protection for the first four weeks.

Chloroquine (Nivaquine or Avloclor) two weekly and proguanil (Paludrine) two daily are now considered to be the least effective. They should only be used if there is no suitable alternative.

A new very effective drug – Malarone – is now available on prescription. It is expensive but has the advantage of fewer side effects than Lariam or doxycycline. It can be started the day before travel and continued for only seven days after leaving.

All prophylactic agents should be taken after or with the evening meal, washed down with plenty of fluids. And with the exception of Malarone, all should be continued for four weeks after leaving the last malarial area.

Diagnosis and cures

Even those who take their malaria tablets meticulously and try to avoid being bitten may contract a malaria that is resistant to prophylactic drugs. Untreated malaria is likely to be fatal, unless prompt treatment is obtained.Travellers to remote parts are encouraged to carry a treatment to cure malaria, since a high fever can develop rapidly over hours. Presently quinine and Fansidar is the favoured regime. This should be obtained from a doctor before departure. Another popular cure called Halfan has been recognised as causing some deaths and is no longer a recommended treatment.

You should visit a doctor or hospital as soon as you experience malarial symptoms: any combination of a headache, flu-like aches and pains, a rapid rise in temperature, a general sense of disorientation, and possibly nausea and diarrhoea. Carrying a thermometer is always wise. Local doctors regularly deal with malaria, and any laboratory or hospital will be able to give you a quick malaria test.

Malaria takes at least a week to incubate but can take much longer. Continue prophylactic drugs after returning home as directed, and, if you display possible malaria symptoms up to a year later, then get to a doctor and ensure that he/she knows you have been exposed to malaria.

Finally, if you have a fever and the malaria test is negative (which does not completely exclude malaria), you may have typhoid, which should also receive immediate treatment. Where typhoid testing is unavailable, a routine blood test can give a strong indication of this disease.

Bilharzia

Dr Vaughan Southgate, Natural History Museum, London

Bilharzia or schistosomiasis is a common debilitating disease afflicting perhaps 200 million people worldwide. Those most affected are the rural poor of the tropics who repeatedly acquire more and more of these nasty little worm-lodgers. Infected travellers and expatriates generally suffer fewer problems because symptoms will encourage them to seek prompt treatment and they are also exposed to fewer parasites. But it is still an unpleasant problem, and worth avoiding.

When someone with bilharzia excretes into fresh water, the eggs hatch and swim off to find a pond snail to infest. They develop inside the snail to emerge as torpedo-shaped cercariae, barely visible to the naked eye but able to digest their way through human or animal skin. This is the stage that attacks people as they wade, bathe or shower in infested water.

The snails which harbour bilharzia are a centimetre or more long and live in still or slow-moving fresh water which is well oxygenated and contains edible vegetation (water-weed, reeds). The risk is greatest where local people use the water, bearing in mind that wind can disperse cercariae a few hundred metres from where they entered the water. Wading in slow-moving, reed-fringed water near a village thus carries a very high risk of acquiring bilharzia, while swimming in a rocky pool below a waterfall in a forest carries a negligible one.

Water which has been filtered or stored snail-free for two days is safe, as is water which has been boiled or treated with Cresol or Dettol. Some protection is afforded by applying an oily insect repellent like DEET to your skin before swimming or paddling.

Previous page Girl selling oranges, Larabanga

Above left Mona monkey in Baobeng Fiema Sanctuary, where they are regarded as sacred

Above right Bay duiker, one of several common but elusive small antelopes of the Ghanaian rainforest

Below Elephant, commonly seen on foot in Mole National Park

Bottom Sacred crocodile, Paga

Cercariae live for up to 30 hours after they have been shed by snails, but the older they are, the less vigorous they are and the less capable they are of penetrating skin. Cercariae are shed in the greatest numbers between 11.00 and 15.00. If water to be used for bathing is pumped early in the morning from deep in the lake (cercariae are sun-loving) or from a site far from where people excrete there will be less risk of infestation. Swimming in the afternoon is riskier than in the early morning. Since cercariae take perhaps 10 to 15 minutes to penetrate, a quick shower or a splash across a river followed by thorough rubbing dry with a towel should be safe. Even if you are in risky water longer, towelling off vigorously after bathing will kill any cercariae in the process of penetrating your skin.

Only a proportion of those cercariae which penetrate the skin survive to cause disease. The absence of early symptoms does not necessarily mean there is no infection, but symptoms usually appear two or more weeks after penetration: typically a fever and wheezy cough. A blood test, which should be taken six weeks or more after likely exposure, will determine whether or not parasites are going to cause problems. Treatment is generally effective, but failures occur and re-treatment is often necessary for reasons that aren't fully understood, but which may imply some drug resistance. Since bilharzia can be a nasty illness, avoidance is better than waiting to be cured and it is wise to avoid bathing in high-risk areas.

Other diseases
Sleeping sickness
This is carried by tsetse flies, which look like oversized houseflies and have a painful but (sleeping sickness aside) harmless bite. Tsetse flies commonly occur in low-lying game reserves in Ghana; they bite in daylight and are attracted to blue clothing. Sleeping sickness has a patchy distribution within a small limit of the tsetse fly's range; it is a minor threat to travellers and treatable.

AIDS and venereal disease
HIV and other sexually transmitted diseases are widespread in the region to a degree that is unimaginable in Western countries, and AIDS-related deaths in many African countries have reached epidemic proportions. The risk attached to having unprotected sex with anybody but a regular partner is prohibitively high. Condoms and femidoms offer a good level of protection against HIV and other sexually transmitted diseases. The additional use of spermicide pessaries further reduces the risk of transmission. If you notice any genital ulcers or discharge, seek prompt treatment.

Hospital workers in Africa deal with AIDS victims on a regular basis. Contrary to Western prejudices, health professionals do realise the danger involved in using unsterilised needles, and you are unlikely to be confronted with one in a town hospital or clinic. If you need treatment in a really remote area where supplies are a problem, you might be glad to be carrying a few needles and hypodermic syringes in your medical kit.

Meningitis
This is a particularly nasty disease as it can kill within hours of the first symptoms appearing. The tell-tale symptoms are a combination of a blinding headache, a blotchy rash and a high fever. Immunisation protects against the most serious bacterial form of meningitis and is usually recommended for

Ghana. Other forms of meningitis exist but there are no vaccines available for these. Local papers normally report localised outbreaks. If you show symptoms, get to a doctor immediately.

Rabies

Rabies is carried by all mammals – beware the village dogs and small monkeys that are used to being fed in the parks – and is passed on to man through a bite, or a lick of an open wound. You must always assume any animal is rabid (unless personally known to you) and seek medical help as soon as possible. In the interim, scrub the wound with soap and bottled/boiled water then pour on a strong iodine or alcohol solution. This helps stop the rabies virus entering the body and will guard against wound infections, including tetanus. If you intend to have contact with animals and/or are likely to be more than 24 hours away from medical help, then vaccination is advised. Ideally three pre-exposure doses should be taken over four weeks. If you are bitten by any animal, treatment should be given as soon as possible, but it is never too late to seek help as the incubation period for rabies can be very long. Tell the doctors if you have had pre-exposure vaccine. Remember if you contract rabies, mortality is 100% and death from rabies is probably one of the worst ways to go!

Tetanus

Tetanus is caught through deep, dirty wounds, including animal bites, so ensure that such wounds are thoroughly cleaned. Immunisation gives good protection for ten years, provided you do not have an overwhelming number of tetanus bacteria on board. If you haven't had a tetanus shot in ten years, or you are unsure, get a tetanus toxoid injection and a tetanus booster as quickly as possible. Keep immunised and be sensible about first aid.

Insects

Even if you take malaria tablets, do all you can to avoid mosquito bites. The imperative reason for this is the increasing level of resistance to preventative drugs, while of lesser concern are several other mosquito-borne viral fevers which could be present in low- and medium-altitude parts of the region. The *anopheles* mosquito which spreads malaria emerges at dusk, as do most other disease-carrying mosquitoes, so you will greatly reduce your chances of being bitten by wearing long trousers and socks after dark and covering exposed parts of your body with insect repellent, preferably a DEET-based preparation such as Repel 100 or Jungle Jell. Sprays or roll-ons of this sort are not available in Ghana, so bring one with you. The *anopheles* mosquito hunts mostly at ground level, so it is worth putting repellent on your ankles, even if you wear socks. When walking in scrub and forest areas by day, you should also cover and spray yourself, since the *aedes* mosquito which spreads dengue is a day-biter (solid shoes, socks and trousers will in any case protect you against snakes, sharp thorns and harmless but irritating biters like midges).

Like many insects, mosquitoes are drawn to direct light. If you are camping, never put a lamp near the opening of your tent, or you will have a swarm of mosquitoes and other insects waiting to join you when you retire. In hotel rooms, be aware that the longer you leave on your light, the greater the number of insects with which you are likely to share your accommodation.

Once you are in bed, the best form of protection is a net, which is not normally supplied in hotel rooms in Ghana. Mosquito coils, which are widely available and cheap in Ghana, will also reduce (but not eliminate) the biting rate, and (even though strains of mosquito have evolved that are skilled at flying in turbulent air) so will a fan. Far better, though, is to carry your own permethrin-impregnated net, which will protect you against everything. Nets and impregnation kits are available from Trailfinders Travel Clinic, MASTA at the London School of Tropical Medicine and Hygiene, and from British Airways Travel Clinics (see page 78).

Minute pestilential **blackflies** spread river blindness in parts of Africa between 19° north and 17° south. You're at risk only near fast-flowing rivers and rapids, where they breed. The flies bite in daylight. Long trousers tucked into socks will help keep them off. Citronella-based repellents don't work against them.

Tumbu flies or **putsi** occur in hot, humid climates, where they often lay eggs on drying laundry. When a person puts on clean clothes or sleeps on a fresh sheet, the eggs hatch and bury themselves under the skin to form a crop of 'boils', each of which hatches a grub after about eight days before the inflammation settles down. In putsi areas, you should dry clothes and sheets in a screened house, or in direct sunshine until they are crisp, or iron them.

Jiggers or **sandfleas** latch on if you walk barefoot in contaminated places, and set up home under the skin of the foot, usually at the side of a toenail where they cause a painful boil-like swelling. They need picking out by a local expert; if the flea bursts during eviction, douse the wound in spirit alcohol or kerosene – or more jiggers will infest you.

There are several unpleasant illnesses which can follow a **tick bite** in Africa, including Lyme disease, but the good news is that even if a tick is carrying disease organisms, it will not inevitably infect you. You are less likely to be infected if you get the tick off promptly and do not damage it. Remove any tick as soon as you notice it on you – it will most likely be firmly attached to somewhere you would rather it was not – grasp the tick as close to your body as possible and pull steadily and firmly away at right angles to your skin. The tick will then come away complete as long as you do not jerk or twist. If possible douse the wound with alcohol (any spirit will do) or iodine. Spreading redness around the bite and/or fever and/or aching joints after a tick bite imply that you have an infection which requires antibiotic treatment, so seek advice.

To balance the warnings, it should be stressed that the overwhelming majority of insects don't bite people and, of those that do, the vast majority are entirely harmless. Mattresses or walls of grotty hotels quite often contain bedbugs and fleas, both of which are essentially harmless.

Skin infections

Any insect bite or small nick gives an opportunity for bacteria to foil the body's defences. It will surprise many travellers how quickly skin infections start in warm, humid climates, and it is essential to clean and cover the slightest wound. Creams are not as effective as a good drying antiseptic such as dilute iodine, potassium permanganate (a few crystals in half a cup of water) or crystal (or gentian) violet. One of these should be available in most towns. If the wound starts to throb, or becomes red and the redness starts to spread or the wound oozes, antibiotics will probably be needed; flucloxacillin (250mg four times a day) or cloxacillin (500mg four times a day) or, for those allergic to penicillin, erythromycin (500mg twice a day) for five days should help. See a doctor if the infection does not start to improve in 48 hours.

Fungal infections also get a hold easily in hot, moist climates, so wear 100% cotton socks and underwear and shower frequently. An itchy (often flaking) rash in the groin or between the toes is likely to be a fungal infection which will need treatment with an antifungal cream such as Canesten (clotrimazole) or, if this is not available, try Whitfield's ointment (compound benzoic acid ointment) or crystal violet (although this will turn you purple!).

Sun and heat
The equatorial sun is vicious. Although it is impossible to avoid some exposure to the sun, it would be foolish to do so needlessly. Tanning ages your skin and it can cause skin cancer. If you are coming to Africa from a less harsh climate, let your body get used to the sunlight gradually or you will end up with sunburn. Take things too far and heatstroke – a potentially fatal condition – may be the result. Wear sunscreen and build up your exposure gradually, starting with no more than 20 minutes a day. Avoid exposing yourself for more than two hours in any day, and stay out of the sun between 12.00 and 15.00.

Be particularly careful of sunburn when swimming or snorkelling. A shirt will protect your shoulders and a pair of shorts will protect the back of your thighs.

In hot and particularly in humid weather, you may sweat more than normal. To counter the resultant loss of water and salt, you should drink more than usual and eat extra salt if you develop a taste for it (salt tablets are useless). Prickly heat, a fine pimply rash caused by sweat trapped under the skin, is a harmless but very uncomfortable and common problem when you are first exposed to a humid tropical climate such as on the coast. It helps to wear 100% cotton clothing, splash regularly with water (avoiding excessive use of soap), dab the area with talc powder and sleep naked under a fan. If it's really bad, check into an air-conditioned hotel room or head for a higher, cooler place.

SAFETY
Marine dangers
The currents off many parts of the Ghanaian coast are highly dangerous, and swimmers risk being dragged away from shore by riptides, strong undertows and whirlpools, particularly during the rainy season and in windy weather. It is common for those swimmers who underestimate the dangers associated with these currents to drown. Quite simply, you should *never* swim in the sea without first asking local advice, perhaps not at all if you are a weak swimmer, and you are advised against going into water deeper than your waist without some sort of flotation device. If you are ever caught in a riptide or whirlpool, it is generally advisable *not* to immediately fight the current by swimming to shore, but to save your strength by floating on your back or swimming parallel to shore until the tide weakens, and only then to try to get back to land.

The coastal residents of Ghana evidently view beaches in a less aesthetic way than we do. It is customary in most seaside towns and villages for the beach to serve as a communal toilet. While this may not constitute a health threat in most circumstances, dodging between freshly deposited turds does tend to take the edge off a pleasant stroll on the sand, and imagining what the last tide washed away would certainly put me off swimming. Fortunately, most beaches that are regularly visited by tourists are no longer put to the, um, traditional use.

Don't swim or walk barefoot on the beach, or you risk getting coral or urchin spines in your soles or venomous fish spines in your feet. If you tread on a venomous fish, soak the foot in hot (but not scalding) water until some time after the pain subsides; this may be for 20–30 minutes in all. Take your foot out of the water to top up otherwise you may scald it. If the pain returns, re-immerse the foot. Once the venom has been heat-inactivated, get a doctor to check and remove any bits of fish spine in the wound.

Snakebite

Poisonous snakes are widespread but rarely encountered since they generally slither away when they sense the seismic vibrations made by a walking person. You should be most alert to snakes on rocky slopes and cliffs, particularly where you risk putting your hand on a ledge that you can't see. Rocky areas are the favoured habitat of the puff adder, not an especially venomous snake but potentially lethal and unusual in that it won't always move off in response to human foot treads. Wearing good boots when walking in the bush will protect against the 50% of snakebites that occur below the ankle, and long trousers will help deflect bites higher up on the leg, reducing the quantity of venom injected. Snakes rarely attack people unless provoked, most snakes are harmless, and even venomous species will only dispense venom in about half of their bites. To give an example, in South Africa, where venomous snakes are widespread, fewer than ten snakebite fatalities are recorded annually – more people die from being struck by lightning!

In the event of a snakebite, be aware that most first-aid techniques do more harm than good. Cutting into the wound is harmful, tourniquets are dangerous, and suction and electrical inactivation devices do not work. The victim must be taken to a hospital which has antivenom. While being transported, remember that the venom will spread more slowly if the victim stays calm, and if the bitten limb is splinted and kept below the height of the heart. If you have a crêpe bandage, bind up as much of the bitten limb as you can, but release the bandage every half hour.

- NEVER give aspirin; you may offer paracetamol which is safe.
- NEVER cut or suck the wound.
- DO NOT apply ice packs.
- DO NOT apply potassium permanganate.

If the offending snake can be captured without risk of someone else being bitten, take it to show the doctor, but be aware that a decapitated head can dispense venom in a reflex bite.

Wild animals

The dangers associated with African wild animals have frequently been overstated in the past by the so-called 'Great White Hunters' and others trying to glamorise their chosen way of life. In Ghana specifically, there are few situations in which you would be likely to encounter potentially dangerous large mammals. Furthermore, most wild animals fear us far more than we fear them, and their normal response to human contact is to flee. The likelihood of a tourist to Ghana being attacked by an animal is very low, but it may be worth giving a quick overview of the situation with certain animals.

The need for caution is greatest near water, particularly around dusk and dawn, when **hippos** are likely to be out grazing. Hippos are responsible for more human fatalities than any other large mammal, not because they are aggressive but because they tend to panic when something comes between them and the safety of the water. If you happen to be that something, then you're unlikely to live to tell the tale. Never consciously walk between a hippo and water, and never walk along river banks or though reed beds, especially in overcast weather or at dusk or dawn, unless you are certain that no hippos are present. Watch out, too, for **Nile crocodiles**. Only a very large croc is likely to attack a person, and then only in the water or right on the shore. Near towns and other settlements, you can be fairly sure that any very large crocodile will have been disposed of by its potential prey, so the risk is greatest away from human habitation.

There are only a couple of places in Ghana where a hiker might stumble across an **elephant** or **buffalo**, the most dangerous of Africa's terrestrial herbivores. Elephants almost invariably mock charge and indulge in some hair-raising trumpeting before they attack in earnest. Provided that you back off at the first sign of unease, they are most unlikely to take further notice of you. If you see them before they see you, give them a wide berth and bear in mind they are most likely to attack if surprised at close proximity. If an animal charges you, the safest course of action is to head for the nearest tree and climb it. Black rhinos are also prone to charging without apparent provocation, but they're now very rare except in a few reserves where walking is forbidden.

There are campsites in Africa where **green monkeys** and **baboons** have become a pest. Feeding these animals is highly irresponsible, since it encourages them to scavenge and may eventually lead to them being shot. Monkeys are too small to progress much beyond being a nuisance, but baboons are very dangerous and have often killed children and maimed adults with their vicious teeth. Do not tease or underestimate the strength of a baboon. If primates are hanging around a campsite, and you wander off leaving fruit in your tent, don't expect the tent to be standing when you return.

The dangers associated with large **predators** are often exaggerated. Most predators stay clear of humans and are likely to kill accidentally or in self-defence rather than by design. Lions are an exception, but it is uncommon for a lion to attack a human without cause – in the highly unlikely event that you encounter one on foot, the important thing is not to run, since this is likely to trigger the instinct to give chase. A slight but real danger when sleeping in the bush without a tent is that a passing hyena or lion might investigate a hairy object sticking out of a sleeping bag and decapitate you through predatorial curiosity. In areas where large predators are still present, sleeping in a *sealed* tent practically guarantees your safety – provided that you don't sleep with your head sticking out, or at any point put meat in the tent.

Part Two

Accra

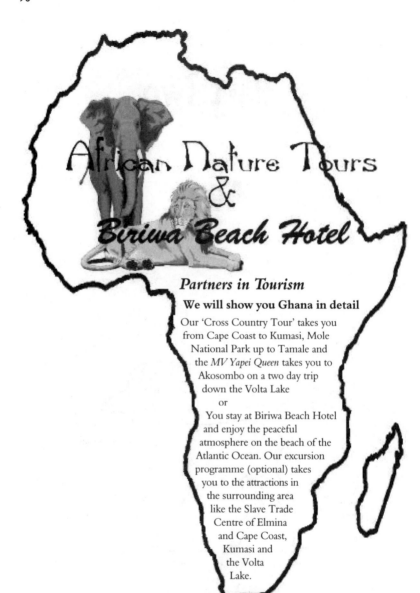

African Nature Tours & Biriwa Beach Hotel

Partners in Tourism

We will show you Ghana in detail

Our 'Cross Country Tour' takes you from Cape Coast to Kumasi, Mole National Park up to Tamale and the *MV Yapei Queen* takes you to Akosombo on a two day trip down the Volta Lake

or

You stay at Biriwa Beach Hotel and enjoy the peaceful atmosphere on the beach of the Atlantic Ocean. Our excursion programme (optional) takes you to the attractions in the surrounding area like the Slave Trade Centre of Elmina and Cape Coast, Kumasi and the Volta Lake.

Info: www.biriwabeach.com.gh
Address: P.O. Box 479, Cape Coast/Ghana
Tel: +233-42-33333/33444
Fax: +233-42-33444/33666
e-mail: bbh@ghana.com

Accra

It is tempting to introduce Accra as Ghana's historical capital, or something similarly portentous. This is, after all, a city that started life in the 15th century, when the Ga people who still live in the area settled on the west side of Korle Lagoon to found a small village from where they traded with passing Portuguese ships. Later in the same century, near what is now Brazil Lane, the Portuguese built a lodge that was burnt to the ground by locals shortly after it was constructed. No traces of this lodge remain, but modern Accra can still lay claim to three fortified buildings dating from the mid-17th century – Dutch Fort Ussher, British Fort James and Danish Osu Castle. Furthermore, in 1877, when what are now Nairobi, Johannesburg and Addis Ababa were no more than tracts of empty bush, Accra became the capital of the British Gold Coast colony.

Knowing the above, Accra has to be classed a disappointment. The old forts, the city's most obvious draw cards, at least on paper, are closed to the public, their whitewashed stone exteriors patrolled by camera-sensitive military personnel. Osu Castle, the seat of government since colonial times, cannot even be approached closely, since the surrounding streets are barricaded on all sides. And the smaller Ussher and James forts now serve as prisons – approachable, yes, but wholly untouchable. Alone among Accra's historical buildings, the colonial-era lighthouse near Fort James offers an informal welcome to the curious visitor – ask nicely and you may even be allowed to climb the 82-step spiral staircase for a gull's-eye view over old James Town and Ussher Town.

Accra is a modern city, emphatically so, with a population drawing ever closer to the two million mark and an urban landscape of giddy incongruity – scruffy lanes lined with open sewers and colonial-era homesteads lead to untended open spaces, grandiose Independence monuments and arches, dazzling modern skyscrapers and run-down concrete blocks harking from the headiest days of Soviet town planning. The more you try to pin Accra down, the more elusive it seems, and it is in this respect – the way in which the former Danish outpost of Osu, say, still feels like a separate entity to Ussher Town, or Adabraka – that Accra is, if not a historical city, then certainly one whose modern schizophrenia reflects its distant past.

We found Accra to be one of those cities that rewards casual exploration – punctuated in this drenching humidity by frequent stops to sip the juice from a decapitated coconut or gulp down a chilled soft drink. Tourist attractions, it is true, are few and far between, but both James Town and Osu have a certain fading charm, while the frenzied central market area and – even more – Adabraka are vibrantly, brashly modern without ever feeling in any way threatening. Add to this any number of garden bars, inexpensive restaurants and live music venues, and Accra in all its modernity becomes as likeable and absorbing as most African cities.

Not the least of Accra's attractions is its amiability. Hectic it may be, chaotic in places, but as far as visitors need be concerned, there must be few third-world cities of comparable size with such a safe and relaxed mood. I arrived in Accra with defences formed by years of East African travel. Within 24 hours, I realised how wholly inappropriate these defences were. The closest thing to hassle that we encountered in Accra was the relentless horn-blowing of taxi drivers (and can any city be patrolled by such a high proportion of empty taxis?) to whom a white pedestrian evidently spells custom. Yet, remarkably, the selfsame taxi drivers were always happy to point us to a shared taxi if that's what we wanted, rather than try to hustle us into an overpriced charter ride.

In summation, those who have only a short time in Ghana would probably be well advised to spend as little time as is necessary in a city which has little to offer in the way of targeted sightseeing. For those with the time to enjoy Accra – well, enjoy...!

GETTING THERE AND AWAY
By air
All international flights arrive at Kotoka International Airport, one of the most centrally located international airports that I'm aware of in an African capital, a mere 4km from Sankara Circle and roughly 500m east of Liberation Avenue. Assuming that your passport and visa are in order and you have an onward ticket, the immigration and customs procedures are quick and straightforward. Until recently, immigration wouldn't stamp more than 30 days in your passport, regardless of what visa you had or how long you intended to stay. These days, they seem automatically to grant visitors a 60 day stamp, but you might want to check this should you intend to spend longer than a month in Ghana.

It appears that visitors are no longer required to fill in a Currency Declaration Form (which states exactly how much money you are bringing into the country and sometimes used to be checked against your bank receipts and remaining cash or travellers' cheques on departure).

There *are* money exchange facilities at the airport, and while the rate isn't particularly great, it makes sense to change enough money into local currency to get a taxi to your hotel and (should you be arriving after banking hours) to see you through to the next banking day. If you fly in during the wee hours of the morning, then you shouldn't expect foreign exchange facilities to be open, and will probably be glad of having a few spare US$1 bills rather than relying on the taxi drivers to provide you with change.

As soon as you leave the terminal building, you'll be mobbed by taxi drivers. As things stand, there would be nothing preventing you from pushing past them all and hopping into a passenger taxi in the direction you want to go, though it's probably fair to say that if any one public transport route in an African capital is likely to attract light fingers, then it's the one from the airport. My inclination after a long flight and loaded down with luggage would be to save your first acquaintance with Accra's bemusing public transport routes for later in the day. A passenger taxi from the airport to anywhere in central Accra really shouldn't cost more than US$2.50, but you'll be asked for a lot more and, again, while you certainly ought to negotiate the fare, this probably isn't the moment to get overtly confrontational.

Should your flight be scheduled to arrive after dark, it might be wise to make an advance booking at a mid- to upper-range hotel, depending on your budget: the Granada, Shangri-La and Golden Tulip are all close to the airport. Be aware that many hotels graded three-star or above have a shuttle service to and from the airport, but you ought to check whether this is the case when you book (or get your travel agent to check it), and should also ascertain until what time it runs. (Balanced against the argument for booking a hotel in advance is that on the last three occasions when we've flown into a West African capital scheduled to arrive after dark, various delays meant we actually arrived the next morning, so that a pre-paid hotel booking would have been a waste of money.)

For internal flights to Kumasi and Tamale, contact **Airlink** through any travel agency or through Ghana Airways.

By road

There are numerous different bus and tro-tro stations in Accra, some serving specific lines and others a specific cluster of destinations. The most important stations to travellers are the main STC station on Ring Road, a short distance east of Lamptey Circle, Kaneshie station on Winneba Road about 1km northwest of Lamptey Circle, and Tudu station in the city centre north of Makola Circle.

I would strongly advise travellers heading out of Accra to use an STC bus, assuming that they are going far enough to make it worthwhile (the STC buses charge full fare to their end destination even if you 'drop' along the way). From the main STC station, buses leave once an hour to Kumasi and Takoradi, and several times daily to Cape Coast. At least one Kumasi bus daily continues northwards to Tamale, Bolgatanga and Bawku. You should arrive with half an hour to spare to be reasonably certain of getting a ticket, but at worst you could take a City Express bus from the City Express station 100m down the road. Telephone 221912 to check current timetables – the people are very helpful on the phone.

All tro-tros and other buses to destinations along the coast and north towards Kumasi leave from Kaneshie station on a fill-up-and-go basis – you'll rarely wait more than 30 minutes for a vehicle to leave for anywhere you want to go to. STC buses and tro-tros to destinations in the east leave from Tudu station. Destinations for STC buses heading in this direction include Aflao (on the Togo border), Ho and Akosombo. For some destinations east, for instance Shai Hills and Prampram, you may have to pick up a tro-tro from Tema station (just south of the Novotel) to Ashaiman and change vehicles there.

Wherever you are going, hail a taxi to take you to the right station – the drivers know exactly from where vehicles leave for even the most obscure destinations, and at around US$1 per charter ride it saves immense hassle and asking around. Likewise, when you arrive in Accra, it really is worth the small price of a taxi to get to your hotel swiftly and simply.

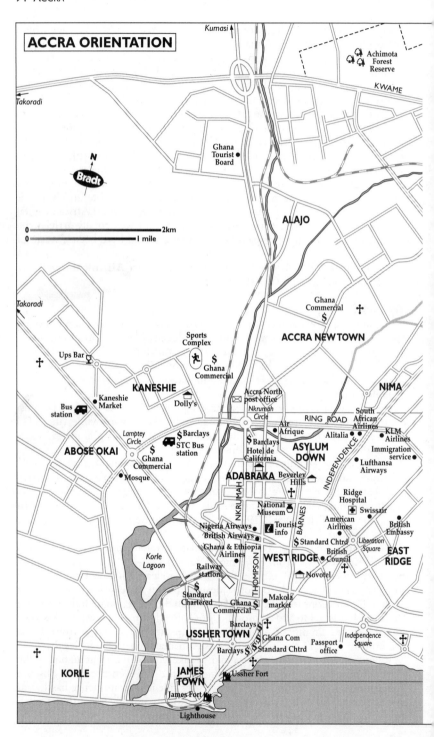

ACCRA ORIENTATION

Kumasi

Takoradi

Achimota
Forest
Reserve

KWAME

N

Bradt

0 ——————— 2km
0 ——————— 1 mile

Takoradi

Ghana
Tourist
Board

ALAJO

ACCRA NEW TOWN

Ghana
Commercial
$

NIMA

Sports
Complex

Ups Bar

Ghana
Commercial
$

KANESHIE

Dolly's

Accra North
post office

Nkrumah
Circle

RING ROAD

South
African
Airlines

KLM
Airlines

Kaneshie
Market

Bus
station

Air
Afrique

Alitalia

Lamptey
Circle

Barclays

Immigration
service

ABOSE OKAI

STC Bus
station

Barclays

ASYLUM
DOWN

Lufthansa
Airways

Ghana
Commercial

Hotel de
California

Mosque

ADABRAKA

Beverley
Hills

Ridge
Hospital

Swissair

National
Museum

Tourist
info

American
Airlines

British
Embassy

Korle
Lagoon

Nigeria Airways
British Airways

Standard Chtrd

Liberation
Square

EAST
RIDGE

Ghana & Ethiopia
Airlines

WEST RIDGE

British
Council

Railway
station

Novotel

Standard
Chartered

Ghana
Commercial

Makola
market

USSHER TOWN

Barclays

Ghana Com

Passport
office

Independence
Square

Barclays

Standard Chtrd

KORLE

JAMES
TOWN

Ussher Fort

James Fort

Lighthouse

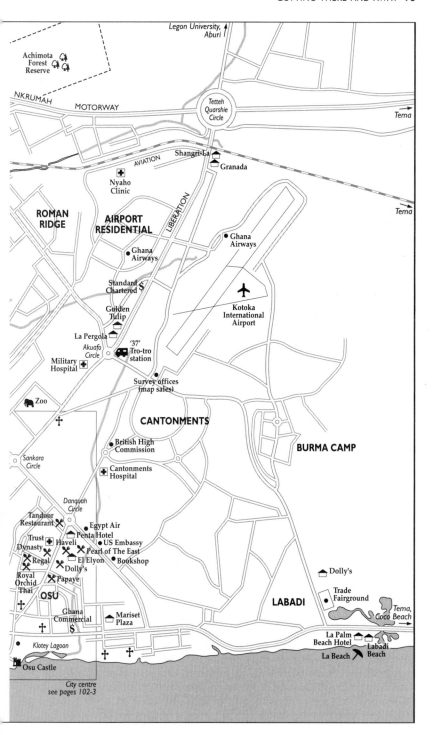

ORIENTATION

Central Accra is bounded to the south by the Atlantic Ocean and to the west by Korle Lagoon. In other directions, it is bounded by Ring Road, which starts at the old Winneba Road on the seafront immediately west of Korle Lagoon, before running northeast via Lamptey Circle to Nkrumah Circle, then east from Nkrumah to Sankara Circle, and then southeast from Sankara Circle via Danquah Circle to the junction with Labadi Road near the seafront.

Tourists who spend some time in Accra will probably come to regard Nkrumah Circle as the city's most significant landmark. Not only is it the local transport hub of the city, but it marks the intersection between Ring Road and Nkrumah Road, the latter the main north-south thoroughfare through Accra's commercial heart of Adabraka (in the north), Ussher Town and James Town (on the seafront). Running parallel to and east of Nkrumah Avenue, Kojo Thompson and Barnes roads are arguably the city's second and third most important north-south thoroughfares, the former well supplied with budget accommodation, the latter effectively the eastern border of the most built-up part of the city centre, and notable for two important landmarks, the National Museum and Novotel Hotel.

The suburbs that lie within Ring Road can be divided into three broad clusters. In the west are the three central suburbs mentioned above, essentially the commercial city centre. Of these, Adabraka is the main haunt of budget travellers since it is dotted with cheap accommodation, bars and restaurants, while the older suburbs of Ussher Town and James Town are of some historical interest. To the west of this, bounded roughly by Barnes Road to the west and an imaginary north-south line running between Sankara Circle and Independence Square, lies a cluster of more spacious, green suburbs comprising from north to south: Asylum Down, North Ridge, East Ridge, West Ridge and Victoriabourg. The main thoroughfare through this part of Accra is Independence Avenue, which connects Sankara Circle on Ring Road to the seafront at the south end of Barnes Road. The most easterly suburb is Osu (aka Christiansbourg), another old part of town focused towards Osu Castle and bisected by Cantonments Road, an important commercial centre notable for its many restaurants.

Several important trunk roads fan out from Ring Road. The main road to Winneba and the West Coast leaves Ring Road at Lamptey Circle, the main road to Nsawam, Kumasi and the north leaves from Nkrumah Circle, while Liberation Road, which leaves from Sankara Circle, heads past the airport to Tetteh Quarshie Circle and the Kwame Nkrumah Highway for Tema and other destinations east of Accra. At the very southeast of Ring Road, Labadi Road heads to La Beach, Coco Beach and Tema via the coast.

GETTING AROUND

Accra is serviced by a remarkably cheap and efficient system of tro-tros, passenger (shared) taxis and dropping (charter) taxis, though getting to grips with the main routes used by passenger vehicles takes time and a certain degree of trial and error. In my opinion, travellers who are spending only a couple of days in Accra may as well stick to dropping taxis, which can be picked up practically anywhere and at any time. You're unlikely to have to pay more than US$1 for a ride within the bounds of Ring Road, though you may sometimes have to negotiate to get a fair price, and fares do seem to be higher on days when traffic is particularly heavy. Dropping taxis to places outside Ring Road – La Beach, the STC bus station, Accra Zoo or the airport – will cost more than US$1, but will still be very cheap by international standards.

Passenger taxis and tro-tros are absurdly cheap (less than US$0.20) depending on the route, and we heard and experienced nothing to suggest there is any serious need to worry about pickpockets and the like, especially on the taxis. Once you are reasonably well oriented to Accra, the system is quite easy to assimilate. The most important local transport hub is Nkrumah Circle, and you can pretty much assume that you'll find a shared taxi or tro-tro from here to wherever you want, at the worst involving one change of vehicle. Shared taxis to the Novotel Hotel (via Farrar Avenue and Barnes Road) and to Osu leave from the southeast side of the circle, while those to Sankara Circle, '37', the airport, La Beach and Nungua leave from the northeast side behind the Shell garage next to the overpass. Minibuses heading right down Nkrumah Road to James Town can generally be picked up by waiting on the west side of Nkrumah Road immediately south of the circle. Tro-tros to destinations slightly further out of town, for instance Legon University and Aburi Botanical Gardens, generally leave from the northwest side of the circle.

An important tro-tro station in the city centre is Tema Station on Independence Avenue below the Novotel Hotel, where you can pick up tro-tros to coastal destinations in the direction of Tema as well as northeast along Independence Avenue to Sankara Circle and along Liberation Avenue past the airport. Outside Ring Road, a landmark worth knowing is 37 station at Akuafo Circle on the junction of Liberation Avenue and Gifford Road, where you'll pick up shared taxis to most destinations including Nkrumah Circle (via Sankara Circle), Osu (via Cantonments Road and Danquah Circle) and Nungua (via Burma Camp Bypass and La Beach).

WHERE TO STAY
There are several hundred hotels and guesthouses scattered in and around Accra, ranging from a half-dozen with world-class facilities to innumerable budget hotels aimed primarily at the local market. What follows is a representative selection of some of the best places in each range; it is bound to be less than fully comprehensive, and readers are invited to let me know about any new finds.

Upmarket: Three to five star; US$100 and above
Labadi Beach Hotel PO Box 1, Trade Fair, Accra; tel: 021 772501/2/3/4/5; fax: 021 772520; email: labadi@ghana.com.
It isn't difficult to see why Labadi Beach is the only established hotel in Ghana to be awarded a five-star grading. The most striking feature of the hotel is the rare attention to detail noticeable not only in the architecture and the lush landscaped gardens (complete with large reed-fringed dam and adult and children's swimming pools), but also in the standard of service. The location, too, is a major boon, adjacent to one of the country's most attractive and lively public beaches, practically opposite the Trade Fair grounds, and yet only ten minutes by taxi from the city centre. Facilities include tennis courts, sauna and health club, an excellent business centre, a poorly stocked curio and bookshop, three highly regarded restaurants, a free hourly airport shuttle, and 15-channel satellite TV in every room. According to a Ghanaian resident of ten years, the

hairdressing and beauty salon here is very good and reasonably priced. The rooms are as good as any available in the capital, with the bathrooms in particular less cramped than is often the case in international-class hotels. Rooms cost US$230/270/520 single/double/suite inclusive of an outstanding buffet breakfast.

La Palm Royal Beach Hotel PO Box OS 3000, Accra; tel: 021 771666/700; fax: 021 771717; email: enquiries@la-palm.com.
Situated 200m from Labadi Beach Hotel, the recently opened La Palm is Accra's only other five-star hotel, overlooking La Beach but without direct access to the shore. The hotel grounds are centred around a first-class swimming pool area, and the communal areas and rooms are tastefully decorated with a contemporary look. Facilities include an excellent restaurant, satellite TV in all the rooms, and a good shop selling curios, books and newspapers. La Palm is the flagship hotel for the Golden Beach chain, and effectively serves as its head office. Whether this hotel is the best hotel in its range is a matter of taste, but it certainly represents the best value for money at US$153/163 single/double.

Golden Tulip Hotel PO Box 16033, Airport, Accra; tel: 021 775360; fax: 021 775361; email: goldtulip@ncs.com.gh.
This 230-room four-star hotel, part of the Dutch chain, lies out on Liberation Road towards the airport, and is the only hotel in Accra to approach the standard set by the two beach hotels. It is well situated for access to the city centre and the airport, and the facilities are easily the equal of the Labadi – swimming pool, tennis courts and mini-golf course, good restaurants, an excellent curio and bookshop, and a business centre. Drawbacks include the relatively uninspiring grounds and distance from the beach. Rooms cost US$215/250 single/double including a good buffet breakfast.

Accra Novotel PO Box 12720, Accra; tel: 021 667546; fax: 021 667533.
Part of the French Novotel chain, this four-star hotel lies on the southern end of Barnes Road, and its height makes it something of a landmark in the city centre. Very much a businessman's hotel, the Novotel is the obvious choice if you plan on doing a lot of walking around the city centre, but the atmosphere is negligible and the rooms are not as plush or spacious as those at Accra's other four- and five-star hotels. Facilities include a swimming pool, tennis court, business centre, outstanding restaurant, curio shop and satellite TV in all rooms. Room rates are US$140/160 single/double including a good buffet breakfast.

Hotel Shangri-La PO Box 9201, Accra; tel: 021 776993; fax: 021 774873.
Situated on Liberation Road, a short distance past the airport, this hotel is very popular with Accra residents. The major strength is the communal areas, which make tasteful use of natural materials and ethnic art and crafts, and are centred around a palm-fringed fountain and large, illuminated swimming pool. Facilities are comparable to those of the hotels listed above, and include a business centre, book and imported newspaper stall, gymnasium, sauna, tennis court, horse-riding and a good restaurant known for its pizzas. Accommodation in s/c chalets with AC, fridge, satellite TV and large private safe costs US$110 single, US$140 small double or US$175 large double.

Nogahill Hotel PO Box C511, Cantonments, Accra; tel: 021 500121/2; fax: 021 501002.
This is a highly regarded three-star hotel situated on First Link Road in the suburb of East Legon, close to Osu and the airport. Facilities include a swimming pool, international restaurant, pizza restaurant and confectionery, and satellite TV in all rooms. Rates are comparable to the Shangri-La.

Mid-range: one to three star; US$100 and under
Niagara Hotel & Niagara Plus PO Box 4079, Accra; tel: 021 230118; fax: 021 230119; email: niagara@ighmail.com.
The Niagara Hotel on Kojo Thomson Road in Adabraka is one of the most popular hotels in this range, as much for the excellent and responsive management style as for the rooms, which are nevertheless good value at US$65/85 single/double with hot water, AC and satellite TV. This is a good hotel to contact as a first base in Accra, as they respond quickly to emails (a rarity in Ghana) and you might also want to ask about an excellent combination deal for a hired car with driver and room in the hotel at US$110 per day. The Niagara Plus is a new and identically priced (though perhaps slightly smarter) sister hotel situated in the lively Osu area. Both hotels have good restaurants: Lebanese food predominates at the Niagara, while pizzas are the thing to ask for at the Niagara Plus.

Hotel Paloma Tel: 021 228700; fax: 021 231815; email: paloma@africaonline.com.gh.
Situated on the north side of Ring Road, between Nkrumah and Sankara circles, this is another hotel that is regularly recommended by readers, and it seems outstanding value for money at US$55/60/75 single/double/suite including breakfast. Rooms are all large and comfortably furnished, with satellite TV, AC and hot water, and the suites have kitchenettes. There is a good selection of popular restaurants, as well as an internet café, in the attached shopping arcade.

Coco Beach Hotel Tel: 021 766524.
Situated about 10km out of town, 500m along a signposted junction from Nungua (any taxi heading towards Tema can drop you at this junction), the Coco Beach Hotel is the only relatively cheap beach hotel close to Accra. Chalets with fan cost US$30/40 single/double, while those with AC cost US$40/50. All rooms have TV, hot water and a fridge. A good restaurant serves Western and Ghanaian dishes on the beach.

Frankie's Hotel Tel: 021 773567; fax: 021 773569; email: reserve@frankiesghana.com.
This smart new hotel is situated on the main road through the lively, trendy suburb of Osu. The rooms are relatively small, but clean and modern in appearance, and the location is difficult to beat for nightlife and eating out. US$68/95 single/double.

El-Elyon Hotel Tel: 021 774421; fax: 021 776343; email: elelyon@africaonline.com.gh.
This is a small but smart three-star hotel situated in the lively suburb of Osu, on 18th Lane opposite the Côte d'Ivoire Embassy. Both rooms and facilities

here approach those of more expensive hotels, so it seems very reasonably priced at US$70/85 single/double for an attractively furnished s/c room with AC and satellite TV.

Granada Hotel Tel: 021 775343; fax: 021 774880.
This comfortable two-star hotel next to the Shangri-La on Liberation Road seems good value at around US$80 for a s/c double with AC, so worth heading for if you want to be in relatively suburban surroundings. There is a good bar and restaurant attached or you can eat next door at the Shangri-La.

Penta Hotel Tel: 021 774529; fax: 021 773418.
This pleasant, sensibly priced two-star hotel is centrally located in Osu and has s/c rooms with AC and TV for US$45/50 single/double

Taj Guesthouse Tel: 021 778760.
Also in Osu, on the road towards the US Embassy, this Indian-run hotel (with attached Indian restaurant) is also good value at US$50/60 single/double with AC.

Mariset Plaza Tel: 021 774434; fax: 021 772085.
Situated at the southern end of Osu, just off Labadi Road, this three-star hotel with swimming pool has s/c double rooms with satellite TV for US$80/90.

Moderate: ungraded to one star; US$20 (1998 US$35) and under

If you want to stay somewhere quite central, you'll find a string of hotels in the moderate price range on Farrar Avenue within easy walking distance of the bars and restaurants of Adabraka. The best of these is probably the **Hotel President** (tel: 021 223343), which has s/c doubles with AC and TV for US$16 (1998 US$25), as well as cheaper rooms with fans and a good patio bar and affordable restaurant. Next up, and a bit seedier, the **Avenue Club Hotel** (tel: 021 222679; fax: 021 234813) has a lively outdoor bar and rather nice s/c rooms with AC, TV and fridge for US$8/13 double/twin (1998 US$19/23). Further down, on the junction with Samora Machel, the **Beverley Hills Hotel** (tel: 021 224042; fax: 021 242532) also seems good value at US$20/30 s/c double/twin with AC and TV (prices quoted in US dollars).

On Kojo Thompson Road, a short way south of the intersection with Castle, the **Hotel Avenida** (tel: 021 221350; fax: 021 221321) is as good value as any of the above. Here, a s/c AC double with cold water only costs US$12 (1998 US$17), while a s/c AC double with carpet, TV and hot running water costs US$21 (1998 US$23). Nearby, on Chatfield Road, the **Hotel St George** (tel: 021 224699) has good s/c rooms with AC, fridge, TV and hot water for US$11/13 single/double (1998 US$23/27).

Two hotels in this range lie on Ring Road east of Nkrumah Circle. The **Ringway Hotel** has seen better days and seems poor value at US$15/20 (1998 US$20/25) for a s/c single/double. The **Adeshie Hotel** (tel 021 221307) by contrast is very plush and reasonably priced at US$20 (1998 US$34) for a s/c double with AC, TV and phone.

Tucked away in North Ridge right next door to Lemon Lodge, the popular **Korkdam Hotel** (tel: 021 223221; fax: 021 223424; email: korkdam@

africaonline.com.gh) has AC s/c rooms for a very reasonable US$9/13/20 single/double/suite (1998 US$14/20/28).

An odd little place on the beachfront near Independence Square, perfectly positioned to catch the evening breeze, the **Riviera Beach Hotel** is rather run-down but not without a certain appeal, and reasonable value with s/c rooms at US$8/13 (1998 US$16/23) single/double with hot water and fan. It also has a quiet, sea-facing bar and serves tasty meals in the US$3–4 range.

Shoestring: ungraded; US$8 (1998 US$12) and under

There's no shortage of shoestring accommodation in Accra. Absolutely the cheapest option, with the bonus of a brilliant location for nightlife and eating out, is the **Salvation Army Hostel**, close to the US Embassy in Osu. Accommodation here is in four-bed dormitories and costs US$1.50 per bed.

Otherwise, the place to head for in search of a cheap room is Adabraka, where a cluster of affordable hotels and hostels lie within 500m of the junction of Castle and Kojo Thompson Roads. A good starting point, right on the junction, the **Hotel de California** (tel: 021 226199) is not quite the lush beach hotel that the name might lead you to expect, notwithstanding the shady palm and mango trees in the grounds, but a creaky old colonial building complete with high ceilings, lazy fans, wooden floors and patio bar. This place is difficult to beat on the combination of price, atmosphere and location, and it's a reliable place to meet other travellers (as well as a clique of 'guides' and other hangers on) – I personally enjoy staying here but it received mixed reports from readers of the first edition. Rooms using communal showers cost US$2.50/3.00 single/double (1998 US$6/7). The breakfast is good value.

Opposite the Hotel de California, the **Hotel Crown Prince** (tel: 021 225381) doesn't have much atmosphere, but the rooms seem fair value at US$3.50/5.00/6.50 (1998 US$7/8/12) single/double/suite (the first two with fans, the last with AC). Similar in standard, and two blocks away on Adama Road, the **Date Hotel** (tel: 021 228200) is OK at US$5/6 for a single/double using communal showers and US$8 s/c double, though recent reports of theft from the rooms should be heeded.

On Castle Road, about 500m east of Kojo Thompson, the **YMCA** is a good place to meet travellers and excellent value at US$2.50 per person. The **YWCA**, barely 100m from the junction with Kojo Thompson, is more basic, and few travellers use it.

Arguably the best-value budget option in Accra is the **Calvary Methodist Guesthouse** (tel: 021 234507), which lies just off Castle Road, on Barnes Road opposite the National Museum. This has s/c rooms with AC for US$3.50/5,00 (1998 US$9/12), a communal lounge with TV, and it serves inexpensive meals.

Back on Kojo Thompson Road, about 500m south of the Hotel de California, the recently upgraded **Kwame Nkrumah Memorial Hotel** is another bargain, charging US$5 for a s/c single with fan or US$6/7 for a s/c single/double with AC and fridge.

There are a few affordable places within a few hundred metres of Nkrumah Circle. The closest is **Aams Hotel**, which is rather run-down but reasonably priced at US$3 for an ordinary double and US$4.50 for a s/c double (1998 US$5/7). On Ring Road, the **Marymart Hotel** wouldn't let me look at a room until I paid the asking price of US$5 (1998 US$9) for a s/c double, from

ACCRA CITY CENTRE

which you're free to draw your own conclusions – one traveller had the same experience and said the rooms were actually very good value. The **Kob Lodge Hotel**, a little further along the same road, seems pleasant enough at US$7 (1998 US$12) for a single with AC.

A more appealing cluster of inexpensive hotels lies in North Ridge, an area with a rather suburban feel despite lying inside Ring Road and being within walking distance of most interesting parts of Accra. The most popular place with backpackers is **Lemon Lodge** (tel: 021 227857), where clean s/c doubles with fan cost US$4 (1998 US$7.50). Similar in price, the nearby **Asylum Down** and **Mavis Hotels** are also very comfortable and the latter hotel has a good garden bar serving cheap meals. Close by, but just outside Ring Road, the **New Haven Hotel** is quiet, pleasant and good value at around the same price for a s/c room with fan.

An excellent set-up, situated on the cliffs close to the city centre, is the **Akama Cultural Village**, which has basic double rooms perched precariously on the cliff for around US$5, and also allows camping. There is a good restaurant, noted for its fresh fruit juice, and cultural activities can be arranged on site. To find it, walk along High Street between the Riviera Beach Hotel and the cathedral, looking out for the signpost which reads 'Behind Baden-Powell House'.

The central **Gasotel Hotel** (formerly the Tropicana) has large, scruffy rooms with double bed, fan but no running water for an uncompetitive US$5 (1998 US$8).

If camping on an out-of-town beach is more your style, the best option is the **Coco Beach Hotel** (tel: 021 776524) five minutes' walk from Nungua on the Tema road, which charges US$3 per person to camp, and has a good bar and restaurant.

WHERE TO EAT AND DRINK

Accra is a pretty good city for eating out, with a diverse range of restaurants to suit all budgets. The main cluster of cheaper bars and restaurants is in Adabraka, between Nkrumah Circle and the Hotel de California, while the more upmarket restaurants are clustered on and around Cantonments Road in Osu. Because of this, and bearing in mind that all else being equal most people would prefer to eat within walking distance of their hotel rather than to cross town, I've clumped restaurants and bars by area rather than by cost or type of cuisine.

Adabraka

This is the best part of town for cheap eating and drinking, with a good selection of restaurants serving meals for comfortably less than US$5, as well as a great many bars. Our favourite place in the area is **The White Bell** on the junction of Farrar Avenue and Kojo Thompson Road. The only open-sided first-floor bar in this part of town, there's usually a good breeze here, not to say cold beer and a reasonably eclectic music selection. Above all, the food is varied, inexpensive, and very good – everything from vegetable curry with rice to a big cheeseburger with chips, and nothing much more than US$3.

Two minutes away, the dining hall at the **Hotel President** looks pretty dismal in atmospheric terms, but the food is good, the price is certainly right at around US$2.50 for a chicken or steak dish, and you can ask to be served in the pleasant garden bar. Another nearby spot for an outdoor drink is the garden bar at the **Club Avenue Hotel**, though food here is restricted to grilled kebabs.

There's a cluster of eating and drinking places along Nkrumah Avenue just south of the Circle. The Chinese food in the **Wok Inn** is not the best in town, but it's certainly very acceptable, and good value at around US$3.50 for a main dish with a huge portion of rice – and the freshly cooked spring rolls really are excellent. The **Waikiki Restaurant** on the opposite side of the road serves various grills for around US$3–4.

Approaching the circle, you'll find all manner of street food, including good spicy kebabs, and the **Terra Nova Bar**, a place we liked for its garden ambience and chilled draught. There are several other bars in this part of town, most notoriously the **Kilimanjaro** and **Piccadilly Night Clubs** – the latter (often dubbed Pick-A-Lady for reasons that will be clear to any single guy walking in this part of town at night) has live music on Wednesday and weekend nights.

On the northeast side of Nkrumah Circle, the spotlessly clean, air-conditioned **City Gardens Chinese Restaurant** does a variety of Chinese and other take-away dishes in the US$2–3 range. There are tables at which you can eat, if you want.

The most upmarket place to eat in this part of town is the excellent Lebanese restaurant in the **Niagara Hotel**, where most dishes will work out at around US$4–5 with rice or chips. Around the corner from this hotel, a new place called **The Orangerie** has an extensive menu of Ghanaian, Western and Chinese dishes in the US$3–4 range – the prawns are particularly recommended. Also relatively upmarket, but cheaper, is the garden restaurant in the **Beverley Hills Hotel**.

Osu

Accra's main cluster of mid- to upper-range restaurants lies on and around Cantonments Road in the suburb of Osu south of Danquah Circle. As a rule, you should bank on spending around US$5–10 per head at the better restaurants in this area, though there are a few cheaper places.

Of the cheaper options, a recommended starting point is **Southern Fried Chicken** on Danquah Circle. This might on the face of things come across as an inferior Kentucky clone, but it actually serves a good variety of very affordable pizzas, curries and burgers alongside the greasy fried chicken. Less appetising and more generic fast food options on Cantonments Road include **Dolly's** and **Papaye Fast Foods**, the former rather dirty, the latter specialising in spicy grilled chicken.

Also on Cantonments Road, **Frankie's** has for some time been known for its excellent pastries, cakes and ice-cream, and the recently opened restaurant and coffee shop have been recommended by several readers.

As is so often the case in Ghana, Chinese restaurants dominate the Osu area. One of the best, and more affordable than most, the **Pearl of the East** on 15th Lane also gives you the choice of eating inside or in the open courtyard it shares with the popular **Mapee's Jazz Club** (live music at weekends) and **Kotton Klub** (live music Wednesday and Sunday, plus darts and pool). Also highly recommended is the **Dynasty Restaurant**, while the **Regal** and **Royal Orchid Restaurants** are reputedly very good.

ACCRA NIGHTLIFE
With thanks to Holger Tills of Tills No 1 Hotel

Accra is an excellent place to go partying, particularly at weekends, but the most popular venues vary depending on the night of the week. Here are some current recommendations:

Afrikiko A short distance from the town centre along the airport road, this is a good place to eat and drink on any evening, but best on Tuesdays when popular salsa dancing lessons are given at 20.00.

Chester's Place Situated in Osu, this lively bar has live music every Wednesday night from 21.00 onwards.

Byewell Also in Osu, this bar hosts live music from 21.00 on Thursday nights.

The Bassline Situated close to the KLM office near Sankoma Circle, this jazz club is more a place for listening to music than for dancing, but it hosts good live jazz or blues most nights except for Sunday, generally starting at around 22.00.

Tweety's This nightclub in Adabraka is known for its Cuban music on Friday and Saturday nights. It is liveliest after 22.00.

Champs This is a Sports Bar type of set-up in the Paloma Centre, with Karaoke nights every Friday.

Macumba One of Accra's oldest and most popular nightclubs, this is open from Wednesday to Saturday, when it generally gets busy after midnight.

Fusion Situated in Osu, close to the Taj Hotel, this relaxed night café is open daily and busiest in the wee hours over the weekends and on Wednesday (the latter is karaoke night). Films are shown at 21.20 on Sundays.

Waikiki Another long-serving and popular nightclub, situated in Adabraka close to Nkrumah Circle, this has a reputation as something of a pick-up joint and is also busiest after midnight.

Ups A short distance from the city centre in Kaneshie, this bar plays great highlife music, particularly on Wednesday night.

Next Door About 10km out of town on the Tema Road, this is a beachfront restaurant and bar, particularly worth visiting on Friday and Saturday nights, when there is normally either live music or a highlife disco.

Golden Tulip Hotel Normally a rather staid upmarket hotel, the Golden Tulip is a good place to see live jazz on Friday and Saturday nights.

Tiptoe Café On 42nd Street, close to Nkrumah Circle, this aptly named bar stays open when everything else has closed – the place for a pre-dawn nightcap!

There are two good Indian restaurants in this part of town: the **Tandoor Restaurant** alongside the Taj Guesthouse and the **Haveli Restaurant** down an unmarked side road opposite the Dynasty Restaurant. The **Lebanese New Club 400** near Sankara Circle has been recommended. For European cuisine, the **Restaurant Sole Mio** serves Italian dishes and pizzas, while the **Chez Marie Lou** is a Swiss restaurant serving various continental dishes.

For something completely different, **Ryan's Irish Pub**, popular with expats and well signposted from Cantonments Road, sustains an Irish country bar atmosphere remarkably convincingly – you could easily forget you're in Africa after half an hour here. Various grills are served at moderate to high prices, and there's a popular weekend barbecue.

Another drinking hole that's popular with expats and Ghanaians alike is the **Fusion Bar** close to the Elf Garage on Embassy Road. The nearby **Connections Nightclub** has been recommended as one of the best in town; it asks a cover charge of around US$2.

Elsewhere in Accra

For the combination of an affordable tasty meal and after-dinner drinking or dancing, catch a shared taxi to '37' station or a private one along Liberation Avenue to the Elf garage between Akuafo Circle and the Golden Tulip Hotel. Here, right behind the Elf garage, you'll find the excellent little **Restaurant La Pergola**, which serves tasty fish, chicken and meat grills as well as various Ghanaian dishes in the US$3.50–4.50 range. Perhaps 100m back towards the circle, continue to **Mr Rees**, a very lively garden bar and dancing spot which plays a good variety of African, American and reggae music, serves cheap draught beer, and boasts several kebab stalls. One advantage of this place for those with cars is that there's enclosed, guarded parking, while those without cars can stumble from the bar right on to a taxi rank from where they can hail a private taxi or catch a tro-tro direct to Nkrumah Circle.

Further out on Liberation Road, past the airport, the restaurant at the **Hotel Shangri-La** has long had the reputation of serving the best pizza in Accra, as well as a variety of grills in the US$5–7 range. A good time to visit is on Friday evening, when it's happy hour from 18.00 to 20.00. There is regular live music at the weekend.

Also on Liberation Road, but very close to Sankara Circle, is the **Afrikiko Restaurant**, a shady garden bar and restaurant, with live music every night (no cover charge), chilled draught beer, and a variety of good salads, burgers and fish dishes in the US$3–4 range. On Independence Avenue, almost immediately south of the same circle, the **Canadian High Commission Restaurant**, open for lunch only, is known for its good, inexpensive meals and sandwiches.

On Ring Road, about halfway between Nkrumah and Sankara circles, the Paloma Shopping Centre boasts a cluster of restaurants, including the **Paloma Restaurant**, which does the usual grills and pizzas and has live music most nights. In the same centre, **Life Westward of Eden Restaurant** is, so far as I'm aware, the only vegetarian restaurant in the country, with dishes starting at US$4. Nearby, the **Bus Stop Restaurant** serves inexpensive Western dishes and ice-cream.

One of the few places in central Accra where you can eat overlooking the sea is the open-air restaurant of the **Riviera Beach Hotel**, which serves tasty meals in the US$3–4 range. At La Beach, next to the Labadi Beach Hotel, are quite a number of bars, inexpensive restaurants, and guys selling freshly grilled kebabs and chicken.

A great place to eat at the seaside is **Next Door Restaurant**, which lies along the Tema Road a few kilometres past the Labadi Beach Hotel. This vast outdoor restaurant serves a wide selection of international dishes – though the Ghanaian specialities are the best bet – accompanied by the sound of crashing waves most of the time, and live music in the evening over weekends.

SAFETY
Accra remains in my view as safe a city as any in Africa – for that matter it is probably one of the safest large cities in the world! In all the correspondence I have received from readers, not one includes a first-hand report of crime in Accra, but a recent note from Ben Clissold serves to remind travellers that nowhere in the world is entirely free from crime, and one should never be complacent.

Ben writes: 'There have been some worrying incidents in Accra. Three volunteers have had bags grabbed by people in passing cars, one in broad daylight. These occurred in La, Teshie Nungua and Kaneshie. There have been a number of cases of petty theft on La Beach, and more worryingly a female volunteer was sexually assaulted outside Jokers on the beach road at night. She is okay but our volunteer organisation as a precaution has recommended that no female volunteers are out alone after dark, which seems like common sense in a foreign country anyway.'

None of which should strike any serious fear into traveller to Ghana; but do be alert and sensible, and adhere to the same rules of urban survival you would in any large, modern city!

LISTINGS (area code 021)
Airlines
Air Afrique On Ring Road East, roughly 300m east of Nkrumah Circle; tel: 230014/5. Airport tel: 777414.

Air Ivoire Trinity House, Ring Road East; tel: 241461.

Alitalia Ring Road Central; tel: 229813/1549; fax: 220759. Airport tel: 772766.

American Airlines Valco Trust House, behind USIS; tel: 231804/5; fax: 231806.

British Airways Cnr Kojo Thompson & North Liberia Rd; tel: 240386/7/8; fax: 231956. Airport tel: 779998.

Egypt Air Ring Road East (near Danquah Circle); tel: 773537 or 760363. Airport tel: 776171.

Ethiopian Airlines Cocoa House, Kwame Nkrumah Av; tel: 664856/7.

Ghana Airways Agostino Neto Rd; tel: 777401. Reservations 228417/1150 or 773321.

KLM Ring Road Central; tel: 224050 or 241560. Airport tel: 775729/6509.

Lufthansa Off Water Road, North Ridge; tel: 221086/4030 or 243893/6. Airport tel: 779052.

Middle East Airlines Tel: 228437. Airport tel: 775492.

South African Airways Tel: 230722/3/4/5; fax: 230726.

Nigeria Airways Danawi Building, Kojo Thompson Rd; tel: 223749/3916.

Swissair Pegasus House, 47 Independence Av; tel: 228150/90. Airport tel: 775634/3363.

American Express
The sole agent for American Express is **Scantravel**, in Enterprise House on High Street, Ussher Town, open from 08.00 to 17.00 Monday to Friday.

Books

An excellent bookshop called **Books For Less**, off Cantonments Road, stocks a huge selection of recent second-hand paperbacks which mostly sell for less than US$1. Second-hand novels can also be bought at a few stalls on the south side of Nkrumah Circle, on Pagan Road near the central post office, and at '37' taxi station near Akuafo Circle.

Accra is the best place in the country (if not anywhere in the world) to pick up historical and other works about Ghana. If casual browsing and bargaining is the way you prefer to make your purchases, then head to the cluster of bookshops and stalls on and around Pagan Road, where you can often pick up the most unlikely books for next to nothing. The bookshop at Legon University, open on weekdays and Saturday mornings, stocks all sorts of oddities, with probably the best range of historical books I could find, as well as plenty of cheap second-hand novels.

For travel guides, maps, and new books, try the **EPS Book Services** on Abafun Crescent, which you can reach by using any transport heading between '37' station and La Beach.

Cinemas

Highly recommended is **Ghana Films**, located at TV3 near the Afrikiko Restaurant and the French Embassy, which shows Ghanaian and other African movies for around US$0.50 a ticket.

Crafts and curios

A good place for general curio shopping is the market at the National Cultural Centre on the seafront on 28th February Road. Here, you can buy just about anything you want, from genuine *kente* and other local cloths to carvings, masks and statues from all over Ghana and elsewhere in West Africa. It's also a good place to pick up colourful dyed shirts and cheaper trinkets such as imitation *kente* wallets and bead necklaces. The one drawback to doing your curio shopping here is the high level of pushiness and histrionics – this is certainly not the place to go if you want a life-affirming experience.

Unless you're tremendously pressed for time, you may prefer to do your curio shopping in a more haphazard way. Most curios sell primarily to Ghanaians, not to tourists, and for all but the most esoteric requirements (face masks, for instance) you'll find that there are stalls selling interesting items all over the city – around '37' and the Golden Tulip Hotel, on Ring Road next to Danquah Circle, and on La Beach, for instance. Alternatively, the main markets – Makola in the city centre and Kaneshie on Winneba Road – also stock a wide range of textiles and beads, and although the markets are generally more busy than the National Cultural Centre, the stall owners are not as dependent on the tourist dollar, so the atmosphere is less pushy.

For more serious buyers, a group of skilled craftsmen operate out of the Trade Fair Centre opposite La Palm Hotel. Finally, if your budget is up to shipping it home, surely the ultimate in Ghanaian souvenirs must be your very own customised coffin, carved Posuban-style in whatever shape you like (elephant, boat, minibus, whale!) at the celebrated coffin shop in Teshie on the Tema Road.

For those with a more serious interest in high quality Ghanaian art, it is recommended that you pay a visit to The Loom – the oldest and probably the best art gallery in Accra (and in the whole country). Some paintings can be bought for as little as the equivalent of US$15–20, but it is also suitable also for people willing to spend more for quality work. The Loom also sells souvenirs, craftwork and postcards, has very helpful and reliable staff, and absolutely no bargaining is involved. The owner of this award-winning gallery is a former journalist and broadcaster for the Ghanaian and British media, and she is very knowledgeable about Ghanaian art history. The Loom is located on Nkrumah Avenue in Adabraka, between the Terra Nova Bar and Wok Inn Restaurant.

Embassies and high commissions
Algeria 87 Tito Ave; tel: 776719; fax: 776828.
Australia *contact Canadian High Commission.*
Austria 45 Water Road, North Ridge; tel: 225716/9; fax: 221983.
Belgium Mile 4, Independence Ave; tel: 776561; fax: 773927.
Benin 80 Volta St, Second Close, Airport; tel: 774860.
Bulgaria 3–5 Kakramadu Road, East Cantonments; tel: 772404; fax: 774231.
Burkina Faso 772/3 Asylum Down; tel: 221988.
Canada 42 Independence Ave; tel: 778555/6; fax: 773791.
China 6 Agostino Neto Rd; tel: 777073; fax: 774527.
Cote d'Ivoire (Ivory Coast) 918th Lane, Osu; tel: 774611/2.
Denmark 67 Dr Isert Rd; tel: 226972/1385; fax: 228061.
Finland 73rd Rangoon Close; tel: 776307; fax: 774513.
France 12th Road, off Liberation Av; tel: 228571/04 or 774080; fax: 775904.
Germany 6 Ridge St, North Ridge; tel: 221311/26; fax: 221347.
Guinea 4th Norla St, Labonie; tel: 777921; fax: 760961.
India 9 Ridge Road, Roman Ridge; tel: 775601/2; fax: 772176.
Italy Jawharlal Nehru Rd; tel: 775621/2.
Japan 8 Tito Ave; tel: 775615/6; fax: 775951.
Liberia Odiokwao Rd; tel: 775641/2.
Mali Liberia Rd; tel: 775160.
Netherlands 89 Liberation Rd; tel: 773644 or 231991/2; fax: 773655.
Niger E104–3 Independence Av; tel: 224962 or 229011.
Nigeria Tito Ave; tel: 776158/9; fax: 774395.
Norway *Resident in Lagos*
Russia F586/1 Ring Rd East; tel: 775611; fax: 772679.
South Africa Plot 10, Klottey Crescent, North Labone; tel: 764500/1; fax: 764484 or 762381.
Spain Lamptey Ave ext; tel: 774004; fax: 776216.
Sweden 11th Lane, Osu; tel: 773145; fax: 773175.
Switzerland 9 Water Rd, North Ridge; tel: 228185/25; fax: 223583.
Togo Togo House, Cantonments Circle; tel: 777950/4521.
United Kingdom 1 Osu Link; tel: 221665; fax: 221745.
United States of America Ring Rd East, Osu; tel: 775347/8/9; fax: 776008.

Foreign exchange
The best banks for changing foreign currency and travellers' cheques are Barclays and the Standard Chartered Bank, with the latter generally offering the best rates for cash or travellers' cheques. Both have head offices on Bank Road, 100m from the High Street Post Office in Ussher Town, and branches

in Adabraka and Osu. Until recently, one generally got a better exchange rate for hard currency cash at any of the dozens of forex bureaux dotted throughout the city, but in late 2000 we came across no forex bureau offering a better rate than the Standard Chartered Bank – possibly a temporary quirk caused by the ongoing devaluation of the cedi over the course of that year, so it's worth looking around for the best rate. Few forex bureaux accept travellers' cheques, an exception being the Sacred Lady Forex Bureau opposite the White Bell in Adabraka. In an emergency, there is a forex bureau in most of the upmarket hotels, though rates tend to be very poor and most will only change for hotel residents. At cheaper hotels, the receptionist or manager can probably arrange for you to change a small sum outside banking hours.

Credit cards can generally be used to settle bills at the more expensive hotels and restaurants. Visa and MasterCard can be used to draw cash from ATMs outside most branches of Barclays or the Standard Chartered Bank. The Social Security Bank behind the National Theatre handles Diners Club cards, and Scantravel (see American Express above) handles American Express.

Hospitals

For laboratory tests, visit Medlab in SGS House, 14 Ridge Road; tel: 776844. Hospitals and clinics recommended for emergency treatment and other medical requirements are as follows (note that North Ridge Hospital has a doctor present 24 hours):

Military 37 Hospital Liberation Rd near Akuafo Circle and '37' Station; tel: 776111/2/3/4.
North Ridge Hospital Castle Rd near African Liberation Square; tel: 227328.
Nyaho Clinic Aviation Rd, Airport Residential Area; tel: 775341/5291.
Trust (SSNIT) Hospital Cantonments Rd 500m south of Danquah Circle; tel: 776787/7137.

Information for visitors

The Regional Tourist Office is quite easy to locate, along an apparently anonymous side road to the west of Barnes Road between the major intersections with Liberia and Castle roads. The people who work here are reasonably friendly, but making friends is about the only purpose that a visit is likely to serve.

A far better source of current information about Accra is the excellent book *No Worries: The Indispensable Insiders' Guide to Accra*, compiled and published by the North American Women's Association and sold at most large bookshops and upmarket hotels for the equivalent of US$12. Geared primarily at people spending a while in Accra rather than the casual visitor, it provides a useful combination of detailed listings and common-sense advice on everything from swimming in the sea to hiring a domestic servant.

Internet

There are dozens of internet cafés scattered around Accra, with more opening the whole time. Servers tend to be slow by international standards, but rates (often charged by the minute) are very good – about US$1 for 30–60 minutes. The Cybercafé in the Paloma Centre is one of the best, and opens from 07.00 until 23.00 daily except on Sundays when it closes an hour earlier. Other cafés include Yankee Ventures opposite the Paloma Centre, a cybercafé on Kojo Thompson Road opposite the Niagara Hotel, another one underneath the same hotel, the Communications Centre on Castle Road close to the Hotel de California, and five or six places along Cantonments Road in Osu. The British Council is another option, provided you enjoy long queues.

Maps

The KLM/Shell Ghana road map (with Accra on the flip side) is sometimes available in Accra's bookshops and upmarket hotels. For other requirements, head to the map sales office in the Department of Surveys offices on the junction of Airport and Gifford Road, about 500m from '37' Station. Don't buy the 1:1,000,000 one-sheet map of Ghana, which so far as I can see is identical to the KLM/Shell map, but double the price and lacking Accra on the flip. Far more useful is the set of four 1:500,000 sheets which together cover the whole country and cost around US$1 (1998 US$2.50) each.

Be aware that most maps contain some curious omissions, inclusions, displacements and misspellings (one example is the substantial junction town of Ashaiman, only 20km from Accra, which is not shown on any map that I've seen) suggesting they are rather less current than the legend '8th edition Jan 1994' on the 1:500,000 maps would have you believe.

For hikers and walkers, the map sales office sells more detailed 1:50,000 sheets covering most parts of the country. These cost around US$1 per sheet and have proved to be reasonably reliable in my experience. Bear in mind, however, that many are very dated and use unusual or archaic spellings for some towns and villages – so exercise a certain amount of judgement in deciding how far they are to be trusted.

Newspapers

Ghana (like most African countries) must be approached with a certain spirit of sacrifice for those of us whose morning ritual is based around a pot of fresh coffee and equally fresh newspaper. So far as the coffee is concerned, Nescafé is generally the only solution, but a cheap fix on the newspaper front is provided by the gloriously air-conditioned reading room in the British Council on Liberia Road, liberally stocked with British newspapers from three days to one month old, and open from 09.00 to 17.00 Monday to Wednesday and 09.00 to 12.00 Thursday to Saturday. Otherwise, various Ghanaian newspapers are readily available throughout Accra. If you look around, you can also pick up the American weeklies *Time* and *Newsweek*, as well as one- or two-day-old British newspapers, the latter often at inflated prices.

Post

Poste restante addressed to Accra should be collected between 08.00 and 16.30 from the central post office on High Street, near the seafront in Ussher Town. International mail posted in Accra will arrive at its destination more quickly than mail posted from other towns in the country, but it will still most likely take up to two weeks. Mail posted from the post office in the airport is reputedly a bit quicker. For express and courier services, contact DHL on North Ridge Crescent; tel: 227035.

Supermarkets

There are a number of good supermarkets in Accra, selling a variety of imported goods ranging from breakfast cereals to Californian wine, though only those in Osu and the city centre are likely to be of great interest to travellers. In Osu, the Koala Supermarket on Cantonments Road, close to Danquah Circle, is regarded as one of the best supermarkets in the city centre, with a good ground-floor bakery and probably the best selection of imported goods, though sometimes at inflated prices. Also in Osu, Sotrec Groceries has been recommended as the best for fresh bread and meat, while the Ghana Supermarket has an excellent selection of imported wines and spirits, and Tip Top In Town stocks a good range of imported food items at reasonable prices. In the city centre proper, the best range of goods is probably at Multistores on High Street. If you are looking for vegetarian products and herbal teas, try Relish Health Foods on the corner of 11th Lane and 6th Street in Osu.

Swimming
A nominal entrance fee is charged to swim at the public beach at La, which is popular with locals and lined with bars and restaurants. For a swimming pool, the pick is the one at the Shangri-La Hotel, where non-hotel residents pay around US$1.50 to swim. The other upmarket hotels charge around US$5 to non-residents.

Telephone
International telephone calls can be made from the telecommunication offices near the Central Post Office on High Street, on Cantonments Road, and on Nkawam Road just north of Nkrumah Circle. A little more expensive, but considerably more time effective, are dozens of business centres offering international telephone and fax facilities in Osu, Adabraka and elsewhere.

PLACES TO VISIT
As mentioned in the introduction to this chapter, Accra is not especially rich in sightseeing. There is, however, a fair amount to busy yourself with in and around the city. A walking tour through the city centre, perhaps making some use of taxis, would be a good way to occupy a morning, followed perhaps by an afternoon visit to the National Museum, taking lunch at the adjacent Edvy Restaurant. Less centrally, La Beach, Coco Beach and Next Door Restaurant are perhaps the most obvious tourist attractions for sun-worshippers, though the excellent Du Bois Centre and more mundane Accra Zoo will attract some.

In addition to the places listed below, there are quite a number of places covered along routes in the regional chapters which make for realistic **day trips** (or, using public transport, overnight trips) from the capital. On the west coast, I would lump anywhere as far as Apam in this category, and some people even visit Cape Coast and/or Elmina as a day trip from Accra (on the whole, though, the west coast is more suited to overnight than day trips, not least because of the heavy traffic getting out of Accra in this direction). Other easy targets for day trips include anywhere along the east coast as far as Ada, and most places covered in the chapter *Inland of Accra*.

City centre
Although Accra is well suited for random exploration, the following 'highlights' in and around the city centre are described along a rough route that starts in James Town and follows the main road along the seafront east as far as Independence Square or Osu Castle, before turning back inland past the

National Theatre and British Council to the National Museum, a total distance of roughly 6km.

This is a longer distance than you might think in a city that's not only very busy but also really hot and sweaty. One look at the map, however, and you'll see that several shorter variations are possible. You could also make use of a taxi part of the way – a charter along the 2km run from Independence Square to the National Museum shouldn't cost more than US$2. It's also worth mentioning to new arrivals in Ghana that a walk of this length will seriously dehydrate you should you not drink a lot. One of the most refreshing and healthy drinks on offer is coconut juice – keep an eye out for the coconut vendors who hang out all over the city centre, and will cut a fresh coconut for a pittance.

James Town

The most atmospheric part of Accra, James Town is a pleasure to walk around, with its colourful small markets, colonial-era shops and houses, and strong sense of community. A highlight is the whitewashed 30m high colonial-era lighthouse – you should be allowed to climb to the top for a small tip. Also worth visiting is the old fishing harbour on the beach below Fort James, the second largest harbour in Ghana until the construction of Tema, which is a riot of colourful traditional pirogues in the early to mid morning after the fishermen come in. Shared taxis from James Town to Nkrumah Circle leave from in front of the lighthouse, and you can also pick up a charter taxi here. People here can be very funny about photography – it is difficult to say whether this is because it is forbidden to take pictures of Fort James, or just plain contrariness.

Ussher Town

From James Town, follow High Street northeast and you'll soon cross the ill-defined border into Ussher Town, which is centred around the Dutch-built Fort Ussher (to your right walking up High Street about 500m past Fort James) and, more than any other part of Accra, lays claim to being the true city centre. Even before you reach Fort Ussher, look out for Brazil Lane, the seaward end of which is the former site of a long-vanished Portuguese Lodge, built above the cliff in the late 15th century. Past Fort Ussher, I would turn left from High Street along Bank Lane, a large square around a parking lot where you'll see not only several old buildings, the main banks, and the central post office, but also Fam's Mobile Foods, which has acquired a deserved reputation along the overland truck routes of Africa for its cheap, tasty burgers. At the end of Bank Lane, turn right into Pagan Road, where the pavement spills over with stalls (this is an excellent place to pick up cheap second-hand novels and cassettes of Ghanaian music) until you reach Makola Square, from where you can join the throngs that mass around **Makola Market**, the largest open-air market in Accra and a good place to buy beads and fabrics. Then turn back down Thorpe Road to High Street.

Nkrumah Mausoleum

Set in attractive gardens on the seafront side of High Street between the junction of Thorpe and Barnes roads, the current resting place of Kwame Nkrumah is an altogether colder and more ostentatious affair than its quaintly

Above Palm trees at sunset on the Volta estuary in Ada Foah

Right Coconuts are grown and sold all along the coast – the juice makes for a refreshing and healthy cheap drink.

Below Elmina Castle, the oldest European building in Africa

Above The mud and stick mosque at Larabanga, said locally to date to 1421

Below A traditional compound in Nakpanduri, typical of the mud architecture of the north low-key precursor in Nkrumah's home town of Nkroful on the West Coast. Students of African history in particular shouldn't miss the adjoining museum, which contains photos and other artefacts relating to Ghana's first president.

National Cultural Centre

At the intersection with Barnes Road where High Street becomes 28th February Road, you'll see to your left the National Culture Centre (or Arts Centre), somewhat misleadingly named – at least from a tourist's point of view – since by day it amounts to nothing other than Ghana's biggest craft market. It is a good place to buy practically any type of curio, though readers of the first edition appear to be split evenly as to whether the level of hassle and pushiness is acceptable or not. There is some talk of the cultural centre being moved to accommodate the site of a new hotel development. To the right of the cultural centre are two art galleries, one seemingly for show only, the other with paintings for sale at negotiable prices.

If you are heading on from here to Independence Square, you might want to take a right-hand diversion to the Riviera Beach Hotel, for a cold drink, possibly a meal, and as good a view as you'll get of Osu Castle – though you're advised to ask the hotel staff about safety before wandering down to the beach itself.

Independence Square

Also known as Black Star Square, this conglomeration of Soviet-inspired monuments to pan-Africanism and Ghanaian independence, constructed under Nkrumah, is a stark anachronism, not least – ironically – because of the absolute lack of African influences apparent in its angular design. The thematic centrepiece of the square is Independence Arch; the adjective that springs to mind is ugly (one reader points out: 'I thought the real irony was that, viewed from the right angle, the set of curving arches at the back of the stadium look an awful lot like the McDonald's logo!'). The parade ground between the square and the sea is a barren concrete eyesore, at least when void of the 30,000 people it is intended to accommodate, though it would take a hard heart to be wholly unmoved by the enclosed Flame of African Liberation, lit by Nkrumah himself in 1961.

Osu Castle

Also known as Christiansbourg Castle, this is one of the three main castles on the Ghanaian coast, and it has a more chequered history of occupation than the others. The original castle, much smaller than the modern one, was constructed by Denmark shortly after they bought a piece of land from the chief of Accra in 1661. It was briefly occupied by the Portuguese after the Danish commander was killed in a mutiny in 1679, returned to Denmark four years later, captured by the chief of Akwama in 1693, and sold back to Denmark barely a year later (though the keys of the original castle were never returned to the Danes and remain the hereditary property of the chief of Akwama to this day). After that, the castle remained the Danish coastal headquarters for 150 years, during which time it was greatly expanded, before being sold to Britain along with four other Danish forts in 1850.

The seat of government from 1876 to the present day, Osu Castle etched its name indelibly into the modern African history books on February 28 1948.

This was the day when an anti-colonial demonstration outside the castle, initiated by recently returned veterans of World War II, was fired upon by colonial police, who killed three demonstrators and injured another 237 – a landmark event not only in the history of Ghana, but in the change in tide that led to almost all of Britain's African colonies being granted independence over the subsequent 15 years.

As already mentioned, Osu Castle may not be visited without special permission, and the surrounding roads are cordoned off to prevent close access. The best views of the castle are from the Riviera Beach Hotel and Independence Square. Photography from any angle is absolutely forbidden.

National Theatre

Built by China and opened in 1992, this impressive modern building is host to regular plays and dance performances, and it's well worth checking if there'll be anything on while you are in town (tel: 663449/3559). In any case, you might want to look in to see the small ethnographic display of traditional instruments and carvings. You might also want to pop into the Theatre Gardens for a meal or cold drink.

National Museum

Even if you explore the city centre no further, do pop into the National Museum on Barnes Road, which is open from 09.00 to 18.00 daily except Mondays, and charges an entrance fee of US$1 plus a nominal extra for photography. Most of the displays here are ethnographic in nature, with some excellent examples of traditional crafts ranging from an elaborately carved *oware* board to several *akyeamepoma* (the decorated staffs used by royal spokesmen). There are also reasonable displays at Larabanga mosque and Cape Coast castle. The Edvy Restaurant in the museum grounds does fair meals in leafy surrounds for around US$4 (not open evenings), and it serves cold drinks of all types. The lunchtime buffet on Wednesday has been recommended.

Further afield
Du Bois Centre

Situated at 22 First Circular Road, Cantonments (tel: 773127), this is the former home and now burial place of the prominent American pan-Africanist Dr William E Burghardt Du Bois, leader of all the Pan-African congresses between 1919 and 1927, vocal anti-segregationist and later Communist, and prolific writer and speaker. Visitors are welcome to the centre, which now serves as a research institute and library for students of pan-Africanism, as well as being a memorial to Du Bois himself. Open on weekdays from 08.00 to 17.00, the Du Bois Centre is most easily reached by taking a shared taxi east from '37' Station along Gifford Road, and hopping off after about 1km, roughly 100m after passing Awak Stadium to your right.

Accra Zoo

Fifteen minutes' walk from Sankara Circle, Accra's small zoo is hardly an exemplar, and many visitors find it depressing, which it is – particularly when you see highly sociable animals such as monkeys locked away in confined isolation. On the other hand, as is often the case in small African zoos, most of the enclosed animals were orphaned or injured or born in captivity. More unusually, most of them do seem to be in good physical condition. The only real alternative to the animals' current situation is death (most would die horribly, of starvation or at the hands of a predator, were they to be released into the wild) and it strikes me as somewhat assumptive to transpose our feelings about captivity on to other creatures (lions, for instance, spend up to 23 hours of the day lazing around even in their natural state). This is a good place to see a fair cross-section of Ghana's large mammals and, who knows, perhaps leaving an extra donation might be a more appropriate response to its downfalls than indignant condemnation.

University of Ghana

Situated in attractive grounds 14km from Accra along the Aburi Road, this is the oldest university in Ghana. In addition to a good bookshop and a library rich in colonial documents, the university boasts a mellow botanical garden (behind the Department of Zoology) of special interest to birdwatchers, and – obviously – it is a good place to meet Ghanaian students. To get there, catch a tro-tro from the station located on the northwest side of Nkrumah Circle.

La Beach

This is Accra's best swimming beach, situated in front of the Labadi Beach Hotel, and easily reached by using a shared taxi or tro-tro from Nkrumah Circle or Tema station to Nungua. In addition to the beach itself, which is reasonably safe for swimming depending on the strength of the undertow, there are several shady outdoor bars here, a couple of cheap restaurants, and at least two pool tables, warped ingeniously by the constant exposure to the sun. Thursday night is the best time to come partying here.

Coco Beach

Further out of town, about 20 minutes' walk and signposted from the Tema Road at Nungua, near Teshie, this is another good beach, based around a resort that's popular with overland trucks and a good place to head for if you fancy camping near Accra. In addition to the good bar and restaurant, there's live music here most weekends. It's worth stopping in Teshie to look at the fantastic coffin shop – sculpted in shapes from beer bottle to cars – and the excellent arts and crafts gallery on the opposite side of the road.

Kaneshie Market

This large market lies along the Winneba road about 1km past Lamptey Circle, next to the synonymous tro-tro station. In terms of what you can buy, it differs little from Makola Market in the city centre, but it is generally quieter and less frequented by tourists, so the pressure to buy is minimal.

Part Three

The Coast West of Accra

INTRODUCTION

It is hardly surprising that Ghana's coast lies at the centre of its tourist industry. But what *is* remarkable – I daresay unique – is that such a magnificent chunk of tropical coastline should support a tourist industry based almost entirely around historical sightseeing. The reason for this is not that the beaches of the west coast fail to live up to every archetype of white-sanded, palm-fringed tropical nirvana – many of them do, even if riptides and currents pose a potentially fatal threat to swimmers in several places. No, it is that Ghana, alone in Africa, bears tangible physical evidence of an episode as barbarous and shameful as any in the recorded history of the continent: the trans-Atlantic slave trade.

For the sake of historical accuracy, I think it important to stress that the west coast of Ghana is scarcely unique in having supported a substantial slave trade before 1850. On the contrary, the large-scale trade in human lives arrived much earlier at several other parts of the West African coast, whereas Ghana remained relatively immune as a result of its importance to the international gold trade. Even in the mid-18th century, by which time the slave trade out of Ghana had peaked, a greater volume of slaves was being exported annually from French Dahomey alone than from the entire coast of what is now Ghana.

What makes Ghana different to any other part of West Africa is simple. Elsewhere along the coast, trade was generally conducted out of makeshift buildings of which nothing is left today. In Ghana, by contrast, the slave trade was run out of a string of solidly built forts and castles, many constructed at the height of the gold-trading era and later adapted to include slave dungeons. The most substantial of these castles and forts are still standing today, the scratched walls of their dank dungeons a graphic reminder of two centuries of cruelty and despair, from the Fort of Good Hope in the east to Fort Apollinia in the west, via the imposing whitewashed castles that dominate the beachfronts of Cape Coast and Elmina.

The west coast of Ghana is neatly divided in two by the twin towns of Cape Coast and Elmina, which lie 15km apart, roughly halfway between Accra and the Côte d'Ivoire. Formerly the Gold Coast headquarters of Britain and Holland respectively, Cape Coast and Elmina today form the main tourist focus in the region, their fully restored castles holding immense historical significance and impact. Both towns, however, warrant further exploration, as in different ways they both retain something of the mood of an older Africa, not merely in terms of historical buildings, but in their tangible sense of community. An added attraction of Elmina is that it boasts what is perhaps the country's most impressive selection of *posuban* shrines (see box on page 132).

While the immediate vicinity of Cape Coast and Elmina could hardly be described as heaving with tourists, the area does support a tangible tourist industry, and it is thus accorded its own chapter. The other two chapters in this section cover the relatively untrammelled stretches of coast between Accra and Cape Coast, and west of Elmina. Both of these areas are largely ignored by the tourist industry, and thus offer rewarding pickings to independent travellers. True, the relatively upmarket beach resorts at places such as Ankobra, Biriwa and Fete do attract a steady trickle of well-heeled custom, and Busua sometimes hosts a busy backpacker scene. But such places are the exception on a coast that's dotted with strange, time-warped backwaters such as Senya Beraku, Apam, Anomabu, Shama, Sekondi, Prince's Town, Axim, Beyin and Nzulezu stilt village.

Towards Cape Coast

For many visitors to Ghana, the coastal belt between Accra and Cape Coast will be remembered as nothing more than a blur of small towns and weaving taxis as seen from the window of an STC bus or tour coach. For most of its length, the main coastal road connecting Accra and Cape Coast lies just far enough inland that it offers few obvious indications that it runs along the coast at all. And yet, connected to the main road by a series of short feeder roads, this area is studded with a tantalising array of time-warped small towns, run-down forts, and palm-fringed beaches, bypassed by the overwhelming majority of visitors to Ghana.

Whether one chooses to explore this area will be a question of temperament and available time. It would be an exaggeration to claim that any of the forts has an impact commensurate to that of the immense castles at Elmina or Cape Coast, or that the region boasts any upmarket resort better than Elmina's Coconut Grove, or one natural attraction comparable to Kakum National Park near Cape Coast. Frankly, if you have only a couple of days available to explore the coast, then the case for hopping into that STC bus or tour coach direct to Cape Coast or Elmina is strong.

It is different altogether for travellers with time on their hands, or a yen for getting off the beaten track. If it is beaches you are after, they don't come much better than Fete, a small town which lies only an hour's drive from Accra, and boasts two of the finest (and, except at weekends, quietest) upmarket resorts in the country. For the historically minded, Senya Beraku, Apam and Anomabu are obvious highlights, the first two offering accommodation in centuries-old forts, the last the site of a fine mid-range beach resort. Closer to Accra, the attractive Kokrobite Beach is the site of a private music academy, and recommended to those who wish to learn more about Ghanaian music. Also of interest are the relatively substantial towns of Winneba and Saltpond, the former offering some of the cheapest beachfront accommodation in the country, and the isolated Biriwa Beach Resort between Anomabu and Cape Coast.

KOKROBITE BEACH

Located no more than 30km west of Accra by road (though the heavy traffic on the western outskirts of Accra can make it feel a lot further), Kokrobite Beach is best known as the site of the Academy of African Music and Arts Ltd (AAMAL), founded by the internationally known Ga percussionist Moustapha

WEST TO CAPE COAST

Tettey Addy. This is a good place to spend time if you'd like to be instructed in African drumming or music, and it also hosts a popular drumming and dancing show every Saturday and Sunday afternoon. The beach here is also good, though the potentially dangerous undertow means that you should ask before you swim, and it is earning an unenviable reputation as the one place in Ghana where casual theft is a regular problem – don't take any valuables to the beach.

Getting there and away

Those with private transport should follow the coastal road west of Accra for approximately 22km before turning left at the signposted junction for Kokrobite. Using public transport, there are normally direct tro-tros between Kaneshie Station in Accra and Kokrobite, though they may take ages to fill up. Alternatively, any other vehicle heading towards Winneba from Kaneshie station can drop you at the junction for Kokrobite, from where it is 7km to the beach. There isn't that much transport along this stretch of road, so you might have to charter a taxi.

Where to stay and eat

At AAMAL, you can camp inexpensively or take a room, the latter very good value at comfortably under US$10 double. The restaurant serves top-quality seafood. For more information about AAMAL, tel: 021 665987 or 027 554042, or fax: 021 667533.

For cheaper accommodation at Kokrobite, **Big Milly's Backyard** (aka Wendy's Place) is a perennially popular backpackers' set-up, run by an Anglo-Ghanaian couple, and offering dormitory beds for US$3 and rooms for US$6/8 single/double. Facilities include a bar and restaurant, a book swap service, and professional massages. You can also participate in the AAMAL drum and dance lessons at around US$3 per hour, and the live music performances on Saturday nights.

FETE AND SENYA BERAKU

Roughly 40km southwest of Accra as the crow flies, the somewhat isolated twin towns of Fete and Sentya Beraku form an obvious first port of call for unhurried travellers heading west from the capital. Set only 6km apart, and connected to each other by a dirt road covered by regular shared taxis, these two small towns are both attractive travel goals, albeit for very different reasons.

The main point of interest at Senya Beraku is the 18th-century Fort of Good Hope, which boasts a dramatic cliff-top position overlooking a beach covered in colourful fishing boats and reportedly safe for swimming. The town itself is larger than you might expect, unbelievably run-down and populated by perhaps the noisiest children in Ghana. Nevertheless, it is not without some curiosity value, notably a clutch of old churches and – bizarrely – a group of cracking concrete graves that date from the early 20th century and stand right in the middle of a road (or at least what appears to have been a road before it was eroded to its present topographic state).

Senya Beraku first attracted the interest of Holland in the 1660s when a small trading lodge was built there, to be abandoned shortly afterwards. In 1704, the Dutch returned to the site, and with the permission of the Queen of Agona they started work on what would turn out to be the last fort they were to build in West Africa. Originally a very small, triangular construction designed to facilitate a low-key trade in gold, the Fort of Good Hope – would it be too heavy-handed to note the irony? – ended up serving almost exclusively as a slave trading centre. In 1724, the fort was extended to cover more or less its present area, and a large slave dungeon was built into the southwest bastion. The Fort of Good Hope was handed to Britain as part of the 'fort exchange' treaty of 1868, and apparently fell into disuse at some point during the colonial era, since by the time of independence it was a partial ruin. In the 1980s, the fort was restored as a joint historical monument and resthouse.

If Senya Beraku, with its combination of beautiful coastal setting, grandiose European fort, slave dungeons, crumbling buildings, eroded streets and abject poverty, could be seen to encapsulate much of what is disturbing about modern Africa, Fete's attractions are altogether more uncomplicated. This, in a nutshell, is prime sun 'n' surf territory. The small town sprawls over a low hill down to two attractive sandy beaches, both of which now host a good resort hotel, and it is rapidly establishing a deserved reputation as an isolated upmarket beach retreat the equal of anywhere along the coast.

Getting there and away

Both Senya Beraku and Fete lie roughly 15km south of the main road between Accra and Winneba. Either town is reached via a reasonably good dirt road, leaving the main road about 2km west of Awutu Beraku. This road passes through the small town of Ojobi (notable for its bright pink church) and then about 5km before reaching the coast it forks, with the left fork going directly to Fete and the right fork directly to Senya Beraku. The best place to pick up public transport heading this way is not at the junction itself but at Awutu Beraku, where regular shared taxis leave for both Senya Beraku and Fete. It is advisable to pick up a taxi heading specifically to the town you want to visit.

Although the occasional shared taxi runs along the 6km road directly connecting Senya Beraku to Fete, you might be in for a long wait. The alternative is to hire a charter taxi (this shouldn't cost more than US$2 one way) or to walk, the latter a reasonably attractive option in one direction, provided that you're not carrying luggage.

If you are coming direct from Accra, tro-tros to Senya Beraku leave reasonably regularly from Kaneshie Station.

Where to stay and eat
Upmarket
Tills No 1 Hotel Tel: 027 559480 or 021 304890; fax: 027 558247; email: tillsbeach@yahoo.com; web: www.till.net/TillsNo1.
Set on a beautiful beach 500m from Fete town, this plush hotel, owned by a German resident in Accra, offers outstanding value for money in its price range, with eight standard rooms at US$35/40 single/double and four suites at US$55 (all with hot shower, AC, satellite TV and fridge). The restaurant serves excellent seafood and grills in the US$5–10 range, while facilities and activities include beach and indoor games, mini-golf, canoe trips, fishing, windsurfing, drumming and dancing lessons, as well as minibus excursions with a driver.

Whitesands Beach Resort Tel: 021 303889; fax: 021 774064; email: whsands@ighmail.com.
Whitesands is a promising new development on the lovely beach immediately east of Fete town. The buildings, influenced by Hopi Indian architecture, are quite unlike anything else you'll see in Ghana and blend well with the surroundings. At present, Whitesands is aimed primarily at day trippers from Accra, but a few attractively decorated rooms are available in the manager's house at US$50/60 single/double on week nights and US$60/75 over the weekend. More rooms are likely to be added during the next year or two. In addition to good watersport facilities, the resort has a beachfront restaurant and bar serving grills and seafood. A day entrance fee equivalent to US$2 is charged.

Shoestring
Oddly, when you consider the shabbiness and isolation of Senya Beraku itself, the **Fort of Good Hope** easily ranks as the most organised of the various forts now serving as a resthouse. Double rooms with electric light and fan cost US$4. Other facilities include a communal lounge, clean shared toilet and shower, gift shop, bar with fridge, and restaurant serving chicken or fish with fried rice or chips for around US$3. The staff, too, seem unusually well-tuned to the needs of travellers. Bearing in mind that this fort at one point served as a slave dungeon, the very slickness of this operation (slick, that is, by Ghanaian standards) does teeter on the edge of tastelessness. Then again, you could argue that any economic uplift offered to this town by tourism must outweigh historical sensitivities. Still, it's difficult to imagine that anybody would want to hold their wedding reception here, though the facility is advertised.

The only other accommodation in Senya Beraku is the **Anthill Hotel** behind the taxi station, which has acceptable double rooms for US$3 (fan supplied on request).

WINNEBA
The largest coastal settlement between Accra and Cape Coast, Winneba is the traditional capital of the Afutu, whose King Ghartey IV was the prime initiator behind and president of the Fante Confederation of 1868–73. Winneba was also the site of a reasonably important British fort from 1673 until 1812, when the town was evacuated by its settler community following an Ashanti invasion in which the British commander was tortured to death (for decades after this, passing British ships fired a broadside when they passed the site of the fort). Traces of the old fort can be seen in the Methodist church built on the same site by missionaries in the late 19th century. Otherwise, Winneba's compact town centre has the atmosphere of a historical port, all winding alleys, malodorous fishy markets and fading colonial buildings, but no individual buildings of great historical interest, so far as I am aware.

For travellers, Winneba is most attractive for its busy fishing harbour and the expansive beach that lies immediately to its west. You might want to take a look at the old European and Royal cemeteries, which face each other about 300m from the fishing harbour, and hopefully you'll have more luck than us trying to locate the worthwhile *posuban* shrine that reportedly lies between town and beach. The one time of the year when Winneba changes status from diverting backwater to must-visit is on the first weekend of May, when it hosts the Aboakyer Festival. This 300-year-old festival, probably the most famous in the country, is centred on the 'deer hunt', in which Winneba's two oldest *asafo* companies, dressed in full traditional regalia, compete to be the first to hunt down and capture alive an antelope using only their bare hands. The festival carries on throughout the weekend, climaxing twice: on Saturday when the deer hunt takes place amid much noise and colour until one or other company wins, then at 14.00 on Sunday when the captured animal is sacrificed to the oracles at the Pemkye Otu fetish.

Getting there and away

Winneba lies about 6km south of the main road between Accra and Cape Coast. From whichever direction you are coming, you'll be unlikely to find transport heading directly into Winneba. Instead, take a tro-tro to Winneba junction (also known as Swedru junction) from where regular shared taxis make their way to the old town centre.

Where to stay
Budget

Situated about halfway between Swedru junction and Winneba, the recently opened **Hunters Lodge** (tel/fax: 021 229661) is an unexpectedly plush set-up with nine rooms ranging in price from US$12 (single with double bed) to US$30 (suite). All rooms are s/c with AC, satellite TV, fridge and hot shower. Counting against an otherwise excellent hotel are the bland setting and the distance from the beach.

Shoestring

Winneba's nominal tourist hotel is the **Sir Charles Tourist Centre** (tel: 0432 22189), a sprawling chalet complex right above the beach about 1km from the town centre. The rooms are incredibly run-down, but it's difficult to quibble with the price of US$2.50 for a s/c room with double bed, or US$3.50 for a similar twin. (1998 US$6–14). The restaurant is in a circular hall of absurdly vast proportions; the menu is correspondingly small (fish with rice or yam when we visited!) and prices lie somewhere in-between. Assuming that run-down but cheap is what you are looking for, the one problem with the Sir Charles is that it is remarkably ugly: the brutal 1970s architecture and tackily fading pink and blue paint combine to negate any visual pleasure that might otherwise be extracted from the beachfront location. Fortunately, the beach stretches west for a few kilometres, and it is very beautiful once you wander 50m away from the resort.

Altogether less aesthetically confrontational is the **Winneba Resthouse** (or 'Army Resthouse' as it's also known), which lies within the College of Education Southern Campus off the road between the town centre and the Sir Charles. This place has a great view, perched on a hilltop facing a beach to the west, and the large s/c double rooms with fan are really good value at US$3.50 (1998 US$5). The only drawback is the distance from the beach – a good ten-minute walk.

There are a couple of cheap hotels along the road between Winneba and the junction, but they are no better than the ones in town – in any case, it is difficult to see why any tourist would bother coming to Winneba only to stay in the scruffy suburbs miles from the sea. Worth mentioning, however, is the **Yes Motel**, in a field about 300m (and signposted) from the Cape Coast side of Winneba junction opposite the tro-tro station. Again, it's difficult to see *why* any traveller would stay here with such good options available near the beach, but if you do then it is indisputably good value – basic room with double bed, fan and bathroom shared with one other room for US$2 (1998 US$3.50) and large s/c twin with two double beds, fan and sitting room attached for US$4 (1998 US$7.50). The Yes Motel has a bar but no restaurant – there's plenty of cheap chop available at the junction and Western food at a smart garden restaurant called **Hut de Eric** on the Accra side of the junction.

APAM

Memorable for its picturesque fishing harbour laden with colourful pirogues, Apam would perhaps be my first choice were I in a position to stay in only one place between Accra and Cape Coast. The centrepiece of the town is Fort Leydsaamsheid (Fort Patience), built by the Dutch in 1697, captured by the British in 1782, returned to the Dutch three years later, then finally handed back to Britain in 1868. Now a resthouse, this must be about the smallest extant fort on the Ghanaian coast, and the cramped dimensions of the prison cell suggests that it was never used to store slaves to any serious extent, if at all. The most impressive thing about the fort is its position, on top of a sharp little hill which offers a great view over the town and harbour to one side, and a pretty, secluded beach to the other. Several other buildings in Apam strike me as being of some antiquity, including the turn-of-the-century Methodist church and the house belonging to Chief Quaye.

Getting there and away

Apam lies about 15km south of the main Accra–Cape Coast road. The junction at Ankamu is easily reached by tro-tro coming in either direction, and regular shared taxis run from the junction to the town.

Where to stay and eat

Fort Patience doubles as a shoestring **resthouse**. There are seven small bedrooms, each containing one three-quarter bed, and going for US$1.50 per person. The only facilities are bucket showers. There is no restaurant in the town, but you can buy a fair selection of food and drinks around the market and tro-tro station. The only other accommodation in the area is the **King Pobee Hotel** at least 1km out of town, just off the road towards the junction and close to the police station – any shared taxi coming from the junction will know where to drop you. Clean but scruffy s/c rooms with fan cost US$3.50.

MANKESSIM

The busy junction town of Mankessim may not be much to look at today, but it is widely regarded to be the focal point from which the Fante expanded into much of what is now south-central Ghana. The Fante tradition is that Mankessim was founded by three priests who went by the name of Obunumankuma, Oson and Odapagyan, an event that evidently occurred at least half a century before the Portuguese reached the Ghanaian coast. Mankessim has had its moments in more recent history too: it was here in 1868 that the chiefs of the Akan states of south-central Ghana met to form the Fante Confederation, of which Mankessim served as *ipso facto* capital under the presidency of King Ghartey IV of Winneba until the confederation disbanded in 1873.

The most likely reason you'd want to stop at Mankessim is to see the famous *posuban* that lies about 500m from the central traffic circle along the same road as the tro-tro station. This must be about the largest shrine of its sort in Ghana, a peculiar three-storey construction adorned with around a dozen life-sized human sculptures (see also page 129). You might also want to ask about visiting a sacred shrine called Nananompow – Grave of the Fathers – traditionally thought to be where the three founding fathers of Fante were buried, as well as the seat of the Fante gods. The most interesting days to visit Mankessim are Wednesday and Saturday, when there is a good market.

Getting there and away

Mankessim is an important transport hub, easily reached by tro-tro from Winneba, Cape Coast and points in between.

Where to stay and eat

The impressive **Manna Heights Hotel** (tel: 042 33856 or 020 8110400; email: mannaheights@choice-radio.com) is perched on an isolated, breezy hilltop about 2km from Mankessim, and reached via a signposted turn-off from the Saltpond road. The lack of sea views and distance from the beach suggest it is not aimed specifically at tourists, but otherwise it has to rank as one of the best deals in its range on the Ghanaian coast, and would make a useful base from which to explore this stretch of coast. Facilities include a swimming pool and excellent restaurant. Large, smart s/c rooms with satellite TV, AC and a hot bath cost between US$27 and US$33.

The only accommodation within the town limits is the central and very reasonably priced **Clare Palace Hotel**, about 200m from the tro-tro station. Rooms are all s/c with fan and cost US$2.50/3.50 single/double. The hotel has a restaurant and rooftop bar.

SALTPOND

Saltpond is often regarded to be Mankessim's coastal twin, lying about 8km to its southwest and about 1km from the main road towards Cape Coast. Very few travellers pop into Saltpond, but it's an interesting enough place. The narrow roads and colonial architecture are reminiscent of a smaller version of Cape Coast, and there's a very pretty beach. Of historical interest, 200m from the hospital, is a stunning *posuban* shrine, which dates to 1687, and is decorated with perhaps a dozen life-sized human statues as well as a menagerie of dragons and vultures.

At Abanze, on the Cape Coast road about 2.5km from Saltpond, lies **Fort Amsterdam**, which dates to 1631 and was the first fort built by the British on the Gold Coast. The original fort was destroyed in an attack by the people of Anomabu in 1811, to be restored as recently as 1951. Perched on a hilltop, Fort Amsterdam affords excellent views over a busy fishing beach and the Etsi Lagoon to the village of Kormantse, from which its alternative name of Fort Cormantin derives. The slaves held in Fort Amsterdam, sold mainly to the Caribbean plantations, became known as Cormantins – according to the fort's caretaker there are several rivers and other geographical features in the West Indies whose modern name derives from this term. Among the prominent Afro-Americans to have traced their roots to Kormantse is Louis Armstrong.

Getting there and away

Shared taxis connect Saltpond to Mankessim and Anomabu. Coming from elsewhere, you can disembark from public transport at Saltpond junction and then walk or hire a taxi to cover the last 1km or to the town centre.

Where to stay and eat

The **Palm Beach Hotel** at Saltpond junction is an incongruous high-rise concrete eyesore redeemed by the views it offers over the town and beach, and the rooms, which are very good value at US$9 for a s/c double with AC, TV, fridge and balcony (1998 US$17). There is no restaurant, but the rooftop bar would be a nice place to sit in the evening. Also near the junction, the **Nkubeom Hotel** has more basic double rooms for around US$5 (fan only) or US$8 (AC).

The only lodging in the town centre is the very acceptable **Naatoa Guesthouse**, where s/c rooms with fan cost US$4/6 single/double, and one double with AC is available at US$8. There are no proper restaurants in Saltpond, but several places sell cheap chop. For a drink, the Victoria Beach Resort on the beach looks to be a good bet, with a disco on Friday and Saturday night.

ANOMABU AND BIRIWA

The small seaside town of Anomabu, situated about halfway between Mankessim and Cape Coast, had been an important trading centre since before Britain settled at Cape Coast, when it served as the coastal trade outlet

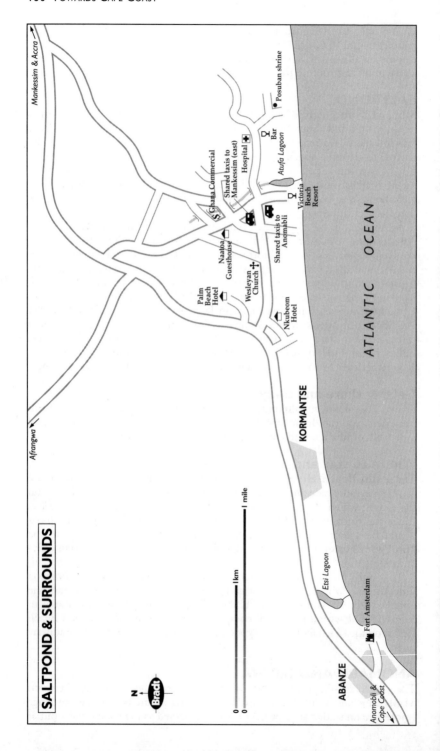

SALTPOND & SURROUNDS

Mankessim & Accra

Afrangwa

Ghana Commercial

Shared taxis to Mankessim (east)

Hospital

Bar

Atufa Lagoon

Posuban shrine

Naatoa Guesthouse

Victoria Beach Resort

Shared taxis to Anomabii

Wesleyan Church

Palm Beach Hotel

Nkubeom Hotel

KORMANTSE

ATLANTIC OCEAN

Etsi Lagoon

Fort Amsterdam

ABANZE

Anomabii & Cape Coast

1km

1 mile

N

Bradt

for the Fante Empire based at Mankessim. Anomabu has a strong history of independence, despite having been settled intermittently by various European powers. In 1630, the Dutch built a fort at Anomabu, only to abandon it in 1664 due to pressure from Britain. After the British constructed Fort Charles on the beach in 1674, Anomabu became perhaps the biggest slave emporium on the Gold Coast, dealing mainly with the freelance 'ten-percenters'. Britain left Anomabu in 1731, largely as a result of disagreements with the local traders, and destroyed the fort so that it couldn't be captured by a rival power. The French then settled at Anomabu for a period, attracted by the established trade in slaves, but they were expelled by Britain in 1753.

Anomabu today has more to occupy visitors than first impressions might suggest. Away from the somewhat mundane main road, the skyline is dominated by a large, sandstone church and the fort, constructed by the British over the foundations of the older Fort Charles in 1756. One of the most solidly constructed pre-20th-century buildings anywhere on the Gold Coast, Anomabu's fort was extended upwards by one storey during the mid-19th-century reign of King William IV, since when it has been known as Fort William. It now serves as a prison, and entrance is forbidden for security reasons (as is photography from most angles), but there is nothing preventing you from walking around the perimeter.

Adjacent to Fort William, there's a substantial ruin which, according to one knowledgeable local, actually predates the fort. About 100m further east, on a beach dotted with coconut palms and (be careful!) fresh turds, there's a sanded-up swimming pool in the rocks, probably dating to the 18th century – a good spot from where to take a discreet snap of the fort. Look out to sea and you'll see the rock after which Anomabu is named – seasonally the site of a breeding colony of gulls.

Several of Ghana's most notable *posuban* shrines lie in Anomabu. There are in all seven shrines in the town, one built by each of the seven asafo companies, and all are easy to find. Don't miss the shrine belonging to Company Three, an improbable assemblage of sculpted animals ranging from a cheetah to a whale, adorned with several smaller carvings of animals in grotesque proportions. This shrine is situated about 50m from the main road facing the Ebenezer Hotel behind a contorted strangler *ficus* tree that's one of the most impressive of the town's 70-plus gods. There are also three substantial *posuban* shrines tucked away in the tight network of alleys lying immediately west of the fort, notably the shrine built by Company Seven, shaped like a European ship and the size of a small house. The oldest shrine, built by Company One, is not as impressive to look at, but it is of special importance as the site where a new village chief must be sworn in – symbolised by the lock and key depicted on the shrine.

You're free to wander around Anomabu and look at the shrines, and you're unlikely to be asked for money unless you take photos. Be warned, however, that the moment you do show a camera you'll not only be expected to pay a separate libation at each shrine (which gets costly!), but are likely to get caught up in all sorts of unpleasantness. (See also *Posuban shrines* box on pages 132–3.)

Alongside the main road next to the Ebenezer Hotel, you may notice a small memorial, erected in 1937 to commemorate Anomabu's most famous son, George Ekem Ferguson (born Ekow Atta in 1864), a trained geographer and

POSUBAN SHRINES

Unique to Ghana's central coastal region, *posubans* are the eye-catching and often elaborately decorated concrete shrines that dot the urban landscape of many Fante settlements, reaching something of a garish zenith in such ancient trading centres as Elmina, Anomabu and Mankessim. These shrines are the work of *asafo* companies, the patrilineal military units that are a feature of most Akan societies. *Asafo* companies are traditionally responsible for the defence of their town, but these days they are perhaps more significant for their ceremonial function and for their activity and influence in the arts and local politics. Most towns in the region boast at least five rival companies, and some boast up to 12. Each company is identified by number, name and location, with Number One Company generally being the longest established unit in any given town, as well as the most important and influential in terms of links to the chieftaincy. In Anomabu, for instance, a new chief is always sworn in at the *posuban* built by Number One Company, which is adorned with a symbolic padlock and key.

Many *posubans* originated as storage houses, used to hold not only arms but also the company regalia, and they are often decorated in a manner that is both richly symbolic and – to the outsider – decidedly cryptic. The extent of this decoration varies enormously from town to town. You could easily walk right past most of Cape Coast's *posubans* without noticing them, since at best they are decorated by one small mural. In Elmina and Mankessim, by contrast, the most important shrines are multi-storey affairs decorated with up to ten life-size human forms, and complex enough in their symbolism to keep you guessing for several hours.

Perhaps the most surprising thing about the *posubans* of the Ghanaian coast is how little they owe to any other African artistic tradition – unique to the area these *posubans* may be, and ancient too by all accounts, but were you to show a picture of a typical shrine to most Europeans, they'd

natural linguist who was perhaps the single most important pioneer in expanding Britain's knowledge of the Ghanaian interior before his death in battle near Wa at the age of 33.

The small, rather nondescript fishing village of **Biriwa**, a few kilometres west of Anomabu, is best known for its superb beach, something of a hippy hangout in the 1970s, but these days used almost exclusively by patrons of the Biriwa Beach Hotel (see *Where to stay*).

Getting there and away

Anomabu is bisected by the main coastal road between Mankessim and Cape Coast, and tro-tros heading between these towns will drop you right in front of either hotel. When you are ready to move on, it's easy to find a seat in a passing tro-tro in either direction – just walk outside your hotel to the main road! If you are coming to Anomabu directly from Accra or Takoradi, you may be tempted to use the STC bus which stops at the Ebenezer Hotel for a meal break – bearing in mind that you'll have to pay the full fare even if you disembark here.

be hard pushed to guess in what continent it had been photographed. One renowned shrine in Anomabu just about conjures up Africa by depicting lions and leopards (sitting somewhat incongruously alongside a whale and several surreal antelope-like creatures), which cannot be said for the best-known *posuban* in that town, several metres long and built in the shape of a European warship. Other famous shrines in the region are dotted with European sailors (clad in blue and white) and overgrown clocks, while one startling shrine in Elmina depicts the story of Adam and Eve. It's the sort of thing that's bound to annoy arty ethno-purists, though personally I find it fascinating to see this strange melding of exotic and indigenous influences in a town such as Elmina, a place where Africa and Europe have, after all, been rubbing shoulders for more than five centuries.

Despite vigorous questioning of local elders, I was unable to establish when, why and how these elaborate *posubans* were constructed. Most of the shrines I saw look as if they took their present form in the post-independence era. It is my understanding (and I'm open to correction on this) that the actual sites of the shrines often *are* centuries old, but that the shrines themselves are resculpted every few decades to reflect changes in fashion and recent additions to the long list of symbols and proverbs boasted by each *asafo*. One of the few shrines to reflect their age directly is the one in Saltpond, which is dated 1685.

Details of important individual shrines are given under the town where they are found. For most short-stay visitors, the obvious place to go *posuban* viewing is Elmina, though the selection found in Anomabu is arguably more varied and interesting, while the main shrine in Mankessim (traditionally regarded as the first capital of Fante) is probably the largest and most elaborate in the country, and the one in Saltpond among the most bizarre. Most of the shrines lie on main roads, so viewing them is free, but a donation of around US$1 per shrine will be expected if you want to take photographs.

Where to stay and eat
Upmarket
Biriwa Beach Hotel PO Box 479, Cape Coast; tel: 042 33333/444; fax: 042 33555/666; email: bbh@ghana.com; web: www.biriwabeach.com.gh.
This German-owned hotel started life about 15 years ago as a restaurant, since when it has expanded to become one of the most homely upmarket retreats in Ghana. Positioned on a high bluff overlooking Biriwa's fantastic beach, the hotel has about ten attractively decorated s/c double rooms, all with AC and bath, for US$60. The restaurant remains outstanding, with a varied menu that reflects not only its proximity to the sea, but also its German ownership. A variety of day trips can be arranged through the hotel, as can two-week trips around northern and eastern Ghana.

Moderate
Anomabu Beach Resort Tel: 042 33801; fax: 042 35801; email: anomabu@hotmail.com.
This exceptionally beautiful resort, which opened in 1999, lies on a palm-lined

beach to the west of the town centre. Although not luxurious, Anomabu Beach Resort is very comfortable, with an idyllic setting, and informed by an organic sense of aesthetics that has few if any peers on the Ghanaian coast. Large mud-clad and thatched double bungalows with a fan cost US$30, while standing tents are available at US$12 per double, and camping costs US$3 per person (all prices quoted in US dollars). Facilities include paddleboat and sailing boat hire. The raised wooden restaurant serves good meals in the US$3–4 range between 07.30 and 21.00.

Budget

On the main road, at the Cape Coast end of Anomabu town, the friendly and central **Ebenezer Hotel** (tel: 042 33673) has large s/c rooms with carpet, fan, hot water and private balcony for US$4.50/6.50 single/double (1998 US$5/7), and similar rooms with AC for US$8. The ground floor restaurant, where most STC buses between Accra and Takoradi stop for a break, serves excellent and inexpensive chop. On the opposite end of the main road, the marginally smarter **Hotel Mariesabelle** (tel: 042 33673) charges US$3.50/6.50 for s/c singles/doubles with fan (1998 US$4.50/7.50) and US$8 for s/c doubles with AC (1998 US$17). The restaurant here serves good meals in the US$2–3 range, and ice-cold drinks, best enjoyed on the rooftop balcony.

MOREE

This large village (or should that be small town?) about 5km northeast of Cape Coast is the site of Fort Nassau. This was the first fort built by the Dutch on the Gold Coast, using bricks brought from Holland, and it served as their headquarters from its construction in 1612 until the capture of Elmina Fort in 1637. Now a substantial ruin, Fort Nassau is clearly visible on a hill above the town, where the standing walls are interspersed with the circular, mud, fish-smoking ovens so characteristic of this part of the coast. More engaging than the ruined fort, however, is the view from the hill: on one side, Moree stretches out in all its corrugated-iron-roofed glory; on the other side is a beach as beautiful as any in Ghana, dotted with typically colourful fishing boats.

Moree lies only 2km from the main Accra road (though it feels so isolated that could be 200km). At the junction you'll find some of the most dilapidated taxis in Ghana waiting to trundle down to Moree in blissful, pothole-dodging lethargy. Alternatively, direct shared taxis between Moree and Cape Coast take about 15 minutes. There is no formal accommodation in Moree, but you could ask about a room in a private house or try camping on the beach.

Cape Coast, Elmina and Surrounds

While Ghana might have a less clearly defined tourist circuit than many African countries, the twin towns of Cape Coast and Elmina – situated less than 15km apart – form its obvious focal point. In addition to some great beaches, notably those at Brenu, Ampenyi and Coconut Grove, the region is notable for the castles at Cape Coast and Elmina, the largest and best preserved buildings of their type in West Africa – and in the case of Elmina Castle, the oldest extant European building of any type in Africa. While historical sightseeing and lazing on the beach are the core tourist activities in this area, both of its major towns are lively and rewarding social centres, bound to be enjoyable to any who want to absorb themselves in the intricacies of modern urban Africa. For natural history lovers, meanwhile, the regional highlight is likely to be Kakum National Park, renowned for its 40m high canopy walkway, but also the most accessible place to seek out Ghana's elusive forest fauna.

CAPE COAST

The first capital of Britain's Gold Coast colony and modern capital of Ghana's Central Region, Cape Coast is steeped in history. Architecturally, it has little in common with the old Swahili towns of Africa's east coast; in atmosphere, however, the streets and alleys of the town centre share with, say, Lamu or Mombasa a comfortable, lived-in feel, and a genuine sense of community – this is one of those towns where the distinction between administrative, business and residential districts is so blurred as to be meaningless. Cape Coast is a fascinating town to explore, its relative antiquity reflected not only in an endlessly surprising range of architectural styles spanning three centuries, but also in the organic shape of the old town, with roads hugging the curves of low hills.

Cape Coast was probably founded in the early 15th century. Its English name is a derivation of *Cabo Corso* – Short Cape – the name given to it by the Portuguese captains Joao de Santarem and Pedro de Escobar in 1471. Two contradictory traditions relate to the origin of Cape Coast's vernacular name: Oguaa. One tradition holds that Oguaa is a derivation of the Fante word *Gua* (market) and that Cape Coast was originally founded as a market town. The other explanation is that it derives from that of the village's founder, a hunter from Efutu remembered by the name Egya Oguaa.

While the truth of the local traditions is difficult to verify, we do know that by the time the British captains John Lok and William Towerson reached the

Gulf of Guinea, in 1555 and 1556 respectively, Oguaa was a fishing village of roughly 20 small houses enclosed within a reed fence and presided over by a chief who went by the rather intriguing name of Don Juan. Nothing more is heard of Oguaa for two generations, until 1610, when a Portuguese lodge was built at an undetermined site on the outskirts of the village, which by that time probably extended from the beach north to what is now Jackson Street.

The rapidly growing village changed hands several times in the 17th century. In 1652, the abandoned Portuguese lodge was occupied by Swedes, then a mere six years later it was captured by the Danes, who signed a treaty with the Efutu paramount chief allowing them to construct a larger, triangular fort at nearby Amanful. The new fort fell briefly into the clutches of the Dutch – the dominant European power in the region at that time, with large forts at nearby Moree and Elmina – before it was taken over by Britain following the Anglo-Dutch War of 1664–65. From that time onwards, Cape Coast was Britain's headquarters on the Gulf of Guinea, and from 1672 onwards the British begin work on expanding and converting the fort to become modern-day Cape Coast Castle.

By the late 17th century, Cape Coast had grown from a small fishing village to one of the largest and most important trading ports along the coast. In 1693 the Paramount Chief of Efutu moved his capital from the inland village of Efutu to what is now Victoria Park, on the west side of modern-day Cape Coast Castle. Two years later, a visitor estimated the number of houses in the small town to exceed 500, and it is clear that by this time the modern town centre had more or less assumed its present shape.

Cape Coast's importance derived from its position as the link between the maritime trade routes of the European powers and the terrestrial trade routes through to the Sahel. Throughout the 18th century, Cape Coast's economy was dominated by its role at the heart of the trans-Atlantic slave trade – at any given time before 1807, when trading in slaves was abolished by the British parliament, there would have been up to 1,500 captured individuals awaiting shipment in the dungeons of the expanded Cape Coast Castle.

Following the re-establishment of legitimate trade from the Gulf of Guinea in 1821, all British castles along the coast were formally taken over by the British Crown and placed under the governor of Sierra Leone. Cape Coast served as the administrative headquarters of Britain's castles from 1828 until 1874, when it became the first seat of government of Britain's Gold Coast colony. Three years later, this role was assumed by Accra, and although Cape Coast has hardly slid into backwater status since, one still senses that the town centre would be instantly recognisable to a time traveller from the Victorian era.

Getting there and away

Two direct STC buses run directly between Accra and Cape Coast daily, leaving at 09.00 and 15.00 and taking roughly three hours in either direction, the exact timing strongly dependent on how quickly the bus can get through the outskirts of Accra. The hourly STC buses between Accra and Takoradi also stop at Cape Coast, and will drop you there provided that you don't mind paying the full fare to Takoradi (which currently elevates the cost of a ticket from around US$1.50 to US$2, a negligible sum by international standards). There are also two STC buses daily between Takoradi and Kumasi, stopping at Cape Coast. The STC bus station is opposite the Methodist church.

CAPE COAST TOWN CENTRE

Bradt

N

KOTOKURUBA

ABOOM WELLS

Palace Hotel

Aloumie Krom Bar

Kotokuruba Market

Taxis (within Cape Coast and to Elmina)

JOHNSTONE

KO

ABOOM

Vec Guesthouse

Goil

Mighty Victoria Hotel

J P BROWN

Fort Victoria

CORONATION

KAWANOPOTO

Cathedral

Amkred Guesthouse

Sammo Guesthouse

ROYAL

Shell

ROYAL

Coastal Forex Bureau

Elf

Minibuses to Takoradi

QUEENS

BEULAH

Joyce lovers spot

GARDEN

ATLANTIC OCEAN

Dan's Paradise Hotel

Tro-tro to
Kakum NP

ROWE

RESIDENTIAL

Shell

SARBAH

Lorry
station

OTOKURUBA

Odas
Internet
Café

Coconut
Delight

ASHANTI

Savoy
Hotel

London
Bridge

JERUSALEM

Crab Shrine

Fort William

LIGHTHOUSE

COMMERCIAL

Communication
spot

NTSIN

Mobil

JACKSON

CHEETAM

Heritage
House

KING

Chapel

Cape Café &
Methodist
bookshop

AGGREY

Barclays

CHAPEL
SQUARE

Shared taxis
to Elmina

Standard
Commercial

Ghana Commercial

RUSSELL

Calex internet

Bars

Law Courts

Belgrave
Memorial
Hall

Anglican Church

Curio
stalls

Castle
Restaurant
(closed)

Cape Coast Castle

0   250m
0   200 yds

There are also regular tro-tros from Cape Coast to most main coastal towns from Takoradi to Accra. Tro-tros to Accra and other destinations along the Accra road east of Cape Coast generally leave from the vicinity of the main lorry station on the junction of Sarbeh and Residential roads. Tro-tros to Kakum National Park leave from Kotoka station near Kotokuraba Market. Shared taxis to Elmina and other local destinations leave from Kotokuraba taxi station. Tro-tros to Takoradi and points west along the coast leave from in front of Joyce Lovers Spot at the Elf garage at the junction of Elmina and Jukwa roads.

Where to stay
Upmarket
Sanaa Lodge Tel: 042 32391/570/788; fax: 042 32898.
This white double-storey building, which lies a couple of kilometres west of the bridge across the Fosu Lagoon on a rise near the Ministry of Health, is the only genuinely upmarket establishment in Cape Coast. Thirty rooms are available ranging from US$60/75 single/double to US$85 for a family room. All rooms have AC, hot bath, satellite TV, fridge and balcony. The hotel has an attractive view over the beach, and facilities include a large swimming pool, a hairdressing salon, a gift shop, a conference centre, and a good poolside grill, restaurant and cocktail bar. Several readers have written to recommend the standard of service and facilities as among the best in Ghana.

Moderate
Cape Coast Hotel Tel: 042 32919; fax: 042 33457.
Despite the lack of atmosphere and bland location, this is a very pleasant tourist-class hotel, and exceptional value at a negotiable US$25 (1998 US$40) for a large s/c double with AC, fridge, satellite TV, balcony and hot bath. A disadvantage of staying here is that it lies on the traffic circle at the junction of Jukwa Road and the Cape Coast bypass, a good 30-minute walk from town, though you can easily pick up a shared or charter taxi at the traffic circle.

Fairhill Guesthouse Tel: 042 33322; fax: 042 33323.
This homely but rather out-of-the-way hotel has very good s/c doubles for US$20 (1998 US$34) with AC, TV and video (there's a library of videos to watch), fridge and hot water. It is a bit difficult to find, perched on an isolated hill in the marshy area to the west of Fosu Lagoon. With private transport, the guesthouse is about 1.4km and clearly signposted from next to the Goil garage on the Cape Coast bypass about 500m from the traffic circle mentioned above. Without private transport, I'd get a taxi out there, though once you know the way it's only 10 minutes' walk from Jukwa Road where you can pick up shared taxis to the town centre.

Nana Bema Lodge Tel: 042 32103/230; fax: 042 32616.
Perched on a hill with good views over the town, this rather smart new place is the most central option in its price range. A selection of different rooms range from US$26 for a standard s/c double to US$55 for an executive suite with two bedrooms (prices quoted in US dollars). All room have AC, and a TV, fridge and hot water.

Budget

The current pick in this range is the long-serving and reasonably atmospheric **Savoy Hotel** (tel: 042 32805/68), which offers very affordable accommodation within easy walking distance of the town centre. The rooms range in price from US$6.50 for a s/c double with fan and hot water to US$8 for a s/c double with AC and US$10.50 for a suite. (1998 US$14/18/25). A decent restaurant is attached, or you can eat on the balcony.

Also relatively central, the new **Mighty Victoria Hotel** (tel: 042 30135) has large rooms with hot water and fan for US$7/10 single/double. There's no AC, but the rooms are very airy, and much smarter than other hotels in this range. A good inexpensive restaurant is attached.

Dan's Paradise Lodge (tel: 042 32942), situated on the same hill as the Nana Bema Lodge, has a rather tacky atmosphere arguably compensated for by the quality of the rooms. A s/c double with AC, hot water, and a bed large enough to sleep a rugby team costs US$8–10, depending on whether you want TV, fridge and radio (1998 US$20–25). The path up to the hotel is steep enough to justify taking a taxi if you have luggage. There's a fair restaurant attached with meals costing around US$3.

Other budget options include the **Amkred Guesthouse**, where adequate s/c doubles with hot water cost US$8/10 with fan/AC (1998 US$14/18), and the **Vec Guesthouse**, which has rather cramped s/c doubles with AC for US$10.

One place you needn't bother yourself about at present is the **Catering Resthouse**. Formerly owned by the government, and presumably now privatised, this place has been closed for three years, and I've been unable to ascertain when – and indeed whether – it is ever likely to resume business.

Shoestring

The **Palace Hotel** is a well-established and recommended backpackers' haunt, situated some 15 minutes' walk from the castle on Aboom Road, close to the junction with Aboom Wells Road. Large clean rooms with fan and basin cost US$2.50/3.00 single/double (1998 US$7/8), while s/c doubles cost US$3.50 (1998 US$10). The communal showers are well kept and appear never to run out of water. There's a good bar downstairs, a reasonable restaurant upstairs, and grilled kebabs on the pavement in the evening.

Similar in standard, and popular with travellers whose feedback is mostly positive, the three-storey **Sammo Guesthouse** is conveniently close to a tro-tro station, and less than ten minutes' walk from the castle. Several types of room are available, starting at US$2 for a rather cramped single with fan using communal showers, and going up to US$5.50 for a large s/c double (1998 US$5–13). The breezy rooftop bar is one of the best places in Cape Coast for a drink and meal, though recent reports suggest meals may not always be forthcoming.

An attractive out-of-town option is the **Sarahlotte Hotel** in Osa Estate, which lies about 4km from Cape Coast centre along the Elmina Road, a mere 50m from the beach and no more than 500m from the intersection with the main Takoradi–Accra road. A small family-run place, this has a variety of rooms ranging from a large non-s/c double with fan for US$4.50 to a s/c double with fan, TV and fridge for US$6.50 (1998 US$10–15). Meals can be prepared on request, or you could eat in town – all shared taxis and tro-tros between Cape Coast and Elmina run right past this place.

Where to eat and drink

Situated right next to Cape Coast Castle, the former **Castle Restaurant** used to be *the* place to eat in the town centre, as much as anything for its breezy beachfront setting. The restaurant burnt to the ground in May 1998, since when it has undergone a series of transformations worthy of a soap opera: after being closed for longer than a year, it briefly re-opened as the Xylophone in mid-2000, but had closed again when we passed through Cape Coast in early December of that year. The latest development, according to a traveller who passed through in January 2001, is that it has now re-opened as the **Oasis Beach Resort**, and is 'a great place to spend an evening watching the setting sun, with a menu pretty much the same as the Sanaa Lodge but cheaper, simpler and not quite as tasty.'

Similar in standard, but lacking the view, the bar, and the propensity for regular mutation, the central **Cape Café** (aka Women's Centre) is housed in a well-ventilated room off Commercial Street above the Methodist Bookshop (opposite Barclays Bank). Open from 08.00 to 20.00, this friendly little place serves a good range of local and Western meals and pizzas in the US$1–2 range. Cold drinks are also available, but alcohol and smoking are forbidden. An attached shop stocks some lovely local fabrics. The Women's Centre is a non-profit organisation that provides shelter to the homeless.

The **Courthouse Canteen**, in the Court Building less than 100m from the entrance to Cape Coast Castle, is the works canteen in the basement of the courts complex above, and serves substantial portions of inexpensive local cuisine in a functional but perfectly adequate setting with clean toilets.

Near to London Bridge, **Coconut Delight** prepares memorable fresh fruit juices, as well as good spring rolls and various other snacks and light meals, including breakfast.

Of the more central hotels, the **Savoy Hotel** has a good restaurant, with meals in the US$2–3 range, and the added attraction that you can eat outdoors. Another attractive place for an evening meal is the **Sammo Guesthouse** – the food is good and reasonably priced, and although the ground-floor restaurant lacks atmosphere, you can ask to eat at the rooftop bar, which usually catches a breeze and offers a good view over the town. There is also good food available at the **Mighty Victoria Hotel**.

Less central, the **Assasa Pa Vegetarian Paradise** has a great location on the beach at the western edge of Fosu lagoon. All food here is vegan. Salads and starters cost less than US$1 while main meals cost around US$2. No alcohol is served, but fruit juices are available.

Also some distance from the town centre, the **Aloumie Krom Garden Bar and Restaurant** is in a closed courtyard, so it can get rather stifling, but otherwise it is a good place for a chilled beer and local meal. It's particularly convenient if you're staying around the corner at the Palace Hotel.

For street food, head to Ntsin Road, which positively buzzes at night, exuding the aura of sociability and community typical of Cape Coast. There are a few sweaty drinking spots on Ntsin Road, but our favourite central drinking hole is the **Communication Spot** on Commercial Road, not least because of the breezy first-floor balcony from where you can watch Cape Coast go by.

During the day, you can normally buy fresh coconuts for drinking from a vendor who stands in front of the Mobil garage on Jackson Street, while pineapples and other fruits are sold by vendors along Ntsin Street near the castle.

Where to visit
Cape Coast Castle
This World Heritage Site warrants at least two hours' exploration, at least if you want to see it properly. Visitors must pay for a ticket to see the castle at the entrance: the charge is US$2.50 per person for a self-guided tour (with a useful pamphlet provided when it's available), or US$5 per person with a guide. The ticket is good for one visit only, except by special arrangement. Photography is permitted at no extra fee. If you don't specify that you will do a self-guided tour, the ticket office might well charge you for a guided one.

It is widely accepted that the modern Cape Coast Castle stands on the site of the Swedish Fort Carolusbourg, built from wood in 1653 and fortified with stone the next year (note that there is little foundation for the claim that the original Portuguese lodge at Cape Coast stood on this site). After Cape Coast was captured by Britain in 1665, the fort was expanded to be comparable in size and strength with the nearby Dutch fort at Elmina, and in the 1680s the slave dungeons were constructed in such a way that they were accessible only from the seaward side of the fort. A second phase of expansion, prompted in part by the notorious leakiness of the roof, took place roughly between 1760 and 1795. By the end of this period, the castle had assumed its modern, loosely pentagonal shape, and practically no traces of the original Swedish fort remained.

It is difficult to know quite how to react to Cape Coast Castle. For all the horrors that have taken place within its dungeons, the first thing that impresses about the building is its architectural scale. And the pervading mood, far from being sinister or evil, is innocuously bureaucratic. The castle has been so sanitised as to be – well, if not quite unreal, then wholly un-African, remote from everything around and outside it. I don't know what to make of the recently whitewashed bastions adorned with neat rows of freshly painted black cannon; or of staff so breezily well-trained that you half expect them to spout 'have a nice day' as they hand you a ticket; or of the gift shop that lies within the castle, or of the lively and aesthetically pleasing Castle Restaurant on the adjacent beach – or of the only 'washroom' that I've ever seen in anglophone Africa. I mean, for goodness sake, if you cannot call a urinal a urinal, then how on earth are you supposed to take in the fact that you are inside a building which for a time stood at the heart of *the* greatest involuntary diaspora in human history?

The museum helps place things in perspective – it houses an absorbing, sobering sequence of displays charting the origin and mechanisms of the slave trade, the scale of the resultant diaspora, and its aftermath in the hands of inspirational black leaders such as Marcus Garvey and Martin Luther King. It is emphatically worth taking a guided tour, to help interpret what you see. But, ultimately, it is the time you spend in the slave dungeons that cuts most closely, their stone walls still marked by the desperate scratching of those imprisoned within them. There are three dungeons in all. The oldest was built before 1790 on the south-eastern bastion. The later male dungeon was built below Dalzel's Tower in 1792, while the female dungeon is on the eastern wall, near the exit to the sea that bore the grim nickname 'Door of No Return'. A couple of years ago, a symbolic invitation was issued to two descendants of slaves which saw them return through the door of no return, thus effectively breaking the chain. There is a sign on the other side, now, that says 'Door of Return'.

Those buried in the courtyard of the castle include the Reverend Philip Kwakwe (1741–1816), a native of Cape Coast who became the first Anglican priest of African origin. Also buried here is the novelist Letetia Elizabeth Landon (1802–38) and her husband George MacLean (1801–47), governor of Cape Coast from 1830 until 1843 and Judicial Assessor of the town from 1843 until his death.

Around the old town

Several of the hills in Cape Coast have been fortified at some point in their history. Only two such out-forts now survive, Forts Victoria and William, both part of a chain of lookout posts which were used for signalling purposes, and are still clearly visible from the governor's rooms at the castle. Fort Victoria, to the northeast of the castle, was constructed in 1837 on the site of a ruined fort built in 1712 and formerly known as 'Phipp's Tower'. On Dawson's Hill, Fort William is now a lighthouse and has been since 1855, but it was constructed over the older Smith's Tower, built of mud and stone in 1820. Both forts are in good condition and welcome visitors.

Otherwise the centre of Cape Coast may lack individual landmarks, but it is certainly well endowed with Victorian-era buildings, especially along Commercial and Jackson streets and Beulah Lane – and there is even a bust of Queen Victoria standing in her namesake park to prove it! Many of these old buildings are solidly constructed brick homes with an enclosed upper-floor balcony. The area around Dawson's Hill is one of the best preserved parts of the old town, with Coronation Street in particular boasting several two- and three-storey buildings architecturally characteristic of Cape Coast in the mid- to late 19th century. Particularly notable is the now derelict building near the junction with Commercial Street, built as a hotel in the 1880s and later a convent.

Possibly the oldest unfortified building in Cape Coast, is the three-storey former Government House opposite the Methodist church off Jackson Street. It is known that this building was leased to the government by one Caroline Jackson in 1850, but it is unclear how much older it actually is – it seems reasonable to assume it was built before or during the period 1817–22 (when John Hope-Smith was governor), and it may conceivably have been built in the late 18th century. Government House has recently been restored and re-named Heritage House. It now houses the tourist information office, as well as an internet café and drinking spot.

Near to this, on Royal Lane, the former Convent of St Mary is perhaps the best-preserved building of its kind in Cape Coast. Originally built by an Ashanti prince in around 1850, this building was bought by a community of nuns in 1891 and served as a convent until 1975, since when it has been only intermittently occupied. It currently houses the Coast Forex Bureau.

There are a few *posuban* shrines in Cape Coast, but none is very impressive. At the centre of the traffic circle on the junction of Ashanti and Commercial roads, there is a small *posuban*-like sculpture of a crab. Although recently placed there, this statue has a great significance as the crab is one of the important symbols of Cape Coast – one tradition has it that the village was first founded because of the good crab meat available, and that it was originally called Kotokuraba (crab village), still the name of the town's main market and the nearby tro-tro station.

Near the above junction, London Bridge is a rather odd and unimposing little bridge dating to the late 19th century and appropriately garnished with painted Union Jacks and the like – it's worth crossing if only to have a fruit juice at Coconut Delight.

Assin Manso

This small town, which lies about an hour from Cape Coast along the Kumasi road, was formerly an important stop along the slave trade routes of the 18th and 19th century. It is located on the banks of the Ndonkor Nsuo (Slave River), where slaves were bathed and checked for fitness before being taken to the coast for shipment out of Africa. As a symbolic gesture, the bodies of two slaves – Samuel Carson from the USA and a women known as Crystal from Jamaica – were flown to Ghana in July 1998 to be re-buried here. Visitors are welcome to see the graves and to wander along the riverbank. Regular tro-tros leave in this direction from Kotokoruba station in Cape Coast, and they will drop you outside the large building which serves as the seat of the traditional council, where it would be courteous to pay your respects before you look around.

Listings
Books

A limited selection of cheap paperback novels is stocked at the Methodist Bookshop on Commercial Road. Two excellent and inexpensive books giving a historical background to Cape Coast are sometimes available at the Castle curio shop. These are the *Cape Coast and Elmina Handbook*, edited by Kwame Arhin of Legon University (Institute of African Studies, 1995) and *Cape Coast in History* by James Erskine Graham Jr (Anglican Printing Press, 1994). Here you can also ask about the useful *Central Region Tourist Map* with large maps of both Cape Coast and Elmina on the reverse.

Curios

Although a number of curio stalls are situated opposite Cape Coast Castle, prices are generally rather high, due to the number of package tours that stop here. The shop in the Cape Café is regarded to be a good place to buy high quality fabrics in a hassle-free environment, and at reasonable prices.

Foreign exchange

All the major banks are represented, with the Standard Chartered on Chapel Square normally offering the best rate of exchange for cash and travellers' cheques, no commission charged. Barclays Bank, on Commercial Road, generally offers a poorer rate, but you can draw local currency on a Visa card at the ATM outside. There are several forex bureaux dotted around town, of which Coast Forex on Royal Road offers the best rate for cash, though at the time of writing it was no better than the bank rate.

Internet

The Odas Internet Café on Commercial Road only has two computers, but it offers the best rates for browsing, and the service seems to be unusually speedy. Celex Internet, close to Cape Coast Castle, is more expensive but has more machines. There is also an internet café in Heritage House, the same building that houses the tourist office.

Tourist information

The regional tourist office in Heritage House is probably the best source of up-to-date information about Cape Coast and other places in Central Region, though the not unfamiliar prevailing attitude seems to be that all the answers must be in the handful of pamphlets and maps they stock. It's not that you'll meet with an unhelpful response – on the contrary, the staff couldn't be more obliging – it's just that it doesn't appear to have occurred to anybody involved that tourists visit a tourist information office to get information.

KAKUM NATIONAL PARK

Less than an hour from Cape Coast by private vehicle or tro-tro, Kakum National Park – along with the contiguous Assin Attandaso Game Production Area and Pra Suhien Forest Reserve – protects a patch of rainforest that not only ranks among the most extensive remaining pristine habitat of its sort in Ghana, but is also the most accessible to the casual visitor to the country. Covering a total area of 607km², the protected area is classified as moist, semi-deciduous forest, and like any true rainforest, it is characterised by high rainfall figures (especially between May and December) and a humidity level averaging around 90%. Although vital purely in conservation terms, forests such as this often form important watersheds – the rivers that rise in Kakum, for instance, provide water to more than 130 towns and villages, Cape Coast among them.

The Kakum complex of reserves protects at least 40 large mammal species, including giant forest hog, six types of duiker, bushbuck, bongo, forest elephant, various flying squirrels, leopard, spot-nosed monkey, Diana monkey, mona monkey and black-and-white and olive colobus. None of these mammals is likely to be seen by day visitors, but it is possible to arrange overnight camping trips to Antikwaa Camp, where elephants in particular are encountered with some frequency. Kakum is an excellent place to see forest birds, with roughly 275 species recorded, though to see even a tiny proportion of these you would need to spend a couple of days in the area and do some early-morning guided walks. A full checklist of large mammals, birds and reptiles, together with detailed notes and line drawings of the more common and interesting species, is included in the outstanding 124-page *Field Guide to the Kakum National Park*, written by Roell, Helsens and Nicolet, and available at the park headquarters for around US$3.

The diversity of Kakum's flora is such that there are parts of the forest where the number of plant species per hectare comfortably exceeds 200! This vegetation is divided into five broad layers. The sparsely vegetated floor of the forest interior is dominated by herbaceous plants, above which a layer of shrubs reaches up to about 4m. The upper three layers together form the canopy: the lowest layer consists of spreading trees reaching a height of around 18m, above which lies the main closed canopy of larger trees, typically around 40m high, and then finally there are the emergent trees, many of them very old, reaching a height of up to 65–70m.

The main tourist attraction at Kakum is the much-publicised canopy walk. Constructed in 1995, this 350m long, 40m high wood-and-rope walkway is suspended between seven trees and broken up by a number of viewing platforms. Unique in Africa so far as I'm aware, the canopy walk offers a rare opportunity to actually look into the forest canopy, a breathtaking experience

KAKUM NATIONAL PARK

Assin Foso

Twifo Praso

Assin Attandaso
Game Production Reserve

Aboabo
camp

Ahomaho

Afiaso

Asueso

Asueso Forest Reserve

Afia

Esikuma

Obuo

Brisco 1

Membasoma Gor
(Brisco 2)

Antwikwaa

Kakum National Park

Twifo Praso

Kakum

Ankaaku

Domana

Nemini

Nkyenna

Mfuom

Kruwa

Obengkrom

Park HQ
& canopy walk

Pro Suhen
Forest Reserve

Tourist
Resthouse

Abrafo

Jukwa,
Cape Coast

N

Bradt

0 _____ 10km
0 _____ 5 miles

DOMANA ROCK SHRINE

Consisting of a cool three-storey high natural cavern formed by one large rock balanced on three others, the Domana Rock Shrine is associated locally with a paramount deity known as Bosom Kese. A community-based ecotourist project has recently been set up in the area, offering not only a guided visit to the sacred cavern for around US$1 per head, but also canoe trips on the 500m wide, forest-fringed Pra River for US$2 per head. The river offers good fishing, birding and butterfly-viewing. A seven-bedroom guesthouse has been constructed to accommodate tourists. Accommodation cost US$3.00 per night, and local meals can be prepared on request.

Domana is most easily visited as an extension of a trip to Kakum. From the main national park entrance and canopy walk, drive north for a further 8km or so to Ankaako Junction, where a left turn will lead to Atobiase junction after about 15km. Turn right here, and you will reach Domana after approximately 5km. Using public transport from Cape Coast, head to Kotokraba Bus Station and ask for one of the tro-tros that ply the route through to Atobiase.

Please note that the above details are based on a brochure I picked up in Takoradi and information sent to me by the executive director of the project; I have not visited the shrine, nor do I know of any other travellers who have been there. Pre-booking is not necessary for guided tours, but it is recommended that accommodation reservations are made in advance. These and other enquiries are best directed to the Friends of The Earth Society in Takoradi (tel: 031 21050; email: friends@africaonline.com.gh) or Ghana Tourist Board office in the same town (tel: 031 22357).

in itself (though emphatically *not* for those with a poor head for heights), and one that will immediately excite birdwatchers. Be warned, however, that the canopy walk can get quite busy, especially at weekends, when the whole exercise starts to feel a bit frogmarched, something that's reflected in the price of US$10 for the first hour (including the 15–20-minute walk in either direction from the park headquarters) plus another US$1 for every extra hour (students with valid ID are charged half-price, as are volunteers with proof of their status). Bearing this in mind, you'll get the most from the experience by being at the headquarters as soon as possible after the opening time of 08.00. Better still, should you be spending the night in Abrafo, you can arrange the previous afternoon to be met by a guide before 08.00, when everything is quiet and the forest is at its most atmospheric. Before heading out on the walk, spend a few minutes looking around the informative natural history displays in the information centre.

We felt that the canopy walk dominated thinking around the park headquarters to an extent that became mildly irritating, an impression that has subsequently been echoed by several readers. This richly diverse forest has so much more to offer than one (perhaps slightly over-hyped) novelty, and those with the time and an interest in natural history are encouraged to think about doing a more general walk. This costs US$2.50 per person for the first hour plus US$1 per extra hour, and you can arrange on the previous afternoon to be met before 08.00 the next day – the early morning is the best time to see birds and monkeys (though not butterflies, of which 400 species have been recorded in the area, since they tend to peak in activity in the mid- to late morning).

Recent developments at Kakum include an overnight stay on a camping platform close to the park headquarters (see *Where to stay*), as well as guided night walks, which cost US$5 for up to three people and US$1.50 per additional person. With suitable equipment, an overnight camping trip deeper into the park would be an even more alluring option, but this no longer seems to be offered.

Situated on the eastern edge of Kakum, 40km from Cape Coast along the Assin Fosu Road, the village of Mosomagor is famed locally for its Nyamebekyere Kukyekukyeku Orchestra, which plays traditional music on wind instruments crafted from local bamboo. In addition to putting on performances for tourists, the orchestra offers musical lessons, and can arrange day hikes into Kakum and overnight stays at a tree platform two hours' walk from the village. An entrance fee of less than US$1 per person is charged to visit the village, while an orchestral performance costs US$15 for up to five people. It is best to make any arrangements a few days in advance; for contact numbers and details of accommodation in the village see *Where to stay* below.

Getting there and away
The Kakum National Park headquarters is clearly signposted along the Jukwa Road roughly 33km from Cape Coast. You can easily get there either by chartering a taxi or by using a tro-tro heading to Jukwa from Kotoka station in Cape Coast, and with an early start you can be at the headquarters when it opens at 08.00. If you intend sleeping over at the nearby tourist resthouse, then you're advised to get out of the tro-tro at Abrafo, leave your luggage at the resthouse, and walk the last 1km to the park headquarters.

Where to stay and eat
Most people visit Kakum as a day trip out of Cape Coast, but it is possible to stay overnight locally at the **Tourist Resthouse** in Abrafo, about 1km south of the park headquarters. This is a pleasant enough place, charging US$3 (1998 US$7.50) for a basic double without running water or fan. Reasonable meals and a limited range of semi-chilled drinks are served at the covered tables in the garden.

The restaurant at the **park headquarters** has improved greatly of late. A variety of local dishes are on offer, mostly for around US$1, and cold drinks and beer are on sale. No accommodation is available at the park headquarters, but travellers with their own tent can **camp** on a tree platform ten minutes' walk away for US$1.50 per person. Fires aren't permitted at the campsite, so you will have to eat at the restaurant in the park headquarters.

It would be possible to use **Hans Cottage Botel** (see 150) as a base from which to explore Kakum. There is no real logistical advantage in doing this, as opposed to heading there as a day trip directly from Cape Coast, but the atmosphere of the Hans Cottage does seem more in keeping with that of Kakum than does anywhere in Cape Coast.

At **Mosomagor** village on the eastern side of the park, a small local resthouse charges US$3 per person for basic accommodation. Meals can be

HANS COTTAGE BOTEL

Tel: 042 33621/3; fax: 042 33623; email: hcottage@yahoo.com.

This very attractive and original set-up, situated at Efutu about 8km from Cape Coast centre along the road to Kakum National Park, is not only an excellent place to spend a night or two, but well worth visiting as a day trip from Cape Coast, and would make a convenient brunch stop en route back to Cape Coast after a morning walk at Kakum. The centrepiece of the 'botel' is a double-storey wood-and-thatch restaurant built on a stilted platform over a small lake and connected to the shore by several wooden walkways.

The main attraction here is the dozen or so crocodiles resident in the lake, easily lured to the surface by throwing bread in the water to attract the fish on which they feed. The lake also supports a plethora of colourful lizards and a varied avifauna. Aurally, things are dominated by the ceaseless chattering and swizzling that emanates from various weaver colonies around the lake (we identified village, golden and Viellot's black weaver), but several types of kingfisher also appear to be resident, and herons and egrets are well represented – patient photographers with adequate lenses could find it very rewarding.

The rooms form a separate unit about 100m from the platform, centred around a residents-only swimming pool. Different types of room are available to suit different budgets: a smart s/c double with AC, fan, TV and hot water costs US$12 (1998 US$30), whereas a 'backpacker' double with fan and use of hot communal showers costs US$4.50 (1998 US$10). Camping is permitted at a negotiable rate, with access to the AC conference room when it's available. The restaurant is a great place to sit, and it serves a good variety of reasonably priced meals – mostly in the US$3–4 range – as well as chilled drinks of every variety.

Hans Cottage Botel lies to the left of the main Kakum road at Efutu. Coming from Cape Coast, you can't really miss it if you have private transport or are sitting in the left side of a tro-tro. To find a tro-tro from Cape Coast heading in this direction, go to Kotoka station.

provided. It is also possible to walk out to a tree platform two hours from the village and sleep in the forest at a charge of US$8 per person. For more details, contact the Ciltad/Agoro Project Management, PO Box 711, Cape Coast; tel: 042 30265/7; fax: 042 30264; email: ghcr@ghana.com.

ELMINA

Situated on the thin strip of land that separates the shallow Benya Lagoon from the Atlantic, Elmina is a fascinating small town, at least the equal of nearby Cape Coast in terms of historical sightseeing, though often overlooked by tourists in favour of its larger neighbour. The town started life as a fishing and salt producing village roughly 700 years ago and, despite having served as first the Portuguese and later the Dutch headquarters in West Africa, an overgrown fishing village is basically what Elmina remains today, the rich harvest of the surrounding ocean supplemented by the production of salt from the brackish lagoon. Back in its economic heyday, however, Elmina lay at the heart of the West African gold trade.

Known by the Portuguese as *Aldea das Duas Partes* ('Village of Two Parts' – a reference to the lagoon), Elmina has probably gone by its modern name only since the Dutch took over in 1637. Nevertheless, the name Elmina is almost certainly derived from a Portuguese term which referred to this whole stretch of coast – *Da Costa de el Mina de Ouro* (The Coast of Gold Mines) – though some sources suggest, without any apparent foundation, that Elmina is derived from the Arabic phrase *el mina* (the harbour).

Traditional accounts suggest that Elmina has been settled at least since AD1300, when it was chosen as the capital of Kwaa Amankwaa, the founder of the Edina state, originally a matrilineal chieftaincy though its monarch was selected on patrilineal lines after 1680. The site was probably chosen because of the Benya lagoon, an excellent venue for salt production. An important trade route developed in prehistoric times between the salt mines of Elmina and the goldfields of the Bono Empire (around what are today Tarkwa and Obuasi), and it was due to this that the Portuguese were able to buy gold with such ease when they first landed at Elmina in 1471.

Our best idea of Elmina's wealth and political set-up prior to the arrival of the Portuguese comes from a contemporary account of a meeting held in 1482 between the Portuguese captain Diogo de Azambuja and King Caramansa (probably an erroneous transcription of the common Edina royal name Kwamina Ansah). The narrator writes that Caramansa 'was seated on a high chair dressed in a jacket of brocade, with a golden collar of precious stones ... his legs and arms covered with golden bracelets and rings ... and in his plaited beard golden bars' and that 'his chiefs were all dressed in silk [and] wore rings and golden jewels on their heads and beards'. The same account goes on to describe the king as a man 'of good understanding, both by nature and by his dealing with the crews of the trading ships' and that 'he possessed a clear judgement ... as one who not only desired to understand what was proposed to him, who not only listened to the translation of the interpreter, but watched each gesture made by Diogo de Azambuja; and while this continued, both he and his men were completely silent; no-one as much as spat, so perfectly disciplined were they'.

In 1482, with the permission of Caramansa, the Portuguese began work on the earliest incarnation of the Castle of St George, a rather humble building by comparison with the modern castle. Within five years, several Portuguese traders had settled around the fort, and Elmina had been elevated to city status by the King of Portugal. Elmina remained the Portuguese centre of operations for more than 150 years, though their grip on the fortress gradually waned towards the end of this period. In August 1637, St Jago Hill was taken by the Dutch and the castle was bombarded by cannons, forcing a Portuguese surrender that effectively ended their period of influence in West Africa.

From 1637 until 1872 (when Holland sold all her Gold Coast forts to Britain), Elmina was in many respects the Dutch equivalent to Cape Coast. The Castle of St George was substantially expanded shortly after the Dutch took possession of it, and it was further renovated and expanded throughout their centuries of occupation. In 1665–66, a second fort was established on St Jago Hill, ensuring that no other rival power could take Elmina with the same ease as the Dutch had. A French trader, describing Elmina in the 17th century,

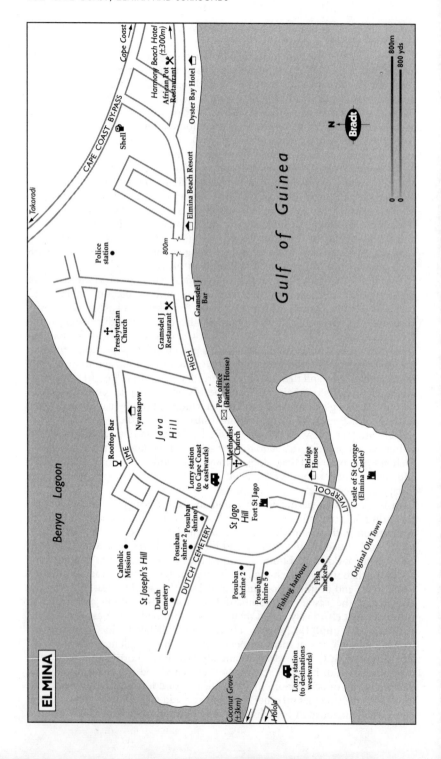

ELMINA

Benya Lagoon

Gulf of Guinea

Cape Coast

CAPE COAST BY-PASS

Takoradi

Harmony Beach Hotel
African Pot Restaurant (±300m)
Oyster Bay Hotel
Shell
Elmina Beach Resort
800m

Police station

Presbyterian Church
Gramsdel J Restaurant
Gramsdel J Bar
HIGH

Nyansapow
Java Hill
Post office (Bartels House)
Methodist Church
Rooftop Bar
LIME

Lorry station (to Cape Coast & eastwards)

St Jago Hill
Fort St Jago
Bridge House
LIVERPOOL
Castle of St George (Elmina Castle)

Original Old Town

Catholic Mission
St Joseph's Hill
Dutch Cemetery
DUTCH CEMETERY
Posuban shrine 2
Posuban shrine 1
Posuban shrine 2
Posuban shrine 5
Fishing harbour
Fish markets

Lorry station (to destinations westwards)
Coconut Grove (±3km)
Hlolai

800m
800 yds

wrote that it was 'very long, containing about twelve hundred houses, all built with rock stones [and] divided into several streets and alleys'. Old maps show that the small town centre had assumed much of its modern shape by the late 18th century, perhaps earlier. It would appear that the town has seen surprisingly little development since it was abandoned by the Dutch, partly because the British were already well ensconced at nearby Cape Coast, but more significantly perhaps because its very location between ocean and lagoon precluded the sort of expansion that has taken place in Cape Coast since the late 19th century.

Much of Elmina's fascination today lies in the way the former Portuguese and Dutch capital has returned to its fishing village roots. There is something decidedly odd about watching the colourful pirogues sail in and out of the lagoon, much as they might in any other small Ghanaian port, except that it is happening right in front of what is the oldest European building in West Africa. And this is the sort of paradox that one repeatedly encounters in a town which has a mood so inherently African juxtaposed against an urban landscape moulded almost entirely by exotic influences. Elmina's apparent contradictions are epitomised by the large *posuban* shrines that lie to the east of St Jago Hill, monuments unique to this part of Ghana, yet which – on the basis of appearance alone – could as easily have come from practically anywhere in the world.

Getting there and away
Elmina lies about 2km off the main Takoradi–Accra road, and it's connected to Cape Coast by a regular stream of tro-tros and shared taxis. In most circumstances, your best bet in heading to Elmina is to catch public transport to Cape Coast, then use a local vehicle to Elmina – there are regular STC buses to Cape Coast, as well as tro-tros from Takoradi. The same is true when you leave Elmina – you can pick up a shared taxi to Cape Coast from Chapel Square, and find transport on from there (bearing in mind if you are heading to Takoradi that you'll pass Takoradi station on your way into Cape Coast).

Where to stay
Upmarket
Coconut Grove Beach Resort PO Box 175, Elmina; tel: 042 33637/48/50 or 021 225155; fax: 042 33646; email: coconut@africaonline.co.gh; web: coconutgrovehotels.com.
Set on a superlative palm-lined beach about 3km west of central Elmina, Coconut Grove is rightly regarded to be one of Ghana's premier beach resorts, and is very popular with Accra residents, particularly those with families. The rooms are large and attractively furnished, with hot showers, satellite TV and fridge, and range in price from US$73/90 for a single/double to US$124 for a detached suite and US$146 for a family cottage (prices quoted in US dollars). The spacious landscaped grounds incorporate a large swimming pool close to the beach, as well as a golf course, and a variety of watersports are available. An excellent restaurant serves meals in the US$5–7 range, while an internet café is in the pipeline.

Elmina Beach Resort PO Box 100, Elmina; tel: 042 34359/33742; fax: 042 33714/34359; email: ebr@africaonline.com.gh; web: www.goldenbeachhotels.net.

Formerly part of the international Best Western chain, now merged into the Ghanaian Golden Beach Hotels group, this plush, international-standard unit lies about 1km northeast of the town centre on a ruggedly rocky stretch of coast. With its elegant decor, blasting AC throughout, and aura of breezy trans-Atlantic efficiency, Elmina Beach Resort feels less resort-like than Coconut Grove, but the two are on a par in terms of service and facilities. In addition to a great swimming pool area, the hotel has good business facilities, an excellent restaurant, and satellite TV in every room. Timeshare units are currently under construction. Prices start at US$54/64 for a s/c double in the low season (Jan 5 to Feb 20 and May 1 to July 15), at US$72/84 in mid-season (Feb 12 to April 30 and Sept 21 to Nov 5), and US$90/100 in the high season (the rest of the year).

Moderate
Coconut Grove's Bridge House *Booking details as for Coconut Grove Beach Resort*
The opening of this new hotel in early 2000 means that finally there is some decent tourist-class accommodation in Elmina's historic old town. Better still, it is housed in one of the town's oldest buildings, with a patio bar facing the fishing harbour and castle. The air-conditioned rooms are comfortable rather than luxurious, but excellent value at between US$35 and US$50 – and the setting, assuming you want to soak up the nocturnal atmosphere of the old town, really is unbeatable. The hotel runs a regular shuttle between Bridge House and the beach resort, where residents have free access to all facilities.

Harmony Beach Hotel Tel: 042 33678/9; fax: 043 33681.
Situated on the Cape Coast Road about 2km from the town centre, this comfortably bland hotel lies very close to the beach but – somewhat bizarrely – faces the main road and has no direct beach access. The s/c rooms all have AC, satellite TV, fridge and telephone, but somehow the whole package doesn't quite seem to justify an asking price of US$44 for a standard double and US$55 for an executive double (prices quoted in US dollars).

Oyster Bay Hotel Tel: 042 33605/6; fax: 042 33643; email: obh@gh.com.
Situated next to the Harmony Beach Hotel, Oyster Bay is a more inherently attractive set-up, hugging a rocky stretch of coast, and with a saline swimming pool in the rocks below the dining area. Large s/c rooms with AC, TV, fridge and fan cost US$35 double. It's fair value, though the restaurant has gone downhill of late, and the rock pool is reportedly often dirty.

Shoestring
While Elmina boasts an excellent range of tourist-class accommodation, travellers on a budget are surprisingly poorly catered for. The only cheapie in the town centre is the **Nyansapow Hotel** (tel: 043 33955), a pleasant enough place, consisting of a double-storey building centred around a large, open courtyard. Smart, clean, s/c doubles with fan and running water cost US$6 (1998 US$7.50). There is a bar on the ground floor, but no restaurant.

The only alternative, so far as I am aware, is the **Holola Guesthouse** in the suburb of Bantoma, about 1km from Elmina Castle along the Pershie road. The rooms are of a similar standard to the Nyansapow, but more expensive at

US$10 s/c double, and the inconvenience of its location, not to say the quantity of mosquitoes that breed in the neighbouring salt flats, make it something of a last resort.

Rumours that **Fort St Jago** will one day be converted to a resthouse have been doing the rounds for the best part of a decade, but there was still no sign of this translating into reality when we looked in towards the end of 2000.

Where to eat

The best place to eat in the town centre is the snappily named **Damina St George's Castle Restaurant**, situated on a northern rampart of the castle which is accessible without paying the castle entrance fee. Open from 08.00 to 21.00, this restaurant offers the winning combination of a historical setting, breezy location and good meals in the US$2–3 range (the highly recommended lobster is a bit more expensive). The usual soft drinks and beer are served, and while service could be speedier, it does at least come with a smile.

The **Gramsdel J Spot**, which spans High Street on the Elmina side of town, consists of a rather stuffy indoor restaurant on the town side of the road, and a more comfortable wooden platform bar perched on the opposite side of the road above the beach. The menu here isn't extensive, but the spicy fish and chicken stew is very tasty and reasonably priced at around US$1.50 per plate, and the beers are reliably chilled. Nearby, there is a pleasant rooftop bar on Lime Street, about 100m west of the Nyansapow Hotel, overlooking the salt ponds in Benya Lagoon.

Some distance out of town, more-or-less opposite the Oyster Bay Hotel, the **African Pot Chop Bar and Restaurant** consists of a boozy ground-floor chop bar and a more sedate air-conditioned restaurant upstairs. A good selection of Western, Chinese and Ghanaian dishes are available in the US$1–3 range.

Aside from the above places, your options amount to heading for one of the chop stalls around the market, or wandering out of town to one of the upmarket hotels – if you go for the latter option, the **Coconut Grove Beach Resort** has the most attractive location and serves excellent food in the US$4–6 range. The filling snacks at the **Elmina Beach Resort** are very good value at around US$2 per plate.

What to do

The obvious place to start a walking tour of Elmina is **St George's Castle**, perched on a rocky promontory between lagoon and ocean. Freshly whitewashed as of 1995, the castle is now maintained as a historical monument and museum, and there is an entrance fee of US$2.50 per person, plus an additional fee of US$2.50 if you would like a guided tour – well worth doing. The castle is if anything more architecturally impressive than its Cape Coast counterpart, much of it four storeys high, and it offers excellent views across to the beach and over the town. Founded in 1482, St George's Castle is the oldest extant colonial building in sub-Saharan Africa, though it has been so extensively rebuilt and extended over the centuries that even its mid-17th-century shape is radically different to its modern one. (I think you could convincingly argue that the 'oldest building' tag hangs more meaningfully on the small Church of Senhora Baluarte on Mozambique Island, barely altered in architectural terms since it was constructed in 1522.)

The original St George, a small rectangular fortress, was sufficiently substantial to withstand three Dutch naval bombardments, before it was captured as a result of the bombardment from the top of St Jago Hill. The modern fort must cover about ten times the surface area of the original; the only recognisable relic of pre-Dutch times is the former Portuguese chapel, converted by the Dutch to an auction hall for slaves, now a museum with displays that concentrate on local history rather than the slave trade.

You may want to linger awhile at the pretty **fishing harbour** and fish market directly in front of the castle. Dozens of colourful pirogues can be seen here, making their way in and out of the sheltered Benya Lagoon every morning beneath the small bridge over its mouth. Immediately east of the castle and the harbour, between lagoon and ocean, lay the **original old town**, depicted in several paintings and lithographs before it burnt to the ground in 1873 as a result of a British naval bombardment.

To get from the castle and fishing harbour to what, I suppose, has to be termed the modern **old town**, you must follow Liverpool Street north over the bridge across the lagoon mouth. During Elmina's prime in the early 19th century, this area is where the wealthiest citizens lived, many of them mulattos or prosperous Dutch merchants who married Elmina women and settled in the town. Immediately after you cross the bridge, you'll see a cluster of these houses running up the right side of Liverpool Street, large double-storey buildings now trimmed of many of their more ornamental touches. Built in the 1840s, this cluster of buildings consists of Bridge House (partially destroyed during heavy rains in 1981, more recently renovated as a hotel), Quayson House, the twin Viala Houses and Simons House (now a complete ruin).

From here, a left turn into the road that runs alongside the north bank of the lagoon will, after no more than 20m, bring you to the steep and easily found path to the top of **St Jago Hill**. A wonderful panoramic view over the fishing harbour and the town centre is to be had from the top of this hill. It also provides an excellent vantage point over St George's Castle, something that was exploited by the Dutch in 1637 when they dragged four cannons to its peak and bombarded the castle, forcing a Portuguese surrender. **Fort St Jago** was built on top of the hill in 1665–66, so that the Dutch could be certain that they wouldn't lose possession of the castle in a manner similar to the one they had used to gain it. The resultant relatively modest fortified garrison post was named Fort Coenraadsburg by its Dutch constructors, but for reasons that are unclear it is generally known today by the older Portuguese name for the hill. Though several extensions were made after 1666, the essential shape of the fort is little changed since that time.

When you walk back down to the base of St Jago Hill, turn right, following the road that runs alongside the harbour away from Liverpool Street before curving inland. Here, over the space of perhaps 200m, is Elmina's main concentration of *posuban* **shrines** (see also page 132). The first two, on the left side of the road a few metres after it curves inland, belong to Asafo Companies Five and Two. The shrine built by Asafo Company Five is a double-storey affair with several life-sized figures carved on the ground floor and – strikingly – a ship with three naval officers on the upper one. Number Two Shrine consists of four life-sized carvings of people surrounding an older man in a bright blue robe and flanked by two aeroplanes. Most impressive, however, is the shrine built by Asafo Company Four at the junction with Dutch Cemetery Street: a variation on the story of Adam and Eve. Unlike in smaller towns, it isn't normally a problem to photograph the shrines in Elmina without being asked for a payment.

Turn left into Dutch Cemetery Street if you want to nose around the old **Dutch Cemetery**, inaugurated in 1802 and moved to its present site at the base of St Joseph's Hill four years later. Well maintained, the graveyard boasts several marble tombstones as well as a large, neo-classical cenotaph dating to 1806. Turn back along Dutch Cemetery Street, passing the shrines built by Asafo Companies Two and One, and you can take a left turn into Lime Street. This is the site of **Dolphin House**, built in the late 19th century by the merchant Fred Dolphin at the foot of the road running to the top of St Joseph's Hill. Once distinguished by its multi-arched façade, Dolphin House had become very run-down prior to collapsing entirely in late 1999. Walk up this hill to see a clutch of impressive mission buildings, including a large **Catholic church** dating from the 1880s, and a view over the salt ponds in Benya Lagoon.

When you walk back to Dutch Cemetery Street, turn left and follow it to Chapel Square, at the intersection of Liverpool and High streets and marked by an attractive Methodist church. A left turn into High Street will bring you to what is perhaps the best-maintained building of its vintage in Elmina, the stone **post office**. This was built some time between 1825 and 1850 as the domestic dwelling and trading quarters of the merchant C H Bartels (son of Governor Bartels), and it later served as a hospital during the colonial era.

TOWARDS TAKORADI

The stretch of coast between Elmina and Takoradi has three obvious highlights: the beach resorts at Brenu Akyinim and Ampenyi, both of which can be visited as a day trip from Elmina, and – closer to Takoradi – the off-the-beaten-track town of Shama with its historic fort.

Brenu Akyinim and Ampenyi

The small village of Brenu Akyinim, 15km west of Elmina, is known for its attractive and reasonably safe swimming beach, a substantial chunk of which has been fenced off to form the Brenu Beach Resort, charging an entrance fee of US$0.50 which ensures that the villagers do their ablutions elsewhere. Swimming is not advisable unless you check current conditions with the locals, but Brenu is a great place to lounge in palm-fringed, white-sanded perfection, and facilities are suited to those on a budget. Brenu forms an easy goal for a day trip out of Elmina.

A bit further west lies the village of Ampenyi and Ko-Sa Beach. This beach is as pretty as any on the Ghanaian coast, and although it is less popular than Brenu, it boasts a natural rock pool where swimming is reliably safe and pleasurable.

Getting there and away

In a private vehicle, you need to first head out along the Takoradi road for about 15km until you reach Ajensudo junction, where the respective turn-offs to Brenu and Ampenyi lie about 500 apart and are signposted. The distance between the main road and either beach is about 5km and the roads are in good nick.

There is no direct transport between Elmina and Brenu Akyinim (and note that 'Akyinim', pronounced 'A**ch**inim', is also, rather confusingly, the name of a suburb in Elmina) or Ampenyi. This means you will first need to catch a tro-tro to Ajensudo junction; any westbound transport from Elmina will oblige. Here you'll find a few shared taxis to Brenu and Ampenyi. These taxis fill up rather slowly, but since the full fare for six passengers works out at less than US$1 you could always treat yourself!

Where to stay and eat

At Brenu, the gorgeous **Brenu Beach Resort** has an excellent restaurant serving mostly seafood dishes in the US$4–6 range, as well as minerals and alcoholic drinks. There is no accommodation at the resort, but the **Celiamen's Hotel** behind the tro-tro station has basic but adequate s/c rooms with a fan costing US$3/4 single/double (1998 US$6/7). There is a bar attached to the hotel, and the friendly owner can arrange a meal courtesy of the lady who runs the beach resort restaurant.

Situated right on the beach at Ampenyi, the **Ko-Sa Guesthouse** offers simple accommodation in local-style grass huts using clean communal showers and toilets for US$10/15 single/double. It is a nice homely place, but the prices seem relatively steep for a room without a fan – exaggerated in late 2000 by being one of the few places in this price range anywhere in Ghana to quote a US dollar rate. Simple meals are served to advance order, and drum lessons are offered at US$5 per person.

A couple of hundred metres from Ko-Sa Guesthouse, the **Royal Ampenyi Beach Resort** is an attractive rustic beach bar of inexplicably vast dimensions (the entire population of Ampenyi could, I suspect, squeeze into the compound). Quite why what is possibly the largest bar in western Ghana should adorn the beachfront of humble Ampenyi is anybody's guess – aside from a blaring radio, there was no sign of life behind or in front of the bar when we dropped in.

Komenda

The mouth of the Komenda River was a focal point of Anglo-Dutch rivalry in the 17th and 18th centuries, as testified by two ruined forts on the opposite banks. Fort Vreedenburg was built by the Dutch in 1682, and Fort English by the British five years later. Little remains of these forts, so Komenda is probably worth visiting only if you have private transport and an insatiable interest in old ruins – the 5km turn-off is signposted from the main Cape Coast–Takoradi road.

Shama

This small, out-of-the-way town makes for a diverting overnight excursion en route between Cape Coast and Takoradi. Shama is the site of Ghana's third-oldest fortified building, the Fortress of St Sebastian, built and named by the Portuguese in 1523. In 1640, the all-but derelict fort was captured by the Dutch, who completely rebuilt it following a brief British occupation in 1664. The ground plan today is almost identical to the Portuguese original, but an extra storey was added by the Dutch. Later in the fort's career, strong buttresses were constructed to prevent the soft foundation rock from being washed away – hence the high semi-circle of steps leading to the main entrance.

Hotel Applause

Fort St Sebastian

Elmina &
Takoradi

Tro-tro

Small
Posuban
shrine

Old Church

Market

Bar

N

SHAMA

Shama's fort is well maintained and looms imposingly above the central market. Entrance costs roughly US$1 inclusive of a guided tour – you might be asked extra to take photographs. So far as we could see, the only other building of any great vintage in Shama is the Methodist church built opposite the fort in 1893. Also of interest is the fish market on the mouth of the Pra River, a short walk to the east of the town centre. During the gold-trading era, Shama was renowned for the seaworthy canoes that were crafted on an island a short distance upstream of the Pra mouth, and even today it is possible to organise a canoe ride up the river from near the market.

Getting there and away

Any tro-tro heading between Cape Coast and Takoradi can stop at Shama junction. A steady flow of shared taxis ply the 4km road to Shama.

Where to stay and eat

At the multi-storey **Hotel Applause** (tel: 031 23941), a s/c double with fan and hot shower costs a very reasonable US$4 (1998 US$7.50). There used to be a great rooftop bar and restaurant at the hotel, but while the rooftop is still there, as are the views, the bar seems to have shut up shop.

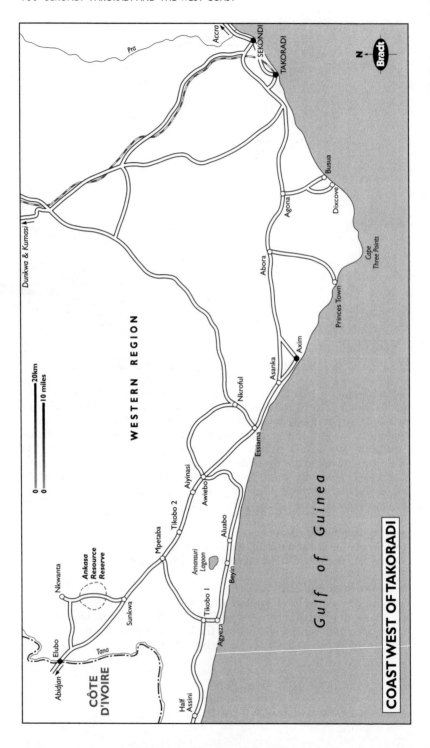

COAST WEST OF TAKORADI

Sekondi-Takoradi and the West Coast

The coastline of Ghana's Western Region may see relatively few tourists by comparison to the areas covered in the preceding two chapters, but it is no less worthwhile. The twin cities of Sekondi-Takoradi, the regional capital and gateway to the west coast, is admittedly of less inherent interest than Cape Coast or Elmina, but it is still an amenable place to spend a night or two, boasting a bustling central market, a pretty beach, the historical Fort Orange, and – most unexpectedly – the opportunity to see wild monkeys within a few hundred metres of the city centre.

The beaches to the west of Takoradi are, in my opinion, the most stunning in Ghana, none more so than the palm-lined slices of tropical nirvana at the blissfully isolated Ankobra and Axim Beach Resorts near Axim. The beach at Busua, though less beautiful, is excellent for swimming, and lined with a row of resorts and guesthouses to suit all budgets. For the historically-minded, there are old colonial forts at Dixcove, Princes Town, Axim and Beyin, the last of which forms the normal base from which to visit the unique stilt village of Nzulezo. For nature lovers, the coast around Princes Town presents some interesting rambling opportunities, while extensive new developments at the Ankasa Resource Reserve have elevated this formerly neglected tract of rainforest to one of the country's prime hiking and birding destinations.

SEKONDI-TAKORADI
Sekondi-Takoradi is probably the third largest urban conglomeration in Ghana, with a total population approaching 300,000. Takoradi is the larger, more modern and more industrialised of the twin cities, which lie about 10km apart on the coast roughly halfway between Accra and the Côte d'Ivoire border. Many travellers pass through Takoradi since it has good road and rail links, as well as an adequate beach and an excellent selection of hotels and restaurants.

Formerly an obscure fishing village, Takoradi was earmarked for development as a harbour in 1920, and officially opened as such in 1928, and became the most important port in the country until the development of Tema. The compact city centre, emanating from the circular central market, has a busy, modern feel without approaching the chaotic atmosphere of, say, Kumasi. Below the city centre is an attractive suburban area that runs along the beach to the west of the golf course.

Sekondi, in direct contrast to its upstart twin, is visibly steeped in history. A solid Dutch fort was built there in 1690 over the foundations of a lodge built

50 years earlier, and the town has served as the administrative capital of Western Region and an important naval base from the very earliest colonial times right up to modern day. Very few travellers make the 20-minute tro-tro ride from Takoradi to Sekondi, but those who do will be amply rewarded. The Dutch Fort Orange is still in use as a lighthouse, and the family who live there seem happy to let visitors wander around the fortifications, which offer a great view over the town. The railway station is a fine piece of colonial architecture, while the harbour, with its backdrop of green hills, is bustling with colourful fishing boats. Above the harbour, the quarter still referred to locally as the 'European Town' is a compact jumble of crumbling turn-of-the-century buildings, with an atmosphere as rich as it is depressing.

On the fringes of central Takoradi, a three-hectare patch of forest on Monkey Hill supports tenacious populations of the localised olive colobus monkey and more widespread spot-nosed monkey. A census in 1999 counted 12 colobus and 41 spot-nosed monkeys, suggesting that neither species is likely to persist indefinitely within this suburban enclave unless the local authorities recognise their tourist potential and accord the hill formal protection as a park or small nature sanctuary. For the meantime, it is easy to visit Monkey Hill informally, ideally at around 17.00, when the odds of seeing both types of monkey are better than even. The turn-off to the top of the hill lies about 100m from Sekondi Circle (the roundabout north of the Ahenfie Hotel) along New Takoradi Road.

Getting there and away

Direct STC buses between Accra and Takoradi take roughly four hours in either direction. The first bus out of Accra leaves at 05.00, after which there is one bus every hour on the hour until 17.00. Buses out of Takoradi also leave throughout the day, leaving every hour on the half-hour. You generally want to arrive at the STC station 30 minutes before the bus leaves to be sure of getting a ticket. There are also two STC buses daily to Kumasi via Cape Coast, leaving at 08.00 and 13.00 and taking around five hours; it is probably advisable to book seats for these buses a day ahead of when you intend to travel.

Direct tro-tros run between Takoradi and practically every town of substance on the coast west of Accra. Tro-tros to Elubo, Beyin, Half Assini, Dunkwa and most other points west of Takoradi leave from the lorry station on the opposite side of Axim Road to the STC station, though those to Agona Junction (for Busua and Dixcove) and Axim now leave from a newer station on the same side of Axim road as the STC station, but about 500m further north toward the main traffic circle at the junction with the Elubo Road. Tro-tros to Cape Coast and other points east of Takoradi leave from the station at the corner of Cape Coast and Ashanti roads. Tro-tros to Sekondi leave from a back road off Kintampo Road.

For details of the twice-daily train service to Kumasi, see *Getting there and away* under Kumasi on page 262.

Where to stay

Despite its low profile as a tourist centre, Takoradi boasts Ghana's largest concentration of hotels outside of Accra and Kumasi, including a couple of dozen mid-range places which cater primarily to local businessmen. The following listings, though selective, are far from comprehensive; readers are welcome to pass on new recommendations.

Upmarket
Africa Beach Hotel PO Box 250, Takoradi; tel: 031 25148; fax: 031 21666.
Oddly, this is the only real beach resort among Takoradi's myriad hotels, and
for that reason alone probably the first choice in its range. The hotel is centred
on a large swimming pool and open bar/restaurant area, and the comfortable
rooms all come with AC and satellite TV. The rack rate of US$70 is negotiable
for extended stays.

Atlantic Hotel The largest and once the smartest hotel in Takoradi, situated
between the beachfront and city centre, this has been closed for renovation for
some years. The signpost proclaiming that it will eventually re-open as a
Holiday Inn probably shouldn't be taken too seriously.

Hillcrest Hotel PO Box 634, Takoradi; tel: 031 22773/22277; fax: 031
24381; email: hilcrest@ghana.com.
This is the only three-star hotel in Takoradi, situated between the city centre
and beach, close to the site of the disused Atlantic Hotel. This is a blandly
international hotel, and what it lacks in character is compensated for by
excellent facilities, including a business centre, a swimming pool, AC and
satellite TV in all rooms, and a good Western-style restaurant. US$60 double
(quoted in US dollars).

Planters Lodge PO Box 1096, Takoradi; tel: 031 22233; fax: 031 22230;
email: planters@africaonline.com.gh.
Set in large grounds separated from the beach by the golf course, Planters Lodge
is probably the most ambient upmarket hotel in Takoradi. The accommodation,
in Swiss-style chalets, is very attractive and comfortable, and facilities include a
tennis court, business centre and excellent restaurant. Double rooms with AC
and satellite TV cost US$80 during the week and US$60 over weekends.

Takoradi Beach Hotel Tel: 031 21021/22496; fax: 031 21022/21031.
This is a bland multi-storey monolith set back from the beach behind the
Africa Beach Hotel. Neither as slick as the Hillcrest or Planters, nor as
attractively situated as Africa Beach, it seems poor value at US$70/80 for a
double with AC and satellite TV, the routine 20% discount notwithstanding.
It is, however, one of the city's better conference locations.

Moderate
Melody Hotel Tel: 031 24109/28875; fax: 031 28874.
This new hotel, conveniently situated opposite the STC bus station, is
currently the best value in its range. Large double rooms with AC, fan, satellite
TV, hot bath and fridge cost US$16 (1999 US$25). The restaurant serves good
meals, with several Indian dishes available.

Guesthouse Maggi PO Box 0684, Takoradi; tel: 031 22852.
Set in a quiet suburban garden not far from the beach, this pleasant guesthouse
has double rooms with AC, TV, fridge and hot shower for US$30.

Harbour View Hotel PO Box 619, Takoradi; tel: 031 23576; fax: 031 24944.
This relatively central hotel, situated on Sekondi Road above the harbour, has

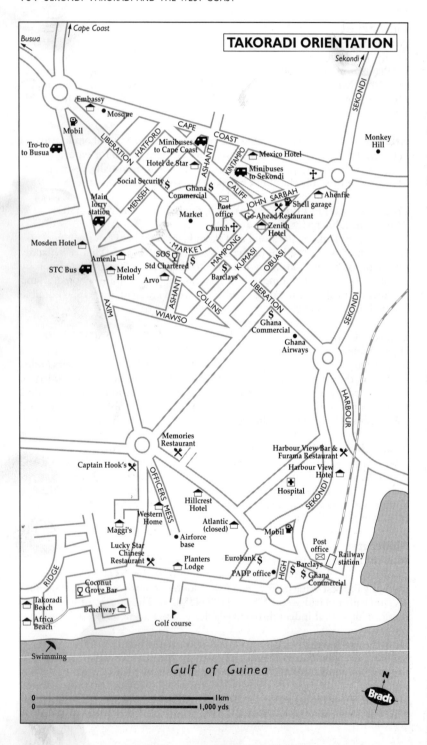

TAKORADI ORIENTATION

Busua

Cape Coast

Sekondi

SEKONDI

Embassy
Mosque

Mobil

Tro-tro to Busua

Monkey Hill

LIBERATION

HATFORD

CAPE

COAST

ASHANTI

KINTAMPO

Minibuses to Cape Coast

Hotel de Star

Mexico Hotel

Minibuses to Sekondi

Ahenfie

Shell garage

MENSEH

Social Security

Ghana Commercial

CALIFF

JOHN SARBAH

Main lorry station

Market

Post office

Go-Ahead Restaurant

Church

Zenith Hotel

Mosden Hotel

Amenla

MARKET

SOS

Std Chartered

MAMPONG

KUMASI

OBUASI

STC Bus

Melody Hotel

Arvo

ASHANTI

Barclays

COLLINS

LIBERATION

AXIM

WIAWSO

Ghana Commercial

Ghana Airways

SEKONDI

HARBOUR

Memories Restaurant

Captain Hook's

OFFICERS' MESS

Hillcrest Hotel

Harbour View Bar & Furama Restaurant

Harbour View Hotel

Hospital

Western Home

Maggi's

Atlantic (closed)

Airforce base

Mobil

SEKONDI

Lucky Star Chinese Restaurant

Planters Lodge

Eurobank

PADP office

Post office

Barclays

Railway station

RIDGE

Coconut Grove Bar

Takoradi Beach

Africa Beach

Beachway

Golf course

HIGH

Ghana Commercial

Swimming

Gulf of Guinea

N

0   1km
0   1,000 yds

Bradt

comfortable s/c rooms with AC at US$10/15 (1998 US$15/25).There's a good outdoor bar and Chinese restaurant in the same complex.

Budget
There are several good options in this range, with the pick arguably being the new **Mosden Hotel** on the first floor of the Mankessim White House next to the STC bus station. All rooms here have a hot bath and satellite TV; those with fan only cost US$6.50 and those with AC cost US$8. Although breakfast is included in the room price, it is for one person only, and the extra breakfast is quite expensive for what you get.

On the other side of the city centre, the large multi-storey **Ahenfie Hotel** (tel: 031 22966) has s/c doubles, a good restaurant, a garden bar, and a disco where – take note – 'all shirts must be tucked into trousers except jumper'! Rooms with a fan cost US$6/8 single/double, while those with AC cost US$13 double.

Opposite the central market, the new and somewhat enigmatically named **Hotel You 84** is a real bargain. All rooms are self-contained and have hot water; those with fan only cost US$6 while those with AC and TV US$8.50. The ground-floor restaurant serves good local meals.

Located between the city centre and the beach on Officers Mess Road, another definite recommendation is the **Hotel Western Home** (tel: 031 23728), a small place consisting of half a dozen air-conditioned s/c doubles with hot water from US$6.50 upwards.

Shoestring
The **Beachway Hotel**, 20 minutes' walk or US$1 by taxi from the city centre, is without doubt the most attractive cheap hotel in Takoradi, if not along this entire stretch of coast. Set in leafy grounds, this creaky, four-storey colonial building has large balconies facing the beach and the golf course. Rooms using communal showers range in price from US$3 for a single to US$4.50 for a large double (1998 US$4–8). There is a pleasant garden bar and restaurant serving food by advance arrangement only.

In the city centre, and more convenient if you are literally just crashing the night in Takoradi, you have the choice of half-a-dozen cheapie hotels, all of which charge very similar rates. Top of the list is the well-maintained **Amenla Hotel**, which has large, clean rooms with fans and running water. Rooms using communal showers cost US$2.50 single or double (1998 $4/5), while s/c doubles with fan only cost US$4 (1998 US$7.50) and those with AC cost US$5. Around the corner, the **Hotel Arvo** is a bit more run-down, but it has identically priced rooms and is definitely the second choice in this bracket.

Next best is probably the **Zenith Hotel**, notable more for its colonial architecture and idiosyncratically decorated courtyard than for the large but rather run-down rooms costing US$2/3 single/double (1998 US$4/5). Still, it's a clear notch above the identically priced **Mexico Hotel** and **Hotel de Star**, and for that matter the less central and slightly more expensive **Embassy Hotel**.

Where to eat
If you are staying in the city centre, one of the best places to eat is the air-conditioned, non-smoking **You 84 Restaurant**, on the ground floor of the synonymous hotel, which serves great local food in the US$1–2 range. The nearby **SOS Restaurant**, which has an air-conditioned, ground-floor bar as

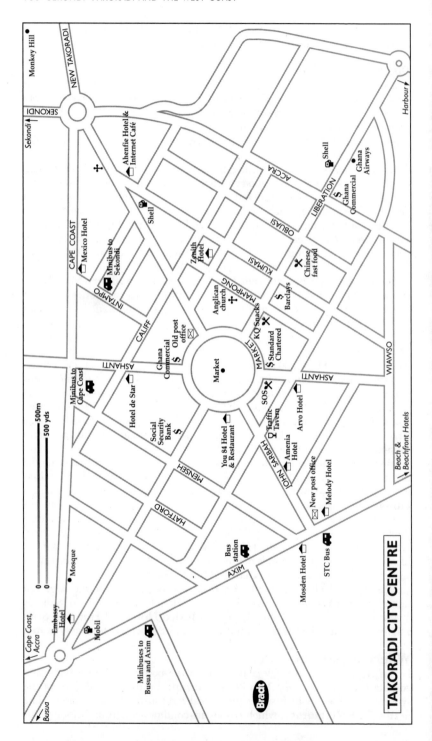

TAKORADI CITY CENTRE

well as a first-floor restaurant spilling on to a balcony overlooking the market circle, seems to have gone downhill of late and served nothing but unappetising burgers when we last looked in – still the balcony is a nice spot for a drink. Other affordable central eatery-cum-boozers include the **Go-Ahead Restaurant** next to the Shell garage, **Chinese Fast Food** on Liberation Road, and **Traffic Tavern** near the Arvo Hotel. There are smarter restaurants, complete with air-conditioning, in the **Ahenfie** and **Melody Hotels**.

A bit further from the centre, a lively place to spend the evening is the **Stomach Cure Garden** next to the Harbour View Hotel. This open-air bar with chilled beers has a great view over the harbour by night. There's a guy who grills kebabs and such outside the bar, or you can eat excellent Chinese food for around US$5–6 per head, excluding drinks, at the air-conditioned **Furama Restaurant** next door.

Our current favourite in Takoradi is the **Memories Restaurant**, a couple of hundred metres from the Hillcrest Hotel. In addition to an air-conditioned indoor restaurant, this place has a great semi-open bar with overhead fans, or you can sit in the large garden. The menu of Chinese, Western and Ghanaian dishes is varied and mostly excellent – with nothing costing more than US$2.

There're a couple of decent places near the beach and golf course. The **Lucky Star Chinese Restaurant**, popular with backpackers staying at the Beachway Hotel, is similar in standard and price to the Furama – it, too, has a comfortable garden area and air-conditioning indoors. **Twin Cities Chinese Restaurant** is at the eastern end of the golf course. There is no garden and the façade is threadbare but the food is excellent and moderately priced and the service friendly and relatively quick. They provide a very good take-away service in 15 minutes from phoning in the order (tel: 031 23888).

The smartest restaurant in Takoradi is undoubtedly the German-owned **Captain Hook's** on Beach Road, which specialises in seafood, pizzas and grills. The food is unquestionably superb, as are the atmosphere and decor, and although it feels a bit dear if you've been in Ghana for a while, by international standards it is very reasonably priced. Pizzas and pastas fall in the US$4–5 range, meat grills in the US$5–7 range, and seafood is US$7 upwards.

Listings
Cultural shows
An excellent dance group named Kundum Obrenpong goes around to the different hotels in the area to perform. They are easy to contact to arrange for performances: PO Box 1056MC, Takoradi, Ghana. (They are located in the northern part of Takoradi in the section of town called Astoria.)

Deep-sea fishing
The marlin fishing is exceptional. Excursions can be arranged through the owner of Captain Hook's restaurant – at US$600 per day! – albeit for 3–4 persons. He also does an inshore charter for 4–6 people and whale-watching trips can also be arranged from November to February.

Foreign exchange
All the major banks are represented, with the Standard Chartered as usual offering the most favourable rates. Case Forex Bureau on John Sarbah Road

and Esam Forex opposite the Amenla Hotel are two of the best places to exchange cash quickly.

Internet
There are a few internet cafés signposted around town, though most seem not to actually offer the service! A reliable bet, offering excellent rates and a good half-dozen computers, is the café in the building in front of the Ahenfie Hotel. There is also a good internet café on Liberation Avenue diagonally opposite the Barclays Bank.

Tourist information
For up-to-date details on developments in Ankasa and Bia Resource Reserves, visit the helpful PADP office, on the second floor of the building next to the Fan Milk Depot on High Street, close to the railway station (tel: 031 25322; email: padp@africaonline.com.gh; web: www.wildlife.gov.gh). The Office will close September 30 2001. Watch the update newsletter (see box page XIV) for relocation details.

BUSUA, DIXCOVE AND BUTRE
Only 20km east of Takoradi, the village of Busua lies on a beach that is widely regarded to be among the best and safest in Ghana, for which reason this small fishing village has played host to a steady influx of backpackers since the 1960s. Recent years have seen Busua attract a marginally more upmarket crowd than in its hippy heyday, particularly following the refurbishment of the long-serving Busua Beach Resort. But it is also true that the village has never before been blessed with so many affordable lodgings and restaurants, most of which are run by locals rather than out-of-town businessmen. The beach remains magnificent, the village and fishing harbour in particular are very colourful, and the friendly, backpacker-oriented atmosphere makes it tempting to label Busua as West Africa's answer to the legendary Twiga Lodge in Kenya and Cape Maclear in Malawi. Busua, in a nutshell, is a great place to chill out for a few days.

Twenty minutes' walk from Busua, **Dixcove** is more a small town than a village, a compact settlement of run-down alleys and crumbling colonial-era buildings, which impart a definite sense of – well, if not history exactly, then certainly historical continuity. Like many other Ghanaian ports, Dixcove has long been the site of a European fort, but was probably settled by local fishermen for centuries before that. In 1692, Dixcove (or Dick's Cove as it was then known) was chosen by the British as the site of a fort, construction of which was completed in around 1696. For the best part of two centuries, Dixcove Fort was the only British property in the Dutch-controlled part of what is now the Ghanaian coast, for which reason it is said to have survived more attacks than any other fortress on the Gold Coast. The fort was captured by the Dutch in 1868 and renamed *Fort Metalen Kruiz*, only to be returned to Britain in 1872 along with all other Dutch forts on the Gold Coast – oddly, however, the Dutch name stuck and it is known as Fort Metal Cross today. The fort is the obvious focal point for visits to Dixcove, and the caretaker will lead an informative tour by request, as well as arrange rooms for travellers. It is also interesting to watch the colourful fishing boats on the busy beach.

About 3km east of Busua as the crow flies, the little visited village of **Butre** can be reached by a fairly direct footpath, by boat, or – rather more circuitously – by road. Butre lies on a wide sandy swimming beach in a large bay adjacent to a small river estuary and protected by a well-wooded peninsula. The main point of interest here is the substantial but somewhat overgrown ruin of Fort Batenstein, perched on a tall hill above the village and reached via a short, steep footpath. Originally constructed by the Dutch in 1656, Batenstein was rebuilt in the 18th century, abandoned due to slow trade between 1818 and 1829, eventually to be handed over to Britain in 1872, after which it fell into disuse. The views from the fortifications are exceptional. For a negotiable fee, villagers in Butre can take visitors by canoe upriver to the site of a derelict British palm-oil factory near Sese. You will probably be expected to visit the welcoming chief on arrival at Butre, and asked to sign the visitors' book. There is currently no accommodation in Butre, nor any restaurant other than a few chop bars, but there is some talk of ecotourism development over the next few years, possibly as the trailhead of the mooted NCRC Heritage Trail (see *The Coast Between Dixcove and Axim* page 172).

The deserted Nunu Busua Island, in the bay below the village, can be visited by boat from Busua. There isn't a lot to see on the island, but there's nothing stopping you from camping overnight and leering at the mainland if the mood takes you. Swimming out to the island cannot be recommended – even if the tides don't put you off, the proliferation of stinging jellyfish should!

Getting there and away

Dixcove and Busua lie no more than 2km apart and roughly 20km east of Takoradi as the crow flies. To reach either town, follow the main Elubo road east of Takoradi to the junction town of Agona, then take the left turn signposted for Busua Beach Resort. This road splits at Asane, about 6km south out of Agona, with the left fork reaching Busua after another 4km and the right fork reaching Dixcove after about 5km. So far as I'm aware, no tro-tros connect Takoradi directly to Dixcove and Busua, but there are regular tro-tros from Takoradi to Agona, from where tro-tros run every hour or so to both Dixcove and Busua.

There is no direct road between Busua and Dixcove. If you want to travel between the two, you have three options: to catch a tro-tro back to Agona and change vehicles there, to charter a private taxi between the two, or to walk. The two towns are connected by a 1.5km footpath, which takes about 15–20 minutes to walk. The path leaves Dixcove from alongside the fort and Busua from the opposite side of the estuary next to the fishing harbour. Do be aware that you'll have to wade through the estuary at Busua, which is safe enough at low tide when the water is thigh height, but dangerous at high tide, according to some locals. We've received several second-hand reports of robberies along this footpath since 1999, and in early 2001 heard personally from a group of three Peace Corps Volunteers who were mugged along the way. Based on this, it would be extremely risky to walk between Busua and Dixcove with luggage or any valuables on your person (based on the circumstances of the recently reported mugging, I'd be dubious about it even with a local guide). If you decide to risk it, leave all your valuables behind and take a guide.

Butre lies 3km east of Busua, and can be reached along a direct footpath which follows Busua Beach for about 500m before ascending low cultivated hills which offer some lovely views over the ocean. A signposted dirt road to Butre leaves from the Agona–Busua road a few hundred metres south of Asane, but so far as I'm aware it is not covered by public transport. Should you have your own vehicle, head along this road for about 3km, then turn right at Tentum (aka Tontu) and you will reach Butre after another 4km.

Where to stay
Upmarket
Busua Beach Resort Tel: 031 21210/857/859; fax: 031 21858; email: bbr@ghana.com.

This popular resort re-opened in all newly renovated glory in late 1996, since when it has acquired a justified reputation as one of Ghana's top beach hotels, and more recently been bought out by the Golden Beach Hotels Group. Set in large landscaped grounds, right on the beach, it has excellent watersport facilities as well as a swimming pool, curio shops, tennis court, 35-seat tourist coach for hire, restaurant and (coming in 2001) a three-hole golf course. By international standards, Busua Beach Resort is remarkably good value: plush s/c rooms with AC and satellite TV cost US$40/50 single/double and suites cost US$70. A new feature of this hotel are budget rooms aimed at backpackers, which cost US$5 per person with fan or US$10 per person with AC (all quoted in US dollars).

Budget
The **Alaska Beach Club** on Busua beach has simple double rondavels (round huts) for US$5 non-s/c or US$10 s/c, all with fan (1998 US$15). In the first edition of this guide, I recommended the Alaska for its idyllic beachfront position, but I've since received a few complaints about the noise at night, theft from rooms, and rude management (though these should be balanced against just as many favourable reports). We ate here on our most recent visit to Busua, and it seemed secure enough, not to say reasonably friendly, though certainly the blaring music wouldn't bode well for an early night.

Less atmospheric, but otherwise better value, **Dadson's Lodge** is the first place you'll pass to your right coming from the tro-tro park. A clean double-storey building, it has a variety of rooms ranging from non-s/c with fan for US$3.50/5.00 single/double (1998 US$5/10), as well as a few new s/c 'suites' for around US$7. There's a friendly atmosphere in the ground floor restaurant, and the food looks good and reasonably priced.

Shoestring
The best bet in Busua is **Sabina's Guesthouse**, a friendly, family-run place with basic, clean rooms for US$3/4 single/double (1998 US$5/7.50). Another recommendation in this range is **Mary's Place**, which normally has rooms at a similar price. (Mary had been ill when we last looked in, and she wasn't up to taking in tourists.)

In Dixcove, the caretaker at Fort Metal Cross can provide travellers with a basic room for around US$2. The only other formal accommodation in Dixcove is the **Quiet Storm Hotel**, the conspicuous, blue-and-pink building on a slope to your right as you enter the town. It's nothing very special, and lacks the vibe of the Busua hotels (which for some might be an attraction), but is good value at US$2/3 for a single/double room with fan, using communal

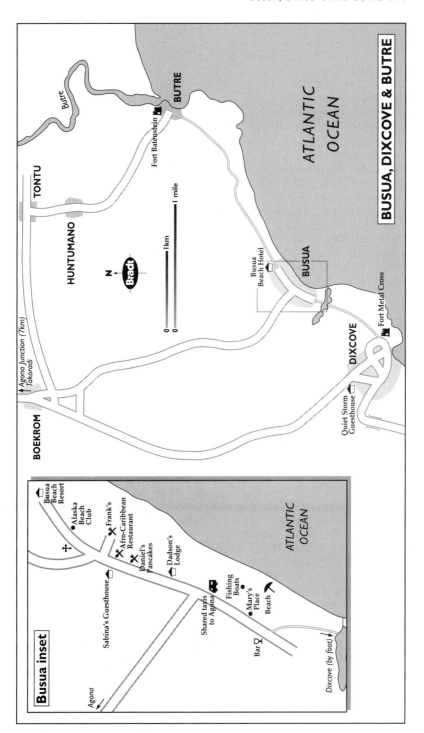

BUSUA, DIXCOVE & BUTRE

bucket showers (1998 US$$7.50/10). The signpost had been taken down in early December 2000, but the hotel was apparently operating – I was told it was full but quoted a room rate. A more recent report suggests it has closed down entirely.

Where to eat
Aside from the upmarket restaurant at the Busua Beach Resort, your choices within town are between the outdoor restaurant at the beachfront Alaska Beach Club, the indoor restaurant at Dadson's, or a cluster of excellent and reasonably priced backpacker-oriented eateries clustered between Sabina's and the Alaska. These are **Daniel the Pancake Man** ('world-famous' pancakes, great fruit juice, and a vast menu of main dishes), **Frank's Restaurant** (lobster and other fresh seafood), and the new **Afro-Caribbean Restaurant** (good atmosphere in the evenings).

Reached from Busua by a short causeway, guarded by a dozen dogs, **Black Mamba's Restaurant** is a new and highly recommended German-run eatery. You can eat on a shady terrace overlooking the bay, and there is a vast menu from which to choose – everything is freshly cooked, servings are generous, and pizza is something of a speciality. Expect to pay around US$5 for a main course.

THE COAST BETWEEN DIXCOVE AND AXIM
The area between Dixcove and Axim has stagnated economically since the 1970s, when a crippling outbreak of a disease known as Cape St Paul's Wilt struck the extensive coconut plantations on which the local economy was based. It is, however, a region of great natural, historical and cultural importance, centred on arguably the most scenic stretch of coast anywhere in the country. Unfortunately, tourist facilities in the region are currently rather limited, with the only formal accommodation in the region being available at Prince's Town, where several rooms are available to travellers. Several other villages along the coast could be visited as day trips in a private vehicle, or using the tro-tros that connect them to the main Takoradi–Axim road.

The area is of particular interest to adventurous hikers, who could, at present, walk between most coastal villages using an existing network of local footpaths. Following an ecotourism assessment in early 1999, the NCRC has come up with the concept of a Heritage Trail through the region, which will run from Butre to the Ankasa Resource Reserve via Cape Three Points, Prince's Town, Egyambra and Axim. The idea is to link the region's various natural and cultural sites by supplementing local footpaths with some new and more scenic trails, all of which will be signposted, and serviced by a series of community-managed ecotourist lodges and campsites. This, it is hoped, will not only attract tourism to a neglected corner of Ghana, but also ensure that the economic, environmental and social benefits of this tourism are spread throughout the rural communities involved.

The Heritage Trail is still a gleam in the eyes of the NCRC, and it is unlikely that any tangible developments will occur here before 2002. However, local footpaths that are open to adventurous travellers already cover many legs of the mooted trail. In large part based on the generous input of the NCRC, I have tried to highlight where this is the case, notably under the sections on Prince's Town and Egyambra, in the hope that it will generate greater interest in these hiking and rambling opportunities concurrent to the development of formal ecotourism facilities.

The major problem facing travellers along several stretches of this trail is that formal accommodation between Dixcove and Axim exists only in Prince's Town. It should, however, be possible to camp in most villages, with the permission of the local chief. Given this, and the lack of a formal tourist infrastructure, it is recommended that you engage the services of a local guide and buy the appropriate 1:50,000 survey sheets in Accra (0402A1 and 0403B2).

Akwidaa

This substantial fishing village, bisected by the Ezile Estuary, lies about 10km southwest of Dixcove as the crow flies. Also known as Esile or Akodaa, it boasts a couple of great beaches, notably the one in the cove immediately west of the village, which isn't settled, and is therefore very clean and quiet. It is possible to arrange canoe trips with local fishermen into the mangrove swamps upriver, where a large variety of birds as well as monkeys are likely to be encountered, especially towards dusk and shortly after dawn. Of minor historical interest is the ruined Fort Dorothea (or Fort Akodaa), situated on a rock promontory immediately south of the old town centre.

Getting there and away

There is reasonably regular public transport between Akwidaa and Agona junction on the main Takoradi road.

It is also possible to hike between Dixcove and Akwidaa. The more straightforward route is to follow the roughly 12km long road via Achowa, but this runs inland, and offers little in the way of scenic interest or shade. An alternative but slightly longer route passes through Mediya, an ancient and interesting village which lies about 4km from Dixcove by road, and is dotted with the clearly visible remains of many old buildings. Onwards from Mediya, an interesting bush track leads to Chavane across thick, overgrown farmland and a series of small and rather precarious bamboo bridges, as well as a dark, shaded passage where many butterflies and birds can be seen and heard. En route to Chavene, Breman is a small village where you can witness the palm-oil production process. From Chavene, the road continues to Kwamanfokrom through a rubber plantation, the management of which is willing to offer information on request. From Kwamanfokrom, it is a further 5km to Akwidaa by road.

For details of hiking between Akwidaa and Cape Three Points or Prince's Town, please see the section on Cape Three Points.

Where to stay and eat

There is currently no accommodation, but the community has reportedly begun preparations to construct small beach huts that can be used as tourist accommodation. A study is currently underway assessing the feasibility of constructing an eco-lodge in the village – this is considered to be vital to the success of the Heritage Trail, as one would otherwise have to hike between Dixcove and Prince's Town in one day. There are several bars in Akwidaa (but no electricity) and the local people are eager and willing to cook if requested.

Cape Three Points

Situated about halfway between Akwidaa and Prince's Town, Cape Three Points is the most southerly point in Ghana, and the site of a 19th-century lighthouse, where the friendly caretaker is always happy to show visitors around. The panoramic views from the low cliffs around the lighthouse are stunning, and whales sometimes come close to shore between November and January. At the base of the cape lies a small fishing village and a sandy beach.

A short distance inland of the cliffs, the Cape Three Points Forest Reserve protects an area of relatively untouched coastal forest, perhaps the most extensive remaining example of this habitat in the country. Although totally undeveloped for tourism, this small and vulnerable reserve is regarded as having a biodiversity rating as high as that of Ankasa, and is reputedly still home to small numbers of several large mammal species (a survey is planned for 2001) as well as a diversity of birds.

Getting there and away

An extension of the road between Agona junction and Akwidaa continues on to Cape Three Points. For hikers, the scenery from this 10km stretch of road is somewhat monotonous, but at present no coastal footpath exists as an alternative. Shared taxis between Agona and Akwidaa don't normally continue to Cape Three Points, but it should be possible – and not dauntingly expensive – to charter one of them to take you there.

In the other direction, Cape Three Points is linked to Prince's Town by a well-marked and scenic footpath that leads to Aketechi then follows the sandbar dividing the ocean from the 2.5km long Ehunu Lagoon. This walk takes about two hours, which means that one could visit Cape Three Points on foot as a round day trip from Prince's Town, possibly breaking up the walk by canoeing across the lagoon. Canoes are probably best arranged from Prince's Town, as the villagers at Aketechi on the eastern side of the lagoon reputedly ask exorbitant fees.

An alternative route between Akwidaa and Prince's Town offers the opportunity to walk inside the Cape Three Points Forest Reserve. To do this, however, it is *essential* to be accompanied by a knowledgeable local guide, as there are many tracks in the forest and one might otherwise get lost. The hike involves a 3–4km walk through cultivation to the forest boundary. The trail within the reserve is about 8km long, shady, and of great interest to butterfly and bird enthusiasts, with the small possibility of encountering monkeys. The trail exits the forest close to Aketechi, from where one can follow the footpath alongside the lagoon, or try to arrange a canoe.

Where to stay and eat

There is no formal accommodation, but it is normally possible to stay at a room in the lighthouse. A proper eco-lodge is likely to open as and when the Heritage Trail is established.

Prince's Town

Rather isolated, yet easily the best-equipped stop for tourists along this stretch of coast, Prince's Town is notable not least for the impressive list of aliases it has acquired (Prince's Terre, Princesstown and Prusi for starters). Set on an attractive and largely unspoilt stretch of coast on the eastern bank of the Nyila

River mouth, Prince's Town is visited by very few travellers, partially as a result of its distance from the main Takoradi–Elubo road. The centrepiece of the small town is Fort Gross Friedrichsburg, a near ruin at the time of independence, but now fully restored and functioning as a resthouse. Entrance costs slightly less than US$1.

Fort Gross Friedrichsburg has a rather unusual history. It is the only fort in Ghana with Germanic associations, built as it was by the Brandenburg Africa Company, a latecomer to the European struggle for dominance of the Gold Coast, formed in 1682 as a representative of Prince Friedrich of Brandenburg. After landing at the village then known as Pokesu in 1683, the Brandenburgers were ceded the promontory on which the fort now stands, in exchange for which they offered the village protection against the Dutch and other slave raiders. By the 1690s, Fort Gross Friedrichsburg had become the most important smuggling centre on the coast, simply because the officials received so few ships from Brandenburg that they were forced to trade illicitly with other nations to make a profit.

In 1716, the Brandenburgers abandoned their fort to John Connie, an Ahanta chief who had already acquired the nickname 'King of Prince's Terre' for his role at the centre of a trade network so powerful that it caused a temporary decline in the fortunes of nearby Dutch ports such as Dixcove and Axim. Over the next decade, the fort was the centre of a series of military clashes between the Dutch and John Connie, and word of the Ahanta chief's victories over a European power made him something of a folk hero in the slave plantations of the Caribbean (Connie is evidently the source of the John Canoe festivals that have been celebrated in the region ever since). Gross Friedrichsburg was finally captured by the Dutch in 1724 and re-named Fort Hollandia; it remained under Dutch control for almost 150 years before being handed to Britain as part of the treaty signed in 1872. Despite all this, the most striking thing about the fort today is how little it looks like a military building – on first glance, it could easily be mistaken for an old colonial governor's residence or something similar.

Aside from the fort, Prince's Town forms the base for several interesting day trips, normally arranged through the fort's caretaker. The most popular goal in the area is the crocodile pond at the village of Egyambra, which lies about two hours walk from Prince's Town, and can also be reached by a boat along the Kpani River. Although Egyambra can be visited independently of an overnight stay at Prince's Town (see *Egyambra* page 176), Prince's Town is currently the most popular and probably the easiest base from which to visit it.

Immediately east of Prince's Town lies the beautiful Ehunu Lagoon, a 2km² expanse separated from the ocean by a narrow, sandy – and practically uninhabited – beach that is reputedly safe for swimming. Canoe trips on the lagoon can be arranged with the caretaker at the fort for around US$3 per person; there is a good chance of seeing black-and-white colobus monkeys from the boat, especially in the early morning, and you can also ask to be taken to a bamboo forest and a traditional palm-wine distillery. It is also possible to walk from the lagoon on to Cape Three Points, which lies about two hours each way from Prince's Town, or into the Cape Three Points Forest Reserve – both possibilities are elaborated on under the *Getting there and away* section for Cape Three Points (page 174).

Getting there and away
Prince's Town is 18km from Abora junction on the main Takoradi–Elubo road and is signposted. Any vehicle heading between Agona and Axim can drop you at the junction, where you'll probably be in for a long wait – there's not a lot of transport, but you should get through eventually, except perhaps after heavy rain when the road has tended to become impassable in the past.

Details of the hike from Cape Three Points and to Egyambra are covered under those headings.

Where to stay and eat
Fort Gross Friedrichsburg doubles as a resthouse. Four double rooms with a fan are available at around US$2.50 each, and there is a communal bucket shower. Meals can be prepared with notice, or there are a couple of chop shops in the village.

Egyambra
Situated about 6km west of Prince's Town as the crow flies, Egyambra (aka Agyembrah) is of interest mainly for a sacred crocodile pond, which offers a similar but less publicised experience to the one at Paga on the Burkina Faso border. For a negotiable fee of around US$7–10, the fetish priest at the pond will call a crocodile to be fed, chanting as he pours a (traditional?) bottle of coke into the water. When the crocodile arrives, it feeds on one (of two) chickens provided by the visitor. At this time, there is an opportunity to take photographs, but the crocodile soon disappears back into the water with the chicken in its mouth. In addition to the fee, each party of visitors must provide a chicken, a cockerel and two bottles of coke.

Getting there and away
A rough 15–20km road connects Egyambra to the main Takoradi–Axim road at Anyame. Public transport along this road leaves from Axim and Agona Junction (near Busua) and is reasonably frequent. Since the crocodile ceremony only takes place in the morning, travellers wanting to experience it should get an early start.

A more popular option is to visit Egyambra by foot or canoe as a day trip from Prince's Town, something that is easily arranged with the caretaker at Fort Gross Friedrichsburg. From Prince's Town, one can, for a small fee, hire a canoe up the Kpani River as far as Miamia, passing through mangrove swamps teeming with birds on the way. It is also possible to walk along the beach to Miamia, which will take about one hour, with views over the sea and the river and mangroves. It is possible to stop off at the *Akpeteshie* distillery on the riverbank between Prince's Town and Miamia to observe the distilling process. The beach at Miamia is very beautiful and perfect for swimming, as the sea is very calm, but it is only kept clean on the eastern part where several private villas have been built. From Miamia, a roughly 1.5km trail continues to Egyambra via the beach and then around a rocky outcrop surrounded by a mass of brightly coloured flowers, while offering good views of the sea.

Keen hikers – especially those who travelled to Egyambra by canoe – could think about continuing westward on foot towards Axim, a roughly 10km walk along the beach, with the option after roughly 7km of staying overnight at the superb Axim Beach Resort. The trail towards Axim follows a lovely coastline of palm-lined beaches, shady lagoons, interesting rock formations, and small fishing villages (where one should greet the locals). It would be advisable to take a guide along this route, which is currently used by few tourists.

Where to stay and eat

Egyambra currently has no accommodation, though there is probably nothing stopping you from asking permission to camp, and there are a few chop bars.

AXIM

The largest town on the coast west of Takoradi, Axim (pronounced more like *Azsim*) is also the site of Ghana's second-oldest fort. The triangular Fort São Antonio dates to the Portuguese era, and although its exact year of construction is not on record, most authorities reckon it to be around 1515. Positioned on an outcrop, with excellent natural protection in the form of a few small rocky islands and a reef, the fort was captured by Holland in 1642 and remained under Dutch control until it was handed to Britain in 1872. Unlike St George's Castle in Elmina, nominally the oldest European building in Africa, the basic shape of Fort São Antonio's bastions has changed little since the 16th century. The three-storey building that rises above the main fortifications was added during the period of Dutch occupation, but is recognisable from an etching dating from 1682.

Axim was once one of the busiest trading posts anywhere on the West African Coast. In the late 17th century, more gold was traded through Fort São Antonio than any other Dutch fort, and in the 18th century the surrounding area became an important source of cotton and timber. In the colonial era, Fort São Antonio was used as a regional administrative centre, and it continued to house government offices into early 2000. Since then, the offices have been moved elsewhere, and the fort has opened up formally to tourism, with the probability that it will start operating as a resthouse as of early 2001.

Aside from the fort, which is one of the most impressive in Ghana, there is little about Axim today that betrays its historical significance. In the first edition of this guide I described the town as 'the most characterless port in Ghana, chronically run-down and rather unwelcoming', an assessment which, in hindsight, seems unduly harsh. It helps, of course, that the town's most important tourist attraction is now open to the public, especially as the vantage point offered by the fort over the beachfront is thoroughly arresting. But on re-visiting Axim, I found it to be a rather interesting town: friendly, atmospheric, and refreshingly untouristed.

Whatever else one might think about Axim, there is no denying it lies close to two beaches of almost breathtaking perfection. These are Ankobra Beach, about 3km northwest of town, and Awangazule Beach, a similar distance to the southeast. Both of these beaches are serviced by comfortably rustic and reasonably priced resorts (see *Where to stay* below); either one of them is alone worth coming this far west of Takoradi to stay at.

Getting there and away

Regular tro-tros connect Axim to Takoradi in the east, to Essiama to the west, and to most other towns along the west coast.

Where to stay and eat

22400

22241

Moderate

Ankobra Beach Resort Tel: 0342 22349/399/400/401/683.
Situated about 500m south of the main Takoradi–Elubo road, from where it is
clearly signposted about 5km west of the Axim turn-off, Ankobra Beach
Resort is built along an idyllic palm-lined beach close to the mouth of the
Ankobra River. In addition to having an attractive layout, the resort places a
strong emphasis on cultural and historical excursions, for instance to the
various slave forts and Nzulezo stilt village near Beyin. Accommodation is in
rustic but comfortable detached and semi-detached bungalows, strung out
over several hundred metres through the tall palms. Self-contained rooms are
good value at US$15 (1998 US$25) for a double with standing fan, US$18.50
(1998 US$35) for a double with roof fan, or US$28 (1998 US$55) for a family
bungalow with AC. The open-air restaurant is atmospheric and the food
excellent. If you are reliant on public transport, any tro-tro heading along the
main road can drop you at the signposted junction, from where it's a five-
minute walk to the resort. Note that while the beach at Ankobra is safe, we
have had reports of travellers wandering along the beach between Ankobra and
Axim being mugged.

Axim Beach Resort Tel: 021 402394.
This spanking new resort, which opened in September 2000, lies to the
southeast of Axim on a rocky promontory overlooking a pristine and virtually
uninhabited expanse of palm-fringed beach stretching eastwards towards the
Awangazule Lagoon. The setting is the stuff of desert island fantasies, and the
beach itself is reputedly safe for swimming, though conditions may vary from
one day to the next, so do ask local advice before taking the plunge.
Accommodation consists of six circular s/c chalets with fan and cold shower,
decorated in tasteful African style, at a very reasonable US$12 double. The
open-air restaurant serves local dishes for around US$2, and has the usual stock
of refrigerated drinks. The resort is signposted from the feeder road between
Axim and the Takoradi–Elubo road, about 1km from central Axim and close to
the hospital. When we visited, getting there involved a rather circuitous detour
through a fishing village, but a direct 2km track between the feeder road and
the resort should have been cut by the time this guide goes to print.

Budget

The **Frankfaus Hotel**, roughly 100m uphill from the tro-tro station and
main traffic circle, is a reasonably comfortable double-storey building,
overpriced by comparison to similar establishments elsewhere in Ghana (less
noticeable at 2000 exchange rates than it was a couple of years earlier). A small
non-s/c double costs US$5 (1998 US$12) while a s/c double with bucket
shower costs US$6.50 (1998 US$15).

The only other place to stay in Axim at the time of writing is the **Hotel
Monte Carlo**, about ten minutes' walk and signposted from the tro-tro
station. Here, a rather grubby double with fan sets you back around US$4
(1998 US$9) – as with the Frankfaus, grossly inflated by Ghanaian standards,
especially as the communal toilets reek and the ambience is zero.

Fort São Antonio is scheduled to open as a resthouse before the time this
book goes to print, and in terms of atmosphere and location it will definitely

supersede the other budget options in town. According to the caretaker, at least six rooms will be available, presumably at budget rates comparable to other forts along the coast (none of which charges in excess of US$5 for a room).

For local eats, try the **Friend's Snack Bar** around the corner from the Frankfaus Hotel. There's no shortage of places to sink a beer or two: the **Christ The King Spot** near the post office is notable not only for its monumentally improbable name, but also for having a balcony (facing away from the sea, sad to say) while an **anonymous open-air beachfront bar** next to the fort has a lively, inclusive atmosphere underscored by happy, blaring music.

NKROFUL

This small town 4km north of the main Takoradi–Elubo road is noted as the birthplace of Kwame Nkrumah, Ghana's first president, and the site of the small mausoleum where the former president was buried after his death in 1972. Frankly, this Nkrumah Mausoleum is a rather underwhelming sight by comparison with the vast Nkrumah Mausoleum in Accra (which in any case is where Nkrumah's body now lies). It is easy enough to find, however, lying within the bright pink information centre – children, lots and lots of them, will show you how to get there, not to say drape themselves over the memorial, shove their way in front of the camera, etc.

If you want to visit the mausoleum, ask any vehicle travelling along the main road to drop you at Essiama, from where regular and inexpensive shared taxis go directly to Nkroful. There is now a rather good budget hotel in Nkroful, the **B & Q Guest Inn** (tel: 0342 22377), where clean, smart s/c doubles cost US$5.50 with fan only or US$7 with AC and TV, and suites cost US$11.50. A restaurant and bar are attached.

You could also stay in Essiama itself. The **Motel de Miegyina**, which lies behind the Goil garage on the Axim side of the main junction, could hardly be cheaper at US$2 for a basic double. Rather nicer is **Maggie's Guesthouse**, 100m further up the road, which has double rooms with AC for around US$10 and serves good meals on request. For those who enjoy getting off the beaten track, Essiama is worth exploring, notably the road to the beach, which is lined with substantial but decaying residences built by miners in the 1920s and 1930s.

BEYIN AND NZULEZO

The seaside village of Beyin is the site of Fort Apollonia, the last fort to be built by Britain on the Gold Coast, constructed in 1770 with the permission of the Nzema chief, Amenihyia. Fort Apollonia was built in a different manner from any other fort in the country, with a substantially stronger seaward bastion that not only served a defensive purpose, but also contained the cells used to store slaves. Beyin's fort was built to endure, using rock quarried from a site 10km away. It has retained its original shape, despite having been shelled during the war between the British and the French, and having been abandoned for long periods of time. It was renovated in the late 1950s, and converted to a resthouse in the 1970s, in which capacity it served until 2000. Following a recent agreement reached between the Ghana Museums & Monuments Board and the University of Pisa in Italy, however, the fort will soon be converted into a historical and ethnographical museum dedicated to the Nzema people of the area.

Arguably one of Ghana's travel highlights, and certainly a more singular experience than Fort Apollonia, **Nzulezo Stilt Village** (aka Mzulezo) lies on the freshwater Lake Amansuri about 5km from Beyin. Supporting a population of roughly 500 people, Nzulezo is one solid construction raised above the water, consisting of a central wood and raffia walkway with perhaps two dozen individual houses on either side of it. Quite why the people of Nzulezo decided to build their village above the water is an open question – especially as they are not primarily fishermen but agriculturalists, whose fertile fields lie about 1km north of the lake. The villagers welcome tourists, except on Thursdays, which are sacred. Having paid the entrance fee in Beyin (see below) you may wander around freely and take as many photos as you like (you'll be asked to send them copies of the best results).

Nzulezo can only be reached by dugout canoe and the 5km, one-hour ride there is as rewarding as the village itself. It follows the Amansuri River through areas of marsh and open pools fringed by palm thickets and jungle until it opens out on to the dark, reflective waters of the lake. It's a lovely trip, especially in the early morning cool, and you should see plenty of birds. Pygmy geese and lily-trotters abound on the lily-covered pools. Purple and squacco herons are often flushed from the reeds, and a variety of colourful bee-eaters, rollers and kingfishers perch silently on low branches. Hornbills and plantain-eaters draw attention to themselves with their cackling and chuckling – keen birdwatchers and photographers could happily spend an additional morning on the water without visiting the village. Note that it is hot out on the water, and there is no shade once on the lake, so remember to take bottled water, wear a shady hat, and liberally slap on the sunblock.

Getting there and away
Beyin lies along a dirt road that follows the coast south of the main Takoradi–Elubo road. Coming from the direction of Takoradi, the junction for Beyin is at Awiebo, something that you don't really need to know if you are using public transport, since Takoradi and Beyin are connected by direct minibuses taking three to four hours in either direction. Heading towards Elubo, there are a few direct vehicles daily, but if nothing is going, you could catch a vehicle bound for Half Assini as far as the village known as 'Tikobo One' and there pick up a shared taxi to Elubo.

A canoe to Nzulezo can be organised through the Beyin office of the Ghana Wildlife Society (GWS), which has recently started a project for the sustainable development of the lagoon and its tourist attractions. The boat takes about one hour each way and the cost of the return trip is currently fixed at around US$3 per person, half of which goes to the village and half to the boatmen.

Where to stay and eat
Fort Apollonia will soon close as a resthouse, which means that the inexpensive local guesthouse which opened close to the fort in 1999 to handle its overspill is currently the only place to stay in Beyin. At least one new guesthouse with better facilities is currently under construction on the sea shore in front of the castle. There's a bar next to the fort with an electric fridge, and local food such as fried yam and *kenkey* is available at stalls along the main road. There is talk of a resthouse being built at Nzulezo.

ANKASA PROTECTED AREA
One of Ghana's most exciting emergent ecotourist destinations, the Ankasa Protected Area is comprised of the contiguous Nini-Suhien National Park and Ankasa Resource Reserve, which together form a highly accessible 509km^2 chunk of wet evergreen rainforest, bounded on the south by the Ankasa River and on the north by the Nini River. Ankasa is regarded as having the greatest biodiversity of any reserve in Ghana. Up to 300 plant species have been counted in one hectare, with over 870 vascular plant species so far on record for the reserve. The list of more than 70 resident mammal species includes forest elephant, bongo, giant forest hog, red river hog, chimpanzee and several types of duiker and monkey (of the latter, mona monkey, spot-nosed and black-and-white colobus are most common, though the localised Diana monkey and white-crested mangabey are also present). A checklist of 190 bird species includes a great many forest-obligates, with the localised and elusive white-fronted guinea fowl being of particular note. The checklist does not include the many savannah species found in the surrounding farmland. The reserve also protects a prodigious variety of butterflies (600 species), reptiles and amphibians.

Until recently, Ankasa was one of several protected areas in Ghana that made few concessions to attracting visitors. Over the last couple of years, however, the reserve has undergone an extensive tourist development programme, implemented by the Protected Areas Development Programme from a base in Takoradi. Already in place are three rustic and inexpensive overnight camps, as well as two short nature trails and a 25km stretch of good gravel road along which visitors are free to walk and cycle. A fourth camp is scheduled to open in 2001, which will be part of a three-day hiking trail ending with a canoe ride down the Tano River, along with a restaurant and visitors centre at the main Ankasa gate. Within the lifespan of this edition, it is hoped that observation towers, overnight trails and bird hides will follow, along with a private camp aimed at upmarket visitors, mountain bike and canoeing trails, and possibly the establishment of salt licks and hides where rare forest animals can be observed. While experience suggests that broad-ranging plans of this nature should perhaps be viewed with a degree of scepticism, the astonishing rate of progress since I first set foot in the reserve in 1998, and the evident commitment of the guides and rangers, is massively encouraging. For details of progress, contact the Protected Areas Development Programme (PADP) at 031 25322 or padp@africaonline.com.gh, or drop into their Takoradi office next to the Fan Milk Depot on High Street.

The entrance fee for non-Ghanaian adults currently works out at around US$2, but this will probably soon climb back to the 1999 rate of US$5. The same goes for guide fees (US$0.50 per hour), vehicle entrance fees (US$0.50), still photography fees (US$0.30) and video fees (US$3).

Getting there and away
Ankasa gate and campsite lie 6km north of the main Takoradi–Elubo road, along a signposted turn-off 21km east of Elubo, and can be reached in any vehicle. The best day to get to the reserve using public transport is Monday (local market day), when you can catch a tro-tro from Aiyinasi or Elubo to Sowodadem and then another tro-tro from Sowodadem directly to the Ankasa gate. On other days, your options are either to charter a taxi to the gate from Elubo or Aiyinasi (this shouldn't cost more than US$8 one-way) or else to ask a tro-tro heading along the main road to drop you at the junction and hitch or walk the last 6km. If you go for the latter option, it's a pleasant walk on gentle slopes, and you can break the walk at a small bar in Amokwasuazo.
Do note that when you arrange transport to Ankasa, you should make it clear that you want to visit the reserve and not the synonymous town.

Once Elubo Camp opens – some time during 2001 – it will also be possible to approach Ankasa direct from the town of Elubo on the Côte d'Ivoire border. The entrance gate and camp lie 5km from the town: there is no public transport, but you could walk or charter a taxi.

Where to stay and eat
Three camps are currently operating, with a fourth scheduled to open in 2001. At Ankasa gate, within ten minutes' walk of two of the camps, a wooden restaurant spanning the Ankasa River was in an advanced state of construction in late 2000, and is scheduled to open in early 2001, serving local meals and the usual drinks. Sleeping at any of the camps currently costs less than US$1, but this rate was set prior to the dramatic plunge in the exchange rate in early 2000 and is bound to increase soon. At the time of writing, discussions are underway to settle on a new price, which – given that lights and gas furnishings are to be offered – is likely to be set at around US$10 per person, or US$50 per party for exclusive use of that camp.

Ankasa and Lophira Camp

About ten minutes' walk west of Ankasa gate, the synonymous camp is reached via a footpath through the staff quarters. This lovely camp lies in a clearing encircled by tall forest and close to a small waterfall. Accommodation consists of two open-sided huts designed to sleep a total of 12 people. Kerosene lamps, mosquito nets and camp beds are supplied on request at no extra charge, but you will need to bring your own bedding – not that you'll really need to sleep under anything more substantial than a net in the hot, sticky climate. Facilities include a toilet, shower and kitchen with gas cooker and utensils supplied. At the time of writing, visitors need to bring their own food, but the camp lies within easy walking distance of the soon-to-open restaurant. Also ten minutes walk from Ankasa gate and the restaurant, but to the east, the new **Lophira Camp** is similar in design to Ankasa, but has a more remote feel. The 2.5km Baka Trail can be explored from either camp.

Nkwanta Camp

Situated 8km by road from the Ankasa gate, this camp is named for the nearby village of Nkwanta, an ancient trading post mentioned in literature dating to 1640, but recently evacuated by the park authorities. The camp lies in a fantastic stand of bamboo forest often referred to as the Bamboo Cathedral. According to the guides, it is visited by black-and-white colobus monkeys most mornings, and the nearby forest regularly turns up fresh bongo spoor (though this elusive antelope has yet to be seen by the guides). Little more than 100m from the camp, the mango trees and plantains around the abandoned village are a favoured haunt of elephant during the fruiting season of March to May. Accommodation and facilities are pretty much identical to those at the other camps, though the distance from the gate will enforce self-catering, even after the restaurant opens.

The 3km Paa Ngrant Trail leads out of Nkwanta Camp. This is the remnant of an old logging trail last used in the early 1970s. The area for about 2kms around Nkwanta was selectively logged and old concrete concession markers can still be seen. The trail currently extends to the high-tension transmission line that bisects the reserve. This opening gives an unusual opportunity to observe savannah species in the middle of a rainforest and a better chance to see animals such as elephant and bongo, which regularly cross the gap. Past the power line, the pristine rainforest reasserts itself. The trail currently goes to Dyers Camp at the Suhien River Falls (approximately 20m high and truly beautiful). No facilities are yet available at this site though tents are permitted. The trail is being extended northwards to provide a 3–4 hour hike to a granite outcrop known as Brasso Hill, at 167m the highest point in the reserve. A range camp and facilities similar to Nkwanta will be built here in 2001. From Brasso, a trail which is currently under construction will wend westwards to Mpeasem on the Tano River (about 2–3 hours), from which, a motorised canoe will take you to Elubo (about 2hrs).

Elubo Camp

This camp lies at the western edge of the reserve, about 12km from Nkwanta and 5km from the town of Elubo. Two enclosed chalets have been constructed but are currently being used as a patrol post for the WD staff. The new park headquarters will be situated nearby and the camp will revert to tourism use when its construction is completed. Facilities are similar to the other camps. Once this camp is running, it will – together with Nkwanta and Ankasa Camps – complete what might be viewed as an informal hiking circuit, allowing visitors to hike between the three overnight camps using the (otherwise little-used) main roads that connect them.

ELUBO

Everything about Elubo screams 'border town', from the exceptionally chaotic market spilling over on to the main street, to the hissing money changers and mandatory clowns who try to overcharge you for everything on the basis that you've probably just crossed into Ghana from Côte d'Ivoire. As a result, Elubo is the sort of place you'll probably want to pass through as quickly as possible. Redeeming features include the street food – the beef kebabs on sale here are as tender, tasty and generous as any we had in Ghana – and (especially if you *have* come from the more expensive Côte d'Ivoire) a couple of very reasonably priced hotels

Getting there and away

Regular tro-tros connect Elubo to Axim and Takoradi, as well as to Abidjan in Côte d'Ivoire. If you are travelling from Elubo to a point before Axim, you may have to change vehicles in Aiyinasi.

Where to stay and eat

The **Hotel Cocoville**, surprisingly large and upmarket in this remote neck of the jungle, is situated about 200m from the lorry station overlooking the Tano River, with a view of the remnant forest patches on the Ivorian bank and (less picturesquely) a steady stream of locals coming to soap themselves down. The rooms here are indisputably good value at US$5 for a s/c double with fan or US$8 for a s/c double with AC and TV (1998 US$10/17). You can eat pretty well in the restaurant or at the waterfront garden bar – meals are a little expensive by Ghanaian standards at around US$5, but portions are generous.

Of the cheaper places, the **Hotel Falun** opposite the lorry station is clearly the best option. Clean rooms with double bed cost less than US$3 and there are regularly refilled tubs of water outside the communal bucket showers.

Part Four

Eastern Ghana

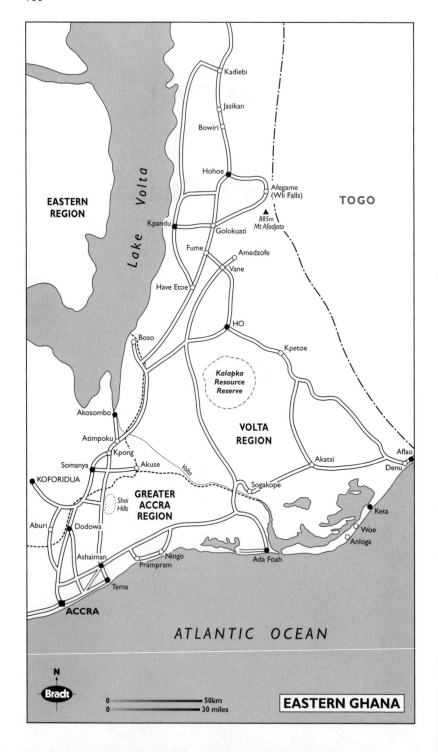

EASTERN GHANA

INTRODUCTION

The east of Ghana, though less geared towards upmarket tourism than the west coast, is a haven for independent travellers, rich in natural beauty and offering a wealth of low-key, low-cost travel possibilities to those with the initiative to take them up. For keen hikers and ramblers, the lush and relatively cool highlands around Ho and Hohoe are studded with the country's highest peaks, as well as a plethora of accessible waterfalls and an excellent little monkey sanctuary at the village of Tafi Atome. The east coast, too, is rich in isolated, out-of-the-way gems, most notably the small ports of Ada and Keta, while the area immediately inland of Accra is notable, among other things, for the tranquil Aburi Botanical Garden and impressive Akosombo Dam on the Volta River.

Travel conditions in eastern Ghana generally conform to those experienced in other parts of the country, a little cheaper perhaps, but no more arduous. Nevertheless, this region will appeal greatly to those travellers for whom travel means *travel* in the chest-thumping, epic journey sense, rather than, say, soaking up the tropical beach atmosphere at Ada. Two exceptional ferry rides run through this part of Ghana: the daily trip from Ada north to Akuse along the Volta River, and the legendary overnight run from Akosombo to Yeji via Lake Volta. And there is also the bumpy overland trip from Hohoe through to the northern capital of Tamale, the closest thing in Ghana to those interminable bone-crunching trips for which many other African countries are renowned. In short, if the term 'off-the-beaten-track' sets your ears pricking, then this is probably the part of Ghana for you.

A less obvious attraction of the east, but one that struck us sharply on revisiting Ghana to research the second edition of this guide, is an almost total absence of hassle. After two weeks on the west coast, where it feels impossible at times to walk a few paces without being subjected to the tedious catcalls of *'Obruni'*, 'White Man' or 'Give me...', we found it immensely refreshing to travel in a region where children tend to greet travellers with an altogether more dignified 'How are you?' or 'You're welcome!' This, I feel, is one part of Ghana where the country's reputation as the friendliest in Africa seems fully justified.

Finally, it should be noted that, while eastern Ghana is currently favoured mostly by backpackers, it does boast a nascent upmarket tourist circuit. The Manet Paradise Hotel at Ada and Volta Hotel at Akasombo are the equal of any hotel in the country, while the last few years have also seen the establishment of good tourist-class accommodation in Ho and on the Keta Peninsula.

The East Coast

Ghana's east coast remains surprisingly underdeveloped for tourism by comparison to the west coast, a situation which – given that Ada or Keta are far closer to Accra than, say, Cape Coast or Elmina – is most probably explained by the relative dearth of landmarks associated with the slave trade. But, while it is true that, the small forts at Keta and Prampram notwithstanding, there is nothing here to compare with the grandiose castles and larger forts to the west of the capital, the east coast does boast at least two very attractive (and very different) beach resorts in the form of Ada Foah and the Keta Peninsula, as well as a system of vast lagoons and estuaries which offer the country's finest marine birding, and (seasonally) the opportunity to see giant turtles laying their eggs on the beach.

TEMA

Ghana's fourth largest city and second largest port (after Takoradi), Tema's population has grown almost tenfold from 35,000 in the early 1960s to more than 250,000 now, mainly as a result of its proximity to Akosombo Dam. Tema is often overlooked by tourists as a result of it being situated only 25km east of the capital, to which it effectively functions as a satellite city. Frankly, this is much as it should be, since Tema really is the dullest of cities, redeemed only by the busy central market area, a lively fishing port and – for nature lovers – an alluringly bird-rich lagoon just as you enter the town along the coastal road from Accra.

Getting there and away

Regular tro-tros to Tema leave Accra from Tema station in the city centre, taking about 45 minutes each way. Travellers staying in the Adabraka area of Accra may find it easier to catch a shared taxi from Nkrumah Circle to Nungua and pick up transport to Tema from there.

Where to stay and eat

It is difficult to imagine why any traveller would want to stay in Tema, since it's so easy to visit as a day trip from the capital, and – contrary, perhaps, to expectations – accommodation is no cheaper. But if you insist, there is plenty of accommodation in Tema, much of it conveniently clustered over a walking distance of about 500m, and all within 50m of a shared taxi route – from central Tema, look for a taxi marked for Community 7, 8 and 9 on the opposite side of the road to the tro-tro station for Accra.

The cheapest rooms are at the **Erica** or **Jakotron Hotel** (though both names are signposted, it appears to be one place) in Community 8; rather scruffy little s/c doubles with fan costing US$8. The nearby **Page Hotel** is far more upmarket, with a restaurant and good snack bar, and AC, s/c double rooms with TV for US$17. Similar in standard, and facing each other as the shared taxis enter Community 9, are the **Hotel du Planet** and **Satellite Hotel**, both of which have s/c doubles with fan for around US$10 and similar rooms with AC for around US$15. Back in Community 8, the **Hotel Lucia** seems a lot smarter and charges practically identical rates of US$10 for a double room with fan and US$15 for a double with AC.

In the middle of the cluster of hotels, basically in one complex, you'll find the **Kabaya Restaurant** and **Golden Ivy Chinese Restaurant**, as well as the pleasant rooftop **Taboo Nightclub and Bar**.

PRAMPRAM AND NINGO

The small towns of Prampram, New Ningo and Old Ningo lie within 10km of each other on the stretch of coast between Accra and the mouth of the Volta. Separated by a long, sandy beach as attractive as any in the country, Prampram and Old Ningo are two of the oldest European settlements in this part of Ghana. Prampram was the site of a small British trading post and fort built in 1742, while Ningo was the site of a Danish fort from 1735 until it was handed to Britain in 1850. Neither fort, however, has survived to the modern day: some traces of Prampram's Fort Vernon remain in the walls of a more modern, but also derelict resthouse near the fishing harbour, and even less remains to be seen of Fort

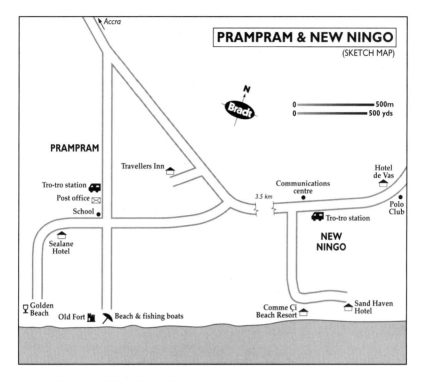

Fredensborg in Old Ningo. The main attraction of the area is the beach, particularly around New Ningo, generally regarded as safe for swimming and dotted with holiday homes – New Ningo even boasts a rather posh-looking polo club. The estuary on the west flank of Old Ningo is also very pretty, its natural beauty enhanced by the colourful fishing boats moored on the beach.

Getting there and away

All three small towns lie about 6km to the south of the main Accra–Aflao road, along a road which on paper forms a roughly 20km-long southward loop. In practice, no vehicles can complete this loop at the time of writing, since the bridge over the estuary on the west flank of Old Ningo is being reconstructed and is open to foot passengers only. Prampram is the main transport hub in the area, but there is no direct tro-tro transport between it and Accra – you will almost certainly have to change vehicles at Ashaiman, a busy junction town to the north of Tema. If you are coming to Prampram from the direction of Ada, ask to be dropped at Dwahenya (also known as Prampram junction) and wait for a lift to Prampram there.

Regular shared taxis connect Prampram to New Ningo and Old Ningo (or more accurately at the time of writing, to the edge of the bridge across the lagoon, from where it's a five-minute walk to Old Ningo).

Where to stay and eat

Visitors to Prampram have two hotels from which to choose. At one end of the scale is the **Prampram Sealane Hotel** (tel: 024 208830/1), about 500m and signposted from the lorry station. This place is definitely aiming for the Accra weekend crowd with its green neat grounds, reasonable bar and restaurant, and comfortable s/c twin rooms with TV and hot water for US$12 with fan or US$17 with AC (prices as in 1998). At the opposite end of the scale is **Sam's Place**, tucked away in the alleys behind the lorry station, and offering grotty rooms at around US$3 (1998 US$5). Don't, incidentally, be led astray by signposts to the **Travellers Inn** on the New Ningo side of town, which consists of a bar and supermarket, but has no accommodation.

On the Prampram side of New Ningo, along a 200m dirt road leading from next to the communications centre down to the beach, the new **Sand Haven Beach Resort** (tel: 024 369134) consists of two comfortable rooms (with more under construction) in a hut sharing an equipped kitchen with fridge, toilet and bath for US$10 per room. On the other side of New Ningo, the **Hotel de Vas** near the Polo Club has basic but adequate rooms for US$1.50 (1998 US$2.50).

The ambience-deficient **Golden Beach Resort** in Prampram, five minutes' walk from the Sealane Hotel, serves chilled drinks on a rather desolate beach dominated by the massive hulk of an abandoned cargo ship. Similar but nicer is the **Comme Çi Resort**, which lies in large beachfront grounds on the western side of New Ningo close to Sand Haven. The only place to eat Western food is the Sealane Hotel in Prampram.

ADA

The port of Ada lies on the mouth of the Volta River, which was readily navigable for several hundred kilometres inland before the construction of the Akosombo Dam in the 1960s. Among the most celebrated visitors to Ada was Henry Stanley, who sailed there from London in a Thames pleasure launch several months after his renowned 'discovery' of Livingstone in Tanzania. It was Stanley, in the company of Captain Glover, who took the first steamer across the perilous Ada Bar and up the Volta.

Ada is the traditional core of the Ada nation, one of the most important and cohesive empires on the pre-colonial Gold Coast. Oral tradition suggests that the Adali – the people of Ada – arrived in their modern homeland from somewhere to the east (probably Benin or Nigeria) prior to the late 17th century and eventually settled at Big Ada. The nation expanded in the early 18th century, as several lesser chieftaincies in territories along the Volta pledged their alliance to the Ada Matse (King), who is today the paramount chief over ten major clans occupying an area of almost 20,000 km² south and east of the Volta.

The wealth and influence of the Ada Empire was based on its strategic position at the mouth of the Volta River, from where it traded as far upriver as Yeji, and the limitless source of raw salt that is the Songor Lagoon. Both these assets were coveted by neighbouring powers, for which reason the empire spent much of the 18th and early 19th century fighting territorial wars, often with Danish backing. Oddly, despite Ada's significance as a combined river and ocean port, only one rather small fort is ever known to have been built there, Fort Kongensten, constructed by the Danes in 1783 and long-since vanished.

Ada probably peaked in importance in the 19th century, but its autonomy became increasingly tenuous after 1850, when the Danes sold their Gold Coast assets to the British. Following the Dutch evacuation of the coast in 1872 and

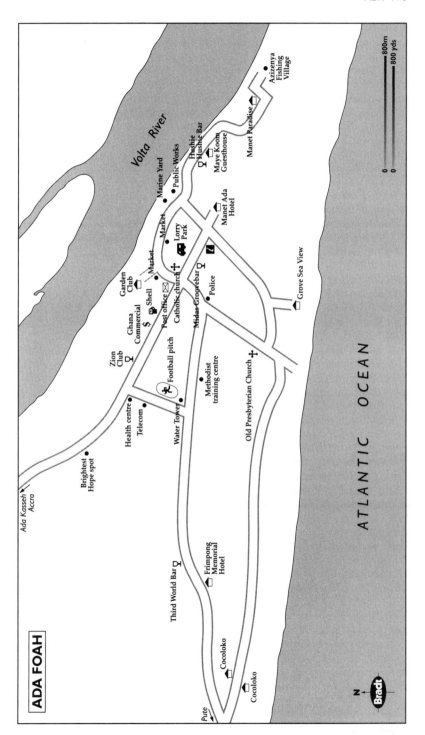

ADA FOAH

the British victory over Ashanti two years after that, Ada become an *ipso facto* Crown colony, and the traditional role of the Ada Matse was severely compromised. As some indication of how British colonisation neutered the role of the paramount chief, it is said that all but one of the four Matse who were enstooled between 1876 and 1927 died in suspicious circumstances, and the stool was held vacant for 25 of those years. By contrast, only two Matse have ruled since 1927: Dake II (1927–77) and Abram Akuaku III (1977 – present day).

Today, Ada is something of a backwater, with nothing but a few faded colonial-era buildings to show for its illustrious past. The superb beach and riverfront scenery, however, combined with a range of activities and accommodation to suit all tastes and budgets, make it a worthwhile stop in its own right, as well as the most obvious base from where to explore the lushly vegetated lower regions of the River Volta, whether by chartered canoe or via the public ferry to Akuse.

For more detail about the history of Ada and surrounds, I recommend C Amate's informative and well-written book *The Making of Ada*, published in 1999 and on sale at the Manet Paradise Hotel.

Getting there and away

Ada consists of three discrete settlements: Ada Kasseh lies on the main Accra–Aflao road, at the junction of the road to Big Ada and Ada Foah, which lie 15km and 20km respectively to its south. From the point of view of travellers, Ada Foah is the most important settlement, since it lies closest to the river mouth as well as to most of the accommodation in the area. If you can't find direct transport to Ada Foah from elsewhere on the coast, you'll have no difficulty getting a tro-tro to drop you at Ada Kasseh, from where regular tro-tros run up and down to Ada Foah.

It is also possible – in theory – to arrive at or leave Ada Foah by river ferry to Akusi near Akasombo, or to catch a motorised canoe across the Volta to Anyanui for Keta (see *Around Ada* below).

Where to stay and eat

All the accommodation listed below lies in or around Ada Foah, the main tourist focus in the area. If, however, you should get stuck at the junction town of Ada Kasseh, the **Garden Club Hotel** is a surprisingly smart-looking local hotel with rooms in the US$5–10 range. There is no accommodation in Big Ada; the closest place is the basic **No Problems Guesthouse** along the road between Big Ada and Ada Foah.

Upmarket

Manet Paradise Holiday Resort PO Box 66, Ada Foah; tel: 0968 22276/398; fax: 0968 22275/397.

This superb three-star hotel with 45 rooms lies in compact landscaped grounds on the bank of the Volta about 1km from the centre of Ada Foah. In addition to a swimming pool area beneath shady palms, the hotel offers good water-sport facilities, tennis and volleyball courts, boat trips and other local excursions in the company of knowledgeable guides, and deep-sea fishing trips. Modern air-conditioned rooms with satellite TV cost US$50/60 single/double, while suites cost US$110. The restaurant, the best in Ada, serves a good range of Ghanaian and international dishes starting at around US$3.

Moderate
Manet Ada Hotel *Contact details as for Manet Paradise Holiday Resort.*
Recently acquired by the owners of the Manet Paradise, and closed for
renovation in late 2000, this centrally-situated multi-storey hotel is likely to fill
the gap between the upmarket Manet Paradise and various budget options
when it re-opens in late 2001.

Budget
The **Garden Club Annex** behind the post office seems slightly overpriced
for what it is – a slightly run-down and undistinguished local budget hotel –
but for the time being it is the only place in town offering affordable rooms
with a fan. Ordinary doubles cost US$5, while s/c doubles cost US$8. A short
distance from the town centre along the road to the Manet Paradise, the **Maye
Krom Guesthouse** is scheduled to open in early 2001, and looks likely to be
a more promising bet in this range. Neither of these hotels has a restaurant,
but the supermarket attached to the Maye Krom is probably the best in Ada.

Shoestring
The **Cocoloko Beach Camp** was established in late 1999 by the owner of the
Estuary Beach Club, a popular backpackers resort on the estuary mouth which
was destroyed by floods a year before that. The camp, which is set within view
of the beach, about 30 minutes' walk west of the town centre, consists of about
a dozen clean but basic reed huts (no fans or nets) set among the sand and
palms, and charges US$4.50 per double. Meals and drinks are available.

Very similar in conception, the **Grove Sea View Resort** has arguably a
better location, closer to the town centre and right on a safe swimming beach.
The basic huts also lack fans and nets, and cost US$3 double. There is a bar,
and meals are available at around US$2.

Several drinking spots and chop shops are dotted around Ada. The
Brightest Hope Spot has been recommended for simple local meals, while
the **Hushie-Hushie Bar** next to the Maye Krom Guesthouse is a good place
for a drink.

Around Ada
The main point of interest in Ada itself is of course the beach and riverfront,
but the town does boast a few minor historical landmarks, notably a 19th
century European cemetery and an attractive Presbyterian church built in
1918. The central market is worth visiting on the main market days of
Wednesday and Saturday. An attractive stroll out of town takes you in a south-
easterly direction from the Manet Paradise Hotel towards the estuary, through
the fishing village of Azizanya: this is a very friendly village, on a turd-free
sandy beach lined with colourful fishing boasts and positioned below the tall
palms, and is a good place to watch rural activities such as smoking and sun-
drying fish, and repairing boats and fishing nets. Oddly, the village is also
overrun with domestic ducks – the only place I've visited in Ghana (and for
that matter in Africa) where this fowl is so prolific. The private tourist
information office in Ada started life as an offshoot of the Estuary Beach
Camp, and appears to have lost its sense of purpose since that camp was
washed away a couple of years ago, but it remains a good place to ask about day
excursions from Ada.

Ada's main festival is the annual **Asafotufiami Ceremony,** which is held in remembrance of the military achievements of Ada during the 18th and 19th centuries. The festival always begins on the first Thursday of August, when libation is poured at various ancestral shrines, but is far more colourful on Friday, when a succession of traditional military processions are held around the town, starting at dawn and carrying on until late at night. On Saturday, the festival climaxes with the Durbar, during which the Matse (paramount chief) and various lesser chiefs are carried through the town on palanquins. Festivities continue until the next Thursday, though these are mostly less traditional and so of less interest to tourists. (As one local brochure puts it 'boat races, river cruises, football matches, and people greeting and bidding goodbye to each other'!)

Songor Ramsar Site

This internationally recognised marine wetlands site protects the area around the 115km^2 Songor Lagoon (which lies to the east of Ada) through to Ada and the Volta River Estuary. It is of particular importance for marine and other water-associated birds, with more than 90 species recorded, several of which breed around the lagoon or on islands in the Volta estuary. The area is most rewarding for birders during the European winter, when resident species such as egrets, herons and gulls are boosted by a host of Palaearctic migrants such as terns, sandpipers and other waders, and waterfowl. Three species of marine turtle also breed in the area: green and olive ridely turtle between March and September, and leatherback turtle between September and January. The most interesting mammal found in the area is the manatee, a large aquatic creature whose unusual shape is thought to have given rise to the legend of mermaids.

The area is managed by the Coastal Wetlands Development Project (CWDP), an organisation which has taken an inclusive community approach to conserving these fragile wetlands. The lagoon is important not only for wildlife, but also as a source of protein and as the base of a traditional salt-production industry involving more than 8,000 people. Tourism is actively encouraged, though the only development to date consists of two bird observation platforms, the most accessible of which is in the village of Pute, on the edge of the lagoon some 9km from Ada (no tro-tros run along this road, but taxis can be chartered). The second observation platform, at Lolonya, offers better birding at present, but it cannot be reached from Ada without returning to the main Accra–Aflao road.

It is permitted to look for nesting turtles at the right time of year, though in order to protect these vulnerable reptiles this must be arranged through the CWDP office in the Public Works Department next to the Marine Authority Office. Turtles generally come to shore to lay eggs between 22.00 and 02.00, so these trips can only be run at night. It is hoped, too, that the CWDP will be able to locate the nearest manatee feeding grounds and start running organised boat trips there.

Boat trips

Trips on the Volta River can be arranged through the Manet Paradise Hotel, or through the tourist office (from US$3–9 per hour), or most cheaply with private individuals at a negotiable rate. Popular goals include Crocodile Island, 3–4km from Ada, renowned for its basket-weaving industry, and – although no longer home to crocodiles – a major breeding site for several bird species (including little egret, western reef heron and cormorant) between July and September. Another good excursion is to the mouth of the estuary, about 2km from the town centre.

A couple of interesting public-transport options can be used to explore the river cheaply. The first is the theoretical ferry service which runs up and down the river between Ada and Akuse (15km and a short tro-tro ride south of Kpong), consisting of two boats which leave in opposite directions on alternate days. The newer *MS Oko* starts the upriver journey from Ada at 07.00 on Monday, Wednesday and Friday, arriving at Akuse at about 18.00. The same boat leaves from Akuse at 07.00 on Tuesday, Thursday and Saturday, arriving at Ada at about 16.30. The older *MS Sogakope* leaves Ada at 07.00 on Tuesday, Thursday and Saturday, and Akuse at 07.00 on Wednesday, Friday and Monday. The fare in either direction is US$1 per person. Simple meals are available on board, but not drinks. Both boats stop at Sogakope on the main Accra–Aflao road. Note, however, that this service was not running when we visited Ada in 1998 (diesel shortage), nor when we visited again in 2000 (boats being repaired), and I've had at least two letters from readers who visited in-between and found the ferry was not operational.

A more certain possibility are the boat-taxis that run between Ada Foah and Anyanui on the eastern bank of the Volta on Wednesday (market day in Anyanui). The market here is among the largest in this part of the country, sprawling from the riverbank inland for almost a kilometre, and a great place to seek out anything from authentic local crafts to second-hand T-shirts to, um, fishing nets. The ride across is also fun, leaving from the Ada side at around 08.00, with the option of either returning to Ada by boat or – having crossed the Volta – continuing on the good tar road that connects Anyanui to Keta.

Finally, for serious anglers, the Manet Paradise Hotel offers deep-sea fishing trips in a large motorboat for up to six people at a rate of US$1000 per day.

SOGAKOPE

On the east bank of the River Volta, some 25km upriver of Ada, the small town of Sogakope forms something of a transport hub, since it lies adjacent to the most southerly bridge across the Volta, making it the sole funnel for road traffic crossing directly between Greater Accra and Volta Regions. Sogakope is also the main port stopped at by ferries between Ada and Akuse – at least when these ferries are running. The Vume area, on the opposite side of the river to Sogakope, is rightfully renowned for its painted ceramic pots, which are displayed for sale on the side of the road. Another attraction along the short stretch of road between Sogakope and Ada Kasseh is an ostrich farm, signposted along the main road close to the village of Kpotame; a visit costs less than US$1 per person and can be made independently or through Villa Cisneros.

Aside from changing over vehicles, the only reason you'd be likely to stop off in Sogakope is to visit the **Villa Cisneros Resort** (tel: 0968 22312; fax: 0968 22311; email: cisneros@africaonline.com.gh). This unexpectedly large and upmarket complex lies on the east bank of the river, about 1km downstream from the bridge. Facilities include everything from river trips and excursions to the ostrich farm, to a tennis court and swimming pool. Rooms are fair value, starting at US$26 for a relatively basic single with a fan, and going up to US$51 for a double room with AC and satellite TV, and US$62 for a chalet (prices quoted in US dollars).

The relatively downmarket alternative to Villa Cisneros is the **Volta View Hotel** (tel: 091 27834/46), which lies on the main road despite the name, some ten minutes' walk from the river. The freshly painted rooms, all with TV, seemed steeply priced in 1998 but are good value at current rates: a non-s/c double with fan costs US$3 (1998 US$9), a s/c double with fan US$5.50 (1998 US$17), and a s/c double with AC costs US$7. Should you have to swap vehicles, the garden bar at the Volta View serves ice-cold draught beer and spicy kebabs a mere 20m from the tro-tro station.

AKATSI

This junction town on the Accra–Aflao is where you might have to change vehicles travelling between Ho and Keta or between Aflao and Sogakope. Akatsi is an unremarkable town, whose sole – and somewhat esoteric – point of interest is the John Klu Wildlife Museum, a collection of skins and trophy heads from various big game species shot by the late hunter after whom the museum is named. The museum is housed in a room in the former homestead of John Klu, a long pink building which is still lived in by his family and lies about 200m along a dirt road branching from the main road at the police station.

If the town itself is rather humdrum, the surrounding area is excellent for birdwatchers, comprised as it is of coastal savannah transitional and various wetlands which host large flocks of resident birds and European migrants. This potential is currently being translated into a ecotourist project by the Akatsi District Assembly in partnership with the NCRC, Peace Corps and the Xavi (Havi) community. The main attraction is a one-hour birdwatching and cultural canoe tour on the small and quiet Lotor River which feeds into the Avu Lagoon to the south. For less than US$3, visitors can ride in a traditional dugout canoe with a trained local guide and observe traditional local fishing practices, as well as a variety of birds including pigmy kingfisher, emerald cuckoo, Barbary shrike, pin-tailed whydah and white-throated bee-eater. Located 12km from Akatsi, Xavi can be reached by chartered or shared taxi from Akatsi. Once in Xavi you will easily find an official guide who will organise a boat and walk you to the river, which lies 15-minutes away through stands of baobab and acacia trees.

Also of interest, 6km from Akatsi, off the main road, is the village of Dagbamate, which is home to a famous fetish priest, Hunya Yao, who performs his services every Sunday from 14:00 onwards. Visitors are welcome to observe traditional rites and rituals.

The best place to stay in Akatsi is the **Magava Hotel**, signposted on the Aflao side of town behind the telecommunications aerial. This consists of 20 large, clean s/c chalets, all with fan and TV, for US$5 per double. There is a bar but no restaurant. Cheaper rooms can be found at the **Black Cat Hotel** in the town centre.

KETA AND THE FAR EAST COAST

Probably the least-visited part of eastern Ghana, the roughly 100km stretch of coast between the Volta River and the Togolese border is also one of the most rewarding, and highly recommended to travellers with the inclination to spend a few days away from any established travel circuit. A dramatic feature of this region is the Keta Lagoon, the largest in the country, 40km long and 8km wide. This generally very shallow body of fresh or brackish water is separated from the sea for much of its length by a strip of sand less than 1km wide, causing some concern that many of the settlements on this stretch of coast will eventually be swallowed by the sea. Among other things, Keta Lagoon is a genuine birdwatchers' paradise, and several of its islands are important breeding sites for marine birds.

The main town along the sliver of coast dividing lagoon from ocean is Keta, the site of Fort Pridzenstein, which was built by the Danes in 1784 and sold to the British in 1850. In the colonial era, Fort Pridzenstein served as a prison, a role in which it continued to serve until it was damaged by waves during a storm in 1980. Until recently, the old fort was essentially a ruin, but it is currently being restored and should start functioning as a guesthouse and entertainment centre in early 2001. For a nominal entrance fee, the caretaker will take you to the old slave chambers, and show you a pile of dusty record books dating from the days when the fort was a prison. The attractive beach immediately in front of the fort is unsafe for swimming due to the large chunks of collapsed wall that jut out of the water, but there is safe swimming about 100m to the west.

The fort aside, Keta seems quite incredibly run-down – a result, presumably, of the water erosion that threatens to engulf the town. The large number of crumbling buildings gives Keta a somewhat bleak mood, one that reminded me of parts of the Tanzanian coast in the 1980s, though based on our experience the advanced urban decay is compensated for by the genuine friendliness you tend to encounter only in places where tourists remain something of a novelty. Further in Keta's favour is its beach, very pretty, relatively turd-free and normally safe for swimming (though you should ask local advice first). And finally, there are the birds, which should hold some interest even for those not normally given to twitching – right in the town centre I saw the largest concentrations of pied kingfisher and avocet that I've ever encountered.

While Keta remains the obvious tourist focus in this region, the opportunities for exploration are excellent, aided by the presence of guesthouses or hotels at several points along the coast, including a genuine tourist-class beach resort in the form of the recently opened Lorneh Lodge. As far as sightseeing goes, beaches predominate, but there is also Fort Pridzenstein and the lighthouse at Cape St Paul near Woe, reportedly the oldest lighthouse in the country. Also in Woe, only 50m from the main road, is an observation tower from which birders can check out the various marine species. Extensive shallot farms lie along the edge of the lagoon, especially around Anloga, and the lagoon could reward further exploration by boat – you'll have no difficulty finding somebody to take you out on the water at Keta or elsewhere. The separate Ava Lagoon, the western tip of which lies a mere 50m from the main Keta–Dabala road a few kilometres south of Dabala junction, reputedly harbours a small population of the elusive semi-aquatic sitatunga antelope.

Getting there and away
A good tar road connects Keta to the main Accra–Aflao road at Dabala. You'll have no problem finding transport to Keta from this direction. Coming from

Accra, the best place to find a direct tro-tro to Keta is at Ashaiman. Coming from Ho, you'll probably have to catch one tro-tro to Akatsi, then another to Keta. Coming from Ada, you may also have to do the trip in stages, changing vehicles at Kasseh and Sogakope.

A far more interesting way of approaching Keta from the west, however, would be to take a motorised canoe across the Volta River between Ada Foah and Anyanui, from where the occasional tro-tro covers the 10km or so stretch of road to Savietula junction on the main Keta road. Before doing this, it would be wise to check whether any canoes are likely to be leaving the next day, since they generally only go on market days (Wednesday and sometimes Friday and Saturday). Even on these days, there may be only one boat in either direction. The best source of current advice is the tourist centre in Ada.

Heading east from Keta, most maps show a solid surfaced road following the coast directly to Aflao. In reality, the 5–10km stretch of this road connecting Keta to Azizanze has been engulfed by the narrow bar of shifting sand that separates sea from lagoon (note that Azizanze is not shown on many maps, but it lies about 1km before Blekusu). Local people thus use a taxi-boat to get from Keta to Azizanze, where they pick up a tro-tro to Aflao. These boats leave Keta from in front of the central market 100m from the lorry station, carry around 30 people each, cost next to nothing, and take 30–60 minutes depending on whether they are motorised or not. The boats have to follow a strict course, since the lagoon is so shallow (we saw what appeared to be a man walking on water right in the centre of the lagoon). The best day to travel is market day in Keta, every four days, when you'll rarely wait more than about 30 minutes for something to leave. On other days, transport is less frequent, but you should still get across with ease. When the water level in the lagoon is very low, the boats might be replaced by 4x4s which carry passengers along the sandy beach.

Azizanze has a beautiful position on the lagoon's edge. There are a few stalls selling bread, eggs, etc and you can see where the tar road has literally vanished into the sand. There should normally be a row of tro-tros and shared taxis waiting to go direct to Aflao (certainly this is the case on market days).

The road towards Aflao, once again surfaced and in good condition, passes through a few small villages, palm-lined havens fringed by both lagoon and ocean, and notable for several large, modern burial shrines reminiscent in style of the *posuban* shrines of the Elmina area (see page 153).

Where to stay and eat
Moderate
Lorneh Lodge Tel: 0902 210144.
The smart new lodge, which opened in mid-2000, is situated at Tegbi, 7km from central Keta on the ocean side of the main Dabala road. The main building lies 200m from a safe and very attractive swimming beach, but a second set of chalet-like rooms, currently under construction right on the beach, is scheduled to start operating during the course of 2001. Facilities include a swimming pool, satellite TV in all rooms, and a good restaurant. The large air-conditioned rooms with hot water are stunning value for money at the current rate of US$16/20 single/double.

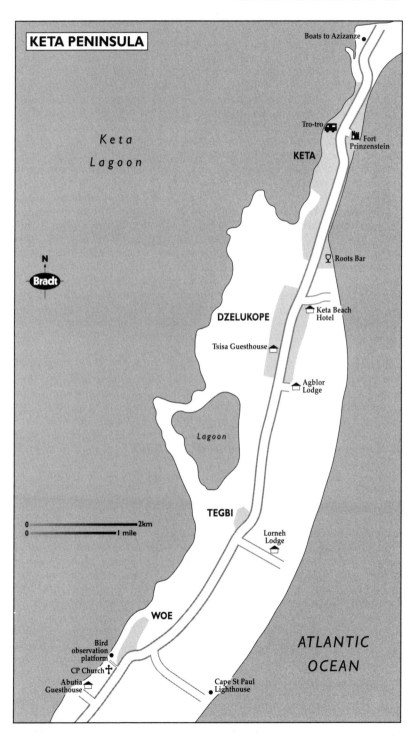

KETA PENINSULA

Boats to Azizanze

Keta
Lagoon

N

Bradt

Tro-tro

Fort
Prinzenstein

KETA

Roots Bar

DZELUKOPE

Keta Beach
Hotel

Tsisa Guesthouse

Agblor
Lodge

Lagoon

0   2km
0   1 mile

TEGBI

Lorneh
Lodge

WOE

Bird
observation
platform

CP Church

Abutia
Guesthouse

Cape St Paul
Lighthouse

ATLANTIC
OCEAN

Budget

The closest hotel to the town centre (at least until such time as the fort starts operating as a guesthouse) is the **Keta Beach Hotel** (tel: 0906 21288), a rather run-down but friendly-enough establishment which used to be popular with Accra weekenders, but these days sees very little custom. Room rates start at US$5/6 (1998 US$7.50/10) for a non-s/c single/double with a fan and using clean communal showers, and go up to US$11 (1998 US$25) for a s/c double with AC, TV, fridge and water heater. Decent if unspectacular fare is served in the restaurant and pleasantly wooded garden bar, and cold beers are available. Coming by road from the west, ask the tro-tro driver to drop you at the hotel, clearly signposted and very close to the main road some 2km before you reach the centre of Keta.

About 1km further out of town, the **Tsisa Guesthouse** is residential and as often as not full. Another 1km further, on the seaward side of the main road, the **Agblor Lodge** is very good value at US$5 for a clean s/c single (with double bed and TV) and suites with two bedrooms for US$10.

Best of all, perhaps, is the **Abutia Guesthouse** (tel: 0906 22239), which lies 500m from the centre of Woe in the direction of Dabala, making it very well-positioned for exploring the lagoon and walking out to the lighthouse. The guesthouse lies in pleasant gardens, signposted 20m from the main road and not much further from the lagoon, and the double rooms with fans are exceptional value at US$3.50 (sharing bath), US$4 (s/c without TV) or US$4.50 (s/c with TV). A restaurant and bar are attached.

Shoestring

The cheapest option at present is the **Larota Guesthouse** in Tegbi, 4km further out of town than the Keta Beach Hotel. This decent family-run place charges US$2.50 for a s/c double with fan and shared showers, and US$4 for a s/c twin with roof fan and hot water. When the fort in Keta opens as a guesthouse, assuming that other forts used for this purpose provide a meaningful guideline to prices, it will probably be slightly cheaper.

AFLAO

This typically chaotic border town, the third largest urban settlement in Volta Region, must be a somewhat disconcerting introduction to Ghana for those coming from Togo. It's one of those places where money changers yell at you from all directions, and you can expect a few blatant attempts at overcharging, especially when you are walking away from the border. For those travelling entirely within Ghana, Aflao lies off any major trunk route, and the only situation in which you'd be likely to pass through the town is if you'd followed the coastal road from Keta and wanted to pick up transport back towards Accra or Ho. Aflao is not without redeeming features, however, most obviously a variety of street food that's second to none in Ghana – wherever you go you'll see women carrying baskets full of crusty baguettes, betraying your proximity to a francophone country.

Getting there and away

Aflao has a lorry station as crowded as any in Ghana, with all manner of tro-tros heading direct to Accra and most points in between. There are also regular

STC and OSA buses to Accra. The most interesting route in or out of Aflao, however, is the coastal one to or from Keta described above.

Where to stay and eat

Should you need to stay the night in Aflao, there's no shortage of accommodation. The **Sanaa Hotel**, the closest place to the lorry station, has adequate rooms for US$4.50/5.50. I'll leave it to you to decide whether you transgress the somewhat cryptic ruling that the 'rate applies to one man one flesh only: Gen 2:24'.

Clustered about 100m apart and roughly 500m back along the road away from the border post, the **Kplom Dedie**, **Prince** and **Ewotsige** hotels all have rooms with double beds for between US$3.50 and US$4.50, with the Kplom Dedie definitely the first choice.

The most upmarket place in town is the **Makavu Hotel**, about 1km from the border, which has s/c rooms with fans for US$8/10 and with AC for US$15. The Makavu has the only restaurant proper in Aflao, as well as an attractive beer garden. Shared taxis run between the border post and a taxi rank in front of the hospital that lies about 50m from this hotel.

The only accommodation along the stretch of road between Keta and Aflao is at Adiafana–Denu, where the one-star **Hotel Vilcabamba** (tel: 0962 354) lies close to the OSA station about 2km before you reach the main junction. Double rooms here start at around US$10.

Inland of Accra

This chapter covers an area which broadly conforms to Ghana's misleadingly titled Eastern Region (Volta Region lies to its east!). The region is broadly bounded by the Volta River to the east, the regional capital of Koforidua to the north, the Akuapem Hills to the west, and the main Accra–Aflao Highway to the south. Regional highlights include the Aburi Botanical Garden in the Akuapem Hills, the under-rated Shai Hills Reserve, the bead factory and market at Krobo-Odumase, the lovely Boti Falls near Koforidua, and the Akosombo Dam on the Volta River.

Most places detailed in this chapter can be – and regularly are – visited from Accra as a self-standing day or overnight excursion. Equally, the area is well-suited to unstructured travel over a few days, with any number of route variations possible, and regular public transport links between practically any two given towns or places of interest. For those travelling further afield, Eastern Region is bisected by a couple of important through-routes. The most significant of these is the road to Akosombo – effectively the gateway to the highlands east of Lake Volta – which bypasses Shai Hills and Krobo Mountain, and comes within a few kilometres of Krobo Odumase. Also worth noting is that the road between Accra and Koforidua via Aburi could be used as a springboard for travels further north, with regular public transport connecting Koforidua to Kumasi.

THE AKUAPEM HILLS AND ABURI

Situated less than an hour's drive inland of Accra, the green and relatively breezy Akuapem (aka Akwapim) Hills, and in particular Aburi Botanical Garden, have long formed a popular goal for a day trip out of the capital, as well as being an excellent area for travellers to start their exploration of the Ghanaian interior. The hills are named for the Akuapem Kingdom, which was founded in 1733 as a result of a rebellion against the oppressive Akwamu Kingdom of the eastern plains, and today consists of 17 townships ruled over by a paramount chief whose throne lies in Akropong.

The Akuapem Hills were one of the first parts of the Ghanaian interior to be settled by Europeans, starting in 1788 with the short-lived tenancy of the Danish Dr Isert. A permanent European presence was established in 1835 with the arrival of the Basel missionary Andreas Riis, who was warmly accepted by Chief Nana Addo Dankwa I and permitted to build a house in Akropong. One of the appeals of this area to European missionaries was the relatively cool

ABURI
(SKETCH MAP)

Royal Garden Restaurant

Aburi Botanical Garden

Akropong, Koforidua

Olyander Guesthouse

Aburi Gardens Resthouse

North gate

Police

South gate

Aburi Bicycle Tours

Taxi

Adomorobf

Post & Telecom

Chief's Palace

Mosque

Market

Nsawam

Carvers & curio stalls

School

School

May Lodge

Accra
Little Acre Hotel(±1 km)

N

Bradt

0   500m
0   500 yds

climate and scarcity of malaria by comparison to the coast. During the mid-19th century, Basel missions were founded at Akropong, Aburi, Abetefi and several other townships in the area, manned by the unlikely combination of German and West Indian priests, whose goal was not solely to spread the gospel, but also to provide education and healthcare. The Akropong Seminary, which was founded by the Basel missionaries in 1848 and is still active today, is often referred to as the Mother of Ghanaian Schools (sadly, so far as I'm aware, none of the original seminary buildings remain).

The main tourist focus in Akuapem today is the **Aburi Botanical Garden**, founded by Britain in 1890 at a site which was already settled by Basel missionaries and had served as a sanatorium for colonial officials in Accra since 1875. Aburi is still a popular weekend retreat with Accra residents, as much for the relatively bracing montane climate as for the lushly scenic setting. The garden, which covers 65 hectares and spans an altitude of 370–460m above sea level, is planted with a mixture of indigenous and exotic trees, notably the avenue of tall palms that leads to the guesthouse, and an immense 150-year-old *kapok* on the main lawn. It is riddled with footpaths from where visitors can see a large variety of labelled trees as well as many birds. In clear weather, the views back to Accra can be amazing. Aburi is also an excellent place to buy curios: at the row of stalls on the junction with the Accra road you'll find drums, fertility dolls, stools *et al* sold in a far friendlier atmosphere than in the capital, and at better prices.

Aburi's attractiveness to adventure tourists has been greatly enhanced by the recent opening of a company called **Aburi Bike Tours and Rentals** outside the southern gate to the botanical garden. The Swiss owners of this company have marked out three self-guided mountain bike trails of 2–3 hours duration as well as some longer guided trails in the vicinity of Aburi, and can provide interested visitors with mountain bikes (in three sizes and fitted with repair kits), maps and a guide. Bicycle hire costs US$3 per bike for the first hour, with the hourly rate decreasing by US$0.30 for each additional hour, while a guide costs an additional US$5 per party per day. The office is open from Thursday to Monday; ring 024 267303 or send an email to aburibike@email.com to make advance enquiries.

A short tro-tro ride north of Aburi, the small town of Mampong (which, ironically, means 'large town', and should not be confused with its more substantial namesake in Ashanti Region) has an important place in Ghana's economic history as the site of the country's first **cocoa farm**, founded by Tetteh Quarshie. Born in what is now Accra in 1842, Tetteh Quarshie was an illiterate, but well-travelled, Ghanaian who lived on Fernando Po from 1870 to 1876 and brought back with him cocoa seeds which would first bear fruit at Mampong in 1879, revolutionising the national economy. The Gold Coast first exported cocoa in 1891, by 1911 it had become the world's largest cocoa producer, and it remains the world's second largest producer to this day. While cocoa was Ghana's leading earner of foreign revenue for decades, it has recently been overtaken by gold. Visitors to Tetteh Quarshie's farm and homestead can see Ghana's first cocoa plant, still in good health, and they will be shown how cocoa is planted and picked.

Although few travellers explore the Akuapem Hills beyond Aburi, it is a fascinating area, not only for the scenery, but for the unusual architectural style of the small towns – evidently influenced by the Basel missionaries.

Worthwhile goals for day trips include the Asenema Waterfall, which lies along a short signposted footpath off the Koforidua road 5km north of Adokrom, a palm tree with six heads on one stem 2km from Mamfe, and the small town of Larteh, home to one of the most renowned fetish priests in Ghana.

Getting there and away

Regular tro-tros to Aburi leave Accra from Tema station. There are also regular tro-tros from Aburi to Mampong, Adokrom, Larteh and Mamre, the latter being where you'll find transport to Koforidua.

Where to stay and eat

Moderate

Little Acre Hotel PO Box CT 1730, Cantonments, Accra; tel: 0876 22078/9 or 22103.

This very pleasant hotel (dedicated, according to the pamphlet, to the glory of God) is set in neat, green grounds about 2km from Abuti along the Accra road. Twin rooms with AC, TV, fridge and hot shower cost US$20. A restaurant and bar are attached.

Budget

The nicest place to stay is the **Aburi Gardens Resthouse**, which is housed in a former sanatorium built in 1875, and overlooks the main lawns of the garden about 200m inside the northern entrance gate. Bedrooms in the main building have three beds each and cost US$3.50 (1998 US$7.50), while s/c chalets, added in 1978, cost US$5–6 (1998 US$10–17), depending on whether they have fridge and TV, and executive chalets with AC cost US$11.50 (1998 US$35). If possible, ring through an advance booking on 0876 22037, especially over weekends and public holidays. The patio bar here serves simple meals for around US$2–3 as well as chilled beers, soft drinks and spicy barbecued kebabs. More substantial, varied and expensive meals are available at the **Royal Garden Restaurant** about 100m away.

If the resthouse in the gardens is full, the **Olyander Guesthouse** about 300m outside the northern entrance has a variety of s/c rooms starting at around US$4 (1998 US$10). Similarly priced accommodation, as well as meals, are available at the rather more run-down **May Restaurant and Lodge** on the south side of Aburi village, about 1km from the southern entrance gate.

For a relaxed drink, **Nora's Spot** above the taxi rank on the road to the south gate of the botanical garden has been recommended, while good, cheap food can be found at **Silvee's**, which has a scenic location close to the north gate.

KOFORIDUA

The capital of Eastern Region, Koforidua was founded in the 1870s by the New Juaben people, who were forced to migrate from Juaben in Ashanti after they staged an unsuccessful (and British-inspired) revolt against the authority of the Ashanti King in Kumasi. Today, Koforidua is a substantial and busy town, with a pleasant atmosphere and an important market – the latter a good place to buy beads on Thursday mornings. Koforidua is also the best base from which to visit the Boti Falls (see below). Otherwise, it offers little of specific interest to tourists.

Getting there and away

Koforidua is an important transport hub, with good bus and tro-tro connections to and from Accra, and north towards Kumasi via Nkawkaw and Begoro. The town is also serviced by regular tro-tros and/or shared taxis to other centres in Eastern Region such as Aburi, Somanya and Akasombo. There is no STC or OSA bus service linking Koforidua and Kumase, but the Kingdom Transport Service runs a decent bus between the two towns.

Where to stay and eat

The large two-star **Saint James Hotel** (PO Box C87, Koforidua; tel: 081 23165/24076), situated about 3km out of town along the Nyamekrom/ Densuegya Road, is the most upmarket lodging in Koforidua. S/c rooms with AC and satellite TV cost around US$25. A good restaurant and bar are attached.

More centrally, the **Partners May Hotel** (where strangers, presumably, may not!) is a pleasant one-star place offering s/c chalet-like accommodation at US$6/9 single/double (1998 US$15/20) with fan and hot water, or US$12 (1998 US$23) double with AC.

For affordable accommodation within walking distance of the town centre, try the **Kes Hotel**, which lies around the corner from Partners May and charges US$5 (1998 US$9) for adequate double rooms using clean communal showers.

Less centrally, a cluster of decent hotels offering accommodation in the US$4–8 range lies within 100m of the junction of Old Estate and Pentecost roads, about 2km northwest of the town centre. I particularly liked the feel of the **Eastland Hotel**, a quiet, friendly place which has clean, compact s/c rooms with running water and fan. It has no restaurant, but there is a bar and local restaurant right opposite. Similar in standard, the **White Rose Lodge**, which has s/c rooms with fan for a similar price as well as doubles with AC, has been recommended by one reader as the best hotel they stayed at in Ghana. A bit smarter, the **Starland Hotel** has s/c rooms with a double bed with fan or AC, and one of the best restaurants in the area. Also in Old Estate, but smarter than the above trio, the new **Capital View Hotel** has been recently recommended for its comfortable rooms in the US$15–20 range, and excellent and reasonably priced restaurant. To get to these hotels, catch a shared taxi from the town centre to Old Estate, or charter a dropping taxi for less than US$1.

The best place to eat in central Koforidua is the **Linda Dor Restaurant** on Oguaa Road. This has a varied menu ranging from steaks and burgers to spaghetti and Chinese dishes, and nothing costs more than US$3. The portions are big and you can eat in or out of doors. There's a second, more central Linda Dor Restaurant next to the Telecom building, with a similar menu, but you can't eat outdoors. Other places you could try are the **Sophisticat Restaurant** on the first floor of the ITTU Building, and the **Commercial Restaurant** on Legon Road. There's also the usual scattering of bars and drinking spots around the market, including the bizarrely named **Joy Container Spot**!

BOTI FALLS

This 30m-high perennial waterfall, one of the most attractive in Ghana, lies on the Pawnpawn River in the Boti Forest Reserve to the northeast of Koforidua. It is impressive at any time of year, but the flow decreases during the dry

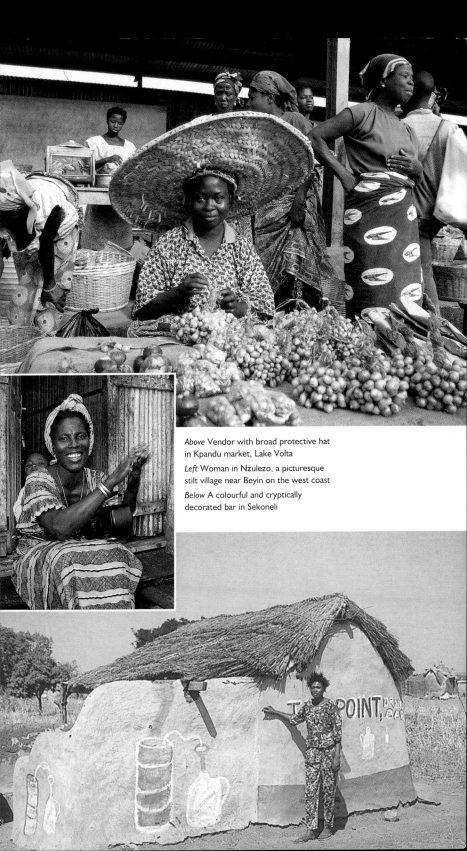

Above Vendor with broad protective hat in Kpandu market, Lake Volta

Left Woman in Nzulezo, a picturesque stilt village near Beyin on the west coast

Below A colourful and cryptically decorated bar in Sekoneli

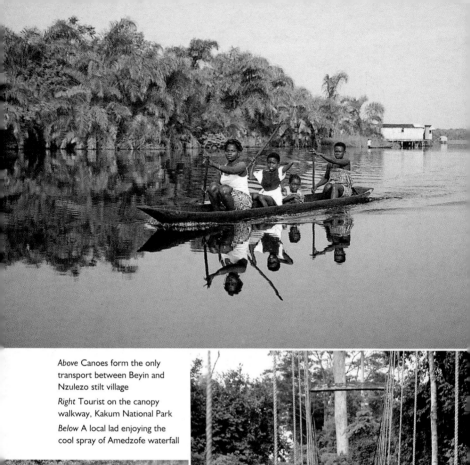

Above Canoes form the only transport between Beyin and Nzulezo stilt village

Right Tourist on the canopy walkway, Kakum National Park

Below A local lad enjoying the cool spray of Amedzofe waterfall season when the waterfall splits into two separate streams. The pool at the base, reached by a sequence of 250 concrete steps, is safe for swimming, provided that you keep clear of the waterfall itself, especially in the rainy season. The scene is made by the surrounding forest, which boasts many enormous trees, including flamboyants with their striking red flowers. An entrance fee of US$0.50 is charged. Do watch out for army ants on the way down – on a bad day they are everywhere, and it might be worth tucking your trousers into your socks to keep them at bay!

The rainforest around the waterfall once harboured chimpanzees and various monkey species. These have reportedly been hunted out, but the forest is still very impressive and supports many different birds and butterflies. It's no problem to arrange a guided walk along the forest paths for a negotiable fee, or to explore the forest fringing the Agogo road on your own. Further afield, you can arrange guided walks to the anonymous caves that lie about an hour from the waterfall, as well as to the so-called 'Umbrella Stone' and a palm tree that reputedly has three trunks. The round trip to all three takes around 2–3 hours, and is tough going in parts, but worth it for the great views and atmospheric jungle setting. The falls may not be running during the dry season.

The Boti Waterfall is a sacred site, and the setting for a celebration every year on 1 July. Many thousands of Ghanaians visit the waterfall on this day, but foreign visitors are welcome to participate.

Getting there and away
Boti Falls lies 21km and 30 minutes' drive from Koforidua. To get there, follow the surfaced road northeast to Huhunya via Kurakan, then take the signposted fork to the left, a 7km dirt road that can be driven in any vehicle. If you're using public transport, a tro-tro from Koforidua to Agogo, a small village shown on no maps, will drop you at the entrance to the falls.

Where to stay and eat
A basic chalet overlooking the waterfall can be rented for around US$3, and camping is permitted at US$1.50 per tent. The friendly caretaker will bring water for washing and arrange for somebody to do your cooking. He keeps two fridges loaded up with ice-cold mineral water, soft drinks and beer, as well as a supply of biscuits and tinned sardines. You can buy other basic foodstuffs at a village 1km up the road, or arrange for the caretaker (who has a car) to run into Agogo to buy you meat or chicken.

THE ROAD TO AKOSOMBO
If you simply want to get to the town of Akosombo (see page 217), a great many tro-tros head there directly from Accra. For those with time to spare, however, two worthwhile and little-visited nature reserves lie practically alongside the Akosombo road. These are Shai Hills Resource Reserve and the Krobo Mountain Community Reserve, both of which would make for easy day trips for motorised Accra residents. Also very accessible from the Akosombo road are the Agomanya bead market and Cedi Bead Factory on the Kpong-Somanya road

Note that travellers using public transport to explore this part of Ghana may well end up changing vehicles at **Ashaiman**, a busy little town at the junction of the main Accra–Aflao highway and the roads south to Tema and north towards Akosombo. Regular tro-tros connect Ashaiman with most of the main lorry stations in Accra. There are a few hotels in Ashaiman should you need to spend the night.

Akasombo – and, for that matter, all the other attractions described in this section – can as easily be approached from Aburi (via Dodowa) and/or Koforidua (via Somanya). In both cases, there is plenty of public transport.

Shai Hills Resource Reserve

Shai Hills is the closest wildlife sanctuary to Accra, and one of the most accessible in the country, since it is bordered by the main Akosombo road. It protects an area of coastal savannah, broken by a range of scenic rocky hills which supports patches of dry evergreen forest rich in endemic plant species. The area now protected by the reserve was home to the Shai people for several centuries until 1892, when they were ejected by the British. There are still a great many traces of Shai occupation in the reserve, including pottery dating to about AD1600. Several active Shai shrines lie within the reserve, but the most important are closed to casual visitors.

Originally demarcated as a forest reserve, Shai Hills was listed as a game reserve in 1962 and, uniquely in Ghana, it has since been fenced off to protect the remaining wildlife. Motorised visitors will be able to explore the reserve from a circular 17km network of fairly good roads (adequate for a saloon car except after heavy rain). Until such time as horseback trails are introduced, however, other visitors must explore on foot with an armed guide, using a combination of roads and footpaths. The reserve is open to day visits between 06.00 and 17.00. Entrance for a non-Ghanaian costs US$2, with a small additional fee charged per vehicle and a fee of US$1 per hour for the mandatory guide. A useful booklet with a map is sold at the entrance gate for next to nothing.

Wildlife viewing in Shai Hills scarcely compares to Africa's major savannah reserves, but there is a fair amount of game around, most likely to be seen in the early morning. The most common large mammal is the olive baboon, which most visitors will see (one troop often hangs around the entrance gate). About 200 kob antelope are resident, and lucky visitors might also encounter the shier bushbuck, and green and spot-nosed monkeys. There are reportedly plans to reintroduce other antelope species, such as roan and hartebeest, though it is difficult to say when these will come to fruition. At the latest count, 175 bird species have been recorded, of which some of the more visible and attractive are the grey hornbill, Senegal parrot and crested francolin.

There are more than ten dams in the reserve, with the one closest to Sayu Camp bordered by an (arguably rather optimistic) game viewing hide, Also of interest is the bat cave about 4km east of Sayu Camp, which can be visited from the road through the park following a 800m foot trail. In addition to the impressive bat colony – several thousands of chirruping individuals, with at least three species represented – this cave once served as the chief's palace, and signs of low protective walls can still be seen.

Getting there and away

The main entrance gate lies on the main Akosombo road opposite Doryumu junction, easily identified by the prominently signposted Midway Spot bar. A second entrance gate, more difficult to pick up, lies about 10km further towards Akosombo, at Sayu Camp. On public transport, the best way to get to

the main entrance gate is to first take a tro-tro from Accra to Ashaiman, from where any tro-tro heading to Doryumu will drop you outside the reserve. If you want to hire a taxi to see the reserve, the closest towns from which you could do this are Dodowa, Somanya, Akusi, or even Akosombo.

Where to stay and eat

Camping is permitted at the main entrance gate for a fee of US$1 per person per night, exclusive of entrance and guide fees. You can also camp at **Sayu Camp** in the north of the park, but you must first report to the headquarters at the main entrance gate. Campers will need to be self-sufficient in terms of food and water.

There is not currently any accommodation in the immediate vicinity of the park, but the rangers told us that an upmarket hotel will open about 500m from the main entrance gate in late 2001.

Another option would be to head to Doryumu, about 2km from the entrance gate. Here you'll find the **Shai Hills Hotel**, an unsignposted cream building on the left side of the Akiyumu Road about 100m from the lorry station. The basic s/c rooms with running water and electricity cost US$3 (1998 US$4) and seem fair value even if the hotel is – in the words of the management – 'not properly functioning' (by which they mean it no longer has a bar or restaurant) and in the words of one traveller 'unfriendly and filthy'. The rooms looked okay in 1998, but nobody was around to show me one when I dropped by in late 2000 – in itself not the best sign – but if they are as dire as my correspondent suggests, then you could try looking around for somebody she describes as 'a lovely bloke called Osmond, who hangs around the taxi park and would have let us stay the night'. There are a couple of bars around the lorry station in Doryumu.

The closest tourist-class accommodation to the reserve is the **Marina Hotel** (tel: 021 767462 or 220510; fax: 021 775009 or 767904), a real gem set in large flowering grounds in the small town of Dodowa on the Accra–Somanya Road. Comfortable s/c rooms with AC, fan, satellite TV and hot bath cost US$12/16 single/double (note that singles have a double bed), and good meals are available at the restaurant in the US$2.50–3.50 range. Dodowa lies 12km from the main entrance gate to Shai Hills, and is connected to both Accra and Somanya by direct tro-tros. To get to the reserve from Dodowa, follow the Somanya road northwards for 4km to Akiyumu junction, where a right turn will bring you to Doryumu after 6km and the entrance gate at the junction with the Akosombo Road after another 2km.

Krobo Mountain Community Reserve

A craggy inselberg that towers above the eastern side of the Accra–Akasombo road, about 5km south of Kpong, Krobo Mountain is the spiritual home of the Krobo people, who settled there for the natural protection it offered against Ashanti slave raids and whose famous defeat of an Ashanti raid in 1764 led directly to the incumbent Ashanti king being destooled. The Krobo were less fortunate when they resisted a British attempt to impose poll taxes in 1892; they were forced off the mountain, which has remained virtually uninhabited ever since.

The Krobo Mountain Community Reserve has recently been developed for tourism with the assistance of a Peace Corps volunteer. A reception centre with summer huts, a shower and flush toilet was constructed at the base of the mountain in 1999, and a number of guided walks are offered, ranging from one to five hours in duration and costing US$1–3 per person. Among the mountain's natural attractions are the rare charcoal tree *Talbotia genetii*, wild baboons, birds, caves and views across to Lake Volta. Of archaeological interest are the ruins of abandoned Krobo villages, still used to enact sacrificial rites, as well as the former chief's palace and the ceremonial 'Dipo Stone'.

Getting there and away
To reach Krobo from Accra or Tema in a private vehicle, follow the Akosombo Road past Shai Hills until you see the signposted junction to your right (about 2km before Akuse Junction) then follow the dirt road to the reception centre. On public transport, the best option is to catch a bus or tro-tro towards Akosombo and ask to be dropped at the junction, from where it is about ten minutes on foot to the reception area.

Where to stay and eat
No accommodation exists on Mount Krobo, though self-sufficient campers are welcome to pitch a tent at the reception area. The mountain could easily be visited as a day trip from Akosombo, Akusi or anywhere along the Kpong–Somanya Road. The closest hotel, however, is the **Traycourt Leisure Centre**, which lies on the west side of the Akosombo road about 3km from the mountain. Set in large grounds, this pleasant hotel consists of several semi-detached s/c doubles with hot water and fan in the US$5–6 range (1998 US$17). The restaurant serves decent food, and there is a large garden bar.

Akusi
This small port on the Volta River is of interest to travellers primarily as the northern terminus of the ferry service from Ada – a service which, at the time of writing, has evidently been suspended. Situated only 8km from the Accra–Akosombo Road, along a turn-off signposted immediately to the north of Krobo Mountain, it would also be as good a base as any from which to visit the mountain and places described under the section *The Kpong–Somanya Road* below.

The unexpectedly smart **Volta River Authority Clubhouse**, signposted to the right shortly before you enter Akusi, has clean singles with a three-quarter bed for US$8 and s/c doubles for US$17, all with AC, while the large green grounds host an inexpensive restaurant and bar, a swimming pool, and tennis courts. More basic, cheaper accommodation can be found at the **Africana Stop Over Inn**.

The Kpong–Somanya Road
Kpong is a small port situated at the junction of the main Accra–Akasombo road and a 10km long tar road leading to the large town of Somanya. The Kpong–Somanya road, which is lined with small towns that merge into each other, is best known for the town of Krobo Odumase. Settled by Krobo people who were evicted from the nearby mountain, this town is regarded to be the centre of the traditional Krobo bead industry.

A great place to see traditional bead-makers at work is Cedi's Bead Factory, which despite a rather humble appearance exports its products as far afield as the USA, Europe, Australia and South Africa. Here you can watch the centuries-old process from start to finish: to make new beads, the bead-makers first crush old bottles into small chips, then arrange them in glazed moulds, before placing them in what looks like a fiery pizza oven for about 45 minutes. They also restore worn beads – some of them many centuries old – by placing them intact in an appropriate mould, then baking them at low heat for about 15 minutes so that they come out shiny as new. The Nene Nomoda family, which runs the factory, claims to have been bead-makers for more than 200 years, and visitors appear to be welcome. There's no charge for looking around, and the family is very welcoming, but if you do visit it would be courteous to buy something from the well-stocked showroom, if only to make things easier for those who follow in your footsteps (at current exchange rates, prices range from US$1 to US$7 for an ordinary necklace; restored old beads are far more expensive). The factory is open daily except for Sunday (tel: 081 24106/8; fax: 021 229168).

Another good place to buy beads in this area is Agomanya Market, a vast expanse of stalls which would rank with Ghana's most worthwhile markets even without the beads. The main market days are Wednesday and Saturday, when at least two dozen bead stalls operate at the southern end of the market, along with many other stalls selling local ceramics and basketwork and the like – few tourists come here, for which reason the atmosphere is not at all pushy.

Getting there and away

Good tar roads and regular tro-tros connect Somanya to Accra, Koforidua, Aburi and most other urban centres in the region, while any public transport on the surfaced road between Accra and Akosombo will be able to drop you at Kpong. Agomanya market lies on the south side of the road 3km from Kpong; the bead and other craft stalls are at the far end of the market from the main road. Cedi's Bead Factory lies about 500m south of the main road; the signposted turn-off is 3km past Agomanya coming from the direction of Kpong. The road between Kpong and Somanya is serviced by a steady stream of tro-tros that will drop you wherever you want along the way. There is a tro-tro park right next to Agomanya Market, and another at the junction 500m from Cedi's Bead Factory.

Where to stay and eat

Using public transport, this area could easily be explored as a day trip from Akosombo or the Traycourt Leisure Centre (see *Krobo Mountain Community Reserve*), while with a private vehicle it could also be visited as a day trip out of Akusi, any of the hotels mentioned under Shai Hills, or at a push Accra, Tema or Ada. There is, however, a fair selection of budget accommodation in the immediate vicinity.

Most convenient is the **Gerted Hotel** in Krobo Odumase, which lies perhaps 500m south of the main road along a motorable track signposted next to the Manya Krobo Community Bank. This is a very comfortable and reasonably priced double-storey building with a rooftop bar and restaurant. Rooms cost between US$4 and US$6.50, depending on whether they are single or double, are self-contained, and have TV.

I'm not aware of any accommodation in Kpong, but at least two basic hotels can be found in Somanya. Of these, the **Palm Hotel** is marginally the cheaper, and probably the nicer. Here, small clean rooms with fan cost US$2.50 single or US$3 s/c double, and inexpensive meals are available. The alternative is the **99 Western Lane Hotel** – decent enough at around US$4.50 for a s/c double with fan, but relatively scruffy, and lacking a restaurant.

AKOSOMBO AND SURROUNDS

The township of Akosombo was purpose-built in 1961 to house the workers involved in the creation of Ghana's largest dam, a clay and rock construction measuring 370m across and 124m from top to bottom, inaugurated by President Nkrumah in 1966. The body of water dammed by Akosombo, known as Lake Volta, is the most expansive artificial lake in the world, with a surface area of roughly 850,000ha, a length of 400km, and a shoreline measuring almost 5,000km.

Aside from affording an excellent view over the dam, Akosombo is important to travellers as the southern terminus of the weekly Lake Volta ferry to the northern ports of Kete Krachi and Yeji (see page 218). In addition to this local passenger ferry service, the more tourist-oriented *MV Dodi Princess* does a joyride to the Dodi Islands every Sunday, leaving at 10.30 and getting back at around 16.00; tickets cost US$10 and can be booked through the Volta Lake Transport Authority, tel: 0251 686. Touristy it may be, but the *Dodi Princess* is tremendous fun, with a live band, plunge pool, good food, and upper and lower deck bars all there to enhance the hedonistic pleasure inherent in sailing across this vast, hill-ringed lake on a sunny day. The boat moors at Dodi Island for 45–60 minutes, when you can either splash around on the small beach, or allow one of the gang of children who make up the boat's reception party to lead you across the island for a small fee.

For the purpose of orientation, it's worth noting that Akosombo township lies some 8km off the main road between Accra and Ho. The junction to Akosombo is at Atimpoku, a small but impressively chaotic urban sprawl straddling the Accra–Ho road on the west bank of the river. Atimpoku's skyline is dominated by a massive suspension bridge, one of only two places where cars are able to cross the Lower Volta. Travellers on a budget are generally better catered for in Atimpoku than in Akosombo, and Aylo's Bay, 500m from the junction, offers perhaps the best access to the river in this area.

Getting there and away
By road

The main regional transport centre is Kpong, situated on the west bank of the Volta some 10km south of Atimpoku and 10km north of the river ferry terminal at Akuse. Kpong is bisected by the main Accra–Ho road, and it is connected by regular tro-tros to Ashaiman (for Accra), Ho and Akuse. Regular tro-tros run up and down from Kpong to Akosombo via Atimpoku and New Senchie, and you'll rarely wait more than five minutes for a seat between any of these places. STC, OSA and other buses travelling between Accra and Ho will generally drop passengers on request at Atimpoku, provided that they don't mind paying the full fare. If you're heading to Ho from Atimpoku, vehicles passing in the right direction might be full when they come past, so it may be quicker in the long run to take a tro-tro to Kpong and board a Ho-bound vehicle there.

THE AKOSOMBO FERRY

Ben Clissold's recent account of the ferry trip from Akasombo to Yeji might make interesting reading for those thinking of heading this way.

'We took the boat up from Akosombo to Yeji. As you said there was no chance of getting a first-class ticket unless you phone in advance and these are still 45,000 cedis. The second-class tickets cost 20,000 cedis but there is no limit on numbers and they don't entitle you to a bed or even a seat on the middle deck of the boat. Third-class tickets cost 13,500 cedis. While we were on the boat there was plenty of food but I know volunteers who got stuck without food for 24 hours. There does always seem to be plenty to drink though.

'Warn people that the ferry takes considerably more time on the return journey from Yeji as it stops several times to pick up yams. Some volunteers were delayed by 36 hours (ie: the whole trip took 70 hours). The other thing that caught us out was when we got off at Yeji at 5pm, some bloke was yelling 'Makongo/Tamale', so we thought we would try to push on to Tamale. But when we got to Makongo there were no tro-tros waiting, and it seems no-one in Makongo owns a vehicle, and there is nowhere to stay – we had to sleep under the shelter for the ferry passengers and get the first tro-tro in the morning.'

Regular shared taxis run around the sprawling hills of Akosombo. From the lorry station, ask for a taxi to 'Mess' for the Volta Hotel, and one to 'Marine' for the ferry jetty and ticket office.

By ferry

The weekly ferry service across Lake Volta leaves from Akosombo every Monday at 16.00. It arrives at Kete Krachi at 05.00 on Tuesday morning and at Yeji on Tuesday evening. It then starts the return trip out of Yeji at around 04.00 on Wednesday morning, stops at Kete Krachi on Wednesday evening and arrives back in Akosombo on Thursday morning. In both directions, the ferry stops at Kpandu, halfway between Akosombo and Kete Krachi, when the water level is sufficiently high, which is generally only in the rainy season.

Three types of ticket are available for the ferry. First-class tickets for an AC, two-bed cabin normally cost US$15 per person for the full trip. Only two such cabins are available, however, so it's advisable to book well in advance (tel: 0251 686). Otherwise, a second-class ticket, which can normally be bought early on the day of departure, costs US$7 per person for the full trip. Third-class deck tickets cost US$5.50 per person for the full trip. Tickets to Kete Krachi are about 20% cheaper than full-fare tickets to Yeji. All tickets are currently about half the price quoted, due to the recent devaluation of the cedi, but it seems likely that first- and second-class tickets will soon increase in price to allow for this.

The cheap daily ferry service between Ada and Akuse would allow you to travel by boat from the Volta mouth all the way to Yeji, using road transport for a mere 30km between Akuse and the Akosombo dam wall. See *Getting there and away* under Ada on page 194.

Where to stay
Upmarket
Volta Hotel Tel: 021 662639 or 0251 731/316; fax: 021 663791; email: voltahtl@africaonline.com.gh.
Part of the upmarket international Accor chain, this hotel is superbly located on a hilltop with a view over the dam wall, and it ranks with the few truly upmarket hotels in the country outside of Accra. Facilities include a large swimming pool area and a good restaurant. There is live music in the bar over weekends. S/c rooms with AC and satellite TV cost US$95/105, while suites cost US$165. The hotel lies more than 1km from Akosombo township; passenger taxis from the lorry station to 'Mess' pass by the bottom of its steep drive.

Moderate
Akosombo Continental Hotel Tel: 021 669586.
Still under construction in late 2000 and set to open in early 2001, this smart-looking hotel seems likely to fill a gap between the expensive Volta Hotel and the various cheaper hotels dotted around the area. It has a great riverfront location between the bridge and Aylo's Bay. Facilities will include a swimming pool.

Budget
In Akosombo township, about 200m and signposted from the lorry station, the **Zito Guesthouse** has comfortable s/c rooms with fan for US$10 or with AC for US$16 (price unchanged since 1998). It also has a pleasant, small garden and serves meals on request.

Along the road connecting Akosombo to Atimpoku, about 5km from the former and 2km from the latter, the **Soundrest Motel** has an attractively rustic setting, with restaurant and bar facilities. The rooms seem good value at US$3.50 for a normal double with fan, US$5.50 s/c double with fan, or US$9 s/c double with AC (1998 US$7/12/17).

On the same road, less than 500m from Atimpoku and the Volta Bridge, **Aylo's Bay Leisure Spot** (tel: 0251 20901; see *Where to eat*) has three air-conditioned double rooms with balcony available at US$23, including a full cooked breakfast.

About 2km south of Atimpoku, at New Senchie, the **Lakeside Motel** (tel: 0251 20712) has a variety of rooms all with one double bed; prices range from US$3.50 for a room with fan using communal showers to US$6.50 for a s/c room with AC (1998 US$10–17). The restaurant has a varied menu and you can eat in the shady, sloping gardens.

Shoestring
Travellers carrying a tent can pitch it at **Aylo's Bay Leisure Spot** (see *Where to eat*) for US$1.50 per person. Otherwise, the **Benkum Motel** in the heart of Atimpoku, only 50m from the lorry station, is the obvious first choice for tentless backpackers. It looks like a dump from the outside, but the rooms are actually very nice and the people seem friendly. Clean s/c rooms with a fan cost US$3.50 (1998 US$7.50) and cheaper rooms using communal showers are also available. There's no restaurant, but the staff will cook breakfast on request, and there's plenty of street food around if you don't want to wander up to Aylo's for a meal. The large courtyard bar can be a lively place for a drink, with occasional live traditional music.

Where to eat

The best restaurant in the area is the one at the **Volta Hotel**, which serves European cuisine in the US$5–8 range as well as a variety of cheaper snacks. At the other end of the scale, Atimpoku is a great place for street food: oyster kebabs and packets of smoked shrimp are two of the local specialities, both probably to be approached with some caution, as it takes only one dodgy chunk of shellfish to debilitate you with food poisoning. A pleasant place to drink nearby is the garden bar opposite Adomi Spot, about 100m along the road towards Akosombo.

Also in Akosombo, about 500m from the ferry port, the lakefront **Volta Transport Club** (aka The Maritime Club) consists of a more than decent and very affordable restaurant and bar set in pleasant, shady gardens exuding an air of faded colonial languor – it's a good place to hang out at any time (except Wednesdays, when it is closed), and especially convenient when you are waiting for the ferry.

Located on the lush riverfront about 500m upstream of the bridge, **Aylo's Bay Leisure Spot** is a great place to chill out over a meal and a few drinks. The restaurant serves tasty plates of fish or chicken with chips or rice for around US$2. Swimming is said to be safe in this stretch of the river (the water is remarkably clear) and a canoe trip from Aylo's to the bridge costs US$2.50 for up to three people. With advance notice, it's possible for groups to organise drumming, dancing and cooking workshops here too.

A similar set-up, though rather less convenient to travellers without private transport, the **Senchie Riverside Resort** overlooks the river about 2km from Atimpoku in New Senchie. The menu here is extensive, with most meals falling in the US$2–3 range, and boat trips can be arranged at under US$10 per hour for up to ten people.

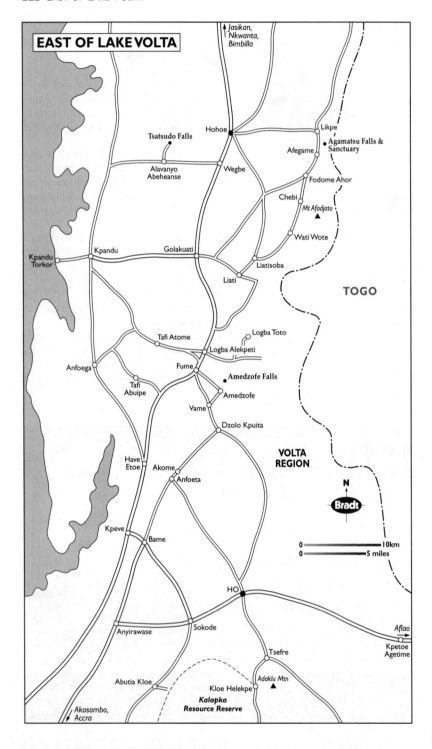

EAST OF LAKE VOLTA

↑ *Jasikan,*
Nkwanta,
Bimbilla

Tsatsudo Falls

Hohoe

Likpe

Afegame

● Agamatsu Falls &
Sanctuary

Wegbe

Fodome Ahor

Alavanyo
Abeheanse

Chebi

Mt Afadjato ▲

Kpandu
Torkor

Kpandu

Golakuati

Wati Wote

Liatisoba

Liati

TOGO

Logba Toto

Tafi Atome

Logba Alekpeti

Anfoega

Fume

● **Amedzofe Falls**

Tafi
Abuipe

Amedzofe

Vame

Dzolo Kpuita

Have
Etoe

Akome

**VOLTA
REGION**

Anfoeta

N

Bradt

Kpeve

Bame

0 ━━━━━ 10km
0 ━━━━━ 5 miles

HO

Aflao

Anyirawase

Sokode

Kpetoe
Agetime

Tsefre

Abutia Kloe

Adaklu Mtn ▲

Kloe Helekpe

↙ *Akosombo,*
Accra

Kalapka
Resource Reserve

East of Lake Volta

This chapter covers the interior of Volta Region, a lushly vegetated and relatively mountainous sliver of land bounded by Lake Volta to the west and Togo to the east. Largely shunned by the package tourist industry – it has been estimated that less than 5% of visitors to Ghana enter Volta Region – this scenic area is increasingly popular with active independent travellers, who are drawn by a compact and generally inexpensive circuit of natural attractions, ranging from the country's tallest waterfall and highest peak to a clutch of obscure but pedestrian-friendly reserves.

A commendable feature of tourism in this part of Ghana is the high concentration of well-run community-based developments. These serve to ensure that virtually all of the revenue raised by tourism is retained locally, to be used for the development of communal resources such as schools and boreholes, while also creating a range of job opportunities at grassroots level. Many of the community projects succeed in subverting the barriers that conventional tourism tends to create between visitors and local people, for instance by offering travellers the opportunity to stay with families rather than in hotels or guesthouses. Perhaps related to this, the ceaseless cat-calls of 'White Man' and '*Abruni*' that are directed at travellers in areas such as the west coast are notable here by their absence, replaced by altogether more agreeable greetings such as '*Akwaaba*' or 'You're Welcome'.

The main towns in this part of Ghana are Ho, Hohoe and Kpandu, all of which form agreeable travel bases and offer good, affordable facilities to backpackers, though they are somewhat lacking in inherent interest. It is the area between Ho and Hohoe that provides the most rewarding travel circuit in the region, centred around the superb community project at Tafi Atome, renowned for its sacred mona monkeys and close to a fascinating *kente*-weaving village, and the scenic hilltop town of Amedzofe. Another very popular destination is the Wli Falls west of Hohoe – reputedly the tallest in West Africa – while worthwhile goals for relatively off-the-beaten-track exploration include a new community project at Adaklu Mountain, the little-known Kalapka Resource Reserve, the *kente*-weaving village of Kpetoe, and a half-dozen small waterfalls in the hills to the south of Hohoe.

HO

The former administrative centre of German Togoland and modern capital of Volta Region, Ho is the largest, busiest town in this part of the country,

HO

Nkwanta

Freedom Hotel
Phil's Country Kitchen

Fiave Lodge
Hotel

Akpenawawu
Hotel

Lorry station

Market

HOUSING

St John's
School

N

Bradt

Barclays $

Mobil
Lord Restaurant

YMCA

MUVIE

Ghana
Commercial $

PRISON

Chances Hotel,
Accra,
Hohoe

Goil garage &
Tourist office

Electricity
station

THIRD

Prison

Volta
Regional
office

Post &
Telecom

Tarso Hotel

Fire station

Hospital

Social
Security
Bank $

White House
Restaurant & Bar

Woezor
Hotel

RESIDENCY

Internet
lounge

PEP Stores

Albert
Kente
shop

Museum

GLALAH

Shell garage &
Books For Less

Shell

Mothers Inn
Restaurant

STARLETS 91

African
Craft market

Arckid
Pleasure
Garden

Alinda Hotel

NURSERY

KASSAH

Ewe Presbyterian
Social centre

JOHNSON

Procha Enterprises

STADIUM

Stadium

0   500m
0   500 yds

Adaklu,
Kingfisher Guesthouse

with excellent facilities for backpackers and good transport connections. Aside from a couple of old colonial buildings (notably the old church and school, and the Ewe Presbyterian Mission at Wegbe, founded in the 1850s), about the only tourist attraction within the town is the Ho Museum next to the hospital, where an investment of US$1 will gain you entrance to an oddly eclectic and occasionally fascinating collection of photographs and artefacts, including displays on the mud-and-stick mosques of the northwest and Ashanti fetish shrines in the Kumasi area. Otherwise, Ho is of limited interest, though it remains a pleasant, inexpensive and well-organised place to take a day or two's break between exploring the many beauty spots that lie within a couple of hours' radius by tro-tro. It is especially worth spending time here over late September and early October, when the annual Yam Festival takes place, climaxing with a chief's durbar in the first week of October.

Getting there and away

Ho is an important transport hub, well connected to most parts of Ghana east of Accra and Lake Volta. Regular tro-tros leave from the lorry station to destinations such as Kpandu, Hohoe, Kpetoe, Akasombo and Accra. Travelling between Ho and eastern ports such as Keta or Aflao, you'll probably have to change vehicles at Akatsi.

Where to stay
Upmarket
Chances Hotel PO Box 605, Ho; tel: 091 28344; fax: 091 27083.
Situated along the Accra road about 3km from the town centre, Chances Hotel is the only genuinely tourist-class unit in this part of Ghana. Set in landscaped grounds at the base of the Kabakaba Hills, it consists of 25 s/c double rooms (soon to increase to 54) and 16 chalets, all air-conditioned with fan, satellite TV, hot water and attractive furnishings. Facilities include a large conference centre, a good restaurant serving international and Ghanaian dishes, and a children's playground. An air-conditioned ten-seat vehicle is available for day and overnight trips at a cost of US$80 per day, including a driver but exclusive of fuel. An on-site internet café is due for early 2001, with a swimming pool to follow by the end of the year. Also in the pipeline are weekend bicycle trips to the Kalapka Resource Reserve and a hiking trail in the Kabakaba Hills behind the hotel. Visa and MasterCard are accepted. Rates, quoted in dollars but payable in local currency, are US$38 double and US$48 chalet.

Moderate
Freedom Hotel PO Box 739, Ho; tel: 091 28158.
Despite it's two-star rating, this excellent hotel lies within a price range affordable to many budget travellers. It is also quite handily situated for those using Ho as an overnight stop, since it lies no more than 500m from the lorry station. The garden, dotted with traditional statues and thatched 'summer houses' is a relaxing place for a meal or a drink (a good selection of Western dishes are available in the US$2–3 range). The 29 rooms range from a single (double bed) with fan using communal showers for US$3.50 (1998 US$7) to a s/c double with fan for US$6 (1998 US$10) and a s/c double with AC, hot water and TV for US$14 (1998 US$20).

Woezor Hotel PO Box 339, Ho; tel: 091 28339/604.
Formerly the government Catering Resthouse, the Woezor Hotel, situated in large grounds on the outskirts of town, is acceptably comfortable, though the rooms are a little frayed at the seams. A s/c double room with AC costs US$7.50 (1998 US$17) while AC stone chalets (which, according to the enthusiastic pamphlet, 'fascinate even the best of architects') cost US$10/12 single/double (1998 US$20/25).

Budget

The pick in this range is the hostel at the **Ewe Presbyterian Social Centre** (tel: 091 26670), which lies in the grounds of the historic Presbyterian church, surrounded by some fine examples of German colonial architecture. The clean, spacious rooms range in price from US$3.50 for a double using communal baths to US$6 for a s/c double with fan and hot water, US$7 for a s/c double with AC and hot water, and US$10 for a large suite with AC, TV and fan (1998 US$6/8/10/14).

More central, the double-storey **Tarso Hotel** is the oldest hotel in Ho – and looks it – though the atmosphere is very amiable and the spacious s/c rooms are very good value at US$4 with fan or US$6.50 with AC (1998 US$6/7).

Less convenient, as it lies about 1km out of town along the Adaklu Road, the **Kingfisher Guesthouse** is good value, with s/c carpeted doubles for US$6.50 (fan) or US$10 (AC).

Shoestring

For a rock-bottom room in the heart of the town centre, look no further than the **YMCA**, where basic but clean doubles cost US$1.50 (1998 US$3.50). So far as I could establish, the rooms are available not only to men but also to couples and single women – but any further queries around the subject of what gender combinations could occupy the rooms and I suspect the bemused receptionist would have had me locked up!

Off the main road between the lorry station and the Freedom Hotel, **Fiave Lodge** is a clean, unpretentious place with a family-run feel. The large, clean rooms all have fans, and they cost US$3–4 (1998 US$4–6), depending on whether they're self-contained and have one or two double beds. Also very close to the lorry station, and similar in price, the **Akpenamawu Hotel** looks rather sordid from the outside, but the rooms are perfectly acceptable and good value.

The once popular **Alinda Hotel** is less convenient, and has seen better days, but the price is right at US$3 for an ordinary double with fan and US$5.50 for a s/c double (1998 US$6/12).

Where to eat

A popular place to eat in the town centre is the **White House Bar**, which serves the usual chilled drinks – including draught beer – along with a limited but tasty selection of stews, pizzas and other snacks for around US$2 per portion. Also recommended is **Mother's Inn Restaurant**, where a plate of chicken with chips or fried rice costs around US$2. At both of these places, you have the option of eating indoors or outdoors, which gives them the edge over the otherwise similar **Lord's Restaurant**, where you are forced to eat indoors (very hot and sweaty). Less central, and more bar than restaurant, **Archid's Pleasure Garden** has an attractively rustic character and gets busy with locals at weekends.

The restaurant at the **Freedom Hotel** is probably the most upmarket eatery in town, serving a good selection of inexpensive, tasty dishes in the US$2–3 range indoors or in the large gardens. Almost next door to this lies **Phil's Country Kitchen**, a lively outdoor bar that also serves filling and inexpensive local meals. On the other side of town, the **Woezor Hotel** offers similar dishes at similar prices, but the atmosphere is a little dingy, except perhaps when there's live music. The food at **Chances Hotel** is excellent and not too expensive at around US$3–5 for a main course, but the location isn't very convenient at night, unless you arrange for a taxi to collect you.

Listings
Books
A branch of Books For Less can be found on the main road close to The White House, though the range of paperbacks in stock doesn't compare to its namesake in Accra. Try also Procha Enterprises for cheap second-hand paperbacks, and the street stalls between the hospital and the Regional Administrative Office.

Crafts
The Ewe, like the Ashanti, are skilled *kente* weavers, and good quality work can be bought at the Albert Kente Shop on Residency Road and Africa Craft Market opposite Mothers Inn Restaurant. Better still, head to Kpetoe, 30 minutes away by tro-tro (see page 229) – this is where most of the cloth sold in Ho is weaved, and prices are generally lower.

Cultural performances
A renowned Ewe cultural troupe, Ziavi Zigi, is based in the village of Ziavi Dzodze, some 3km northwest of Ho on the other side of the Kabakaba Hills. Performances can be arranged for a negotiable fee through the regional tourist office (see below). Cultural performances are also put on occasionally at the open-air theatre in the grounds of the Woezar Hotel.

Foreign exchange
There are branches of Barclays and the Ghana Commercial Bank in Ho, with the former generally offering better rates than the other banks and forex bureaux.

Ghana Tourist Board
Situated in the SIC Building near the Goil garage, the Volta Region tourist office is perhaps the most enthusiastic in the country, and well worth visiting for the latest information on developing tourist attractions throughout the area, especially those with Peace Corps involvement (tel: 091 26560).

Internet
The Internet Lounge, along a side road close to The White House, is the best place to check email or browse the internet, with six computers available at rates slightly more expensive than in Accra. An internet café is likely to open at Chances Hotel in early 2001.

AROUND HO
Kalapka Resource Reserve

Situated no more than 10km south of Ho as the crow flies, this 325km² reserve, gazetted in 1975, has yet to see much in the way of tourist development. It protects an area of gently sloping land, dominated by dry savannah, but with a few patches of forest. Large mammal populations are rather low, though kob antelope, baboon and green monkey are quite common and likely to be seen by most visitors, at least during the dry season (March to June) when game concentrates around the palm-fringed Kalapka River close to the park headquarters. Less conspicuous species include buffalo, bushbuck, waterbuck, Maxwell's duiker, patas monkey and a variety of nocturnal creatures such as bushpig and genet. The area has a reputation for good birding. Although few tourists visit Kalapka at present, and no roads run through the reserve, it is perfectly accessible and day walks can be arranged with the rangers. It is worth noting, too, that the owner of Chances Hotel outside Ho, plans to start running weekend cycling trips into the reserve in 2001.

The dirt road to Abutia Kloe is not without interest, as it passes through some lush semi-forested scenery teeming with birds. On the way, it may be worth asking about the traditionally constructed former German governor's residence that lies on a mango-covered hillside near the village of Abutia Agove, also the site of a famous spring which used to draw people from far and wide during periods of drought. Look out, too, for the *kente* weavers who work in some of the villages around Abutia.

Getting there and away

The only point of entry is through the village of Abutia Kloe, 18km from Ho by road, and connected to it by regular tro-tros. If you are driving from Ho, head out along the Accra road for 9km to Sokode junction, where a left turn will bring you to Abutia Kloe after another 9km. However you get to Abutia Kloe, you must first visit the Department of Wildlife office on the edge of the village, where you will be asked to pay the nominal entrance fee. A 2.5km side-road branching left from Abutia Kloe leads to the rangers' camp on the edge of the reserve. Here you can arrange game walks into the reserve with one of the rangers, who will expect a tip.

Where to stay

There is no formal accommodation at Kalapka or Abutia Kloe, and even without a private vehicle, it is possible to visit Kalapka as a day trip from Ho. In order to get an early start (game being most active in the early morning), it would, however, be preferable to spend the night there. You can pitch a tent (assuming that you have one) at the rangers' camp for a small fee.

Adaklu Mountain

Adaklu is the name of the dramatic inselberg that dominates Ho's southern skyline, as well as the collective name for the 40-odd villages that lie around the mountain's base. Oral tradition has it that the Ewe of Adaklu migrated to the area centuries ago, in order to escape the oppressive rule of King Agokoli in what is now Beyin. When they settled around the mountain, they slaughtered and roasted a cow, and divided out the meat – an act of sharing to which the word Adaklu refers.

The Adaklu area has recently been developed as a community ecotourist project, based at the village of Helekpe, under Peace Corps supervision. The main attraction here are guided hikes to the peak of the mountain, a reasonably demanding 2–4 hour round trip from Helekpe, along which you stand a good chance of seeing some monkeys and a variety of butterflies and birds (as well as giant snails, which are held sacred locally and may not be touched!). In addition, several cultural activities are available at Helekpe, ranging from drumming and dancing performances, to visits to the sacred bats of Avanyaviwofe, and to local *kente* weavers. Costs range from around US$1 per person for a village tour and US$2 per person for a mountain hike to US$5 for a drumming and dancing performance.

Getting there and away
Helekpe lies about 15km from Ho along a fair dirt road. In a private vehicle, head out along the Adaklu road past the Kingfisher Guesthouse and Polytechnic, turning right after 12km at Tsrefre, a small village close to the base of the mountain. Regular tro-tros connect Ho to Helekpe. There is an unmanned visitor centre at Helekpe, but if you arrive with luggage it would make more sense to ask to be dropped at the guesthouse first.

Where to stay and eat
A small **guesthouse** has recently been completed in Helekpe. Double rooms with bedding and nets cost around US$2.50, and communal toilets and bucket showers are available. **Private home-stays** can be arranged for a lower fee. Camping in the village is free of charge, and you can also camp on the mountain for US$2.50 per tent. Meals can be provided to visitors with some notice, and a couple of bars sell minerals and beers.

Kpetoe Agotime
This small town, close to the Togolese border about 30km east of Ho, is renowned throughout Ghana for the quality of its *kente* cloth weavers. Although *kente* weaving is these days largely associated with the Ashanti, the people of Kpetoe claim that the style originated with them and was later adopted further afield after their best weavers were captured during the Ashanti wars. Two types of cloth are made in Kpetoe: the light and popular Ashanti *kente* and the more durable Ewe *agbamevo* (see also *Kente* box on page 286).

The main *kente* factory in Kpetoe, a semi-open concrete construction housing a few dozen weavers, asked us for a fee to look around (in exchange for which they would provide us with 'information'). But there are also plenty of places where weavers work out in the open, and tourists are still so infrequent that you should have no problems just wandering around taking it all in. If you are thinking of buying, prices are far lower in Kpetoe than in the better known *kente* villages of Ashanti, and the atmosphere is more laid-back. Desiadenyo Stores and the home of Madame Felicia Kangni are among the better places to choose from a huge range of cloths and designs.

Kpetoe lies along the main tarred road between Ho and Aflao; there is plenty of transport in both directions and it can easily be visited en route between Ho and the coast, or as a day trip from Ho. If you prefer to spend the night, however, decent s/c rooms are available for around US$4.50 at the

Buggie Hotel about 1km from town towards Ho, and at the more central and marginally nicer **Friends Lodge Hotel**.

THE AVATIME HILLS AND SURROUNDS

Rising from the Lake Volta hinterland towards the Togolese border, roughly halfway between the towns of Ho and Hohoe, the beautiful and lushly vegetated Avatime Hills are rapidly becoming entrenched as one of the most popular destinations in Ghana for enthusiastic hikers and budget travellers. Blessed with a relatively temperate climate, substantial stands of rainforest, a great many bird and butterfly species, and several inexpensive resthouses, the hills offer some excellent opportunities for unstructured hiking and rambling, whether your preference is for day walks or something more ambitious.

The principal town of the Avatime hills – and main tourist focus – is Amedzofe, which now boasts a well-organised tourist office and a good selection of affordable accommodation options. Close to the base of the hills, the village of Tafi Atome – home to several hundred sacred mona monkeys – rivals Amedzofe as the most popular regional travel destination. Less frequently visited attractions include the remote and stunningly situated village of Baikpa, the waterfalls and caves close to Logba Toto, and the fascinating *kente*-weaving village of Tafi Abuipe. While most travellers explore the area on day trips, there are some opportunities for extended hikes – you could, for instance, easily spend a few days working your way on foot from Amedzofe to Tafi Atome (see below) via Biakpa

Amedzofe

A former German mission, Amedzofe is the largest town in the Avatime Hills, the site of a well-known teacher-training college and an attractive 100-year-old church. The town lies at an altitude of more than 600m, and is reached by road via a spectacular 2.5km ascent from Vame. Facing Amedzofe, Mount Gemi is one of the highest mountains in the country, and easily picked out by the 4m tall cross that was erected on its grassy peak in the 1930s by German missionaries – there is a bizarre local legend that the cross doubled as a communication device in World War II!

Tourism in Amedzofe has been formalised under the auspices of the Amedzofe Planning and Tourism Council. All visitors must report to the tourism office to pay a tax of US$2 per person and to arrange guided walks at a small fee. A good target for a short walk is Amedzofe Falls, 45 minutes from town following a dirt road and then a treacherously muddy footpath through lush forest to come out at the three knee-deep pools separating the upper and lower falls. More ambitiously, ask about visiting the valley at the base of the lower fall, said to harbour a population of black-and-white colobus monkeys. Another worthwhile local goal is the peak of Mount Gemi, 30 minutes' walk from town, which offers tremendous views as far as Lake Volta. The tourist office in Amedzofe also arranges guided walks further afield, for instance to Biakpa, Fume (on the main Ho–Hohoe road) and Tafi Atome.

Getting there and away

Amedzofe lies about 35km from Ho, and it is reached by a rough dirt road through Akome and Vame. The most dramatic stretch of this road is the 2.5km ascent from Vame to Amedzofe. Three vehicles plod back and forth between

AMEDZOFE
(SKETCH MAP)

Ho and Amedzofe throughout the day, with one leaving in either direction every hour or so, on average. Note, however, that the vehicles all start out from Amedzofe before 06.30, and the first one generally only gets back at around 10.00, so there's normally a transport lull between these hours. The trip takes slightly longer than an hour in each direction. There may be no transport at all on Sundays.

Heading northwards from Amedzofe towards Hohoe may look straightforward enough on a map, but the reality is complicated by the absence of public transport between Amedzofe and the junction town of Fume on the main Ho–Hohoe road. The simplest way around this is to walk, with the option of using the road directly connecting Amedzofe to Fume, or else taking a Ho-bound vehicle as far as Vame and using the road that connects Vame and Fume. In terms of distance, there's not much to choose between these routes – both of them are around 6–8km – but the Vame–Fume road is a lot flatter and it allows for an overnight stop at the wonderful government resthouse about 1km past Biakpa. The direct route passes through some good forest, but it is steep and slippery in parts and may be tough going with a heavy backpack on. When we first visited Amedzofe a few years ago, we found our way to Fume without any problem, but the tourist office in Amedzofe now recommends you take a guide on the pretext you might otherwise get lost. If you feel like taking a guide, all well and good; if not, don't let anybody coerce you – you'll be unlikely to take a wrong turn (from memory, there are none!) and will come across plenty of passers-by to confirm you're on the right track.

If you're heading to Hohoe and don't fancy walking, your options are either to catch a tro-tro back to Ho and change vehicles there, or to catch a Ho-bound vehicle as far as Akume, where you should be able to pick up some transport to Vame, 8km away on the main Ho–Hohoe road.

Where to stay and eat

The **Amedzofe Government Resthouse** consists of six large double rooms. All rooms have electricity and a private bathroom (there's an outside tap which has running water) and each pair shares a communal sitting room and balcony with views over the forest to Mount Gema and on a clear day to Lake Volta. Rooms cost US$5 double (1998 US$5 per person). They can be booked in advance at Room 24 in Ho Regional Headquarters, though there's little need to book as things stand. Note that the guesthouse isn't actually in town, but on top of the same hill as the large and conspicuous TV transmission tower; to get there, hop off the tro-tro at the junction just as you enter Amedzofe and follow the road signposted for the Ghana Broadcasting Corporation to your right and uphill for about 500m.

A cheaper place to stay is the **blue building opposite Corner House**, on the first junction after passing the turn-off to the government resthouse. A basic double room here costs US$2, using communal bucket showers. The tourist office also arrange **private home stays** for US$2 per person.

The **Vame Government Resthouse** lies on the outskirts of Vame, 2.5km from Amedzofe. It's not signposted, but is pretty much the first building you'll see as you enter Vame coming from Ho, and the dated architecture positively screams 'government resthouse'! The resthouse consists of four single rooms at a bargain US$1 each, all with electricity and fan, some with private bucket showers. The rooms can be booked through the District Headquarters in Ho, though you'd have to be extraordinarily unlucky to arrive and find they are all full. Also in Vame, you'll see several signposts for the **Sikakrom Holiday Resort**, which to the best of my knowledge has never been a functioning entity.

In Akome, about halfway along the road between Ho and Amedzofe, the **Gemini Guesthouse** looks to be a clean and inexpensive little place.

It used to be that very little food was available in Amedzofe, at least after sunset when the chop stalls around the market area close up, but these days you can arrange meals a few hours in advance through the tourist office. There are also a couple of bars next to the market; if you're luckier than us, then the one with the fridge and the one with the beer will be one and the same when you visit.

Biakpa

This remote village, about halfway along the 6.5km road connecting Vame and Fume, is the site of a blissfully isolated **Government Resthouse**, set on a grassy hill facing Mount Gemi and ringed by forest – a gorgeous, little-known spot that will appeal greatly to keen walkers and birdwatchers. Accommodation consists of two double rooms, each with a private dining and sitting room, for the princely sum of US$1.50 per person (1998 US$2.50). There's water for washing, and the friendly caretaker, a stalwart of more than two decades' service, can organise any food you like from the village (well, within reason), and he'll cook it too – but if you're going to take advantage of his services, then do leave him a decent tip. As things stand, this resthouse goes weeks without a visitor, but it might still be worth booking a room through the District Headquarters in Ho (a different entity to the Regional Headquarters).

There is no public transport to Biakpa, but it can be approached on foot either from Vame (near Amedzofe) or from Fume (on the Ho–Hohoe road). Whichever way you come, the walk will take about 45 minutes, and the guesthouse lies about 500m from Biakpa village, in the direction of Fume.

When we last passed through Biakpa, in late 2000, we noticed a locked and fenced-off enclosure called **Unity Gardens** next to the main road on the Fume side of town. We were told locally that this might be developed as a community resthouse or campsite by the end of 2001. I was unable to confirm this.

Logba Alekpeti

This small, bustling town on the main Ho–Hohoe road is of little inherent interest to tourists, but it has quite a strategic location, on the junction for Tafi Atome (5km to the west) and Logba Toto (7km to the east), and only 3km north of Fume (the turn-off for Amedzofe and Biakpa). Logba Alekpeti also boasts a very decent place to stay in the form of the recently opened **Adzotor Hotel**, where clean rooms with a fan cost US$3/4 single/double. A restaurant and bar are attached.

Logba Toto

Set on a steep forested slope facing Mount Gemi, the small and attractive town of Logba Tota is yet another site in eastern Ghana undergoing development as a community tourist project. The main local attraction, about 2km from town, is the Apkonu waterfall, which plunges into a pool where you can swim safely. The cliff above the waterfall is riddled with deep caves that house an impressive bat colony, and are studded with stalactites and stalagmites. A guided trip to the waterfall and caves can be arranged for around US$1 through a village elder called T K Bediako.

Coming in a private vehicle, the 7km turn-off to Logba Toto is signposted eastwards from Logba Alekpeti on the main Ho–Hohoe road. The dirt road initially follows a valley, and is reasonably flat. After about 3km, you'll come to a junction where you need to turn right – from here onwards the road is mostly surfaced, and very steep and winding. Occasional shared taxis run between Logba Alekpeti and Logba Toto, but you could be in for a long wait – it might be worth paying for the extra seats to effectively charter the vehicle.

There is no accommodation in Logba Toto at present, but a community-run guesthouse, currently under construction, is due to open in early 2001. For the meantime, the closest accommodation is in Logba Alekpeti.

Tafi Atome Monkey Sanctuary

Centred around the eponymous village, Tafi Atome Monkey Sanctuary was created in 1993 to protect the sacred monkeys that live in the surrounding forest. The story is that the ancestors of the modern villagers migrated to the area from Brong-Ahafo 200 years ago, and brought with them fetishes for monkeys and tortoises. For many years this taboo protected the monkeys, who were thought to act as spokesmen for the slower tortoises, but numbers had dwindled badly by the late 1980s, largely as a result of the erosion of traditional beliefs by Christianity. Since the creation of the sanctuary, the local monkey population has increased to about 300 monkeys, split across four troops. The habituated troop numbers about 65.

Under Peace Corps guidance, Tafi Atome has developed into the model of a multi-faceted community-based ecotourism project. Naturally enough, the monkeys form the centrepiece of tourist activities; a guided tour of the sanctuary costs US$1 per person for the guide, in addition to a US$1.50 entrance fee (discounted for volunteers and Ghanaians). The monkeys are generally most active before 08.00 and after 16.00, when they often descend to the ground and can be approached quite closely, which means you are most likely to have good sightings if you stay overnight.

Tafi Atome's importance in conservation terms is that it harbours the only Ghanaian population of the nominate race of mona monkey *Cercopithecus mona mona*, distinguished from the Lowe's mona (*C. m. loweii*) of Baobeng-Fiema by its two white hip discs. Given the confusion that surrounds the classification of the *cercopithecus* monkeys, it is possible that, as some authorities maintain, these two types of monkey should be treated as discrete species. At Tafi, you'll be told that their monkeys are the only 'true monas' in Ghana, which could come across as hype, but is perfectly true – though all it means is that *C. m. mona* was formally described before *C. m. loweii*, so that the latter is regarded as a race of the former.

Several other activities are available to visitors spending a night or two at Tafi Atome. These include a guided walk through the village, drumming lessons, forest walks, and an evening session of storytelling, and drumming and dancing – the latter particularly enjoyable judging by the visitors' book. The guides can also organise inexpensive bicycle hire to explore further afield. Worthwhile objectives, all of which are covered in greater detail elsewhere in this chapter, include the *kente*-weaving village of Tafi Abuipe, as well as Logba Tota and Amedzofe.

More generally, we were struck by the lack of hustle that characterises the village. Tafi Atome is a great place to spend a couple of inexpensive and interesting days – and all funds raised from tourism go towards developing the monkey sanctuary or to the development of community projects such as building a much-needed clinic and drilling boreholes. If you are in Ghana at the right time, it's worth knowing that a fetish festival for the monkeys is held in Tafi Atome during the first or second week of February.

Getting there and away

Tafi Atome lies about 5km along a good dirt road that leaves the main Ho–Hohoe road at Logba Alekpeti. There is plenty of transport to the village on Logba's market day, which is on a five-day cycle. On other days, there is the occasional shared taxi from Logba Alekpeti, and the fare is so low that you could rent the whole vehicle for about US$1. Alternatively, you can walk out from Logba Alekpeti, an easy hour's trip along a flat road through lush scenery.

Where to stay and eat
A guesthouse consisting of two double rooms has been constructed for travellers. The building is thatched and unexpectedly cool, but facilities are limited to beds and nets (something you don't see too often in Ghana), and a clean communal ablution block with sit-down toilets and bucket showers. Accommodation in the guesthouse costs US$3 per person, while village accommodation (in a local family house) costs US$2 per person and camping US$1.50. Meals can be arranged for around US$1 per plate, and a couple of shops in the village sell warm minerals, beers and pure water.

Tafi Abuipe
This small village to the southwest of Tafi Atome is one of the major *kente*-weaving centres in Ghana. It is also arguably the nicest to visit, as most of the weavers work outdoors, which gives it a far more organic and aesthetically pleasing atmosphere than Bonwire and the other *kente* villages in Ashanti. With the guidance of the people at Tafi Atome, Abuipe is well-organised to receive tourists, and once you pay the small entrance fee you are free to walk around and photograph as you like. Outside almost every house in the village you'll see a few weavers at work – they are amazingly quick and dextrous – and when we visited the hassle factor and pressure to buy was zero. Having said that, if you are thinking of buying *kente* cloth, Tafi Abuipe is one of the best places to do so – starting prices are almost half of what you'll be asked in Ashanti or Accra.

Getting there and away
From the main Ho–Hohoe road, the most direct route to Tafi Abuipe is via a 5km dirt road which branches westwards immediately to the south of Tafi Mado. In late 2000, this road was good for pedestrians only, since a bridge had collapsed, but I'm told the bridge will eventually be repaired. Once this happens, it could be that shared taxis run directly between Tafi Mado and Tafi Abuipe.

Tafi Abuipe can also be visited from Tafi Atome on foot or using a rented bicycle following a 7km footpath. By road, the distance between the villages is about 14km – follow the Kpandu road for 3–4km, turn left at the first junction, then left again at a small village about 7–8km further on, then continue straight ahead through the last junction, which you'll cross after another 1km or so.

Where to stay and eat
There is no accommodation in Tafi Abuipe at present, though tentative plans exist to build a small resthouse or organise village home-stays. The people at Tafi Atome are involved in promoting tourism to Tafi Abuipe, and should have current information.

KPANDU
This small town near the Lake Volta shore is of interest to travellers primarily as the one place on the eastern shore where you can board or disembark from the Lake Volta ferry, at least during the rainy season when the water level is sufficiently high. The town centre, set about 4km back from the lake, is notable for several turn-of-the-century German buildings, part of a mission

founded there in 1904. The lake port of Kpandu Torkor, connected to the town centre by a steady stream of shared taxis, hosts a bustling market selling not only fish, but all manner of cloths, garments and other foodstuffs. Reputedly even more impressive is the lakeshore market at Aveme Dzemeni, which lies about 10km south of Kpandu and takes place over three days from Monday to Wednesday.

If tourists are an infrequent sight in Kpandu District, the same cannot be said of the Virgin Mary, who evidently makes regular appearances! Two grottos have been established at places where she has been seen. The Catholic grotto, one of the largest in Africa and open to all, is situated on Agbenohoe Hill, a 300m-high inselberg set on the shore of Lake Volta about 8km north of town. The other, under the control of the Ghana Blue Urs (whoever they might be), is at Kpandu Aziavi, 2km south of town, and is again open to all.

Note that the 'K' in Kpandu (and in all other place names in this part of the country that begin with 'Kp') is silent – locals pronounce 'Kp' as a slightly more explosive 'P'.

Getting there and away

Kpandu is connected to Ho and Hohoe by regular tro-tros. For details of the Lake Volta ferry, which stops at Kpandu, see *Getting there and away* under Akosombo on page 218.

Where to stay and eat

So far as I'm aware, there are only two hotels in Kpandu, of which the **First Class Guesthouse**, off the road to the hospital, is clearly the better. Singles with a fan and one double bed cost US$3.50, while a twin with a fan costs US$4 and a s/c double with AC costs US$5.50 (1998 US$5 to US$7.50). The rooms in the main house can be noisy when there's music playing in the bar, so try for an outside room (though on our most recent stay, the blaring hi-fi of old appeared to have been usurped by a more subdued TV).

On the other side of town, the **Refco Hotel** is looking relatively run-down these days, but it is also good value with rooms ranging from US$2/3 for a single sharing bathroom facilities to US$3.50 for a s/c double with fan (1998 US$4–7).

Street food is plentiful along the main road between the Ghana Commercial Bank and the lorry station, and there are a couple of indifferent looking chop bars dotted around town. For a sit-down meal, accompanied by cheap, chilled draught beer, try the **Justice Club**, where in 1998 we had a very good plate of freshly cooked chicken and chips for US$2.50, served with a winning sense of ceremony. The Justice Club evidently doesn't serve food on Sundays, when the next best option is probably the **First Class Restaurant**, under the same management as the synonymous hotel.

HOHOE

Hohoe is the second most populous town in Volta Region, and much like the regional capital it is a decidedly amiable place, busy without being in any way intimidating and offering good amenities to budget travellers. Hohoe makes a useful base from where to explore several local beauty spots (the waterfalls at Agumatsa, Tsatsodo and Liate Wote are all feasible day trips) but it has no inherent qualities that might conceivably invite superlatives.

Getting there and away

Hohoe is connected by regular tro-tros to Ho, Kpandu, Wli and most other towns in the region. Travellers coming to Hohoe from Amedzofe should note that there is no direct transport: you will either have to take a tro-tro back to Ho and pick up a Hohoe-bound vehicle there, or else walk the 5–6km from Vame or Amedzofe to Fume on the main Ho–Hohoe road. Direct transport from Accra to Hohoe generally takes around 3–4 hours. The route is covered by STC buses, which aside from being safer are less often stopped at the ubiquitous police blocks.

Where to stay
Moderate

Note that all of the hotels listed below might in another context be placed in the budget category, but are listed here as moderate in lieu of any option that could truly be considered as tourist class accommodation. All are good value for money, even by Ghanaian standards.

Hotel de Mork PO Box 390, Hohoe; tel: 0935 2082.
This large new hotel is situated in Kpoeta, about 2km from the town centre along the Accra road. Comfortable s/c rooms with hot water and fan cost US$4.50, while large suites with AC, TV, fridge and fan cost US$9. A decent restaurant and bar are attached.

Taste Lodge PO Box 299, Hohoe; tel: 0935 2023.
The smartest hotel in central Hohoe, Taste Lodge is exceptionally good value, charging US$7 (1998 US$20) for a clean and pleasantly furnished s/c double with hot water, AC, fan, TV, radio and fridge. With only five rooms, it is not suitable for large groups. A reasonable restaurant is attached.

Matvin Hotel PO Box 397, Hohoe; tel: 0935 2134.
This was once Hohoe's most upmarket hotel, and it has the grounds to prove it, complete with a large landscaped garden bar overlooking the small Dayi River. With 26 rooms, the Matvin is also by far the largest hotel in Hohoe, and the only one with conference facilities. The rooms are comfortably shabby and very inexpensive: US$3 for a non-s/c room with double bed and fan, US$4 for a s/c double with AC and hot water, and US$8.50 for a suite with TV, AC, fridge and hot water (1998 US$5/10/18). The food is reasonable.

Budget

The **Pacific Guesthouse**, about ten minutes' walk from the tro-tro station via a dirt road through the fields, is a long-serving favourite with budget travellers. A single room with a double bed and fan costs US$3–4 depending on whether it is s/c or not (1998 US$6–9) while s/c chalets with AC and TV cost US$7.50 (1998 US$20). Facilities include running water, a bar and a cosy TV lounge. Breakfast is served but other meals are by special request only.

The newer **Geduld Hotel**, not far from the Pacific, is similar in price and standard, with rooms ranging in price from US$3.50 to US$7.50.

Even further out of town, at least 1km along the Wli road, the **Machill Hotel** is a decent little place where spotless s/c doubles with fan and running

HOHOE

Nkwanta, Bimbilla

Matvin Hotel

Presbyterian Church (1879)

Bar *Wli*

Barclays
$

Small market

Eagle Canteen

Grand Hotel

$ Bank of Ghana

Catholic church

Tanoa Gardens Bar

Hospital

Inatrip Chop shop

Prestige Bar

Lolonyo Chop shop

Sentimental Vein Bar

Post office

Telecom

African Unity Hotel

Lorry station

Shell   Police

← Accra

$ Ghana Commercial

Mobil   Shell

Hohoe District Assembly

+ AME

Taste Lodge

Internal Revenue

Pacific Guesthouse

Electricity station

N

Bradt

Geduld

0   500m
0   500 yds

water cost US$4 (1998 US$7). The absence of food and the distance from town will put off most backpackers, but it is a good choice if you have a vehicle.

Shoestring

Right in the town centre, opposite the prominent Bank of Ghana building, the **Grand Hotel** has a few shabby but very acceptable doubles with fan for US$3 (downstairs) or US$4.50 (upstairs). Showers are communal, and have running water. It's a good place to stay if you want to be close to the action: the atmospheric courtyard bar serves cheap draught beer and sensibly priced meals, and there are several more bars within a block if you hit a dull night. Fortunately, the noise from the bar doesn't penetrate through to the upstairs rooms to a significant degree. The **Africa Unity Hotel** is the only other option in the town centre, and slightly cheaper. It's often full – and one last minute report suggests it has closed – but close enough to the Grand Hotel that you could check it out first.

On the Nkwanta road, about 1km past the Matvin Hotel, the idiosyncratic **Palm Grove Resort** consists of a few small run-down s/c chalets set among the palm trees. There is a bar, and food is prepared to order. It's difficult to know whether to recommend this place or not – the double rooms aren't bad value at US$4, and the rather isolated setting might appeal to some, but I found the aura of disuse rather off-putting.

Where to eat

The restaurant at the **Taste Lodge** has the most varied menu in town, and most dishes cost less than US$3. It would be the definite first choice if you could eat outdoors, but as things stand the dining room is just too sweaty to be a very appealing place to spend an evening. Far better to head to the **Grand Hotel** or **Matvin Hotel**, both of which serve a fair variety of dishes for around US$3 and offer the choice of eating inside or out. For cheaper local dishes, the **Eagle Canteen** and **Inatrip Chop Bar** are recommended.

There are quite a number of good bars in the town centre. In addition to the Grand Hotel, the **Tanoa Gardens Bar** and **Golden Palace Bar** both have cheap chilled draught, and the latter might just serve the spiciest kebabs in Ghana. The **Prestige Bar** was very quiet when we visited, but it should liven up when it hosts live music – check the posters around town for the next date.

AROUND HOHOE
Agumatsa (Wli) Falls

The Agumatsa or Wli ('vlee') Falls, situated on the edge of the 3km^2 Agumatsa Wildlife Sanctuary near the village of Wli Agorviefe on the Togolese border, is perhaps the most popular tourist attraction in eastern Ghana. Despite being billed as the 'largest waterfall in West Africa', it is not especially voluminous, so I would tend to assume that it is the *highest* waterfall in the region. Odd, then, that nobody seems to agree on how high it actually is. A few metres discrepancy I could understand, but it's difficult to know what to make of local estimates that range from 20m via 60m and 1,800ft to 2km, especially when the only figure I can find in print is 400m (surely a reference to the altitude?). Short of leaping from the top myself with a tape measure attached to my waist, I can only guess, but I would imagine that it is in the region of 50–60m high. It is certainly the tallest single drop of water that we saw in Ghana.

As much of an attraction as the waterfall itself is the footpath from Wli village to its base. The flat, easy path leads through thick, semi-deciduous forest for 45 minutes to an hour, fording two rivers (one hot, the other cooler) a total of nine times – there are normally footbridges at all but the first crossing (the most shallow), though these were washed away in early 2000 and are under reconstruction at the time of writing. The sanctuary is thought to harbour some 220 bird and 400 butterfly species. The birding was disappointing when we visited, but the butterflies were dazzling, perhaps because we were walking during mid-morning. You're unlikely to see large mammals on the waterfall trail, though a small number of monkeys reportedly live deeper in the reserve. As you approach the waterfall, you'll hear the roar of plunging water vie with the high-pitched chirping of thousands upon thousands of straw-coloured fruit bats nesting on the adjacent cliffs – this must be an awesome sight towards dusk when the bats go out to forage. There's a large, rather shallow pool below the falls where you can take a refreshing dip, though the water is chillier than you might expect. If you spend the night at Wli, you could ask about the fetish shrine in nearby Wli Afegame.

Having visited the waterfall, a possibility for the fit and adventurous is to explore the network of caves close to the village of Likpe Todium, a village which lies along the main road back to Hohoe. If you want to do this, you must first visit the chief with a bottle of Schnapps, who will organise a guide. The walk to the caves takes about two hours in either direction, and is tough going in parts, though the steep slopes offer great views across to Togo. Some of the caves support large colonies of bats, while one contains the ancient stool of the first Likpe chief.

Note that in December 2000, two different travellers reported being told in Hohoe that Wli Falls was inaccessible due to flooding. Although there was extensive flooding in the area 18 months earlier, this story was nonsense spread by guides who wanted the travellers to do a different day trip with them.

Getting there and away

Regular tro-tros run along the 25km road between Hohoe and Wli. You're unlikely to wait more than 30 minutes for a vehicle and the trip out takes less than one hour. Once in Wli, the Department of Wildlife office, no more than 100m from where tro-tros stop, is where you pay the entrance fee of US$2 per person (proceeds are divided between the Wildlife Department and the community) and organise a mandatory guide (free of charge, but a tip would be in order). Note that the bridge at the Togolese border near Wli was washed away in 1999, so that the border is effectively closed except to pedestrians.

Where to stay and eat

Although most people visit Wli as a day trip out of Hohoe, the small **Falls Guesthouse** has two inexpensive rooms with toilet and shower. The owner of Chances Hotel in Ho intends to build a smarter eco-lodge here in 2001, with prices in the US$10–20 range. It is also permitted to camp at the base of the waterfall.

Tsatsudo Falls

This seasonal waterfall on the Tsatsudo River, near the village of Alavanyo Abeheanse, is very accessible to travellers. It is not as spectacular as the Wli

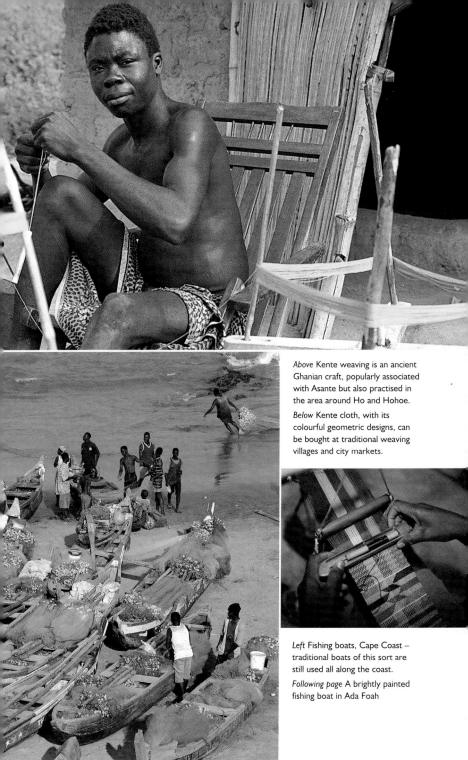

Above Kente weaving is an ancient Ghanaian craft, popularly associated with Asante but also practised in the area around Ho and Hohoe.

Below Kente cloth, with its colourful geometric designs, can be bought at traditional weaving villages and city markets.

Left Fishing boats, Cape Coast – traditional boats of this sort are still used all along the coast.

Following page A brightly painted fishing boat in Ada Foah

Falls, but is just as pretty, consisting of five separate falls, each separated from the one above and/or below by a rocky ledge. The pool at the base of the waterfall is deep enough to swim in properly, but do take care not to bump into one of the many large, submerged boulders. We climbed up a steep rock-face to the ledge separating the bottom fall from the one above, where you could also swim in a pool below a pretty overhang. The route we used to get up (and so far as we could tell the only way up) is not recommended unless you're reasonably agile and sure-footed, since there are a couple of spots where a slight slip would almost certainly lead to a broken limb or worse. So far as animal life goes, frogs seem to be particularly abundant and vociferous here, and the riverine vegetation and cliffs harbour quite a number of birds – we saw what appeared without binoculars to be a pair of auger buzzards and an African goshawk.

Alavanyo Abeheanse lies no more than 20km from Hohoe along a dirt road that branches from the main Ho road at Gibi Wegbe, about 7km from Hohoe. Regular tro-tros connect Hohoe to Abeheanse, which is the first of several villages making up Alavanyo. Before you head out to the waterfall, you must visit the chief and pay a fee of US$2 per head, which allows you to visit the falls as many times and for as long as you like. The waterfall lies about 1km from the village; if you have a vehicle, you can drive to within 50m of it. A guide isn't necessary to find the waterfall, but might be a good idea if you want to explore the higher pools. Overnight camping is permitted at no extra charge, assuming that you've paid your entrance fee. Note that there is no public transport along the road connecting Alavanyo directly to Kpandu.

Liati Wote
This pretty village lies near the Togolese border on the foothills of Mount Afedjato (aka Afadzato) which at 968m is the country's highest peak. Liati Wote is yet another part of eastern Ghana that has been developed for tourism in association with a Peace Corps volunteer, while Mount Afadjato itself has been protected within a community reserve since 1998. Regarded to be one of Ghana's key ornithological sites, the forested slopes of the mountain also host a high diversity of butterflies and relic populations of rare mammals such as the golden cat. The main attraction of Liati Wote is of course the mountain, which can be ascended over an hour or two, and offers great views as far as distant Lake Volta. Also worth visiting is the Tagbo Waterfall, which has a refreshing plunge pool at its base and is surrounded by semi-deciduous forest and is likely to be protected as a community reserve in the near future. The seasonal Tizor Falls also lie close to the village.

Getting there and away
To reach Liati Wote from Hohoe, drive south to Golokwati junction, then turn left at the signposted turn-off. After about 6km, turn left at Liati Agbonyra, then after 4km turn right at Liati Soba, from where it's another 4km to the village. Public transport between Hohoe and Liati Wote is limited to a couple of tro-tros daily, which leave Hohoe from Fodome station near the post office, generally between 12.00 and 14.00. There is also a lorry that leaves Liati Wote once daily between 07.00 and 08.00 and Hohoe daily in the late afternoon or evening.

FROM HOHOE TO TAMALE VIA BIMBILLA

The rough but scenic backcountry route between Hohoe and Tamale runs to the east and north of Lake Volta via the small towns of Nkwanta and Bimbilla. The trip breaks down into three legs, each of which normally takes one day to tackle. Roads are rough throughout: dusty in the dry season, muddy during the rains, and bumpy at all times. There is little point in attempting any leg on a Sunday, since there is even less transport than normal.

The 150km leg from Hohoe to Nkwanta is covered by at least one bus or tro-tro daily. These leave in the mid-morning in either direction, and take up to five hours depending on the current state of the road, which is surfaced for some distance out of Hohoe but deteriorates rapidly after that. The second leg, the 120km trip to Bimbilla, might entail changing vehicles at Kpaso and/or Damanko, and should take about five hours *excluding* delays caused by waiting for vehicles (which might well double the duration of the journey). The final 220km leg between Bimbilla and Tamale is covered by two buses daily in either direction; these leave in the early morning and early afternoon, and take around five hours with a stop at Salaga (see page 304) on the Tamale–Yeji road. For travellers tackling this route in a southerly direction, a daily bus reportedly runs between Bimbilla and Accra, leaving Bimbilla at around 08.00 and taking only six hours to get to Hohoe (via Nkwanta). I've not heard of anybody catching this bus in a northerly direction – perhaps it's normally full when it passes through Hohoe, or possibly it only runs seasonally depending on the state of the road.

Nkwanta is a small but lush town, noted for the colourful yam festival that takes place in November. The **Kilimanjaro Hotel** has been recommended by several travellers as clean and pleasant: a s/c double with a running shower and fan costs around US$3, though cheaper rooms are available, and the restaurant serves decent meals. Close to Nkwanta, the recently gazetted **Kyabobo Range National Park** borders Togo's Fazao Malfacassa National Park and protects habitats ranging from savannah to montane rainforest. Large mammals such as lion, leopard, buffalo, elephant and various antelopes and monkeys are present. Facilities are limited, but camping and guided hikes can be arranged at the Wildlife Department in Nkwanta. The park entrance lies 6km from Nkwanta and is best reached by taxi (expect to bargain hard!). Also of interest, **Shairi** lies at an altitude of 600m on the slopes of **Mount Dzebobo**, the country's second highest peak, only 15km from Nkwanta. Shairi, with a cool, misty climate unusual for Ghana, is known for a nearby waterfall, a fetish shrine, and its picturesque terraced houses.

Bimbilla has rather less going for it, but there's no way of avoiding an overnight stay. The only place to stay is the basic but friendly **Teacher's Hostel**, situated next to the Goil garage some 20 minutes' walk from the tro-tro station, which charges around US$2 for a double room using bucket showers. Reasonable meals are served at the restaurant at the Goil station.

HOHOE TO TAMALE
VIA NKWANTA

TAMALE
Vendi
Dagbon

0   50km
0   25 miles

NORTHERN
REGION

Bimbilla
Napayilli
Damanko

TOGO

Salaga
Kpasa

Makango
Veji

BRONG-AHAFO
REGION

Kumasi

VOLTA
REGION

Nkwanta
Shairi

Teachers
Hotel
Bar &
Restaurant

Bimbilla
(SKETCH MAP)

Goil
Vendi

N

Bradt

Salaga

Tro-tro station

Nkwanta

Bimbilla

Hotel
Kilimanjaro

Tro-tro
station

NKWANTA
SQUARE

Nkwanta
(SKETCH MAP)

Hohoe

Kete
Krachi

Breweniase

Lake
Volta

Jasikan

Bowiri
Lackham

EASTERN
REGION

Hohoe

Golakuati

Kpandu

Ho

Where to stay and eat

There is no formal accommodation in Liate Wote, though a few villagers now offer inexpensive home-stays with decent toilet facilities and mosquito nets. A resthouse is under construction and should be functioning during the lifespan of this edition. Meals can be arranged through local villagers, and cold drinks and snacks are available at **Stella's Inn**.

Lackham Lodge

This is a new multi-faceted community development centred on a 700 acre site called Bowiri Lackham, which straddles the tarred Jasikan road 22km north of Hohoe. Still in its infancy, the tourism aspect of the project is being developed with the assistance of a VSO volunteer, and it promises to open up a part of rural Ghana not currently visited by many tourists. The tourist centre currently consists of a large garden on the roadside, with two summer huts, an ablution block, and a bar. Camping is permitted at a small fee, and accommodation is likely to follow during the lifespan of this edition.

Among the places of interest to be visited in this area are Tepa Abotoase and Kwamikrom on Lake Volta, both of which are important fish markets and boat-building centres. In the hills above Bowiri Lackham, reached via the district capital of Jasikan, the towns of Bordador and Tetteman boast some interesting German architecture and reputedly can be used as the base from which to visit a little-known crater lake. Organised excursions to these places, as well as to a number of fetish shrines and waterfalls in Jasikan district, are likely to be established as tourism increases. As things stand, Lackham makes for an interesting trip, particularly for travellers heading northwards towards Nkwanta, but it should be understood that little exists in the way of prescribed tourist activities.

The regular tro-tros which run between Hohoe and Jasikan will drop visitors at the lodge (ask for Lackham). It is possible to pick up transport northwards from Jasikan to Nkwanta.

Part Five

Central Ghana

INTRODUCTION

This section covers the Ghanaian interior west of Lake Volta, north of Accra, and south of Tamale and Mole National Park. Culturally and geographically, it is a less than cohesive area, but it does tie together in travel terms, since it follows (with only a few diversions) the routes most likely to be taken by travellers heading north from the coast towards Kumasi or on to Tamale and/or Mole National Park.

Within the area described by this section, all roads seem to lead to Kumasi, Ghana's second largest city and the most important route focus inland of Accra. For this reason, the first chapter in the section covers the various route permutations between the coast and Kumasi, while the subsequent three chapters respectively describe Kumasi itself; the many attractions within day tripping distance of Kumasi; and finally the main route between Kumasi and the northern route focus of Tamale.

Readers should note that there is arguably far more to be seen within a 50km radius of Kumasi than there is along the roads that connect it to the coast or to Tamale. For this reason, many travellers bus directly between the coast and Kumasi, and between Kumasi and Tamale. If time is a factor, it would be difficult to argue with this course of action, but for those with the time or inclination to explore off-the-beaten-track, areas such as the Kwahu Plateau to the east of the main Accra–Kumasi road, and the excellent monkey sanctuary at Baobeng–Fiema, offer an incentive to break up the intercity trips.

Between the Coast and Kumasi

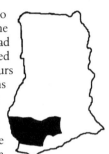

Three main routes link the coast to Kumasi, with little to choose between them, except for how they fit in with the rest of your itinerary. The most popular is the 270km road between Accra and Kumasi, which follows good surfaced roads in its entirety, and can be covered in four to five hours on one of the STC buses that leave in both directions every hour. Less popular, but far shorter, is the 220km road connecting Cape Coast to Kumasi via Yamoransa, Foso and Bekwai, once again surfaced in its entirety and covered by regular buses over three to four hours. The final option is the 225km trip from Takoradi–Sekondi via Tarkwa and Obuasi, which can be covered either by overnight train or by bus along good surfaced roads.

ACCRA TO KUMASI

This is another of the many trips in Ghana that could be done as easily in a few hours as over a week. Kumasi lies a mere four hours from Accra by direct STC bus, but there are a number of interesting sites along the way. In addition to the places listed below, it would be feasible to start your trip by travelling from Accra to Aburi and other places of interest covered in the chapter *Inland of Accra*, terminating at Koforidua, from where it is easy to pick up transport towards Kumasi.

Begoro

This small town lies at an altitude of around 500m on the Kwahu Plateau, the name given to the large area of elevated hilly country that lies between the main Koforidua–Kumasi road and Lake Volta. Rather off-the-beaten-track today, Begoro was chosen as the site of a pioneering Presbyterian Mission in 1875 (look for the arch near the Presbyterian church reading 'Presbyterian Boarding School 1885'), a decision influenced by its pleasant and relatively disease-free mid-altitude climate. Also worth a look is the Fanteakwa's Palace along the road between the tro-tro station and the Sweet Memories Hotel, easily distinguished by its colonial architecture and the large murals of musicians on the outer wall.

Of greater interest than the town itself, however, is the possibility of using it as a base from where to explore the surrounding countryside, which is great walking country notable for its varied birds and butterflies as well as many streams and waterfalls. An obvious target for day visitors would be the Begoro Falls, which lie less than 20 minutes' walk from town. The Begoro Falls drop

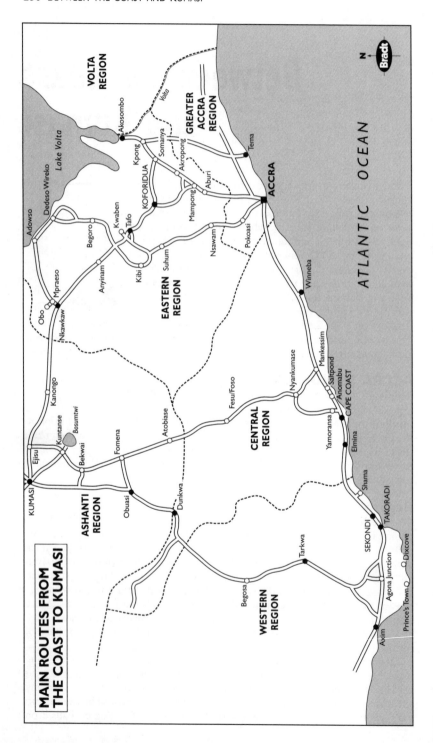

MAIN ROUTES FROM
THE COAST TO KUMASI

about 15m from a large overhang – not much more than a trickle when we visited in the dry season (though even then we were able to wade knee-deep into the muddy pool below the fall for a refreshing natural shower), but reportedly very impressive after the start of the rains.

Getting there and away

The junction town for Begoro is Osriem, which lies on the Kumasi road a few kilometres north of where the main surfaced roads from Accra and Koforidua merge. Begoro lies 20km east of Osriem, and coming from Accra your best bet is probably to hop on a bus bound for Kumasi or Nkawkaw and get off at Osriem, where regular shared taxis head up to Begoro. Coming from Koforidua, there are also direct tro-tros to Begoro.

To reach Begoro Falls, follow the road leading uphill to your left as you enter the tro-tro station. After about 100m, where a storm drain crosses the road, turn right and uphill towards the Presbyterian church, then after another 50m, just before the church, turn left and follow this road for a few metres until you reach a football field. Immediately before the football field, turn right on to the footpath that runs parallel to it before leaving town to descend into a valley. After about ten minutes' walking downhill, you'll reach the river just below the waterfall.

An interesting – albeit very off-the-beaten-track – onward option from Begoro would be to follow a rough back-road to Mpraeso via the shore of Lake Volta. This route, which crosses the Kwahu Plateau through Obooha then descends to Abuoso and follows Lake Volta northwest via Dodeso Wireko and Adowso, promises to be a scenic and rewarding excursion for those with time, patience, curiosity and a fair degree of tolerance for bumpy roads. Tro-tros connect Begoro to Obooha, and Obooha to Abuoso, where a small vehicle-ferry crosses a river mouth on Lake Volta at 14.00 daily (were you to arrive earlier or later, you could presumably hire a canoe to take you across – assuming, of course, that you don't have a vehicle). Irregular tro-tros continue from Abuoso to Nkawkaw, though you might have to change vehicles at Dedeso Wireko, Adowso and Mpraeso. Recent letters from readers suggest that this is not a trip to be undertaken by those who expect a high degree of certainty in their plans, and that for those with private transport it would be wise to check whether the ferry at Abuoso is currently operating.

Where to stay and eat

The only accommodation in Begoro is the aptly named **Sweet Memories Hotel**, which has cosy, clean, s/c rooms with fan for a couple of dollars, as well as friendly staff, and a very effective drinks fridge. For food, you'll find plenty of stalls selling kebabs, bush meat, fried yam and other goodies around the lorry station, all overlooked by the **Dorcas Restaurant**, which does chicken with rice or *fufu* for US$1.50 per plate.

Anyinam

It's difficult to imagine why any traveller would want to sleep over at this moderately sized town situated near the junction where the main roads from Koforidua and Accra to Kumasi converge. Should you be that unimaginable traveller, however, you'll be pleased to hear that there are at least two hotels to choose from. The inexpensive **Mcnsco Hotel**, painted bright blue, is to the left as you enter town from the Accra or Koforidua side, but there is also a newer, rather plush and apparently anonymous hotel right in the town centre, with rooftop bar and restaurant attached, as well as a supermarket.

Nkawkaw

This substantial, readily accessible, but rather scruffy town lies 104km from Kumasi on the main Accra road. Nkawkaw is of interest to travellers primarily as a springboard for visits to Mpraeso and Obo on the northern part of the Kwahu Plateau, but it does boast some memorable features, not least a main street that must rank close to being the most hectic and pedestrian-unfriendly in Ghana. Also noteworthy are the forested mountains rising to the northeast, and the preponderance of fading colonial-era buildings complete with red corrugated-iron roofs and balconies.

Getting there and away

There is plenty of transport to Nkawkaw from all directions. STC buses from Accra to Kumasi will drop you at Nkawkaw, assuming that you don't mind paying full fare to Kumasi.

Where to stay and eat

There's a good choice of budget accommodation in Nkawkaw. A particularly pleasant option is **Bertram's Hotel**, which lies about 500m from the main road, signposted just off the road to Mpraeso. A spacious room with double bed costs US$4, and facilities include clean communal bucket showers and a bar with a fridge. Another good bet, the **Top Way Hotel**, is also on the Mpraeso road, but closer to town, and has rooms with fans for US$2.50/5 single/double.

Plenty of street food is available along the main road through the town centre, but a more attractive option would be to walk out of town about 500m in the direction of Kumasi to the Goil garage. Just behind the garage is a reasonable restaurant with indoor and outdoor seating, serving local fare at around US$2 per plate as well as chilled beers. More fun, perhaps, is to nibble your way around the kiosks and shops that circle the STC parking lot just before the garage – everything from imported biscuits to Californian white wine, as well as the usual grilled chicken and kebabs and chilled sodas and beers, are on offer.

Mpraeso

A district administrative centre, Mpraeso is Nkawkaw's high-altitude twin, perched on top of the sandstone cliffs that lie immediately to the east of Nkawkaw and reached by a road as scenic as any in Ghana, a dramatic series of switchbacks up a jungle-clad slope. Like Begoro to the south, Mpraeso is of less interest in itself than it is for the attractive walking country of the Kwahu Plateau on which it lies.

A more appealing base from where to explore this area, however, is **Obo**, a quiet, small town ringed by forested hills and host to a decidedly odd mixture of dirty old colonial mansions and spanking new, brightly painted holiday homes complete with satellite aerials. It's an unusual town, one that might well appeal to photographers, and the surrounding hills offer some good walking and birding – any child will act as a guide should you want one.

Getting there and away

Regular passenger taxis run along the 10km road between Nkawkaw and Mpraeso. There are also regular passenger taxis between Mpraeso and Obo.

Where to stay and eat

There are three hotels in Mpraeso, all of them dumps. The **Osafa Kantanka Motel**, an unsignposted building next to the Goil garage 100m downhill from the tro-tro station, is the best bet, if only because it is a dump that prices itself accordingly. On paper, the s/c doubles with fan and running water probably sound good value at US$4, but then you haven't seen them. Next up is the **Riverside Hotel**, a bright pink, three-storey dump that might more accurately be called the Trickleside Hotel. Situated on the edge of town about 500m from the tro-tro station (ask anybody for directions), this place seems exceedingly optimistic in asking US$8 for a non-s/c double with no fan. Finally, there is the **Afoarima Hotel**, a dump with eyes that light up when a paleskin comes a-knocking – the rooms are absurdly overpriced at US$8.

Better to stay in Obo, where the **Obo Central Hotel**, basic but emphatically *not* a dump, is a friendly, family-run place with simple rooms for US$2.50. The bar serves chilled drinks, and although there is no formal restaurant, the management will prepare a meal given advance warning.

Bunso Arboretum

Located only 3km from the main road between Accra and Kumasi, the Bunso Arboretum lies in an area of beautiful rolling hills and is home to an extensive variety of plants, trees and herbs including the country's only Brazil nut trees. The arboretum was founded in the 19th century, and is today maintained as a research centre by Ghana's Plant Genetic Resources Centre, which is mandated to undertake the collection and conservation of plant genetic resources in Ghana. Neighbouring fields display identified crop plants, fruit trees and timber species that are either indigenous to Ghana, or which the Plant Genetic Resources Centre is attempting to introduce to the country or region.

The arboretum, which covers 16 hectares of land on a steep hill, has been designated for tourism development through the installation of a Peace Corps Volunteer at in late 2000. As developments progress, visitors will be able to take nature walks throughout the trails and learn more about the local uses for the identified trees, plants and herbs, admire the many species of birds and butterflies, or visit the neighbouring Cocoa College. Plans are in place to open a guesthouse on the premises of the Bunso Arboretum, but until these materialise the surrounding area currently offers many options for visitors in terms of guesthouses, and buying cold drinks and local food.

The Bunso Arboretum is located 3km east off the main Accra–Kumasi road along the Koforidua road. Local transport from Koforidua or the junction is available at any time of the day or early evening. The closest accommodation at present is in New Tafo, roughly 15km south of Bunso and 15km north of Koforidua. The smartest place to stay here is the **Cocoa Research Institute Guesthouse**, which offers AC rooms for about US$30 per night and prepares meals for its guests. Less expensive is the **Echo Guest House**, at around US$6 for a clean double in 2000, and which also serves meals and drinks on the premises.

CAPE COAST TO KUMASI

The shortest route between the coast and Kumasi is the surfaced road which branches from the main coastal highway at Yamoransa, about 1km west of Biriwa and 7km east of Cape Coast. Direct buses between Cape Coast and Kumasi take three to four hours. I'm not aware of any sightseeing along the way. At Yamoransa itself, **Sammy's Hillside Lodge** has decent rooms with a fan in the US$3–4 range, though it's difficult to conceive of any circumstance under which a tourist might want to stay here.

TAKORADI TO KUMASI

The port of Takoradi is connected to Kumasi by a popular overnight train service, which currently leaves in either direction at 20.30 and arrives at around 07.30 the following day, stopping at Tarkwa and Obuasi en route. Tickets can only be booked on the day of departure. Unless you are seriously strapped for cash or a hardened masochist, it's well worth paying the additional fare for a first class sleeper, which costs US$2 at the time of writing (1998 US$4). There are no longer daylight trains along this route.

Takoradi and Kumasi are also connected by a good surfaced road passing through Tarkwa, Begoro and Obuasi. STC and other buses run directly between Takoradi and Kumasi. It is also possible to cover the route in stages using the tro-tros that connect all the towns listed above. The lush scenery along the way is not without some appeal, but none of the towns on this road are regularly visited by tourists, nor do they boast much in the way of prescribed attractions.

Tarkwa

Set in the rainforest inland of Takoradi, this large town is the commercial and industrial hub of a region rich in gold, diamonds and manganese. Although infrequently visited by travellers, Tarkwa has unexpectedly good tourist facilities which cater mainly to local businessmen and the substantial contingent of expatriates who work at the various mines in the area. Lush surrounds and some interesting colonial architecture notwithstanding, it would be difficult to make much of a case for Tarkwa as a tourist attraction, though with advance notice it is possible to arrange tours of the gold mine at Prestea, 18km away, and the manganese works at Nsuta 6km from Tarkwa.

Should you find yourself in Tarkwa, one possible excursion is to the artificial lake at Tarkwa Banso, 45 minutes' walk (or a short tro-tro ride) from the town centre. The lake itself is nothing very special, but the walk there leads through some attractive green scenery, and a small local bar on the lakeshore is a pleasant place for a drink. A second lake lies another ten minutes walk from Tarkwa Banso – anybody will be able to direct you.

Getting there and away

Tarkwa lies about 90km from Takoradi by road; to get there you need to head westwards along the coastal road before turning right at a signposted junction a short distance past Agona. The surfaced road is in fair condition and can be covered in an hour in a private vehicle, or about 90 minutes by tro-tro. The road between Tarkwa and Kumasi via Obuasi is also surfaced and covered by regular buses and tro-tros. There are direct buses between Tarkwa and Accra,

Obuasi & Kumasi

Kandoh's Hotel (1km)

Peace

Hospital

Urban Council

BEGOSO

HOSPITAL

Get in Touch

Standard Chartered

Sag Food Joint

Police

Goil garage

OLD MARKET

Post office

Telecom

POST OFFICE

Barclays

Ghana Commercial

Cold Breezes spot

Tarkwa & Bongo

NZEMA LANE

Corner Bar

Catholic Church

School

TAKWA NABOSO

Lorry station

Railview Hotel

Forestry office

Football pitch

STATION

Railway station

Taxi station

Stadium

Golden Home Hotel

Astoria Bar

Shell

Forex bureau

Fire station

LAY OUT

Morning Light Hotel

ADOM LODGE

Market

LOW COST

STATION

N

Bradt

Adom Lodge

0   300m
0   300 yds

Desperadoes Bar & Restaurant

Takoradi & Accra

Lynka

TARKWA
(SKETCH MAP)

but they are rather slow, so far better to catch a local tro-tro between Takoradi and Tarkwa and use the hourly STC bus between Takoradi and Accra.

All trains between Kumasi and Takoradi stop at Tarkwa. Northbound trains arrive at around midnight, and southbound trains at around 04.30 in the morning. If you want to book a first-class sleeper out of Tarkwa, the station master will phone your reservation through to either Takoradi or Kumasi. Note that the passenger train service between Takoradi, Tarkwa and Accra was suspended when we visited Ghana in 1998 and 2000, though I understand that it was running for a period between our trips.

Where to stay
Moderate
Lynka Hotel PO Box 267, Tarkwa; tel: 0362 20412.
This is the only tourist-class hotel in Tarkwa, situated about 1km from the town centre along the bizarrely named Low Cost Road. Comfortable rooms with AC, hot water and satellite TV cost a negotiable US$30 (quoted in dollars). Facilities include a generator and private water supply, as well as a good restaurant.

Budget
A number of good budget hotels are dotted around Tarkwa. Definitely recommended is the **Morning Light Hotel** (tel: 0362 20355), which lies just off the Accra road about 500m from the railway and tro-tro station. Clean, carpeted double rooms, all s/c with AC, hot bath and TV, cost between US$8 and US$11. Breakfast is served, as are other meals by prior arrangement, but the dining room is rather cramped and stuffy.

Another reliable central option in this range is the **Get in Touch Hotel** (tel: 0362 20592), which has comfortable s/c rooms with AC and TV in the US$7–10 range. An attractive feature of this hotel is the rooftop bar and restaurant with views over the surrounding hills.

Comparatively overpriced at between US$9 and US$18 for a double room with AC and fan, the **Peace Hotel** (tel: 0362 20557) is also less conveniently located, on a dirt road behind the hospital. An attraction for some will be the disco, though this only functions at weekends.

Kandoh's Hotel (tel: 0362 20387) lies about 2km from the town centre in the suburb of Kwabedu. Well signposted, and on a shared taxi route, it is probably the best value of any budget or shoestring hotel in Tarkwa provided you don't mind the out-of-town location. Single rooms with a double bed and fan cost between US$3 and US$5 depending on whether they have TV (satellite) and are s/c, while twins with AC and TV cost US$7.50. There is a bar and restaurant.

Shoestring
The outstanding place in this range, set along a side-road near the market, is the **Golden Home Hotel** (tel: 0362 20583), which has a homely, friendly atmosphere and clean, comfortable rooms with fans for US$2.50 using communal showers and US$4 s/c.

Also close to the market, the **Adom Lodge Hotel** is a functional multi-storey block which lacks for character but has very reasonably priced accommodation. An ordinary double with fan costs US$3, a s/c double with fan costs US$4, and a s/c double with AC costs US$5.

The only other option in this range is the **Railview Hotel**, situated in the heart of the long-haul lorry station and directly opposite the railway station. While this location couldn't be more convenient for catching public transport, it is also very noisy. If that doesn't worry you, the rooms are adequate, and acceptable value at US$2.50/3.50 single/double with fan, or US$6.50 s/c double.

Where to eat
Culinary surprises don't come much better than **Desperadoes Tex-Mex Restaurant**, which serves a wide variety of excellent Mexican and Western dishes in the US$3–4 range. Under the same ownership as Ryan's Bar in Accra and Kumasi, Desperadoes is set in large green grounds along the Accra road, a short walk from the railway station. You can eat out on the patio or in the large pub-like restaurant. Draught beer and a wide range of spirits are served. It is open from 11.00 until midnight.

Just as good in its more low-key and affordable way is **Sag Food Joint** on a short side road opposite the Barclays Bank. In addition to serving a wide range of Western and Ghanaian dishes (pizzas, pastas, curries and seafood, mostly for less than US$2), this air-conditioned restaurant is a good place for breakfast, and stocks a selection of fresh snacks and imported fruit juice and chocolate.

Most of the hotels also have restaurants attached – the rooftop at the Get in Touch Hotel is perhaps the pick, at least in terms of atmosphere – and there are plenty of chop shops around the lorry station and market. For a night out, check whether the **Astoria Bar** next to the Golden Home Hotel is hosting any live music or other performances.

Begoso
Straddling the main tar road towards Obuasi, Begoso is a small, bustling market town set in a lushly forested area about 50km north of Tarkwa. I'm not aware of any particular tourist attractions around Begoso, but the surrounding countryside must have some potential for walking and birding well away from any beaten tourist trail. Any road transport between Tarkwa and Obuasi can

drop you in Begoso, where the **American House Hotel** offers s/c accommodation with AC for around US$5.

Obuasi

Situated some 85km south of Kumasi, Obuasi is Ghana's most important gold mining centre and the home of the Ashanti Goldfield Company. Despite an attractive setting in a valley ringed by verdant hills, Obuasi really couldn't have much less going for it aesthetically. It is, however, a good place to buy locally-produced gold jewellery, and interested visitors can be taken on a tour of the mine by prior arrangement (contact the public relations officer at 0582 494). There is also an attractive golf course behind the Catholic church. In Patakro, on the Kumasi road about 10km north of Obuasi, lies the most southerly of the extant 19th century *Obosomfies* (Ashanti shrine houses) and, in front of it, four statues of similar vintage.

Getting there and away

Obuasi is easy to reach, connected to Kumasi by regular minibus-taxis, and to Tarkwa and Takoradi by less frequent buses. All trains between Takoradi and Kumasi stop at the railway station.

Where to stay and eat

The best hotels in Obuasi are **Miners Lodge** (tel: 024 420386) and the **Coconut Grove Annex** (contact details as for Coconut Grove Lodge in Elmina), both of which fall into the two-star category and charge around US$50/60 single/double. Neither is very central.

A recommended budget hotel is the **Silence Hotel**, which lies no more than five minutes' walk from the lorry station via the market, and has a variety of double rooms with fans ranging in price from US$2.50 to US$5 depending on whether they are s/c and have a fridge. Cheaper still, **New Paradise Lodge** next to the lorry station is neither new nor conspicuously paradisical, but if run-down and seedy don't worry you, it is difficult to argue with a room rate of slightly more than US$1!

The Silence Hotel serves decent local grub, while the **Golf Restaurant**, next to the golf course, serves more Westernised dishes and is popular with expatriates working at the mines.

Kumasi

Ghana's second city, with a population exceeding one million, Kumasi is not only the modern capital of Ashanti Region, but has for three centuries served as royal capital of the Ashanti state. Tradition has it that the city was founded by the first Asantehene, Nana Osei Tutu, who relocated there from his former capital at Kwaman in 1695. Kumasi rapidly acquired the status of largest and most important city in the Ghanaian interior, and was the inland terminus of most of the major 18th-century slave-trading routes to the coast.

Accounts of early 19th-century visitors to Kumasi suggest it must once have been a spacious, attractive city of whitewashed buildings with steep thatched roofs. In the latter part of the century, however, Kumasi became the focus of hostilities between aspirant British colonists and the Ashanti. The old city was burnt to the ground by Sir Garnet Wolseley in 1873, resulting in the Anglo-Ashanti Peace Treaty of March 1874 and a period of prolonged infighting within the Ashanti state. Following the Yaa Asantewaa War of 1900–01, Kumasi (or Kumase as it was then spelt) was annexed to the British Gold Coast colony on January 1 1902.

Today, contrary to any expectations conjured up by the epithet 'Ancient Ashanti Capital', your first impression upon arriving in Kumasi, particularly if you disembark near Kejetia Circle, is less likely to be rustic traditionalism than daunting Third World urbanity. Kumasi is one of the most hectic cities I've visited in Africa, far busier than Accra, and the mood is emphatically modern: the surging throngs of humanity and constant traffic jams that emanate in every direction from the market and lorry station feel positively overwhelming if you arrive from the relatively provincial, traditionalist north of Ghana.

Still, Kumasi ranks in most people's books as one of Ghana's 'must-sees', and what it lacks in terms of old buildings – 'historical Kumasi' amounts to little more than the late 19th-century fort and the colonial-era buildings clustered in the city centre – it makes up for with a number of fascinating small museums (see *Exploring Kumasi* on page 268), and as the obvious base for any number of day or overnight trips detailed in the chapter *Greater Ashanti*.

GETTING THERE AND AWAY

The most reliable transport between Accra and Kumasi are the STC buses which leave in either direction every hour on the hour. In theory, seats must be pre-booked, and I've had a few reports from travellers who've had problems getting a seat on the day of departure, but in my experience, provided you're

KUMASI ORIENTATION

OKOMFO ANOKYE

Bonwire

Jofel Catering

Airport Circle

Airstrip

KOTOKO

ANTOA

ZONGO

EASTERN BY-PASS

ODUMASI

MAXWELL

Prempreh II
Assembly Hall

VAA ASANTEWAA

Justice
Hotel

Menka
Memorial
Hotel

Calvary
Church

The Dish

Accra, Ejisu,
Royal Basin Hotel

Buses for
Accra & Lake
Bosumtwi

MAXWELL

The Beat

HUDSON

Football
Stadium

SIXTH

Tourist
Cottage

VAA ASANTEWAA

ASOKWA

Stadium Hotel

Amissah Hotel

Freeman
Hotel

Noks
Hotel

Elf

N

Hotel de Texas

Ahodjo
Circle

Hotel
Georgia

Shell

Hotel la Belle

Timber
Gardens

0   2km
0   1 mile

Lake Bosumtwi

LAKE

at the STC station 15–30 minutes ahead of departure time, you'll normally be fine. The route used by the buses is via Nsawam, Suhum, Kibi and Nkawkaw, with a scheduled stop at Asiakwa's SOS Village, which has clean toilets and serves a range of inexpensive meals and snacks, as well as cold drinks. You can ask to disembark from the bus before Kumasi, but will have to pay the full US$3.50 fare. Depending on the traffic in Accra, the journey takes four to five hours.

In addition to the Accra service, two STC buses leave for Tamale daily, at 07.30 and 16.00, except on Sundays when only the morning bus runs. There are also direct STC buses connecting Kumasi to Takoradi and Cape Coast, leaving twice daily, and taking around three to four hours to reach Cape Coast and another one to two hours to Takoradi. There is no STC bus to Takoradi, but the buses run by Kingdom Transport Services are almost as good, and leave from a terminal on Odum Road a couple of hundred metres from the STC bus station. Kingdom also runs a daily service to Tamale, leaving at 17.00. It's advisable to book ahead over holidays.

Slower than the STC buses which cover the same route, but nevertheless a popular means of transport between the west coast and Kumasi, is the rail service from Takoradi, stopping at Tarkwa, Dunkwa and Obuasi. One train covers this route daily in either direction, an overnight sleeper that leaves in both directions at 20.30 and arrives at around 07.30 the next day. Tickets may be bought only on the day of departure, starting at 05.30. First-class sleeper tickets, for a two-berth compartment, cost around US$2 at the time of writing. The train is normally punctual and reasonably comfortable, but it's worth paying the slight extra to go first class. No meals are available, and the selection of food on sale at stations is limited, though the dining car does sell drinks and biscuits.

Regular tro-tros leave Kumasi in practically every direction. Tro-tros for destinations to the north and west generally leave from Kejetia station, which is situated below the synonymous traffic circle (the station is closed for renovations at the time of writing, forcing the buses and tro-tros to leave from the surrounding roads). Transport heading south and east – for instance to Accra, Lake Bosumtwi and Cape Coast – leave from Asafo station on Fuller Road.

For short trips out of Kumasi, you can waste a lot of time milling around the chaotic bus station (and more still in the constant traffic jams that surround it), for which reason I generally prefer to catch a shared taxi to a suitable junction and gamble on picking up a tro-tro there. For Ejisu, Effiduase and other destinations east of Accra, the corner of Fuller Road and the Accra Road is a good place to stand. For other destinations, try the appropriate circle on the ring road – Santasi Circle for Bekwai or Obuasi, Sunyani Road Roundabout for Owabi Wildlife Sanctuary, Suame Circle for Mampong etc. The risk attached to doing this is that everything that comes past will be full, but I've yet to wait more than five minutes for a vehicle to stop.

WHERE TO STAY

There are more than a hundred hotels and guesthouses scattered around Kumasi and its suburbs. The following listings represent a few reliable bets in each category, but new recommendations are welcomed.

Upmarket
Hotel Georgia PO Box 2240, Kumasi; tel: 051 24145/23915.
Situated off Ahodwo Roundabout, this multi-storey three-star monolith is
suitable for package groups, with more than 30 rooms, and it has reasonable
facilities including a large swimming pool and satellite TV. Unfortunately, the
hotel is somewhat lacking in atmosphere, and the decor feels slightly frayed at
an asking price of US$80 for a double room (quoted in US dollars).

Pink Panther Hotel PO Box 3142, Kumasi; tel: 051 31924; fax: 051 29296;
email: pinkotel@africaonline.com.
Set in large landscaped grounds in the suburb of Adiebra, outside the circle road,
the Pink Panther is a large new three-star hotel which, assuming you can live
without a swimming pool, easily matches the more established hotels in its range.
Facilities include a conference centre, international restaurant, jazz bar with live
music, business centre and satellite TV with in-house video. US$60 double.

Royal Basin Resort PO Box 537, Kumasi; tel: 051 60144/68; fax: 051 60169;
email: rbasin@africaonline.com.gh.
This top-notch three-star hotel, raved about by several readers of the first
edition, lies about 10km out of town along the Accra Road. Fifteen
comfortable AC rooms with satellite TV are complemented by excellent
facilities, including a swimming pool, gym and jazz club. Recommended.
US$55/75 single/double (quoted in dollars).

Moderate
Cedar Crescent Hotel PO Box 1451, Kumasi; tel: 051 27238; fax: 051
27239.
Situated in the quiet, leafy suburb of Ridge, off Cedar Avenue, this well-
managed and sensibly priced new hotel has large, attractively furnished rooms
with AC, satellite TV and mini-bar. A good restaurant is attached. US$25 for
standard double, US$28 for a suite.

La Vikus Hotel PO Box 4713, Kumasi; tel/fax: 051 22975.
Regularly recommended by readers, this is a very comfortable two-star hotel
with a couple of excellent restaurants on the property and 32 AC rooms in the
US$25–30 range. The only drawback is that it is situated at Santasi Circle,
some distance from the city centre.

Noks Hotel PO Box 8556, Kumasi; tel: 051 24438; fax: 051 24162.
Set in large, flowering gardens in a quiet suburb off Hudson Road, this two-
star hotel is one of the best deals in its range. Doubles with AC and satellite
TV cost US$20 (1998 US$45). A fair restaurant is attached.

Pine Executive Lodge PO Box 3456, Kumasi; tel: 051 26566; fax: 051 26103.
This very pleasant lodge lies on Pine Road, a short taxi drive from the city
centre. The huge rooms all have AC, fan, hot bath and satellite TV. Excellent
value at US$16 double.

Rose's Guesthouse PO Box 4176, Kumasi; tel: 051 24072; fax: 051 23500;
email: roses@ghana.com.

KUMASI CENTRE

Rose's has for years been consistently popular with relatively well-heeled travellers, and it remains probably the first choice in this category, as well as the best value for money. Situated on the Old Bekwai Road a short taxi ride from the city centre, it consists of 14 AC rooms with satellite TV, fridge and en-suite bath and toilet. The attached Ryan's Irish Pub is an excellent place to eat and drink. US$25 double (1998 US$37).

Budget

By far the most central option in the budget range is the **Hotel de Kingsway** (tel: 051 26228), diagonally opposite Vic Baboo's Café. Currently it seems excellent value: twins using communal bath cost US$5.50–6.50, while s/c doubles cost US$7.50 with fan and US$9 with AC. That said, the rooms are rather run-down and should rates once again start approaching the 1998 mark of US$25–35, you'd be well advised to give the Kingsway a miss.

Another very convenient budget option, and more inherently appealing than the Kingsway, is the **Justice Hotel** (tel: 051 22525), which lies along the Accra road close to a rank where you can easily pick up shared taxis and tro-tros into the city centre or out towards Ejisu. Ordinary non-s/c rooms with fan cost US$5.50–7 (1998 US$7–8), s/c rooms with fan cost US$7.50 (1998 US$11) and s/c rooms with AC cost US$9 (1998 US$17).

Several affordable hotels are clustered along Hudson Road, which runs from opposite the Justice Hotel south past the stadium and is covered by innumerable shared taxis. The smartest of these is the **Stadium Hotel** (tel: 051 23647; fax: 051 23731), where s/c singles with double bed and fan cost US$11 (1998 US$17) and double rooms with AC and TV cost US$18 (1998 US$30). A good restaurant is attached. Dropping in price, the **Hotel de Texas** has s/c doubles with fan for US$5 (1998 US$15) and with AC for US$8 (1998 US$20). Further down the same road, the **Hotel La Belle** (tel: 051 27934) seems particularly good value at US$9 (1998 US$15) for a s/c double with AC.

The management of **Vic Baboo's Café** currently have a few double rooms with AC available in a suburban house for around US$7 – ask at the café and they will run you out there. There is also some talk of Vic Baboo's taking over the top floor of the Hotel de Kingsway and converting it to a budget hotel aimed at backpackers. To check this out in advance, give them a ring at 051 28725/23606 or email mahesh@africaonline.com.gh.

Shoestring

Possibly the single most important backpacker crossroads in the Ghanaian interior, the **Presbyterian Guesthouse** ('The Presby' once you feel sufficiently familiar, tel: 051 23879) has been popular for years, as much as anything for the ambience of the ramshackle, double-storey, colonial building, with its wide, wooden balconies overlooking leafy grounds. It also has a great location, two minutes walk from the city centre, and around the corner from the STC bus station. A communal kitchen can be used by travellers for a nominal daily fee. On a good day – electricity, hot running water in the communal shower – the high-ceilinged rooms with fan are great value at US$3 double (1998 US$5). On a bad day – no electricity, cold bucket showers – the atmosphere and opportunity to meet other travellers just about compensates (except perhaps when you are forced to do your socialising in the morning queue outside that solitary communal bucket shower). There are smarter places, true, but when I think of some of the sweaty dumps I've spent US$10–20 to stay at elsewhere in Africa, I have to say that were every town I visited to boast one hotel as affordable, atmospheric and central as The Presby, I'd be a happier and wealthier person.

There are two other shoestring options in the city centre. First is the **Hotel Montana** (tel: 051 32389), tucked down an alley off Odum Road, where large, slightly scruffy rooms with a fan seem good value at around US$2 (1998 US$3.50), especially as the communal shower actually has running water. Closer to the central market and main lorry station, the clean **Nurom Inn Annexe** (tel: 051 32323) has acceptable rooms spanning the US$3–4 range (1998 US$4.50–6).

Less centrally, the **Menkah Memorial Hotel** on the Accra road is a serviceable and reasonably popular cheapie, with clean rooms in the US$4–5 range. A final recommendation in this range is the **Freeman Hotel** (tel: 051 24880) on Harper Road, which has a quiet location and very clean double rooms with fan for US$3 using communal showers and US$4.50 s/c.

WHERE TO EAT AND DRINK

The central and perennially popular **Vic Baboo's Café** has a menu that would take weeks to work through – burgers, pizzas, grills, curries, Chinese, vegetarian in the US$2–3 range – and we've yet to be disappointed. The restaurant is air-conditioned, with separate smoking and non-smoking areas, and it serves the usual range of chilled soft drinks and local beers. There is also an internet café on the first floor (see *Listings* opposite). It is open from 11.00 to 21.00 and closed on Sundays.

The **Windmill Bakery** off Prempreh II Circle has its aficionados, but the lunch and dinner menu is somewhat more varied than the actual selection of dishes. It is, however, a great place for breakfast, with toasted sandwiches providing welcome relief from the regime of omelettes and dry bread. It opens early, but is also closed on Sundays.

Another good central option is **Smart Fast Food** (confusingly also signposted as Golden Flower Fast Food) on Guggisburg Road, which serves the usual meat or chicken with fried rice or chips for less than US$2 per heaped plate. So far as I'm aware, this is the only sit-down restaurant in the city centre that opens on Sunday (though based on our last Sunday visit, you'll need a pretty high tolerance level for wailing cod-gospel music to want to spend much longer here than it takes to gulp down a meal).

Near Kejetia Circle, the **Kentish Restaurant** at the National Cultural Centre serves a selection of uncomplicated Western and Ghanaian dishes at reasonable prices indoors or in the fairly attractive garden. It's a good place to eat should you be planning on seeing one of the musical concerts or plays that are put on occasionally at the cultural centre. On the other side of Kejetia Circle, facing the chaotic lorry station, **Adesheman Gardens** is a contrastingly tranquil place to down a few draught beers, often with live musical accompaniment later in the evening. There's a good, but rather expensive, Chinese restaurant in the gardens (closed Sundays), and plenty of roast kebabs and other chop available in the vicinity.

The more upmarket restaurants are generally found away from the city centre. Most of the more expensive hotels do food. There are good Chinese restaurants in the **Hotel Georgia** and the **City Hotel**, but the long-standing **Chopsticks Restaurant** near Rose's Guest House is considered to be the best in town (interestingly, two different travellers we met on our most recent trip respectively rated the food as the best and the worst they had eaten in West Africa). For Indian food, try the excellent **Moti Mahal Restaurant** in the OAU Hotel. At most of these places you'll be looking at close to US$5–10 for a full meal.

Set in the grounds of Rose's Guesthouse, **Ryan's Irish Pub**, a relative of its namesake in Accra, provides a welcome change of scene if you've been hanging out in 'spots' for a while. The draught beer is sensibly priced, the stock of spirits estimable, and the grill-dominated meals in the US$4–5 range are excellent.

For uncomplicated boozing, **Timber Gardens** on the junction of Lake and Southern Bypass roads is a busy outdoor spot serving cold draught beer, spicy grilled kebabs and chicken, as well as more ordinary chop. The **Old Timer's Bar,** part of the Hotel de Kingsway, is one of the most pleasant drinking holes in the city centre – admittedly rather dead on weekdays, but usually thriving on Saturdays.

For those staying in the Hudson Road area, the **Dish Restaurant** on Sixth Street, 50m from the stadium, is recommended for its good selection of Chinese, Western and Ghanaian dishes in the US$2–3 range – you can eat on the terrace or in the air-conditioned lounge.

LISTINGS
Books and newspapers
A limited selection of second-hand novels can be bought for around US$1 at the stalls on Prempreh II Road close to Vic Baboo's Café, and at the Queensway Bookshop near the British Council. The British Council itself has a stack of fairly recent British newspapers in the air-conditioned reading room.

Cinema
The Rox Cinema on Maxwell Road, more or less opposite the Prempreh Assembly Hall, is open every day and puts on a diverse selection of African, Western, and Asian films.

Foreign exchange
Several forex bureaux can be found dotted around the city centre. Most accept cash only, and at the time of writing they offer a rate no better than the banks. The Standard Chartered Bank and Barclays Bank are situated opposite each other off Prempreh II Circle. Both exchange travellers' cheques without charging commission, but the Standard Chartered normally offers a considerably better rate. It might refuse to change more than US$200 per person in travellers' cheques on any given day. An ATM accepting international Visa cards can be found outside both banks.

Immigration
The visa extension service here is far quicker than in Accra: two or three days as compared with two weeks, and you may even be able to get it done overnight if you can persuade the immigration officers that it's urgent.

Internet

Several internet cafés are dotted around Kumasi. The service at Vic Baboo's Café is one of the best – quiet and air-conditioned! – and can be contacted at mahesh@africaonline.com.gh. Internet access is available at slightly higher rates at the British Council.

Nightlife

Among the livelier nightspots in Kumasi are the Zara Nightclub close to Kejetia Circle and the Foxtrap Nightclub next to the Prempreh Assembly Hall on Maxwell Road. The Old Timer's Bar below the Hotel de Kingsway is reliably lively on Saturday nights. The best place for live highlife music is the Jofel Restaurant near the Airport Roundabout – bands play here most Saturday nights, starting at around 19.00.

Supermarkets

Quite a number of reasonable supermarkets are to be found in the vicinity of Prempreh II Road. By far the most varied selection of groceries in Kumasi is available at the excellent A-Life Supermarket (between the STC and railway stations), which also serves ice-cream cones and other snacks on the veranda café.

Tourist office

The Ghana Tourist Board office in the National Cultural Centre is a useful source of current travel information, particularly if you want to head off the beaten track, and depending to some extent on who you end up speaking to. The office stocks a good map of Kumasi and surrounds.

Tours and guides

Registered local guides speaking most European languages can be arranged at a negotiable fee through the tourist office in the National Cultural Centre. Another good place to obtain a knowledgeable guide is Vic Baboo's Cafe, where you can also arrange local day tours using reliable taxi drivers. Most of the upmarket hotels offer day tours in private vehicles, albeit at a higher price.

EXPLORING KUMASI

The **National Cultural Centre** on Bantama Road, about five minutes' walk out of town from Kejetia Circle, is a good place to start your explorations of Ashanti. The helpful regional tourist office can be found here, and the staff are likely to be clued up on any new tourist developments in the region. There is also an excellent craft market in the cultural centre, recommended by several readers and uniformly regarded to be friendlier and cheaper than its counterpart in Accra.

Situated within the cultural centre, the **Prempreh II Jubilee Museum** offers a good overview of Ashanti history. The museum is named after the popular Asantehene, Nana Osei Agyeman Prempreh II, who ascended to the Golden Stool in May 1931 and reigned until his death almost 40 years later in 1970. Most of the artefacts in the museum relate to the reign of Prempreh II, a largely peaceful period during which the Ashanti Empire, shattered in several respects by the British colonists, re-established much of its former cultural cohesion. Several black-and-white photos are on display, most strikingly a vibrant portrait of the young Asantehene taken at his coronation. There are also a number of royal stools in the museum, one of which is said to be the fake Golden Stool that was handed to Lord Baden-Powell in an attempt to fool the British authorities in 1900, and a photo of the real Golden Stool, which last appeared in public at the enstoolment of the present Asantehene in 1999. Perhaps the most historically significant artefact in the museum is the royal cask which dates back 300 years to the rule of Nana Osei Tutu; contents unknown, since tradition holds that opening it would bring about the fall of Ashanti. The entrance fee of around US$1 covers an informative guided tour. Photography is forbidden.

About 500m further out of town along Bantama Road, situated behind Block C of the Okomfo Anokye Hospital on Bantama Circle, the **Okomfo Anokye Sword** has, according to tradition, been stuck in the same position in the ground for 300 years. The sword marks the spot where the Golden Stool initially descended from the sky, and – in common with the cask mentioned above – it is an important symbol of Ashanti unity. Legend has it that the state would collapse should it ever be pulled out of the ground. The sword is now housed in a small circular building, and a nominal entrance fee is charged to see it. The building is in theory open from 09.00 until 17.00 Monday to Saturday, and 09.00 until 14.00 on Sundays.

Walking back towards town, shortly before Kejetia Circle and lorry station, the **Kumasi Zoo** consists of a few depressingly cramped cages harbouring various primates (many are in solitary confinement, a fate as cruel to a chimp or a monkey as to a person) as well as a rather more aesthetically pleasing duiker-breeding scheme. Altogether more phenomenal than the inmates of the zoo are the thousands upon thousands of fruit bats that rest of their own volition in the trees. This is a quite incredible sight (not to say sound – they chatter away like demented mice), and worth the nominal entrance fee if you've never before seen a large bat colony.

Few people would spend time in Kumasi and not pay a visit to the vast, sprawling **Kejetia Market**, immediately southeast of Kejetia Circle. Reputedly the largest open market in West Africa, this has now been restored to its gloriously hectic former self after it was partially destroyed by fire in 1995. Incredibly, some 10,000 traders operate within the 12 hectare market – many more stalls spill out along the surrounding streets – and excellent overviews can be obtained from the tall building on its western edge. Once inside, the market takes on a labyrinthine aspect, confusing at first, but in fact quite orderly, clothing, textile and food stalls clustered in the west, pottery and metal in the northeast, and tailors in the southwest. Aside from the decidedly smelly part of the market where fish and meat are sold, this is a fascinating place, well worth dedicating an afternoon or morning to, and a great place to buy curios and crafts in an environment where tourists form a fraction of the clientele. Getting lost is part of the fun – the market isn't so large that you are likely to lose your bearings for long – and there is little cause for concern about hassle or theft, but many travellers prefer to explore the market with a local guide.

On Antoa Road, about 1km from the National Museum, **Manhyia Palace** was built in 1926 following the return from exile of Prempreh II's predecessor and uncle, Asantehene Nana Prempreh I. Surprisingly low-key, the palace remains in use today, and it houses a small but interesting history museum open from 09.00 until 12.00 and 14.00 until 17.00 on weekdays (entrance

US$1, photography predictably but for no apparent reason forbidden). The best time to visit the palace is between 10.30 and 13.00 on Adae festival days, which occur every sixth Sunday. The Adae is when the Asantehene receives homage from his subjects, as well as from subservient chiefs – a truly spectacular occasion, with a variety of traditional dress on show, great drumming displays, traditional horns blaring, and all the rest. The Adae dates for any given year are pinned up at the tourist office at the beginning of the year, but unfortunately cannot be predicted further in advance, as they are sometimes shifted or cancelled to accommodate other important events. Casual photography was forbidden under the previous Asantehene, at least without written permission, but it is evidently condoned by his successor Osei Tutu II, who ascended to the Golden Stool in 1999 – several tourists were snapping away when we attended the festival in late 2000.

Back in the centre, near Prempreh II Circle, is the **Kumasi Fort**, probably the oldest building in the city, though not as old as many of the traditional shrines in rural Ashanti. Some sources suggest – wholly inaccurately – that the foundation of the fort, and some of the walls, date to 1820, when Asantehene Osei Tutu Kwame decided to build a replica of the fort at Cape Coast. The fort as it stands today was completed in 1897 by the British using granite blocks transported to Kumasi from the coast. The fortress was surrounded in March 1900, during the so-called 'Ashanti Rebellion', and 29 Britons were trapped within its walls for several weeks before they were able to escape. The Queen Mother of Ejisu, Ohemaa Yaa Asantewaa, the prime initiator of the Ashanti Rebellion, was imprisoned here for a week before being exiled to Cape Coast and later the Seychelles, where she died. A well-maintained British Military Cemetery about 200 northwest of the fort contains the graves of British casualties of the Yaa Asantewaa War.

A highly informative guided tour of the fort, which now doubles as an **Armed Forces' Museum**, costs US$1 and is well worth the expenditure. The tour starts unpromisingly with a collection of weapons and the spoils from various campaigns in which the Gold Coast Regiment has been involved (I was surprised to see how heavily the Gold Coast Regiment had featured in booting the Italians out of Ethiopia during World War II). More interesting, in my opinion, are the many portraits of Ashanti notables (notably Yaa Asantewaa), the first African soldiers to be promoted to various ranks during colonial rule, and two of the World War II veterans who were killed when an anti-colonial protest outside Osu Castle in Accra was fired upon by colonial police. The tour gradually takes on several unexpected dimensions: a potted history of 20th-century conflict, as seen through the collected memorabilia of a relatively obscure African regiment, and, more tellingly, a cruel exposure of the minutiae of colonial arrogance which for many years forbade African soldiers in their regiments to wear shoes. The fort is closed on Sundays.

If you are interested in visiting a traditional **fetish priest** operating within suburban Kumasi, one who welcomes foreign visitors is Akwasi Anokye, who is named after Okomfe Anokye, the first priest of Ashanti. Akwasi lives in house DN24 in the suburb of Daban, and he is in session on Fridays and Sundays (though visits can be arranged with prior notice on other days). Although there is nothing preventing you from visiting the priest privately (don't forget to bring a bottle of Schnapps), his house may be difficult to locate without assistance – one of the guides at Vic Baboo's Café set up our visit.

A reader of the first edition met and bought a painting from one of Ghana's leading painters, Ato Delaquis, who heads the painting department at the Kumasi Art College, and encourages visitors with an interest in art to make contact with him (tel: 051 60329).

Further afield, Kumasi is the obvious base for numerous **day trips** and **overnight excursions** most of which are described in the next chapter *Greater Ashanti*.

BIA PROTECTED AREA

This isolated 305km² forest reserve lies on the Ivorian border west of Kumasi. Administratively, Bia falls into Western Region, and logistically it is remote from any other tourist attraction in Ghana, but since it is most easily visited as a round trip from Kumasi, I have chosen to include it in this chapter. Bia protects an important area of virgin rainforest, noted for its enormous biodiversity. In addition to trees reaching a height of 60m, the reserve harbours more than 80 mammal species, including forest elephant, bongo, forest buffalo, leopard, many duikers and giant forest hog. The ever-expanding bird list now stands in excess of 235, while 650 types of butterfly have been recorded.

Until recently, Bia was known to harbour all eight of the forest-associated higher primates that occur in Ghana ie: mona, diana and lesser spot-nosed monkeys; chimpanzee; white-naped mangabey; and black-and-white, olive, and red colobus. The red colobus is now thought to be extinct in Bia (it has been declared totally extinct in Ghana by primatologists in the USA) but it probably still occurs in the adjoining Krokosua Hills Forest Reserve, now thought to be the only rainforest in Ghana to harbour all eight of the aforementioned monkeys and apes. Krokosua is relatively inaccessible at present, partly due to the hilly terrain, but a large portion of the forest reserve has recently been declared a Globally Significant Biodiversity Area (GSBA) and its protection status is being increased. It may well be developed for tourism and research along the same lines as the Bia Protected Area at some point in the near future.

As with the more southerly Ankasa Protected Area (see page 181), Bia is currently undergoing a very exciting tourist development programme overseen by the PADP in Takoradi. Two camps have already been opened, a third is under construction, and a number of walking trails have been cut through the reserve. Getting here from Kumasi is straightforward on public transport, but it is a long and for the last part bumpy ride, and probably only worth doing if you intend to spend at least three (and better four) nights in the reserve – which is in any case the minimum duration you would need to do justice to the selection of trails and huts on offer.

One of the best walks at present is the Elephant Trail, three hours in each direction from Kunkumso or 40 minutes from Colobus Camp (see *Where to stay* below), which leads to a hide above the scenic Elephant Pool, a good place to see monkeys and birds (elephants are irregular visitors to the pool, and unlikely to be seen on a casual visit). Several more hides and observation posts are planned, along with more trails and possibly a road for game drives. A shorter (3km) loop walk from the guesthouse at Kunkumso takes you to the Apaso Rock, which offers spectacular views of the forest in an area teeming with bird life. The rock and its pools form a shrine for the local people, who believe it to be the home of spirits which exercise a great deal of power, assisting people to have good fortune, and helping barren women procreate. There is an annual yam festival in the honour of these spirits. Visitors are welcome, but are asked to respect the rules and conditions of visiting the rock.

For more details about developments at Bia, contact the Wildlife Department Headquarters in Accra.

Getting there and away

The main entrance to Bia lies at New Debiso (aka Kunkumso), about 240km west of Kumasi along a road which is surfaced for all but the last 94km. A couple of tro-tros run between Kumasi and Debiso daily, taking about seven hours, and passing through Bibiani (Ashanti Goldfields opencast mine), Sefwi Bekwai and Sefwi Wiawso (timber mills). From here the road is gravel and can be very bumpy in the wet season. About 2km past the market town of Asawinso you turn right at the police barrier and take the road to Debiso through the Krokosua Hills and the Village of Asempanye. The Bia National Park HQ is signposted on the left but the park entrance is at New Debiso 23km further on. New Debiso is situated at the top end of Bia National Park on a road junction. The northern road (straight ahead) goes to Debiso (5km) and the western road goes to the border. Both have customs barriers at New Debiso. The entrance gate to Bia National Park is about 20m past the left hand barrier on the left of the road to the border. (If you miss New Debiso, a taxi back there from Debiso takes about 15 minutes.) The Wildlife Department office in New Debiso will show you the nearby gate to Bia.

Where to stay

About 100m from the entrance gate lies **Kunkumso Guesthouse**, a one-storey cabin consisting of two double rooms with bedding provided, en-suite toilet and shower, electricity, and a shared kitchen and dining room with gas stove, pots, plates and cutlery. The current charge is US$15 per person per night. Visitors should bring all their own food. Camping is permitted next to the guesthouse at a fee of US$1 per person.

About 5km west of Kunkumso, **Chimps Camp** is a run-down residential patrol camp which is accessible by road (the last 200m can be exciting driving over a very rough track through a cocoa farm). There is no accommodation here at the moment, but one good house may be turned into a guesthouse in the future.

Deeper into the reserve, **Colobus Cabin** is a raised cabin in the forest, only 4.5km from Chimps Camp along a delightful forest path, or a 12.5km walk from Kunkumso through the forest via Apaso Rock. This has two rooms with double bunks and a front hall with covered veranda. Facilities include pit latrines, water from tanks, and a small gas-bottle kitchen. Once again, visitors should bring all the food and drink they require. The fee is currently US$10 per person.

The new **South Camp** was in an advanced state of construction in early 2001 and should be operational in April of that year. It will consist of two double rooms with kitchen and toilets with a veranda overlooking a waterhole. It is situated in the southern part of the Resource Reserve 25km along an old logging road. The area has plenty of elephant activity, beautiful forest pools and good walks for bird watching. The forest resounds nightly with the cries of the tree hyrax. Fees are the same as Colobus Cabin.

Greater Ashanti

THE ASHANTI KINGDOM

The Ashanti (also spelt 'Asante') are one of the few African peoples whose name is instantly familiar to many Westerners. Undoubtedly, this situation is in part a result of the unique role played by Ashanti in the pre-colonial and modern history of Ghana. No less, however, should it be recognised that the Ashanti owe their notoriety to the fact that, like, for instance, the Zulu or the Maasai, they were one of the few sub-Saharan African peoples to provide effective (if ultimately ineffectual) resistance against Britain's late-19th-century drive for colonialism.

The Ashanti Kingdom only started to take a recognisable modern shape under King Osei Tutu of the Oyoko clan in the dying years of the 17th century. What little is known about Ashanti history prior to this is fogged by myth. This is partly as a result of the ban, placed by Osei Tutu on his subject states, on passing down their own foundation legends to subsequent generations. Some oral traditions claim that the Ashanti people emerged from a hole in the ground near Lake Bosumtwi, others that they descended from the sky. More probable than either of the above scenarios is that the ancestral Ashanti, like other Akan peoples, migrated into modern Ghana from its ancient namesake in what is now Mali some time before the 13th century AD. It is likely that they had settled in their modern homeland north of the confluence of the Pra and Oda Rivers by the early 17th century. The Oyoko clan, generally seen as the true founders of the Ashanti Kingdom, lived in the vicinity of Lake Bosumtwi, an area they called Amanse ('Beginning of Nations'), where they built a capital called Asantemanso (from which the name Asante or Ashanti derives).

For much of the 17th century, the proto-Ashanti consisted of several loosely linked chieftaincies scattered through an area radiating some 30–50km around modern-day Kumasi. All the evidence suggests that the people of this region enjoyed an immensely high standard of living, as a result of the fertility of the soil and their strategic position at the conjunction of the main trade routes to the north and south. In these days, the area was noted particularly for its production of mildly narcotic kola nuts, exported via Salaga to the Muslim states of the Sahel and North Africa. The one thing that these chieftaincies lacked, however, was true political autonomy, since they were all essentially vassal states of the mighty Denkyira Empire, which retained control of the all-important gold trade to the coast throughout the 17th century.

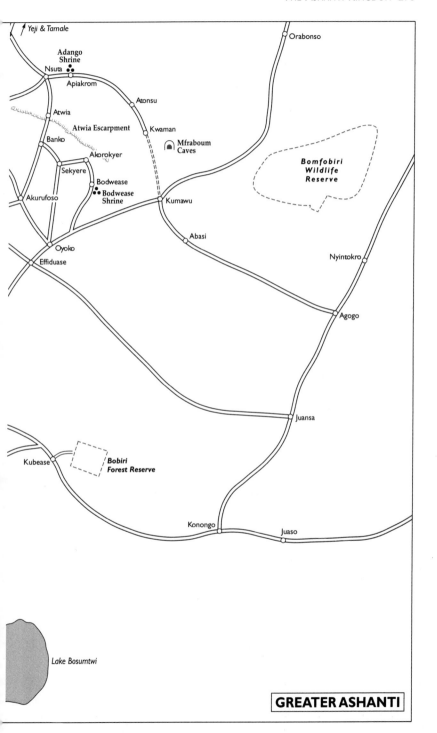

Yeji & Tamale

Orabonso

Adango
Shrine
Nsuta
Apiakrom

Atonsu

Atwia
Atwia Escarpment
Kwaman
Banko
Akorokyer
Sekyere
Bodwease
Bodwease
Shrine
Akurufoso
Kumawu

Mfraboum
Caves

Bomfobiri
Wildlife
Reserve

Abasi

Oyoko
Effiduase

Nyintokro

Agogo

Juansa

Kubease

Bobiri
Forest Reserve

Konongo
Juaso

Lake Bosumtwi

GREATER ASHANTI

The trend towards military unification in Ashanti is thought to have emerged under Oti Akentem, who ascended to the stool of Asantemanso in around 1650. It continued under his successor Obiri Yeboa, who moved his capital to the more central location of Kwamaan before being killed in battle in 1697. Obiri Yeboa's successor to the stool of Kwamaan was Osei Tutu, who with the help of the respected priest Okomfo Anokye would become the first true Asantehene (King of Ashanti), and who is still widely regarded as having been the greatest of Ashanti leaders.

In response to the death of his predecessor, Osei Tutu called upon the states of Juaben, Nsuta, Mampong, Bekwai and Kokofu to form a formal confederation with Kwaaman. Legend has it that when the chiefs of the six states assembled to discuss this union, the priest Okomfo Anokye summoned a golden stool from the sky to land in the lap of Osei Tutu, signifying that he should assume the role of paramount king of the new confederation. It is also claimed that the priest planted three palm (*kum*) trees in various parts of the union, and the first one to start growing was nominated as the site of the Ashanti capital, Kumasi (which means 'under the *kum* tree').

When the Denkyirahene (King of Denkyira) heard about the newly formed Ashanti confederation, he responded by increasing tax demands, and dictating that the union should be dissolved, that each of its chiefs should chop off a finger to send him, and that the Asantehene should hand over the golden stool. The chiefs of Ashanti decided to go to war with Denkyira, though Okomfo Anokye warned that the chief who led Ashanti to victory would not live for more than seven days after the battle, and he advised that Osei Tutu should remain in Kumasi. The Mamponhene (King of Mampong) volunteered to serve as general provided that his stool was made second to that of the Asantehene (the silver stool of Mampong is to this day regarded to be second in importance only to the golden stool of Kumasi). In 1701, the Denkyirahene was captured and beheaded at Feyiase, and his kingdom became the first subject by conquest of the Asantehene.

Using revolutionary military tactics, and fuelled by its growing importance in the emergent slave trade, Ashanti grew from strength to strength in the 18th century. Osei Tutu was killed by snipers while crossing the Pra river and, after a brief period of internal instability, his successor Opuku Ware (1720–50) pursued a policy of military expansion that resulted in most of the Akan states of southern Ghana being subject to Ashanti by 1740. In 1744, Accra was briefly captured by the Ashanti army, and later in the same decade much of what is now northern Ghana fell under Ashanti rule. By the time of Osei Bonsu (Asantehene from 1801 to 1824), the kingdom covered an area larger than that of modern Ghana, spilling over into parts of what are now Côte d'Ivoire, Togo and Burkina Faso.

The 19th-century decline of Ashanti is linked to the parallel decline in the trans-Atlantic slave trade, which lay at the heart of the kingdom's economy. It was more or less sealed in 1896 when Britain occupied Kumasi and deported the Asantehene and several other important dignitaries to the Seychelles. In 1900, led by the aged queen mother Yaa Asantewaa, the Ashanti made one last brave but ill-fated attempt to remove Britain from Kumasi Fort, with the net result that even more of its traditional leaders were deported and Ashanti was formally annexed to Britain's Gold Coast colony. However, while this may have resulted in the core states of the Ashanti confederation losing their autonomy, they have never lost their identity – Britain was practically forced to restore the Asantehene to his stool in 1924, and the King of Ashanti is regarded as being the second most important political figure in Ghana to this day.

It is one thing to sum up the history of the Ashanti, another altogether trying to come to grips with their cultural institutions, rather like asking a foreigner to sum up the British obsession with regionalism and class in a paragraph or two. Every Ashanti is a member of one of seven matrilineal 'families' as well as of his or her clan, and of a patrilineal spiritual group known as a *nton*. Like many African cultures, great emphasis is placed on communality and the subservience of the individual to the nation (as an example, until recent times all land was communal, the nominal property of the Asantehene), yet paradoxically the highest of all Ashanti goals is personal power (one classic Ashanti proverb translates thus: 'If power is up for sale, then sell your mother to obtain it – once you have the power there are several ways of getting her back!').

If you are interested in finding out more, I advise you to seek out one of several books written by Ghanaians and available for next to nothing in bookshops in Accra or Kumasi. Although many of these books are based in parts on dubious historical grounds, they still give much insight into the facts and vicarious truths of Ashanti legend. The most current book, and I suspect among the more credible, is Nana Otamakuro Adubofour's self-published *Asante: The Making of a Nation*, sold at the Palace Museum in Kumasi.

The lush countryside within a 50km radius of Kumasi is regarded to be the core region of Ashanti, since it is occupied by the various states that combined forces under the golden stool in the late 17th century. It is also a region that offers practically limitless opportunities for unstructured travel: not only Ashanti cultural sites such as the new Yaa Asantewaa Museum near Ejisu and a half dozen or so *Abosomfie* (19th-century fetish houses), but also several *kente*-weaving and other craft villages, and natural attractions such as Lake Bosumtwi (the country's largest natural body of water) and several pedestrian-friendly forest reserves.

Travellers generally explore the region using Kumasi as a base (of the places listed in this chapter, only Lake Bosumtwi is more often visited as an overnight excursion than a day trip), and the regional capital is certainly far better equipped than anywhere else in Ashanti when it comes to tourist facilities such as accommodation and restaurants. For those who prefer to get away from tourist hubs, however, a number of small towns might as easily be used as a base for exploring Ashanti, notably Ejisu, Effiduase and to a lesser extent Mampong, and it would also be possible to travel around whimsically staying overnight at wherever you happened to end up. One obvious advantage of steering clear of Kumasi is that it would eliminate the need to navigate the city's legendary traffic jams whenever you want to get out.

With the exception of Owabi and to a lesser extent Bosumtwi, you can travel between virtually any of the places listed in this chapter without returning to Kumasi, making use of the small tro-tros and shared taxis that connect just about any two villages in the area. Under the circumstances, and given that tastes and interests differ, I feel it would be restrictive to describe the places listed in this chapter in the form of a prescribed circuit, so I've chosen to follow them in roughly anti-clockwise sequence, starting with Owabi Wildlife Sanctuary and Lake Bosumtwi.

OWABI WILDLIFE SANCTUARY

One of Ghana's smallest conservations areas, covering a mere 13km², Owabi Wildlife Sanctuary was gazetted in 1971 to protect the chunk of pristine forest surrounding Owabi Reservoir, for many years Kumasi's sole source of drinking water. Crossed by several footpaths, the sanctuary harbours a great many varieties of butterfly, as well as 145 bird species – the raucous pied (or allied) hornbill is the most conspicuous of the forest birds, while the pygmy goose and purple heron can be seen on the reservoir. A fair number of large mammals are present: casual visitors stand a reasonable chance of glimpsing black-and-white colobus and mona monkey in the trees, but are unlikely to see more secretive terrestrial species such as bushpig, bushbuck or black and Maxwell's duiker.

Easily visited in conjunction with Owabi, **Asenemaso Traditional Shrine** is one of the most of unusual of the old fetish houses in Ashanti, since it consists of one large enclosed building rather than four semi-open rooms around a courtyard. Nevertheless, the murals here are excellent, and it is unique in having retained its original ceiling. Asenemaso lies along the Sunyani/Owabi road, 8km from Kumasi, and perhaps 200m past Akuakwa on the junction of the Bibiani Road (see *Where to stay*, below).

Getting there and away
Owabi lies roughly 16km from Kumasi and only 3km from the main Sunyani road. The turn-off to the sanctuary is at Akropong, which can be reached by a regular tro-tro service from Kejetia station. Most tro-tros going from Kumasi to Akropong continue along the Owabi turn-off as far as Esase, from where it's a ten-minute walk to the entrance to the reserve – you may even be lucky and get a lift with a waterworks vehicle. At the entrance gate, you'll have to pay the entrance and guide fees (visitors may not enter the forest without a guide), which shouldn't work out at more than US$2 per person.

Where to stay
There's no formal accommodation at Owabi, but for a small fee you can pitch a tent on the lawn between the entrance gate and the dam wall. The bar at the entrance sells chilled beers and soft drinks, and you shouldn't have a problem finding food in Akropong – it's a fairly large town with a couple of chop bars. Without a tent, it's easy enough to visit Owabi as a day trip from Kumasi. Otherwise, the closest accommodation is at Abuakwa, about 5km from Akropong back towards Kumasi, at the junction of the Kumasi and Bibiani Roads.

LAKE BOSUMTWI
Situated some 30km south of Kumasi in an almost circular crater, Lake Bosumtwi has a diameter of 10km, making it by far the most expansive natural freshwater body in Ghana. It is also the deepest, reaching a maximum depth of about 90m and rising, which has resulted in the submersion of several lakeshore villages within living memory. Debate about the origin of the crater in which Bosumtwi lies was settled by a recent geological study which confirmed it isn't volcanic but the result of a meteorite impact. The lake is a beautiful spot, encircled by raggedly mountainous, thickly vegetated crater walls that reach an altitude of greater than 600m. It also offers ample opportunities for walking, birding, fishing and canoeing. Boat trips around the lake can be arranged through the Paradise Resort or the village for around

US$5 per half hour, while a small passenger boat normally circumnavigates the lake every Sunday ferrying locals between the different lakeshore villages. Plenty of people swim in the lake; there is reputedly no bilharzia.

As you might expect, Lake Bosumtwi is held sacred by Ashanti traditionalists, though the finer details of its exalted status are rather elusive. Some claim that Bosumtwi is where a deity called Twi resides, others that it is visited by the souls of the departed on their passage to eternity. It is also the sacred water body of the Bosumtwi (one of five divisions in the patrilineal *nton* system which the Ashanti and other Akan peoples believe passes a father's attributes to his children), on account of it being as round as the sun, the model for members of the Bosumtwi *nton*. There is a taboo on the use of traditional pirogues on the lake; local fishermen get around by lying on customised tree trunks called *padua*, and using their hands as paddles. An important stone shrine is situated at Abrodwum, on the lakeshore about 1km south of Abono, where libation is poured at traditional festivals or when any bad omen concerning the lake is detected.

The normal base for visits to the lake is Abono, a pretty village on the northern shore, alongside which lies one of the most pleasant upmarket hotels in central Ghana. Picturesque as it may be, however, Abono does lack facilities suitable for budget travellers, and several readers have complained about the level of hassle. Certainly, if our most recent visit is representative, you're unlikely to spend long in the village without being approached by a plethora of prospective guides, children offering you accommodation, teenagers asking you to change foreign notes or coins into local currency, teenagers asking you whether you have any notes or coins from your own country to give them (spot the connection!), people offering you the opportunity to donate to spurious charities, and a persistent old fellow who evidently makes a living from persuading gullible tourists that the chief of Abono has nothing better to do with himself than wander around the village telling gullible tourists that he's the chief of Abono (and while they're about it some cash would be welcome...!).

Getting there and away

Direct tro-tros from Kumasi to Abono take no more than one hour, though you may have to wait a while for something to leave. The alternative is to take a tro-tro to Kuntanase, where you can pick up a shared taxi to Abono. Either way, all vehicles leaving Kumasi in this direction leave from Asafo station, and the total fare to Bosumtwi shouldn't exceed US$1.

Kuntanase can also be approached from Ejisu via a rather poor dirt road. There do seem to be shared taxis along this road, but they are rather infrequent – though cheap enough that you could consider paying the fare for any empty seats. A surfaced road and shared taxis connect Kuntanase to Bekwai via Kokofu.

Where to stay

The excellent upmarket **Lake Paradise Resort** (tel: 051 20164) lies immediately south of Abono across a small reed-lined bay. The resort, which opened in 1999, lies on a landscaped slope leading down to the beach, and has a good first-floor restaurant with a view over the water. Large doubles with AC and satellite television cost US$45.

ASHANTI TRADITIONAL SHRINES (ABOSOMFIE)

The recent renovation of Besease Traditional Shrine near Ejisu, some 20km east of Kumasi, has provided an overdue incentive for tourists to explore aspects of Ashanti tradition which are easily overlooked in the urban bustle of modern Kumasi. The shrine house at Besease, one of ten scattered around rural Ashanti, is a fine example of an *Obosomfie* (plural *Abosomfie*), a building which is traditionally regarded to be the spiritual abode of a particular *Obosom*, the name given to one of the lesser deities who mediate between mortals and the supreme god Nyame. The *Obosom* maintains a permanent presence in its shrine, but manifests itself only on set occasions through the medium of a fetish priest or *Okomfo*, who becomes possessed by the spirit and acts as its mouthpiece. Traditionally, the *Okomfo* is regarded to be the most important member of a community, and he or she works closely with the chief, who will call on the *Obosom* for advice before any important decision is made.

Over the last century, the importance of the fetish houses has diminished. Speak to many Christians in Ashanti, and they will dismiss their traditional beliefs as superstition, yet it is also the case, particularly in rural areas, that many Ashanti people adhere to both systems of faith concurrently. The ambiguities can be difficult for outsiders to come to grips with. At Bodwease Shrine, for instance, the last fetish priest has been dead for a decade, yet the shrine is immaculately maintained by the local community, who believe that the *Obosom* still lives in the shrine and will eventually settle on a human medium, who will be accepted as the new fetish priest by the community.

Most of the extant shrine houses are still inhabited by a fetish priest, who sits in session on specific days (typically Sunday and/or Friday) and is consulted by a stream of locals requiring spiritual advice. A fetish priest can be male or female, and although the role is occasionally hereditary, it can fall on anybody who is called to service by the resident *Obosom*. There are also many fetish priests in Ashanti who operate outside of a traditional shrine house. Tourists are generally welcome to any priest or shrine house, although they will be expected to offer a libation (a bottle of Schnapps or the money equivalent).

The ten 19th-century *Abosomfie* that remain were listed as UNESCO World Heritage Sites in 1980, not solely for their spiritual significance, but also because they form the only surviving examples of traditional Ashanti architecture. Not easy to imagine today, but Kumasi, prior to being razed by the British in 1874, was by all accounts an unusually beautiful city, the wide streets lined by airy houses of a unique architectural style. The typical house of the period consisted of several rooms centred around a quadrangular courtyard and shaded by steep thatched roofs, often rising at an angle of greater than sixty degrees. The lower walls were polished orange, while the upper walls were whitewashed. Another characteristic feature of 19th-century Ashanti homesteads were carved murals of symbols similar to those found on *adinkra* cloth. Much of what is known of pre-colonial Kumasi comes from the verbal accounts of European travellers such as Bowdich (1819) and Winniett (1884), but the handful of black-and-white photographs that survive do provide a visual record of what Kumasi must have looked like in its heyday.

The ten extant *Abosomfie*, some of which are said to be more than 200 years old, are typical pre-colonial Ashanti construction in general appearance, while also boasting certain features unique to fetish houses. With a couple of exceptions, the *Abosomfie* all conform to a ground plan of four rooms facing into a large courtyard. Three of these rooms – the drumming, singing and cooking rooms – are open on the courtyard side, while the fourth, which houses the actual shrine, is screened off and may only be entered by the priest and his assistants. In the courtyard of all the shrines stands a *Nyame Dua* – the altar to the supreme god, which generally consists of a pot wedged on a forked branch. Many of the shrines are littered with a variety of fetishes, most unexpectedly the tortoises which mill around the base of the *Nyame Dua* ('when they die, they don't need coffins, because they have their own...').

For the casual visitor, the most interesting of the traditional shrines is at Besease, about 1km from Ejisu (see *Ejisu & Surrounds* page 282). This is the only ancient building in Ashanti where the roof has been fully restored, and it also contains a number of informative displays. Besease is easily visited in conjunction with the Yaa Asantewaa Museum in Ejisu. Curious travellers who prefer to visit a shrine under less formal circumstances might want to seek out two further shrines in the immediate vicinity of Besease, at Edwenase and Aduko Jachie. There are also superb examples at Bodwease (see *Effiduase* page 289), Apiakrom (see *Mampong* page 291), Patakro (see *Obuasi* page 258) and Asenemaso (see *Owabi Wildlife Sanctuary* page 278).

With the exception of Besease, which to all intents and purposes functions as a museum, none of the fetish houses is formally established as a tourist site. In most cases, the shrines are held sacred by the surrounding community, and many are still occupied by a priest. No entrance fee is charged, but there is no way you enter a shrine without offering a libation in advance and/or a donation afterwards. The mood differed at every shrine house that I visited, and it might well differ from one day to the next at any given shrine, which makes it difficult to offer hard and fast advice. In hindsight, my feeling is that the best approach is to follow the local custom when visiting a chief or fetish priest, which is to offer a bottle of Schnapps as a libation (one bottle would be fine for two people visiting together). Having offered the customary libation, it would not be customary to make an additional cash payment, and I would ignore any hints in that direction (fair enough for them to play the 'customary libation' card, but then they can't have it both ways...). If you prefer to offer a donation, then a reasonable guideline would be the price of a bottle of Schnapps (check this in Kumasi) or the entrance fee to Besease Shrine (about US$1 per person at the time of writing). I was asked for further payments under various pretexts at a couple of the shrines, but when I explained that I was paying what I had been asked to visit Besease Shrine, this logic was accepted in good grace.

A lavish booklet entitled *Asante Traditional Buildings*, published by the Ghana Museums and Monument Board in 1999, and available at most museums in the country, as well as at Besease Traditional Shrine, is highly recommended to those with an interest in the local architecture.

For more affordable accommodation, the **Government Resthouse**, perched on the crater rim along the Abono–Kuntanase road, has s/c doubles with AC for US$15. The stunning views from the resthouse arguably outweigh the disadvantage of being some 5km away from Abono and the lakeshore by road (especially as there is a fair amount of traffic, and the distance is cut to little more than 1km by using a *very* steep footpath). Meals are available. There appears to be some ambiguity about whether advance booking is necessary: in practice, almost certainly not, but it might be worth playing safe and ringing 051 26263 to make a reservation.

The **Lake Bosumtwi Tourist Lodge** in Kuntanase is a clean, comfortable, friendly and very reasonably priced guesthouse: doubles with fans for US$3.50 using communal baths or US$7 s/c. The guesthouse lies in attractive grounds, and meals are served, but it has the drawback of being 13km from the lake, with no view whatsoever.

Paradise Resort aside, there is currently no formal accommodation in Abono. An anonymous and unfinished-looking concrete eyesore, situated between the village and the Paradise Resort, was functioning as a rather squalid budget hotel when we first visited in 1998. Since early 1999, however, it has been closed 'for renovations' – which showed no signs of being underway when we visited Abono in late 2000. If you can live without ventilation (and with the incessant chit-chat that characterises Abono), a couple of villagers rent out rooms at a negotiable US$4 – don't worry about finding them, they'll grab you almost as soon as you hop off the tro-tro. You could eat at the Paradise Resort, or at a couple of local chop shops.

EJISU AND SURROUNDS

The busy little junction town of Ejisu, which lies some 20km from Kumasi at the intersection of the Accra and Effiduase roads, is best known historically as the birthplace and home of Yaa Asantewaa, the Queen Mother who instigated the Ashanti siege of Kumasi Fort in 1900. Today, it is of interest to travellers as the site of a museum dedicated to its most famous daughter, as well as lying within striking distance of three of the region's most accessible *Abosomfie* shrines, all of which are described fully below. Although the Ejisu area can easily be explored as a day trip out of Kumasi, it boasts a couple of decent budget hotels, and could serve a useful base for exploring the Kumasi area.

Getting there and away

Ejisu straddles the main road connecting Kumasi to Accra, 20–30 minutes' drive from the regional capital in a private vehicle. It is also serviced by a constant stream of minibuses in both directions. Coming from central Kumasi, rather than head to the tro-tro station, the best place to pick up transport to Ejisu is at the circle west of the railway bridge at the intersection of Fuller Road and the Accra road (you're unlikely to wait more than five minutes for something to come past). Travellers staying at any hotel along or near the Accra road will easily pick up transport to Ejisu from any taxi stop along the eastbound side of the Accra road.

There are also regular minibus tro-tros connecting Ejisu to Effiduase – just wait at the junction. The taxi station opposite Yaa Asantewaa House is the place to pick up shared taxis to local destinations.

EJISU & SURROUNDS

Where to stay and eat

The **Ejisu Hotel** is a great little budget hotel, situated in the town centre, only 50m and signposted from the main Accra road. The large, clean s/c rooms with fan and running water cost US$3 (1998 US$5), making it one of the best deals in the region. Plenty of street food is available in Ejisu, while sit-down meals can be had at the **Amifas Restaurant**, which lies on the outskirts of town close to the Anglican church. There are also several bars in town.

About 1km from Ejisu towards Besease and Accra, the clearly signposted **Ashanti Art Gallery & Vernacular Travel Lodge** (tel: 027 874574) is a new place with a few comfortable, clean rooms on offer. These range in price from US$6.50 for a double room with a fan (using communal showers) to US$12 for a s/c double with AC. The art gallery is a good place to stop for a cold drink and some unpressurised curio shopping. One drawback of staying here is that no food is served, though you could always wander back to Ejisu for a meal.

Cultural sites around Ejisu
Yaa Asantewaa Museum

This new museum, which opened on August 3 2000 to commemorate the centenary of the Yaa Asantewaa War, is highly recommended to anybody with a passing interest in Ashanti history or culture. The building itself is worth the effort, faithfully constructed to mimic a 19th-century Ashanti chief's palace, with traditional *adinkra* murals on the walls and a steeply angled thatched roof. The nominal admission fee includes an informative guided tour through a series of rooms containing artefacts that either belonged to Yaa Asantewaa (jewellery, bedpan, pots) or else date from her time (war drums, stools, bedding).

The museum lies about 1.5km from the main Accra road. A taxi from Ejisu to the museum costs next to nothing. Alternatively, you can walk – follow the Kuntanase road out of town across the railway tracks, passing the Cocoa Board buildings to your left, and after the first road, and you'll see the distinctive orange museum building to your right after about 500m.

A visit to the museum can be followed by one to the Yaa Asantewaa House in the town centre – not actually the house in which she lived, I'm told, but the one occupied by her ancestors, who generally welcome interested visitors.

Besease Traditional Shrine

The lovely shrine, fully restored in 1998, is the most accessible *Abosomfie* in the region, and regarded to be one of the most important. It has reputedly existed in some form for at least 300 years; the current building probably dates to around 1850 and is where Yaa Asantewaa consulted the spirits before leading the attack on the British fort in Kumasi. The shrine is still in active use today: the priestess, who was called by the spirit more than 30 years ago, lives right next door.

The restoration of Besease shrine – complete with traditionally thatched roof – means that it is the only authentic building in existence to give a clear idea of what much of Kumasi must have looked like in the late 19th century. Inside the shrine, a series of fascinating photographic displays help to place the shrine in its cultural and architectural context. All of which makes Besease the obvious first port of call among the region's *Abosomfie*, even if – as is so often the case – the transformation from cultural site to Cultural Site has arguably robbed it of some of its immediacy. For this reason, I would recommend that anybody with sufficient interest to visit Besease in the first place follows it up with an excursion to at least one *Obosomfie* that has not yet been formalised into a tourist attraction.

Entrance to the shrine costs around US$1; bring along a selection of notes that ensure you can pay whatever cedi sum might be asked for exactly. If gratuitous tipping isn't your thing, you might also think twice about taking up the offer to meet the priestess – a procedure which when we last visited entailed a cursory handshake, followed by a request for money and a turned-up nose when the amount we offered was deemed insufficient compensation for her efforts.

Besease lies about 2km past Ejisu along the main Accra road. The shrine lies about 500m south of the main road and is clearly signposted. If you don't feel like walking from Ejisu, a taxi will cost next to nothing, or you can wait for one of the regular minibus tro-tros that run along this stretch of road towards Konongo.

Atia Kusia Kwame Shrine
Situated in the small village of Edwenase (aka Dwenease), some 5km from Ejisu as the crow flies, this is one of the most elaborately decorated *Abosomfie* in Ashanti. The mural on the south-eastern outer wall is particularly impressive, depicting a male and a female figure, above which lies the famous relief of a crocodile that has been reproduced on the wall of the Prempreh II Museum in Kumasi and the Ashanti Art Gallery in Besease. The shrine, which dates to the early 19th century, is not particularly geared to receiving tourists, and there is no charge for looking at the outside walls. Should you want to take photographs, however, or to look at the unusually well-preserved interior, then bring along a bottle of Schnapps for the priest (who claims to be 95 years old and to have served here since his childhood).

To get to Edwenase by road, follow the Kuntanase road out of Ejisu. Shortly after you leave town, you'll pass the Yaa Asantewaa Museum to your right, then perhaps 1km further cross a bridge spanning the Oda River before passing through the small village of Domuaso. Roughly 5km out of Ejisu, you come to the small town of Omwe and a clearly signposted crossroad where you need to turn left (following the signpost for Accra). Edwenase lies a further 2km along this road, and the *Obosomfie* is clearly visible to your left as you enter the village. A private taxi here and back from Ejisu shouldn't cost more than US$2, or you could catch a shared taxi as far as Omwe and walk from there.

In the right frame of mind, a visit to Edwenase might be treated as a pretext for a gentle ramble through the characteristically verdant Ashanti countryside as much as a goal in its own right. The total walking distance is about 7km in either direction, on reasonably flat roads, which shouldn't take longer than 90 minutes to cover. Given that little or no public transport goes as far as Edwenase, best to take a taxi out should you want to walk in only one direction.

Aduko Jachie
Despite being situated no more than ten minutes' walk from the main Kumasi–Accra road, this elaborately decorated and well-maintained *Obosomfie*

KENTE AND ADINKRA CLOTH

Of all the crafts practised in West Africa, few are more readily identifiable with a particular country than **kente cloth** with Ghana. Strongly associated with the Ashanti, modern *kente* is characterised by intricately woven and richly colourful geometric designs, generally dominated by bold shades of yellow, green, blue, orange and red. However, in its earliest form, before the introduction of exotic fabrics and dyes through trade with the European castles of the coast, *kente* cloth was somewhat less kaleidoscopic, since white and navy blue were the only available dyes.

According to Ashanti tradition, *kente* design originated at Bonwire, the small village close to Kumasi which still serves as the one of the main centres of *kente* production in south-central Ghana. Five *kente* stools were proclaimed by the first King of Kumasi, of which only Bonwire and Adangomase remain active. The Ewe people of Volta Region, the country's other important centre of *kente* production, maintain that they were the first *kente* weavers, and that their techniques were adopted in Ashanti after some Ewe weavers were captured as slaves. While the Ewe claim has a certain ring of truth, the reality is that most people now associate *kente* cloth with Ashanti, where the skills of the finest weavers are to this day reserved for the use of royalty.

These days, much of the *kente* cloth you see on sale in Ghana is mass produced, and considered by experts to have little intrinsic merit. At Bonwire, Adangomase and Wonoo, however, almost every homestead includes a few traditional weavers, who work at looms of ancient design to produce top-quality cloth. Visitors to Volta Region may also like to visit traditional centres of the *kente* craft, such as Kpetoe, a small town on the main Ho–Aflao road, or the small village of Tafi Abuipe near Tafi Atome. The best example of *kente* weaving that you are likely to see in Ghana today is the century-old piece of cloth on display in the National Museum, formerly the property of one of the kings of Ashanti.

Adinkra cloth is popular in many Akan societies, but most strongly

sees very few tourists. The most interesting days to visit are Friday and Sunday, when the flamboyantly dreadlocked fetish priest is in session. Powdered and attired in a manner that vaguely resembles a mime artist, and armed with a limited range of ineptly executed conjuring tricks, the priest here manages to be both mildly intimidating and endearingly Chaplinesque at the same time. Questions of authenticity are bound to cross your mind in the face of all the staginess, but whatever else the act may be, it is not aimed primarily at tourists. On the contrary, many local people take the hammy performance seriously enough to pay what by Ghanaian standards are vast sums of money to have their ills cured by the possessed priest – and judging by the piles of 5000 cedi notes and Schnapps bottles lying around the altar when we visited, business is positively humming. Whether the experience is an exercise in total cynicism or a fascinating insight into African spirituality is difficult to say – but I don't for a moment think that it's tourists who are being ripped off here.

The junction for Aduko Jachie – to your left coming from Kumasi, and prominently signposted for 'Tikrem' – lies about 3km from Ejisu on the associated with the Ashanti. Like *kente* cloth, *adinkra* is generally worn by men in the form of a toga, but its use is reserved for funerals and other relatively sombre occasions rather than for celebrations, and *adinkra* symbolism takes the form of monochrome graphics as opposed to the colourful geometric abstractions of *kente*. Most contemporary *adinkra* cloth is made using a plain white calico textile which is then decorated with various ancient designs using calabash stamps and a dye obtained by boiling the bark of the badie tree, *Bridelia micranta*.

More than 60 different *adinkra* symbols are in use, each of them signifying a specific tradition or proverb. The most popular of these is the rather Chinese-looking *Gye Nyame*, symbolising the omnipotence of God, and is easily recognised since it is depicted on the 100 cedi banknote. Another popular symbol is *sankofa*, heart-shaped with two whirls inside, which has taken on a particular resonance in the post-independence era since it signifies the value of building on one's cultural roots. The *kuntinkantan* design of five interlocking circles depicts the value of pride in one's state or society over pride in oneself, while the *pempansie* (like two opposing figures of '3' linked by a concave bar) symbolises a chain and stresses the importance of each member of a society as part of the whole. While these and other traditional designs remain at the core of most *adinkra* designs, many modern craftsmen are prepared to experiment with variations reflecting the changing nature of Ghanaian society.

The origin of the *adinkra* dyeing technique is uncertain. It is thought to have been adopted by the Ashanti in around 1818, when King Osei Bonsu defeated the Gyaman, whose chief at the time was called Adinkra. Oral traditions differ as to whether the craft originated in the neighbouring territory of Denkyira or in the Jaman kingdom in what is now Côte d'Ivoire, both of which were vassal states of Ashanti during its early 19th-century peak. Today, the main centre of *adinkra* production is the village of Ntonso on the main Kumasi–Mampong road, where it is easy to arrange an informal guide to show you around.

Kumasi road. Any tro-tro heading between the towns will drop you there. Follow the dirt road towards Tikrem for about 1km until you reach Jachie village, and take the first road to your left. The shrine is enclosed within the third building to your right; don't forget to bring that bottle of Schnapps!

BOBIRI FOREST RESERVE

This 21km² pocket of near pristine forest, situated some 30km from Kumasi within walking distance of the main Accra road, has been used as a research site by the Forestry Research Institute of Ghana for some 50 years. The forest supports a rich fauna, most prolifically butterflies, of which nearly 400 different species have been recorded. It is also probably the best site in the region for forest birds, while a variety of monkeys – mona, white-nosed, green, and black-and-white colobus – are present in small numbers. Until recently, few travellers visited Bobiri due to a lack of affordable overnight accommodation, but that is set to change now that the resthouse has reduced its formerly absurd rates to encourage casual visitors.

Getting there and away

To reach the forest from Kumasi or Ejisu, ask any Konongo-bound minibus to drop you at Kubease, about 1km past Hwereso and perhaps 8km past Ejisu along the Accra road. The turn-off to the forest is clearly signposted, and it's a lovely 3km walk out. The first part of the road passes through lush, marshy vegetation, dotted with palms, and absolutely heaving with birds in the early morning (serious twitchers could spend a happy two hours along this stretch sorting out the myriad weavers, waxbills and bulbuls). The only place where you could go wrong here is at the fork 1km out of Kubease, where you ought to head to the right. About 500m past this fork, a signpost and abrupt change in vegetation and drop in temperature signal your entry to the forest proper, after which it's a straightforward 10–15-minute walk to the resthouse.

Where to stay and eat

The **Forestry Resthouse** is a great little place, set in a small clearing in the heart of the forest. Comfortable rooms using communal showers cost US$3/5 single/double, while s/c doubles cost US$7.50. Beers and soft drinks are normally available, and simple, inexpensive meals can be prepared with a few hours notice (all food is bought fresh from Kubease).

BONWIRE

The village of Bonwire is the best-known – and as a consequence the most touristy – of many *kente*-weaving villages dotted around rural Ashanti. According to local tradition, Bonwire was one of five original *kente* stools, which were founded by exiles from Denkyira who settled around Kumasi shortly after 1701, the year in which Denkyira was conquered by King Osei Tutu. Bonwire received royal patronage in the time of King Osei Tutu, and for centuries after the village's most skilful weavers were forbidden from selling cloth to anybody else without the express permission of the Ashanti king.

Bonwire is a good place to buy high-quality *kente* cloth – though rates are far cheaper and quality just as good at the nearby villages of Wonoo and Adangomase. Even if you're not buying, Bonwire makes for a good day trip from Kumasi. The village has a pleasantly relaxed atmosphere, some good examples of traditional Ashanti buildings, and it's no problem to watch the weavers at work. Many of the weavers work indoors or in an enclosed courtyard, so it's easier to find your way around with a guide, who will also be able to provide you with some insight into the various types of cloth and the symbolism of their patterns. Several guides are bound to approach you on arrival; they won't ask a fee but will expect a fair tip.

Getting there and away

Bonwire lies about 20km northeast of Kumasi, from where it can easily be visited as a self-standing day trip. Direct tro-tros leave Kumasi from Manhyia station, close to the synonymous palace, and take about 30 minutes in either direction. Should you be visiting Bonwire as part of more extended explorations, it might be useful to know that the village can also be reached along the (signposted) 3km dirt road that branches west from the Ejisu–Effiduase road a few kilometres south of Juaben. Note, too, that although no tro-tros run between Bonwire and its fellow *kente*-weaving village of Adangomase (see page 293), you could walk or hire a taxi between the two – they lie no more than 2km apart along a dirt road through Amape. Note that no accommodation is available in Bonwire.

EFFIDUASE AND SURROUNDS
Some 40km from Kumasi along a good, surfaced road through Ejisu, the relaxed market town of Effiduase forms a pleasant retreat into small-town Ashanti, away from the main roads and major tourist circuits. Local attractions include the fascinating Bodwease Shrine and scenic Atwia Escarpment, both of which lie to the north of Effiduase towards Nsuta, in an area offering some great off-the beaten-track walking possibilities. In addition to this, Effiduase is conveniently situated for exploring most other places listed in this chapter: the manic tro-tro station has good tro-tro and/or shared taxi links in every imaginable direction, while a couple of good budget hotels lie on the outskirts of town.

Getting there and away
There are direct tro-tros from Kumasi to Effiduase, but it's just as easy to pick up something going along the Accra road as far as Ejisu and to change vehicles there. From the tro-tro station in Ejisu, you'll find shared taxis or minibuses heading to most local destinations, including Ejisu, Bodwease, Mampong, Nsuta and Bonwire.

Where to stay and eat
A couple of exceptional budget hotels lie on the outskirts of Effiduase. Firstly, about 500m from the lorry station, and signposted from the road towards Efface Secondary School, the **Panama Hotel** is a clean, friendly place with a bar and restaurant, running water, and rooms starting at US$2–4 non s/c with fan (1998 US$3–5), or US$4/5 for a s/c double/twin (1998 US$6/9). Another 500m along the same road, opposite the school, the **Lisp Hotel** is not quite as homely, but the rooms are even cheaper at US$3 (1998 US$5) for a large s/c double with fan.

Around Effiduase
Bodwease Shrine
This large shrine, set in the village of Bodwease, is as architecturally impressive as any *Abosomfie* I have seen, and it houses a marvellous collection of fetishes and other artefacts such as bead necklaces, a clay fertility doll, ancient drums, animal bones, and a couple of tortoises. Although the last priest here died some ten years ago, the spirit is still regarded to inhabit the shrine, and locals say that it will eventually select another priest to act as its medium. Until that happens, the gracious old lady who acts as caretaker is willing to show the occasional tourist around the 150-year-old building; she will expect a fair tip, but nothing absurd. Also worth a look is the neighbouring chief's palace, a twelve-room building which is plausibly claimed to be more than a century old. The chief wasn't around when I visited Bodwease, so I was only shown the outer rooms of the palace, but I'm told that he is happy to receive tourists provided they bring the customary bottle of Schnapps. To reach Bodwease, you must first follow the surfaced Kwaman road out of Effiduase for about 8km until you reach Akotusu,

where a dirt road to your left brings you to Bodwease after another 5–6km. Regular shared taxis connect Effiduase to Bodwease.

To Nsuta via the Atwia Escarpment

The winding, 20km dirt road used by tro-tros and shared taxis connecting Effiduase to Nsuta and Mampong passes through a scenic region of hilly jungle, bisected from east to west by the Atwia Escarpment. Studded with several peaks reaching 600m, as well as numerous remote small towns notable for their traditional Ashanti and colonial architecture, this area has much to offer keen hikers and birders. The 1:50,000 survey sheet 0602B1 (on sale for US$1 at the map office in Kumasi or Accra) shows several tracks and footpaths which link the villages at the base of the escarpment to those above it.

One alluring possibility, coming from Bodwease Shrine, would be to walk or catch a shared taxi 2km further north to Akorokyere. From here, you could follow a rough road along the base of the escarpment for about 5km west to Sekyere, then another 2km north to Banko, which lies on the road used by public transport between Effiduase and Nsuta.

Another interesting goal in the area, relatively accessible if you don t mind a bit of walking, is the Abesua (aka Abasua) Prayer Mountain, a tall part of the escarpment where people from all over Ghana come to take advantage of the mountain's prayer answering abilities. The mountain is also notable for the virgin forest of the Ongwam II Forest Reserve, home to many species of birds and small mammals, and for magnificent views of the forest and other scarps in the area. To reach the mountain, ask a shared taxi between Effiduase and Nsuta to drop you at Atwia Adutwam, the forest-fringed village after which the escarpment is named, and which lies near the base of its tallest peak. From here, a 2km walk takes you to the village of Abesua, right at the base of the mountain, where you will be able to organise a guide to lead you along the one-hour walking trail to the top. A twelve-room guesthouse is currently under construction in Abesua, but until such time as it opens the closest accommodation is 8km away at Nsuta (see *Mampong, Nsuta and Surrounds*, page 291). The mountain is easily visited as a day trip out of Effiduase, Nsuta or Mampong.

Bomfobiri Wildlife Sanctuary

Gazetted in 1975, the 53km^2 Bomfobiri Wildlife Sanctuary is centred around the seasonal waterfall on the Boumfoum River after which it is named. The sanctuary harbours a variety of forest mammals, including mona monkey, baboon, bushbuck, black duiker and all three West African crocodile species. A great many birds can be seen along the 2.5km path between the entrance and the waterfall, though it will require some luck to see the reserve's speciality, the bare-headed rock fowl. This is a strange-looking and highly localised bird, loosely related to the crow family, but placed in a monospecific genus unique to the rainforest belt of West Africa.

The entrance to Bomfobiri lies around 10–15km from the town of Kumawu along the Drabonso road. Kumawu itself is easy to reach on public transport, only 30 minutes from Effiduase along a good, surfaced road. Without private transport, getting from Kumawu to the entrance could be problematic. Or more accurately, you can get to the entrance with ease using one of the tro-tros to Drabonso that leave Kumawu every afternoon between 15.00 and 16.00. The difficulty is finding transport back, since vehicles returning to Kumawu from Drabonso are generally full when they come past the entrance. Short of walking back, the only viable option at present is to charter a taxi, which will cost around US$15–20 for a round day trip, and double that if you want to be taken out on one day and picked up a day or two later.

Before heading out to the sanctuary, you are obliged to visit the Department of Wildlife office in Kumawu, clearly signposted as you enter town from the direction of Effiduase. This is where you'll pay your entrance fee (US$2 per person) and collect a guide (US$1 per hour for a day trip, negotiable for an overnight trip). It is also the best place to seek current advice about accommodation and camping, and to organise a taxi charter to the sanctuary.

There is no formal accommodation in the area at present, either in the sanctuary or in Kumawu. In the meantime, travellers with a tent are free to camp within the sanctuary, and they may also pitch a tent outside the Department of Wildlife office in Kumawu the night before they leave for Bomfobiri.

MAMPONG, NSUTA AND SURROUNDS

The seat of Ashanti's second most important chieftaincy, the silver stool of the Mamponhene, Mampong is also one of the largest towns in the region, with a population well in excess of 20,000. It is a rather attractive place, notable for the steep ascent by which it is reached coming from Kumasi, but otherwise unremarkable, except perhaps for the great many fading colonial-era buildings in the compact town centre.

There's not a lot to be said about the smaller and quieter junction town of Nsuta, which lies no more than 10km south of Mampong, but it *is* passed through by all traffic heading to Mampong from Effiduase. Nsuta also offers the closest accommodation to local attractions such as the Atwia Escarpment and Adango Shrine, which makes it a marginally more useful base for exploration than Mampong itself.

Getting there and away

Mampong is connected to Kumasi by a good surfaced road and regular minibus tro-tros. It also has good transport links to Nsuta and Effiduase.

Where to stay and eat

There are two hotels in Mampong. The **Midway Hotel**, about 500m from the tro-tro station along the Kumasi road, has very ordinary rooms for US$2.50 (1998 US$5), using communal bucket showers. The relatively upmarket **Video City Hotel**, closer to the tro-tro station, is a conspicuous, bright-blue building attached to a cinema, with a courtyard centred around an empty pond dotted with traditional statues, and perhaps the driest bar in Ghana. Non-s/c doubles without a fan cost US$3.50 (1998 US$7.50), while nicer s/c doubles with running water and fan go for US$4.50 (1998 US$10).

The **Simple Stores Restaurant** on the main road between the tro-tro station and the Midway Hotel serves local meals and ice-cold drinks indoors or in a courtyard bar.

In Nsuta, the **Eldorado Hotel** has clean doubles with a ceiling fan and private bath for about US$3.50 per night. A bar and restaurant are attached.

Around Mampong
Mframaboum Caves

These can be reached from Mampong by catching a shared taxi to Kwamang (possibly changing vehicles at Nsuta) where the chief can organise a guide. The caves lie two hours from Kwamang on foot, with the last stretch being rather tough – with luck you'll be offered lunch and liquid at a cocoa farm near the caves. There is nowhere to stay in Kwamang, though vague plans to build a resthouse may be abetted by an increase in tourism. Note that Kwamang lies within sight of Kuwamu, but the gorge that separates the towns is passable only on foot, a 5–10km hike depending on who you believe.

Adango Shrine

This small *Abosomfie* in the village of Apiakrom is less architecturally interesting than others of its ilk, but it is studded with some impressive statues, notably a singular figure of a person lying on his back on the floor ('this is how you will lie when God punishes you'). The young fetish priest will show you a history of the shrine, written by his predecessor, in which it is claimed it was founded in 1799 by one Nana Akwasi Acheampong. The priest is a really friendly, straightforward guy, who didn't ask me for a libation and – uniquely – accepted my donation without quibbles or requests for extra payments. He is in session on Fridays and sometimes on Sundays, but you can visit the shrine at any time. To get there from Mampong (or for that matter from Effiduase), you must first catch a shared taxi to Nsuta. Apiakrom lies a short distance out of town along the Kwamaan road – any shared taxi heading to Kwaman will drop you there, but it only takes 15 minutes to walk.

NTONSO AND SURROUNDS

Straddling the main Kumasi–Mampong road, Ntonso is the major centre of *adinkra* cloth design and manufacture in Ashanti. This is the dyed, red-and-black cloth that you often see older Ghanaians wearing draped around them as a toga, especially on Saturdays, since it is the customary attire for funerals. It is not the cloth itself – either plain *kente* or imported cotton – that is made in Ntonso, but the dye stamps: it is possible to buy stamped cloth here, but also to buy the actual stamps. As is the case in Bonwire, the mood in Ntonso is welcoming and the pressure to buy is minimal. There are no organised guides as there are in Bonwire, but it is easy to find an articulate person to show you around and explain the complex symbolism that lies behind the various *adinkra* designs.

Ntonso is also the best springboard from which to visit the *kente*-weaving villages of **Adangomase** (aka Adanwomase) and **Wonoo**. Neither of these villages is as well-known as Bonwire, and both receive very few tourists, but the quality of cloth is just as good, the atmosphere is less pushy, and the prices at Wonoo in particular are considerably better (though not as good as in Kpetoe or Tafi Abuipe in Volta Region). Adangomase and Bonwire are reputedly the only two of the original five Ashanti *kente* stools to survive into the modern era, but Wonoo also has a long tradition of *kente* weaving. As with Bonwire, most of the weaving takes place in private courtyards, so you will need to ask somebody to show you around if you want to see the weavers at work.

South of Ntonso, on the outskirts of Kumasi, the villages of **Ahwiaa** and **Pankrona** are known respectively for their wood carvings and pottery. In both cases, however, you've little chance of seeing the craftsmen at work, and the level of aggro means that they're really only worth visiting if you plan to buy – in which case you can get just as good quality stuff at lower prices in Kumasi itself.

Getting there and away
Any tro-tro heading between Kumasi and Mampong will drop you at Ntonso (or for that matter at Ahwiaa or Pankrona). If you want to continue directly on to Adangomase or Wonoo, specify this, because the junction lies about 1km from Ntonso town centre in the direction of Mampong. There is a station at the junction from where reasonably regular shared taxis and minibuses head to both the *kente*-weaving villages. There are also shared taxis connecting Adangomase to Wonoo. Although no public transport runs between Adangomase and Bonwire, you can walk between the two villages in about half an hour along a little-used dirt road. Note that there is no accommodation in this area.

THROUGH ROUTES: KUMASI TO TAMALE

Wa

Tuna

Mole
National
Park

TAMALE

Sawla

Historical
mosque

Larabanga

Yepei

Damongo

Fufulsu

Damongo Junction

Bole

Historical
mosque

Buipe

Malume

Black Volta

Salaga

Historical
mosque

Bimbilla,
Nkwanta

Bui NP

Bui

Historical
mosque

Banda
Nkwanta

Makanga

Volta Lake

Yeji

Banda

Bamboi

New Longoro

Kintampo Falls

Mengyi

Kintampo

BRONG-AHAFO
REGION

Nsawkaw

Jema

Wenchi

Baobeng Fiema
Monkey Sanctuary

Adobom

Atebubu

Techiman

Nkoranza

Ejura

SUNYANI

Mampong

ASHANTI
REGION

KUMASI

N

0   100km
0   60 miles

Bradt

From Kumasi to Tamale

Most travellers heading northwards from Kumasi travel along the main north–south highway to Tamale, passing through Techiman and Kintampo (note that contrary to the impression created by many maps, the direct stretch of road between Kumasi and Techiman is in poor condition, so most drivers prefer to use the slightly longer but better road via Sunyani). This 400km trip takes about six hours by STC bus, the best way to go if you're doing it in one stretch. Alternatively, it can be broken up using a mixture of shared taxis and tro-tros. The most alluring diversion would be to visit the excellent and readily accessible Baobeng-Fiema Monkey Sanctuary near Nkoranza, though more adventurous travellers might be tempted to head out to the little-visited Bui National Park on the River Volta northwest of Wenchi.

It's worth noting that Mole National Park, covered in the next chapter, does in fact lie along a side road departing from the Kumasi–Tamale road at Fufulsu, on which basis it might reasonably be considered to belong in the present chapter. The reason it has been excluded is that the vast majority of travellers visit Mole on public transport, which is not a realistic option directly from Fufulsu, so that Mole is most often visited in the form of an excursion from Tamale.

SUNYANI

Capital of Brong-Ahafo Region since 1909, Sunyani lies at the heart of one of Ghana's main areas of cocoa and kola nut production. The name Sunyani derives from the Akan phrase *'ason ndwae'*, a reference to a time when the elephants that lived in the surrounding forest provided hunters with a rich source of income in the form of ivory. These days, there's not a great deal of virgin forest left in the region, and the elephants have long since been hunted out, but the substantial forest patch about 1km out of town along the same road as the **Providence Bar** might be worth investigating for birds, butterflies and possibly monkeys. Otherwise, Sunyani battles it out with Koforidua as the least compelling of Ghana's regional capitals, and there is little of interest to travellers in the immediate vicinity.

Getting there and away

Regular tro-tros run along the 130km road between Kumasi and Sunyani, taking about two hours either way. There is also plenty of transport between Sunyani and Wenchi, Techiman and Tamale.

Where to stay and eat

A good budget choice is the **Tata Hotel**, which lies about 1km from the town centre (a taxi there will cost less than US$1) and has large, spotless rooms with fans for US$3.50. Facing this is the similar **King George Hotel**, where rooms fall into the US$3–5 bracket. Unsignposted, on a roundabout a similar distance from the town centre, the smarter **Catering Resthouse** has s/c chalets for around US$20 and the food is rated by expatriates as the best in town.

Under the same management as the synonymous hotel, but some five minutes' walk away, the **Tata Restaurant** serves a variety of tasty, inexpensive local and Western dishes. It also wins the award for the ultimate African misspelling of the word 'spaghetti', in case you're wondering just what 'supergaity' might taste like!

WENCHI

This reasonably large town, linked by regular tro-tros to Sunyani and Techiman on the main Kumasi–Tamale road, is something of a local route focus, but mostly of interest to travellers as the springboard for visits to Bui National Park.

If you need to spend a night in Wenchi, the **Baah Hotel**, 100m from the bus station along the Wa road, has pleasant rooms with a double bed and fan for US$3 non-s/c or US$6 s/c, and the owner seems to keep himself up-to-date with the practicalities surrounding visits to Bui. The only other place we could find is the **Kaaf Hotel**, 200m along the Busia road, which has more basic rooms in the US$2–4 range.

There are no restaurants, but dozens of chop stalls serve inexpensive meals in the lorry station. The breezy **Rooftop Bar**, about 500m from the main traffic circle, serves cheap, ice-cold draught beer and on occasion presents live music.

BUI NATIONAL PARK

The little-visited Bui National Park near the Côte d'Ivoire border protects an area of 1,821km^2 on either side of the Black Volta River, including the large Bui Gorge, long mooted as the site of a possible hydro-electric scheme. Bui is best known for its population of roughly 200 hippos, the largest in Ghana, but it also protects small numbers of several terrestrial mammals, including roan antelope, hartebeest, waterbuck, kob, bushbuck, warthog and green and patas monkeys, most of which are unlikely to be seen by casual visitors. Crocodiles occur in the river, and several hundred bird species have been recorded. Tourist facilities at Bui are basic, but it's a perfectly feasible goal for backpackers, and inexpensive overnight camping and hiking trips can easily be organised through the flexible rangers at Bui Camp.

Bui was originally set aside as a national park with the long-term view of damming the stretch of the Volta that lies within it. There is some talk of this dam being constructed over the next couple of years, which might well improve access but will also presumably affect some of the wildlife populations.

Getting there and away

The park headquarters at Bui Camp lie 8km from the village of Banda and 2km from the village of Bui on the Black Volta. The best route to the camp is from Wenchi. One large tro-tro daily does the 85km run from Wenchi to Bui village via Bui Camp, leaving Bui at 05.30, arriving in Wenchi about three hours later, and starting the return trip any time after that. The tro-tro is normally only half-full when it passes Bui Camp, so you'll have no problem finding a seat when you leave. If for some reason you can't find direct transport to or from Bui, there are at least three tro-tros daily in either direction between Wenchi and Banda, from where it's a reasonably flat 8km walk to Bui Camp. What you shouldn't do is take a vehicle from Wenchi that's going only as far as Nsoko or Mengyi, since you may well get stuck and neither village has any accommodation.

The only alternative to the Wenchi route is the signposted side-road that leaves the main road to Bole and Wa from near Banda Nkwanta, the site of a well-known mosque (see page 336). Motorists should be warned, however, that the signpost at the junction, blithely proclaiming Bui Camp to be 50km away, omits to mention that the unbridged and unfordable Volta River lies about 2km before the camp! For those using public transport, this road is a more realistic possibility, but only on Mondays when a few tro-tros leave Banda Nkwanta for the riverbank opposite Bui in the early morning and start the return trip in mid-morning. Passengers can cross the river in a local canoe.

Bui Camp actually lies some 4km outside the national park boundary, so you'll need to arrange to walk there with a guide. Day walks into the park work out at around US$0.75 per hour guide fee, while overnight camping trips cost around US$2.50 per day, plus there is a US$1 entrance fee. The alternative to entering the park on foot would be to organise a canoe trip out of Bui village.

Where to stay and eat

One of the wooden chalets at Bui Camp is reserved for visitors. The facilities amount to little more than one bed with a foam mattress and no bedding, and a bath where you can take a bucket shower. There is no charge for using the chalet, but a donation will be expected. Camping is also permitted. You should be able to organise local food with the caretaker, and may even be able to buy a few sodas or beers, but it would be prudent to bring some provisions with you, especially if you have thoughts of an overnight foray deep into the park.

At present, the only possibility for those who enter the park overnight is to camp in their own tent. In the near future, however, it is likely that a few tree houses will be constructed next to some established hippo-viewing sites.

There is no accommodation in the villages of Banda, Bui or Banda Nkwanta.

TECHIMAN AND SURROUNDS

Techiman is a substantial and rather ancient junction town straddling the main Kumasi–Tamale road about 60km northeast of Sunyani. The long-standing capital of the Techiman-Bono Kingdom, claimed to have been the first of Ghana's centralised Akan states, Techiman is notable today for its sprawling food market – reputedly the largest of its kind in the country – and is passed through by the river Tono with its sacred fishes and crocodiles (the latter sometimes seen along the stretch of river through town).

For travellers, Techiman forms a significant route focus, and it has long served as the springboard for visits to the popular Baobeng-Fiema Monkey sanctuary (see below). The town is, however, in the process of being developed as a tourist centre in its own right. Two community-based tourist projects have recently started operating in the area – the Tano Sacred Grove and Buoyem Caves – and similar projects have been earmarked for the Kristo Boase Monastery (rocky scenery, occasional monkeys) and a Catholic grotto. A tourist office, which will provide information about local attractions and for elsewhere in northern Ghana, is scheduled to open close to the main traffic roundabout and the Classic FM radio station before August 2001. By this time, walking trails should have opened to all the above sites, along with one in Techiman along the Tono River.

Of the two sites already operating, the **Tano Sacred Grove** is the most accessible, situated at the village of Tanoboase on the main Techiman–Tamale road. It consists of an attractive cluster of sandstone rock formations, now formally protected within a community-run sanctuary, which lie at the source of the Tano River. The stretch of river protected within the sanctuary is believed to house the greatest of the Akan gods, known as Taakora. In addition to its spiritual significance, the sanctuary protects a variety of mammals and birds. Patas monkey and baboon had become very rare here in recent years, but seem to have multiplied in number since the sanctuary was created and a ranger station established. A trip to the grove can incorporate a cultural visit to the village of Baafi, and a hike to the top of a rocky escarpment, boasting a stunning lookout point used during the 18th-century Ashanti-Bono Wars. A fee of around US$1 is levied for a total hike of one to two hours.

The **Buoyem Caves** consist of three large caves, one of which harbours a huge colony of Rosetta fruit bats, situated in a sandstone canyon at the village of Buoyem. A variety of tours are offered by the local community, ranging from a straightforward climb to the caves, to a five-hour hike passing through the lush Mprisi rainforest. A hiking fee of around US$1 is levied. The Buoyem community is proud that the Buoyem Conservation Project is mentioned in the UN publication *Collection of Sustainable Development Success Stories* Vol 4, pages 40–2 (visit www.un.org/esa/sustdev/success.htm). A similar site exists at Oforikrom, 5km east of Techiman, and is also under development for tourism.

BUI IN 2000

The following account of a recent trip to Bui by Ben Clissold should be of interest to anybody following in his footsteps:

Bui was definitely the highlight of my time in Ghana, especially the canoe trip up the Black Volta. This cost around US$3 per boat for the whole day; the maximum number of people per boat is two, and you have to get the guide a boat as well, so it is an advantage if your group is odd numbered. They paddle you up river to see hippos, and even at the end of the dry season this was a pleasant trip, with only a few places were we had to get out and push the canoe. They also let us stop and swim which was lovely and refreshing. Accommodation was very basic and the two beds were so bad we all opted for the floor. We did have a minor midnight disturbance when a cockroach crawled on to one of the girls I was travelling with. There is a well but no other water. We got food cooked for us very cheaply. Transport from the village consists of one tro-tro at 05.00 daily back to Wenchi. You apparently can't get to the road north unless you go back to Wenchi.

Getting there and around

You'll have absolutely no problem finding a tro-tro or shared taxi to Techiman from Kumasi, Sunyani, Kintampo or Tamale. STC buses between Kumasi and Tamale/Bolgatanga pass through Techiman and stop on request, though you will have to pay the full fare.

Tanoboase is located along the Tamale road 7km north of Techiman. The two are connected by regular shared taxis. Once in Tanoboase, anybody will be able to point you to the sacred grove or the ranger station, which lie just outside of town along the dirt road leading east near the north end of town. Buoyem lies approximately 8km from Techiman, and can be reached in a private vehicle by following the Wenchi-road north, and turning right after about 1.5km at the Buoyem signboard, then continuing straight, passing through Mesidan en route. Public transport to Buoyem leaves Techiman from the Wenchi station on normal days, and from the main Kumasi/Market station on markets days (Wednesday, Thursday and Friday). There is no public transport, but a charter taxi should cost no more than US$2.

Where to stay and eat

Should you need somewhere to sleep in Techiman, your best bet is the **Agyeiwaa Memorial Hotel**, which offers a variety of rooms in the US$3–8 range (1998 US$6–15), centred around a shady garden bar, which serves reasonably priced meals and drinks. There are also a couple of cheaper guesthouses dotted around town.

Due to the convenient location, it is easy to visit Tano Sacred Grove as a day trip from Techiman. **Simple lodging** can, however, be provided in the nearby village of Baafi, for around US$1.50 per person including a meal and at least one cultural programme.

In Buoyem, the community-run **guesthouse** consists of two double bedrooms, a lounge, and a shared toilet and bath. There is electricity, and water is supplied daily. Each of the rooms costs US$2. Meals can be provided on request, or visitors can cook using the guesthouse facilities.

BAOBENG-FIEMA MONKEY SANCTUARY

This small sanctuary was created in 1974 to protect the monkey population of the 4km², dry, semi-deciduous forest centred around the villages of Baobeng and Fiema, which lie 1km apart in Nkoranza District. Two monkey species occur here in significant numbers, the mona monkey and black-and-white colobus, but there are also unsubstantiated reports of sightings of green, patas, spot-nosed and Diana monkeys in recent years. The mona monkey population is thought to stand at around 350 individuals, living in troops of 15–20 animals, several of which now have a territory in the forest fringe and adjacent woodland. The black-and-white colobus monkeys, with a population of 165 animals divided into 13 troops, are rarely seen outside the true forest.

The reason why significant monkey populations have survived here but not in most other parts of Ghana is that the inhabitants of both villages regard them as sacred. This tradition has been undermined somewhat in recent years by the rising influence of Christianity, for which reason it is now illegal to hunt monkeys within a 5km radius of either village. Oral tradition dates the monkey taboo to 1831, when the villages were founded, and a special festival is held to this day for the monkeys every November. So serious is the taboo that whenever a monkey dies it is given a formal burial and funeral service by the villagers.

As for how the taboo arose, one story is that Baobeng was founded by a Brong warrior who saw two mona and two black-and-white colobus monkeys guarding a piece of white calico, consulted his patron god, Daworoh, and was told that the monkeys would bring him good fortune. Another story is that Daworoh married Abodwo, the patron saint of Ashanti-founded Fiema, and that the monkeys are their offspring. Yet another tradition is that a former chief who had the ability to turn people into monkeys and back at will, something that was useful in battle, died before he was able to transform some 'monkeys' back into human form. According to this version of events, the colobus monkeys are men and the monas are women, and the two interbreed freely!

The main centre for monkey viewing is Baobeng village, ten minutes' walk from the resthouse, where an entrance fee of US$2.50 (most of which goes towards community projects) must be paid to the game scouts. The mona monkeys that scavenge from the village are particularly tame and they spend a great deal of time on the ground; it is highly rewarding to be able to watch these normally shy forest monkeys interact at such close quarters. The colobus monkeys are shyer and they stick to the trees, but you should easily get a clear view of them, and it's wonderful to see them leap between trees with their feathery white tails in tow. Although the village is the best place to see monkeys at close range, you can also do a guided walk along some of the 10km of footpaths that emanate from it; an opportunity to see some of the many birds and butterflies in the forest, as well as a giant mahogany tree thought to be more than 150 years old.

Getting there and away

The monkey sanctuary lies about 6km along a clearly signposted turn-off running eastwards from the dirt Nkoranza–Jema road. The springboard for visits is Techiman, from where you will need to take a shared taxi to Nkoranza about 25km to the east. From Nkoranza, you shouldn't have to wait too long for a shared taxi heading directly northwards to Fiema, another roughly 25km trip. Ask to be dropped at the resthouse, on the left side of the road about 1km before you enter Fiema. With luck, you can get from Techiman to Fiema in about one hour, and even on a slow day you should be there in two hours. If things don't go according to plan, however, it might be useful to know there is at least one small hotel in Nkoranza

Travellers leaving Fiema for points further north should note that, while shared taxis do run along the road connecting Nkoranza to Jema, they are normally full when they pass the Fiema junction. In other words, rather than trying to head directly between Fiema and Jema, you might be better heading back to Techiman and picking up a northbound vehicle there.

Where to stay and eat

Established as part of a community project, the **resthouse** charges around US$4 for a large, clean room with a double bed or US$2 per person to camp. There is no electricity or running water, but a borehole provides a good supply of water for bucket showers and paraffin lamps are available. At the time of writing, meals can be provided by private arrangement with the caretaker, but this situation is likely to be formalised in the medium term. Beers and soft drinks can be bought in Baobeng village, albeit at rather inflated prices.

KINTAMPO

This moderately sized town lies on the main north–south road, almost precisely halfway between Kumasi and Tamale. It is best known for its waterfall, which is reportedly seasonal, but impressive even when we visited in the dry season. The Kintampo Falls must measure about 25m high, with a wading or swimming pool at the base, easily reached by a series of concrete steps, and a large cave a short distance upstream. The fringing riparian forest is dominated by mahogany trees up to 40m high and looks promising for birding. Also near Kintampo, Fuller Falls is notable for the stream below the waterfall, which disappears underground for some 40m before re-emerging. A nominal entrance fee is now charged to enter the compound around the waterfall.

Getting there and away

There is plenty of direct transport between Kintampo and Tamale, Kumasi, Techiman, Wenchi and Nkoranza. The Kintampo Falls lie 6km from town, a short walk from the Tamale road, and are signposted at the 191km marker. Fuller Falls lie a similar distance from town along a more obscure side road. In either case, the best way to get to the waterfall is to charter a taxi from Kintampo's lorry station – we were quoted about US$4 for either return trip, though a few travellers have reported being overcharged.

Where to stay and eat

The pick of the lodgings is the new **Toronto Hotel**, clearly signposted from the main road through town. Here, a clean s/c double with TV, fridge and fan costs around US$4.50. Going down in price and standard, there's nothing much wrong with the **Midway Hotel** opposite the lorry station, which has large, clean rooms with fan and use of communal bucket showers for US$1.50 (1998 US$3). About 200m back towards Techiman, the **Wood Green Hotel** has clean, s/c rooms with fan and fridge, but no running water, for US$3 (1998 US$5.50) and smaller, scruffier s/c rooms for US$5 (1998 US$8). The **Midway Restaurant** opposite the synonymous hotel is the best bet for a sit down meal, and there are plenty of chop stalls and bars serving chilled drinks dotted between the lorry station and Shell garage.

THE OLD TAMALE ROAD

Once the main trunk route north from Kumasi, the road through Mampong to Ejura and Yeji is now something of a byway, poorly maintained, of limited interest, and likely to be visited only by those travellers who plan on hopping on or off the Lake Volta ferry at Yeji.

The main attraction in this part of the country is **Digya National Park**, the second largest sanctuary in Ghana, protecting a 3,478km^2 knuckle of rolling hills, large, granite inselbergs and varied vegetation jutting into the west shore of Lake Volta. Digya protects one of the most varied faunas of any Ghanaian reserve, including elephant, leopard, possibly lion, warthog, buffalo, bushbuck, waterbuck, reedbuck, kob, roan antelope, six types of duiker and eight primate species. It is rumoured that this part of the lake supports a small population of manatees, large aquatic mammals similar in appearance and closely related to the dugong of the Indian Ocean. The Department of Wildlife office at Ejura must be visited by all prospective visitors to the park, but the park itself is accessible only to self-sufficient campers with a private 4x4. The only accommodation that I'm aware of in Ejura is the Liberty Avenue Hotel, a basic place with rooms for around US$2.50.

Yeji is essentially a port town, and not a particularly attractive one at that. The Lake Volta ferry from Akosombo pulls in here every Tuesday evening, assuming that it's running to schedule, and departs again at around 04.00 the next morning. There's no shortage of accommodation in Yeji: the **Alliance Hotel** has rooms for around US$2.50, or you could try the **Volta** or **Ebenezer** hotels. Heading north from Yeji, a twice-daily ferry to **Makongo** is supplemented by small motorised boats that take around 45 minutes to cross. Regular transport runs along the 160km road between Makongo and Tamale, though you may need to change vehicles at Salaga. There is nowhere to stay in Makongo, so don't cross from Yeji in the afternoon unless you can be sure of reaching **Salaga**, a further 40km along the Tamale road. Here, the **Salaga Community Centre** has a few large, airy s/c doubles with AC for around US$3 (1998 US$7.50) – it lies 500m from the lorry park along the road signposted for the Human Rights Commission, a short distance past a large football pitch.

Part Six

Northern Ghana

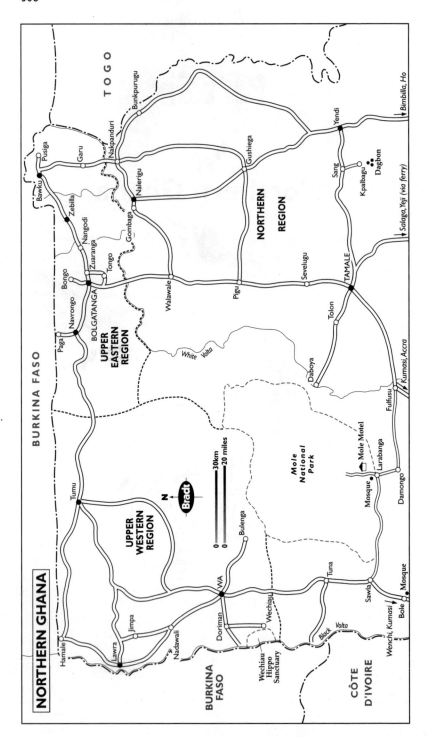

INTRODUCTION

The vast and relatively thinly populated savannah country that lies to the north of Lake Volta and the Black Volta River was annexed to the Gold Coast colony in 1902. Formerly known as the Northern Territory, it is now divided into three administrative regions. The Northern Region is the largest of these, covering an area of 70,384km² (more than one quarter of the country's surface area), and its regional capital Tamale boasts a population of roughly 250,000, which puts it in competition with Tema and Takoradi as the country's third most populous city. Much smaller than Northern Region and – somewhat paradoxically – lying to its north are the Upper East and Upper West Regions, the respective capitals of which, Bolgatanga and Wa, each support a population of between 45,000 and 60,000.

The north of Ghana can in many respects be viewed as a historically and culturally discrete entity from the southern and central regions. Unlike the various Akan groups who live to the south of the Black Volta, the predominantly Mole-Dagbani groupings of the north generally follow patrilineal lines of inheritance and they share a common oral tradition that suggests they arrived in modern-day Ghana in the 12th or 13th centuries following a militarised migration from the Lake Chad region. Historically, the Mole-Dagbani have had far stronger trade and cultural links with the Islamic world than with the Christian Europeans who settled along the Gold Coast, as witnessed by the large number of mosques throughout the region, including several centuries-old west Sudanese-style whitewashed mud-and-stick mosques in the northwest.

Not as dense with tourist attractions as the coast, northern Ghana has a relatively untrammelled, parochial atmosphere that seems far removed from the cosmopolitan bustle of Accra or Kumasi. And, in Mole National Park, the region does boast the country's best and most easily visited game reserve, a patch of open, tsetse-fly-infested savannah where close encounters with elephants are an everyday occurrence on what must be about the most affordable guided foot safaris on the African continent. Close to the entrance to Mole, at the small village of Larabanga, is the oldest and most famous mosque in the country. Another important attraction of the region is the traditional architecture which reaches its peak at Paga on the Burkina Faso border, where large, flat-roofed, mud constructions have grown organically over decades, even centuries, to house as many as a dozen related families. Similar homesteads are to be found around Nakpanduri, on the famed Gambaga escarpment, an area that's also notable for having some of the best scenery and birding in the country, as well as a magnificently positioned and highly affordable government resthouse.

The city of Tamale, itself of marginal interest to tourists, boasts the best facilities in the north, and it's the obvious gateway to the region if only because it's connected to both Accra and Kumasi by daily STC buses and a plethora of tro-tros. Tamale can also be reached by using the weekly ferry service from Akosombo to Yeji on Lake Volta. A second main access road to the north, connecting Kumasi to Wa via Wenchi and Bole, is in worse condition than the main Tamale road, but it's traversed by regular buses and allows you to see several beautiful, old mosques. For convenience sake as much as anything, this chapter describes the north in an anticlockwise loop out of Tamale, with Mole National Park, approachable from several directions, tagged on at the end.

GHANA AIRWAYS

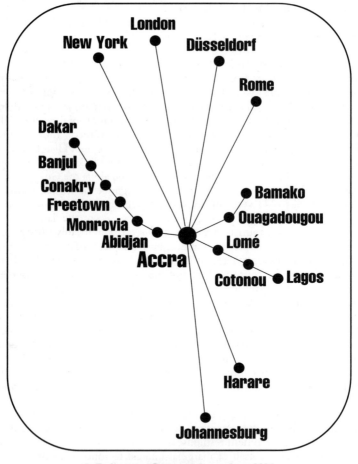

3 Princes Street, London W1
tel: 020 7629 3265; fax: 020 7491 1504
PO Box 7087, Johannesburg
tel: 011 622 4005/4068/4099; fax: 011 615 4625
email: jhbghair@icon.co.za
PO Box 1636, Accra, Ghana
tel: (021) 77 3321; fax: (021) 77 7078

Tamale and Mole National Park

This chapter covers Tamale, the economic and administrative capital of Northern Region, and the normal springboard for visits to Mole National Park, the country's premier savannah reserve and the main tourist focus in northern Ghana. Note that while Mole is covered in this chapter, and is most realistically visited out of Tamale on public transport, the main access road to the national park lies along the main Kumasi–Tamale road, which means that visitors with private transport can go there without ever setting foot in Tamale.

TAMALE

The main route focus in northern Ghana, not to say the largest urban conglomeration, Tamale is hot, flat and quite incredibly dusty: first impressions arriving in the harsh light of day are less than flattering, unless perhaps you're a homesick construction worker, though the sunset, filtered through a misty suspension of fine red dust, can fleetingly make it look like one of the most beautiful construction sites in the world!

Despite being nominated as the capital of Northern Territory less than ten years after the region was annexed to the Gold Coast, Tamale has a rather provincial atmosphere, and it holds little of interest to travellers – the most remarkable aspect of the city is the infestation of whimsically weaving bicycles that makes walking, particularly in the vicinity of the central market, seem positively hazardous. Demented cyclists aside, Tamale's other shortcomings are largely compensated for by a friendly, hassle-free atmosphere, and good, inexpensive amenities.

As for sightseeing, the central market itself is worthwhile, and you'll certainly want to pause to watch the Gonja cloth weavers at work. As a taster for architectural styles found to the north, you could wander past the engagingly low-key palace of the Gulpke Na, clearly signposted on Hospital Road near Barclay's Bank, and consisting of several small, thatched buildings connected by 2m-high walls – be warned, however, that neither photography nor poking around the palace compound are encouraged. You could, however, try to set up a visit to another chief's palace a few kilometres north of town – in a letter dated January 2001, one traveller mentions being taken there by a local teenager, and being free to explore and photograph the low-key but attractive local architecture after offering the chief a handful of kola nuts and a small donation.

Near to the palace is the Centre for National Culture, mentioned

prominently in every piece of travel literature about Tamale that I've come across; I have no idea why. Finally, there are a couple of small dams about 1.5km from the town centre along Education Ridge Road, a good place for a walk and highly promising for birds, though the teak forest which once surrounded the dams has evidently been reduced to tinder .

Getting there and away

Tamale is the main transport hub in northern Ghana. Regular STC buses connect Accra and Kumasi to Tamale, and at least one continues to Bolgatanga and Bawku daily. The weekly air-conditioned luxury express bus between Accra and Tamale costs US$15, leaving Accra at 05.00 on Thursdays and Tamale at 09.00 on Fridays, stopping at Kumasi for 15 minutes. Normal STC buses to Kumasi and/or Accra leave Tamale several times daily starting at 07.00. Coming in the opposite direction, buses from Kumasi to Tamale leave at 07.30 and 16.00 (morning bus only on Sundays). All STC buses leave from the STC bus station behind the post office, where you can also book tickets and make enquiries about current timetables.

Many tro-tros run between Tamale and main towns along the Bolgatanga–Kumasi road. For Mole National Park, a daily OSA bus leaves Tamale at 14.00 to overnight at the Mole Motel before heading back to Tamale at 05.30 the following morning. Without booking a few hours in advance, you'll probably have to stand most of the way. Alternatively, catch a bus connecting Tamale to either Bole or Wa as far as Larabanga (see *Getting there and away* under *Mole National Park* for further details).

Travellers coming to Tamale via the Lake Volta ferry are advised to disembark at Yeji rather than Kete Krachi, since the City Express bus from Kete Krachi to Tamale can takes in excess of 15 hours. For details of transport between Yeji and Tamale, see page 304. For crossing between Hohoe and Tamale via Bimbilla, see page 244.

Where to stay
Moderate
Gariba Lodge PO Box 541, Tamale; tel: 071 23041/2/3; fax: 071 23040.
This comfortable new three-star hotel on the outskirts of town is widely regarded to be the best hotel in Ghana north of Kumasi. Three types of room are available: singles at US$52, executive singles at US$62, and executive doubles at US$72. All rooms are AC with hot showers, satellite TV, a fridge, and international telephone. There is also internet access on site, and a good restaurant. The hotel is located on the Bolgatanga Road just north of the police barrier and the Fan Milk Depot, and south of the Kamina Barracks.

Budget
Formerly the most upmarket option in Tamale, the **Picorna Hotel** (tel: 071 22070) has arguably seen better days, but it still seems good value at US$9/11 (1998 US$20/30) for a s/c single/double with AC and hot water. Located close to the town centre, the grounds are fairly attractive and the food is good.

There are three similarly priced hotels clustered about 1km out of town off Hospital Road. The **Atti Essebe Hotel** is no better than the shoestring places in town, for which reason it seems overpriced at US$5 (1998 US$11) for an unremarkable double with a fan. Far better is the **Miricha Hotel** (tel: 071 22735), which has pleasant grounds and comfortable s/c doubles with hot running water and AC for US$10 (1998 US$18). The more upmarket and highly regarded **Las Hotel** (tel: 071 22158) has a variety of s/c rooms with fan or AC in the US$8–12 range (1998 US$17–23).

Back in the town centre, the **Tohazie Hotel** (tel: 071 23610), formerly the Catering Resthouse, consists of several s/c rondavels costing US$4.50 with fan and US$8 with AC (1998 US$10/17). It's very good value assuming that the water's running by the time you get there. The restaurant has an inexpensive breakfast menu.

A very recent recommendation from a reader is the **Ghana Institute for Literacy and Bible Translation (GILBT) Guesthouse**. Run by a Christian NGO , this offers good value accommodation at around US$8 for a double with AC, and serves cheap meals. It is located in the same road as the School of Hygiene (Ministry of Health).

Shoestring

The most central option in this range is the **Al Hassan Hotel**, which has been popular with backpackers for years, and remains good value at around US$3/4 single/double using communal showers (1998 US$4.50/5.50) or US$5 (1998 US$7) for a s/c double.

Two good Church guesthouses are situated no more than 200m apart on the Bolgatanga road, about 1km past the Macos Hotel. The **Catholic Guesthouse** is outstanding value, offering clean, comfortable, s/c rooms with fan for US$3/4 single/double (1998 US$6/8). The rambling green grounds are an added attraction, along with cheap breakfasts and – a little unexpectedly – a great outdoor bar! The **Christian Council Guesthouse** charges roughly the same price, and it's clean enough, but it seems a poor deal by comparison. Another possibility in this price range is the **Tamale Institute of Cross Cultural Studies (TICCS) Resthouse**, which lies along the same road, a bit further north, and has a fascinating library.

The **Macos Hotel**, clearly signposted about 2km from the town centre on the Bolgatanga road, has the cheapest rooms in Tamale and clean communal showers.

Where to eat

The **Gillipass Restaurant**, on the roof of a three-storey building, is the breeziest place to eat in the city centre, and on a good day also the best, with a wide selection of Western and Chinese dishes offered at reasonable prices. Even if you don't eat here, it's a great place to sip on a chilled beer while you watch the sun set over the city, or stargaze. Directly opposite Gillipass, there's cheaper beer and less breeze at the popular **Point Seven Bar**, where you have the choice of sitting indoors or on the semi-enclosed pavement.

The **Crest Restaurant** in the Al Hassan Hotel is under the same management as Gillipass and serves similar food at about half the price, but the dining room is unbearably hot, even if you switch the fan on, so try to persuade the waiter to let you put your table in the courtyard. Also very reasonably priced, **Sparkles Restaurant** next to the National Cultural Centre is similarly marred by the lack of breeze, though you can at least sit outdoors.

The **Sweet Gardens Chinese Restaurant** on the first-floor balcony of the Las Hotel is popular with expatriates and the food is very good, though you should expect to pay around US$7 per head for a main course with rice.

For Western and Ghanaian dishes in the US$3–5 range, try the restaurants in the **Tohazie** or **Picorna hotels**.

Listings
Curios
Try the stalls around the cultural centre, which have been recommended as far better than most in the country. The busy market is also a good place to buy local crafts and cloths.

Foreign exchange
There are Standard Chartered and Barclays banks in the town centre, both with foreign exchange facilities. Should you be heading on to Mole, make sure you have enough local currency to pay for accommodation, as of late the motel has worked on a far lower exchange rate than the banks, so you win greatly by paying in local currency.

Internet and email
There are several internet cafés. The one between the Al Hassan Hotel and Club Emesta, easily recognised by the prominent Africa Online sign, is recommended.

MOLE NATIONAL PARK
Established the year after Ghana attained independence, the 4,840km² Mole National Park was formally gazetted in 1971 following the controversial resettlement of the relatively few villagers who lived in an area that had formerly been thinly populated due to tsetse flies. Extended to its present size in 1991, Mole conserves an area of relatively flat savannah lying at an average altitude of about 150m above sea level, and broken by the 250m high escarpment on which its only motel accommodation is sited. It is the largest game reserve in Ghana, the most accessible and – at least in terms of general game viewing – the best.

More than 90 mammal and 300 bird species have been recorded in Mole, though several of the larger mammals are thought to be locally extinct or in critical danger of that fate – there has, for instance, been no trace of an African hunting dog noted in more than a decade. In general, however, populations appear to have increased since the last large mammal census was carried out in 1988, and current estimates for the larger herbivores stand at about 800 elephant, more than 1,000 buffalo, and significant populations of hippo, warthog and such antelope species as kob, Defassa waterbuck, bushbuck, roan, hartebeest and grey and red-flanked duiker. Five primate species are present, most visibly the olive baboon, as are 17 carnivores, of which the various mongoose species are most likely to be seen by visitors. Leopard and lion are now mostly known from the occasional spoor, though a pride of three lionesses was sighted at a kill near Lovi in late 1995.

A visit to Mole is easily combined with one to the mosque at Larabanga (see box on page 318), the most famous, frequently visited and reputedly oldest of the half-dozen or so west Sudanese-style mud-and-stick mosques dotted through western Ghana.

Getting there and away

One of Mole's chief attractions for travellers is that it's very easy – if not so comfortable – to reach using public transport. The park lies to the north of the reasonably well-travelled dirt road that connects Sawla on the main Kumasi–Wa road to Fufulsu on the main Kumasi–Tamale road. The turn-off to the park is in Larabanga village, roughly 50km from Sawla, 80km from Fufulsu, and 20km north of Damongo, the district capital of West Gonja. The entrance gate lies 3km along the turn-off from Larabanga and the motel a further 1.5km past the entrance gate, a 60–90-minute walk best undertaken in the cool of the early morning or late afternoon.

The most popular and straightforward approach is directly from Tamale, the terminus for the only bus service that actually goes into the park. This is an OSA bus service which in theory leaves Tamale daily at 14.00, sometimes a couple of hours later, and overnights at Mole Motel after arriving there somewhere between nightfall and midnight. The bus begins the return trip from the motel at between 05.00 and 06.00, depending on the driver's mood, and arrives back in Tamale roughly six hours later. Anybody who is coming from Kumasi and thinking of boarding this bus at Fufulsu (or, more accurately, at Damongo junction, about 3km north of Fufulsu) should be warned that seats are almost always fully occupied when it leaves Tamale. Even if tickets are available, you'll probably have to stand as far as Damongo, where most passengers disembark. Travellers who leave Mole for a destination other than Tamale can use this bus service to get to Larabanga (for Wa or Bole) or Damongo junction (for Kumasi).

Aside from the direct service between Tamale and the motel, at least three other buses daily pass through Larabanga. These bus services are particularly useful coming to or from Wa or Bole in the east. Coming from Wa, City Express buses to Tamale leave at around 06.00 and 17.00, taking about three hours to get to Larabanga. Coming from Bole, a City Express bus to Tamale leaves at 06.00 and arrives in Larabanga two or three hours later. If you arrive at Larabanga on a bus that doesn't continue to Mole, you can either walk to the motel (expect this to take slightly longer than a hour) or else wait for the Tamale–Mole bus to pass through, which will probably be between 17.30 and 18.30.

Leaving Mole in the direction of Bole or Wa, your best bet is to take the Mole–Tamale bus as far as Larabanga, then pick up the first bus heading west, which generally passes through Larabanga before 09.00. If this bus is heading to Wa and you want to go to Bole (or vice versa), disembark at the junction town of Sawla, from where there is plenty of transport in either direction.

If you are heading to Mole as a self-contained excursion from Kumasi on public transport, *don't* make the easy mistake of hopping off a bus at Damongo junction and trying to pick up transport to the park from there. We attempted this a few years ago, eventually having to give up and board a bus to Tamale, and we recently spoke to travellers who attempted (and failed) to do exactly the same thing. The problem is that no tro-tros run along this road and the buses are nearly always full by the time they get to the junction. Better to take a bus up to Tamale and board the OSA bus to Mole there, or (especially if you are interested in ancient mosques) to catch a Kumasi–Wa bus to Bole, spend the night there, then board the Bole–Tamale bus as far as Larabanga the next morning.

EXPLORING DAGOMBA

Tamale lies at the heart of Dagomba, an ancient Mole-Dagbani state founded by an offshoot of the even older Mamprusi. I can find no evidence to suggest that Tamale itself is of any great historical significance: on the contrary, even today Tamale doesn't serve as the seat of the paramount chieftaincy of Dagomba. According to oral tradition, the first Dagomba capital was Yendi Dabari, founded in the mid-15th century, and over the ensuing decades the base from where the militaristic chief, Nyagse, expanded his empire to incorporate a great many smaller kingdoms, most strategically the salt-producing village of Daboya on the White Volta.

Yendi Dabari's influence appears to have declined with the rise of the Gonja kingdom in the early 17th century: in roughly 1620, Gonja expansionists forced the Dagomba chief, Dariziogo, to relocate his capital to modern Yendi, some 30km to the northeast. From around 1750 to 1874, Dagomba was a vassal state of Ashanti, and from 1902 until after World War I the state was split between the British Gold Coast and German Togoland, with Yendi falling into the latter territory. Despite this, not to say the economic ascendancy of Tamale since it was made colonial capital of the Northern Territory in 1907, Yendi remains the modern seat of the Ya-Na (the paramount chief of Dagomba) almost four centuries after it was founded.

Although it's perhaps a rather esoteric pursuit, several of Dagomba's more historic towns can be reached on public transport. There are several tro-tros daily to Yendi from Tamale, a 100km trip that takes about three hours in either direction. Yendi is best visited on Monday or Friday mornings, when the Ya-Na holds an open court in the company of his two dozen shaven wives. The old salt-production centre at Daboya, now better known for its Gonja cloth weavers, lies on the northwest bank of the White Volta, some 60km and two hours by tro-tro from Tamale. Also of great historical interest is the former slave market town of Salaga on the Yeji road, though I understand that few visible relics of its past remain.

Be aware that none of these towns has any formal accommodation so, if you don't want to visit them as a day trip out of Tamale, you'll have to take a tent or rely on making private arrangements.

Driving to Mole should be straightforward enough in a good 4x4, even though the stretch of road between Fufulsu and Damongo is poorly maintained. A 2x4 vehicle with good clearance should get you through, except after heavy rain, but it cannot be recommended. If time is an issue, consider taking a taxi from Tamale. Extravagant, perhaps (it will cost about US$38), but it takes approximately two and a half hours so you could be in Mole in time to see the animals at dusk. Be warned, though – it's seriously bumpy and dusty, and you'll get filthy, but it's worth it if time is tight.

Where to stay and eat

The **Mole Motel** (tel: 0717 22045), built in 1961 on a cliff overlooking two waterholes, is an attractively situated complex marred by an architectural

A NON-HISTORY OF LARABANGA

The mosque at Larabanga may well be the oldest extant building in Ghana. Yet, oddly, nobody seems to agree on just how old it is, or even who built it. Some sources date it to the 13th century, which if not impossible is certainly improbable given that Islam had barely infiltrated the region at that time. In Larabanga itself, locals are fixated on the year 1421 and accredit the construction to an Islamic trader called Ayuba. Meanwhile, a display on Larabanga in the National Museum in Accra states that the mosque was built over the period 1643–75 by Imam Bramah, a theory that seems to be based solely on the somewhat negative evidence that the Imam's original illuminated Koran is still preserved in the mosque (but don't get excited, because you won't be allowed inside the mosque, let alone be shown the Koran).

Local tradition has it that the mosque's founder was travelling through the region when he found the so-called mystic stone that lies on the outskirts of Larabanga and decided, for some unexplained reason, that he would throw his spear from there and sleep wherever it landed. This he did, and during the night he had a strange dream about a mosque, the foundations of which were mysteriously in place when he awoke. Ayuba completed the construction of the mosque and settled at Larabanga. How the date 1421 arose is anybody's guess. All the guides at Larabanga could tell me is that the date appears in a book, which means that it must be right (the book in question would appear to be Jojo Cobbinah's *German guide to Ghana*, a book with a great many merits but no more a work of historical authority than the book you're reading right now!). When pressed on where the book's author got that date, the guides said he had asked around the village – an argument as circular as it is unconvincing. Then again, the early 15th century would tie in with dates given by the Imams of other similar mosques, as well as the period that is generally agreed to be when Islam expanded its hold into what is now northern Ghana. And if this is the case, then, yes, visitors to Larabanga are probably looking at the oldest extant building in Ghana, some 50 years old when the Portuguese set about building their first castle at Elmina. But who knows?

approach that makes no effort to integrate building and environment. Prices at the motel are well within reach of most travellers, and must be classed as reasonable value, though virtually every letter I've received about Mole has complained about food, water or electricity shortages, and what might diplomatically be referred to as poorly trained staff. While these complaints are largely justified, frustrated travellers might take some comfort from the realisation that a triple room here costs exactly the same as the US$25 park entrance fee charged per person per day at most East African national parks (some of which charge an additional US$20 per night for a facility-free camping space)!

Three types of room are available at the motel, all of which have a fan, which works only while the generator is running (typically between 18.00 and 24.00, though this cannot be guaranteed) and a private bathroom with an erratic supply of running water (a bucket is supplied but the onus is on you to keep topping it up). An ordinary double costs around US$20 (1998 US$14), an

It is just as difficult to get to the bottom of Larabanga's status as the oldest and most holy of Ghana's mud-and-thatch mosques. People in Larabanga generally deny the existence of similar mosques elsewhere in the country and, if you say that you've actually seen some of them yourself, they turn up their noses at any suggestion that a 'man-made replica' might be of similar antiquity to their divinely created original. In all probability, the mud-and-stick mosques of Ghana *were* built in close succession along a well-established trade route through the west. Larabanga's claim to be the oldest of these mosques is supported by its reported status over several centuries as a surrogate Mecca for Ghanaian Muslims (a status, I hasten to add, about which I was informed for the first and last time in Larabanga itself). It is difficult to verify – and frankly, after the umpteenth occasion on which the date 1421 and phrase 'man-made replica' had been used to stonewall my enquiries, I found myself actively hoping that someday, somehow, I'd stumble across a piece of evidence that would shatter the atmosphere of smug consensus that appears to consume the good folk of Larabanga on this subject. Can it be pure coincidence that 'Ghana's oldest mosque' also happens to be the one that lies a mere 5km from the motel in Mole National Park? The sense that the people of Larabanga aren't above a bit of conscious mythologising is heightened when you are taken to the mystic stone, a frankly very ordinary chunk of rock which caused the road towards Bole to be diverted because it 'mysteriously' reappeared overnight every time that it was removed by the road constructors.

Whenever it was built, Larabanga mosque, like others of its ilk, is obviously very old, and a truly strange and inspiring sight. Since 1995, the mosque has also been the cornerstone of a Peace Corps, coordinated community tourism project, one of particular importance in that by allowing the villagers to benefit from tourism it has the potential to ease the tension which has marked relations between village and national park ever since the former's traditional hunting grounds were gazetted away without recompense. But it does seem a shame under the circumstances that nobody locally, not even the guides, is able to provide visitors with *any* objective information whatsoever about its history.

ordinary triple US$25 (1998 US$17), and a larger double with a private balcony overlooking the waterhole US$23 (1998 US$20). It is also possible to camp within the motel grounds at a cost of US$2 per person. You will pay less at present if you can do so in local currency.

The communal area of the motel is focused around a swimming pool, which was empty for many years, but since it was repaired in December 1997 has normally been full (though the water is not always clean enough to be very tempting). The bar serves sodas, beers and mineral water, the coolness of which depends on whether it was in the fridge while the electricity was running, and the restaurant serves a limited variety of mediocre meals starting at around US$3–4.

There is serious talk of this motel being taken over by the Golden Beach Hotel chain in 2001. If this does go ahead, it is certain to result in an improvement in overall standards, but may also mean a price hike. Having said that, since Mole is still mostly visited by backpackers and other budget-conscious travellers, it seems likely that any new management will strive to offer some sort of accommodation that doesn't alienate this market. My suggestion is that you speak to other travellers before heading to the motel, or else check with the Golden Beach head office in Accra (contact details as for La Palm Royal Beach Hotel; see page 98).

A recently established alternative to sleeping within Mole, one that may assume greater importance to travellers should Mole Motel change ownership, is the private **resthouse** in Larabanga, run by two brothers and warmly recommended by several travellers. There are a couple of rooms in the resthouse, which has electricity but is not ventilated, which in this stifling climate means most people prefer to sleep on the roof. Either way, the cost is around US$1.50 per person, and meals are available with a couple of hours' notice. The obvious disadvantage of staying here is that you'll need to get between Larabanga and the motel early in the day in order to do a morning game walk, but the tourist office in Larabanga now offers bicycles for hire at around US$3 per day. If you want to see Mole at its best but also keep down costs, a good compromise might be to spend your first night at the motel, do an early game walk, then spend a second night at Larabanga. Bikes can also be hired at the motel for around US$1.

In addition to camping at the motel, several very basic **camping sites** are dotted around the reserve. The only realistic way of staying at one of these camps is to hike there with a ranger. The national park office ceased offering this service a few years ago, but it had reportedly resumed in early 2001, offering tents for hire at US$0.75 with a daily additional charge for camping and for the ranger. The most accessible camping site, Brugbani, 7km from the motel, has a reliable water supply in the rainy season.

What to do

There would be worse ways to pass a day than sitting on the **viewing platform** at the Mole Motel, cold beer in hand, swimming pool 20 paces away, and two waterholes clearly visible below. In the dry season, even this most passive approach to safari-going should reward you with sightings of elephant, kob antelope, Defassa waterbuck, bushbuck, warthog, olive baboon, green monkey and numerous birds during the course of any given day. While you're hanging around the motel, do drop in at the small museum in the staff quarters, which contains elephant skins, skulls and embryos, as well as some good sketches.

Far more exciting than the motel grounds, however, is to head down to the base of the cliff on a **guided game walk** – not that you'll necessarily see a greater variety of mammals, just that you'll get far closer to them, in particular the elephants, which are reasonably habituated to human pedestrians and often allow visitors to approach to within 20m. On foot, you can also be reasonably sure of seeing Nile crocodiles in the dam and of mutually startling a few water monitors – bulky lizards which measure more than 1m long and habitually crash gracelessly to safety when disturbed. A guided walk with an armed ranger costs US$1 per person per hour, regardless of group size, and there are enough rangers for every group to have its own guide. It is customary to tip the ranger. Note that walking in the park without an armed ranger is forbidden, except along the road between the motel and Larabanga.

If the variety of large mammals is limited, the number and variety of **birds** to be seen around the waterholes can be fantastic. Most visitors will notice larger birds such as martial eagle (a pair of which currently nest in the area), white-headed and saddlebill stork, white-backed and palmnut vulture, and various herons and egrets. Colour, too, is not lacking: the noisy but elusive red, black and yellow Barbary shrike is something of a speciality, as is the red-throated bee-eater, a colony of which nests in the vicinity. Also worth looking out for are Senegal parrot, Abyssinian roller, green pigeon and violet plantain-eater. All in all, I saw around 60 species in a three-hour walk; a more experienced West African birdwatcher would doubtless have seen more. If birds are of specific interest, ask for a ranger who is especially knowledgeable. The *Collins Field Guide to the Birds of West Africa* and binoculars can be rented from the tourist centre in Larabanga at a daily rate respectively of US$1.50 and US$3. Those with a strong interest in birds should ask to be guided by Zechariah Wareh, one of the best birding guides in Ghana.

Those wishing to see some of the large mammal species that don't frequent the motel area, or who simply want to experience a genuine wilderness atmosphere, will be disappointed to learn that talk of starting up **overnight excursions** with an armed ranger has been going around for years, but we have yet to hear of anyone who has actually experienced one. Likewise, game drives from the motel haven't been operating for some years, nor are they likely to be restarted in the foreseeable future.

Few visitors would want to miss seeing **Larabanga Mosque**, in the village of the same name some 5km from the motel (see box on pages 318–19). If you're going to be bussing directly in and out of Mole from Tamale, then the best way to do this is to walk out from the motel to Larabanga in the mid-afternoon, then either walk back or wait to catch the late-afternoon bus coming from Tamale. Otherwise, you'll get a chance to spend time at the mosque while you wait to change vehicles at Larabanga – it's only 50m from the main junction and bus station. The official entrance fee (or more accurately viewing fee since visitors may not enter the mosque) is US$1. In addition to this, you may also be asked to make one donation to the tourist project, another to the Imam for upkeep of the mosque, and another as a tip to the somewhat redundant guide or guides. I can't help but feel that most visitors would be more comfortable with a higher one-off, all-inclusive 'official fee' from which every concerned party could get its cut.

Larabanga village is itself a fascinating place, with perhaps the most southerly accessible examples of traditional flat-roofed mud *kraals* in the country, of particular interest to travellers who are not exploring other parts of northern Ghana. Through the Larabanga tourist centre it is possible to organise a stay in a private house, as well as to take a guided tour of the village and a local farm for US$2 per person. Other activities arranged by the tourist centre include bicycle hire and traditional drumming and dancing evenings.

Catering Resthouse (3km) & Navrongo

Bongo

Library

Tourist office

Ssnit House

Catholic Social Centre

Sports field

NAVRONGO

Black Star Hotel

Rocky Base Bar

Madam Rakia All Peoples Canteen

Post office & Telecom

COMMERCIAL

Tro-tros to Navrongo & Bongo

BAZAAR

disused stadium

Ghana Commercial

Mosque

Standard Chartered

St Joseph Hotel

National Investment

Meet Me There Bar

AETEBA

Central Hotel

Comme Ci Comme Ça Annex Bar

Old market

Comme Ci Comme Ça Restaurant

Midway & Streetview Bars

Social Security Bank

New market

Sand Garden Hotel

Goil

AYIA

International Travellers Bar

Shell

Goil

City express buses & tro-tros to Bawku & Bongo

Bar

Fire station

OSA Bus

Taxi

ZUARANGU

Sand Garden Annex Bar

Mobil

Bawku, Nakpunduri

N

Bradt

0 ———— 600m
0 ———— 600 yds

TAMALE

Bus station

Oasis Hotel

BOLGATANGA

Tamale, Kumasi & Accra

Bolgatanga and the Upper East

Because the Upper East Region is so remote from the coast and capital, the few travellers who pass through it are generally backpackers or overlanders en route to or from Mali or Senegal via Burkina Faso. Those who do visit this region will, however, find it offers much in the way of off-the-beaten-track rewards. Bolgatanga, the regional capital, is a chaotic but somehow rather captivating town, and a good base for day visits to the rhyming villages of Bongo and Tongo. Paga, on the Burkina border, is noted for its sacred crocodile pool and lovely adobe architecture, while Navrongo, between Paga and Bolgatanga, boasts a beautiful church with a unique mud-sculpted interior. Rather more remote, but accessible nonetheless, is the pretty Gambaga escarpment, where something of a minor tourist focus is provided by the cheap resthouse in Nakpanduri.

BOLGATANGA

The burgeoning capital of Ghana's Upper East Region may be smaller than Tamale, but it is no less hectic. Bolgatanga, you can't help but feel, is about to do the urban equivalent of bursting at the seams, and it comes as no surprise to discover that the population of this amorphous, bustling city has grown from fewer than 20,000 in 1970 to about 50,000 in 1998. Like many towns in the north, Bolga (as you'll soon come to call it) lacks for specific tourist attractions, though the small, but interesting, ethnographic museum behind the Catholic Social Centre is definitely worth an hour or two. You might also want to pop in at the nearby regional library and Ghana Tourist Board office, the latter your best source of current local tourist information. Bolga's most interesting feature, however, is the busy market, which peaks in activity every three days and is best known elsewhere in Ghana for the fine and often very affordable leatherwork, basketry, colourful straw hats and striped cloth shirts produced by the Frafra people for a predominantly local market. Hat salesmen, heads layered high with samples of their wares, are a familiar sight around town.

Getting there and away

Bolga is an important regional transport hub and you'll have little difficulty finding transport in any direction. The greatest volume of transport runs to and from Tamale and points further south. The Tamale road is serviced by regular tro-tros, plus at least one OSA and City Express bus daily. An STC bus to Kumasi leaves Bolgatanga at 16.30 every Monday, Wednesday and Friday. In the opposite direction, the STC bus leaves Kumasi at 18.00 on Tuesday, Thursday and Saturday.

There are two main lorry stations in Bolga. Tro-tros to destinations further north, such as Navrongo, Paga and Bongo, leave from the old station in the town centre. Tro-tros to destinations in the south and east, such as Bawku and Tongo, leave from the new station behind the Shell and Goil garages on Zaurangu Road. City Express buses also leave from the new station, while the OSA station is near the fire station and the STC station is out of town on the Tamale road.

Note that the only transport to Wa is run by City Express (see *Getting there and away* under Wa on page 334).

Where to stay
Budget
The closest thing to upmarket accommodation in Bolga, the **Black Star Hotel** is widely accepted as the top spot in town. The restaurant certainly looks and feels the part with blasting air-conditioning, swish decor and chattering television. The rooms, by contrast, seem very ordinary at US$5 (1998 US$11) for a double using communal showers and US$8 (1998 US$17) for a s/c double with AC. They might also get noisy at weekends. Nearby, and better value in my opinion, the appropriately named **Central Hotel** has large s/c rooms with AC for US$5/6 (1998 US$8/10) single/double.

Finally, there's the **Catering Resthouse**, a grand folly situated 3km out of town off the Navrongo road. A massive, partially unfinished concrete eyesore with comic modernist pretensions, the Catering Resthouse is redeemed from utter absurdity only by the pleasant s/c chalets with AC, which are excellent value at around US$10 (1998 US$17). The bar and restaurant also seem OK, and it may even host the occasional disco, but ultimately the atmosphere is just too depressing – it's difficult to see why anybody without private transport would want to be isolated in such unattractive surroundings so far from the town centre.

Shoestring
Cheap, and centrally located, the **Sacred Heart Catholic Social Centre** has clean rooms for US$1.50 per person (1998 US$3.50/5.50 single/double), the slight shabbiness of which is compensated for by the excellent communal showers and toilets. Cheap meals and drinks are available from the canteen. There are dorms, too, but these aren't especially cheap and are intended for self-contained groups of at least three people rather than for travellers arriving alone. Also very affordable and central is the **St Joseph Hotel**, next to the old lorry park, where you can get a slightly run-down s/c double with fan for US$3 (1998 US$5).

My nomination for best deal in town, however, is the **Sand Garden Hotel**, 15 minutes' walk from the town centre and ten minutes from the new lorry park off the Bawku road near the fire station. Clean, comfortable non-s/c rooms with a fan cost US$3/4 single/double (1998 US$4/6), using spotless communal bucket showers and toilets, while s/c doubles and rooms with AC cost US$7 (1998 US$9). The large and indisputably sandy garden may be lacking on the aesthetic front but, depending on what's blaring from the tape deck, it's a pleasant enough place for a chilled beer – and the sound system, for once, is far enough from the rooms to allow for an undisturbed night.

Another possibility in this price bracket is the **Oasis Hotel**, a very clean, friendly place which, unfortunately, leaves you stranded in suburbia with few obvious eating options, and is probably only worth thinking about should you arrive in Bolgatanga by STC bus. Large rooms with a fan cost between US$2 and US$4 depending on whether they are self-contained and have one or two beds (1998 US$3.50–5.50). The easiest way to get there is to follow the Tamale road out of town for about 200m past the STC bus station, then turn right into the road signposted for the State Housing Company, then left after about 50m into the side road opposite The Point Bar, then right after about 100m.

Where to eat

The **Comme Çi Comme Ça Restaurant**, on the outskirts of town close to the Sand Garden Hotel, is not quite as indifferent as the name might suggest – on the contrary, it's perhaps the best restaurant of its sort in northern Ghana, offering a varied selection of tasty, attractively presented and substantial Western dishes in the US$3–4 range. You can eat either in the air-conditioned dining hall or in one of several fan-cooled, thatched, outdoor shelters. It's a good place to drink, too, with friendly service and a highly effective fridge. You might want to check the bill, however, as it has a reputation for overcharging.

In the town centre, the restaurant in the **Black Star Hotel** is under the same management as the Comme Çi Comme Ça, and the menu and prices are practically identical. For cheap grilled beef kebabs and whole guinea fowl, try the courtyard bar at the St Joseph Hotel. The usual range of street food is available around the market and lorry parks.

Excursions from Bolgatanga

About 15km north of Bolgatanga, the small town of **Bongo**, a district administrative centre since 1988, lies at the heart of a memorable landscape of massive boulders, magnificent baobab trees and attractive kraals covered in childish stencil-like painted figures. The main attraction here, the aptly named Bongo Rock, emits a convincingly resonant vibrating boom when struck, while the general landscape offers much to photographers. Regular tro-tros to Bongo leave Bolgatanga from the central lorry station, taking about 30 minutes. Bongo Rock lies 20–30 minutes' walk from Bongo; to get there follow the main road back from the tro-tro station past the Catholic church, until after about 300m you see a footpath to your left leading to the taller and more distant of two hills. There's no accommodation in Bongo, but there is a bar serving cool soft drinks and beers about 100m from the tro-tro station in the opposite direction to the Catholic church.

A similar distance south of Bolgatanga, **Tongo** lies at the base of a horseshoe-shaped chain of low mountains, famous not only for their balancing rock formations and the views offered across the border to Burkina Faso, but also for the whistling sound made by the Harmattan wind as it passes through cracks in the rocks from December to February. The mountains above Tongo support the ethnically distinct Talensi people, who live in several small, scattered villages, most notably Tengzugu, where an important oracle and fetish shrine is located in a nearby cave. A popular site of pilgrimage for many Ashanti, who believe the oracle to have mystical curative and visionary powers, Tengzugu Cave lies roughly an hour's walk from Tongo along a rather steep road suitable for 4x4 vehicles only. The cave is visited with increasing frequency by adventurous travellers: initial arrangements must be made through the chief in Tongo, who'll expect the usual gift or payment, and you'll also have to visit the chief in Tengzugu to go through a similar ritual before actually visiting the shrine (only 200m from his palace). It might be worth noting that a party of readers who recently visited the shrine were expected to enter topless – the women in the group reportedly opted out! When you arrive in Tongo, expect to be approached by a few guides offering to set up the trip: make sure that you pick one you like, because you'll be stuck with him after he's taken you to see the chief. Tro-tros to Tongo leave Bolgatanga from the new station and they take about 30 minutes. There is no formal accommodation in Tongo, but this seems likely to change in the near future, and at present you should have no problem finding a hut in which to sleep, or pitching a tent with the permission of the chief. In addition to visiting the shrine, it's possible to arrange longer hiking trips into the mountains. It may be of interest to some readers that relatively formal excursions to Tongo are in the process of being developed by an Accra-based company called Fredina Tours (tel: 021 772494 or 775554).

Also of interest is the sacred bat-tree at **Baare**, 3km from Tongo, though whether it's worth the hassle of visiting yet another chief is debatable, especially as the bats aren't always there and the numbers pale by comparison with the bat colonies you can see in parts of Accra and Kumasi.

Note, too, that **Paga** (see page 330) would make a perfectly feasible day trip from Bolgatanga.

NAKPANDURI AND THE GAMBAGA ESCARPMENT

The Gambaga escarpment, which lies to the east of the main Tamale–Bolgatanga road, is the most significant physical feature in northeastern Ghana, measuring more than 60km from east to west and rising several hundred metres above the surrounding plains. Named after the town of Gambaga, capital of the ancient Mamprusi kingdom, the escarpment is of great interest to birdwatchers and hikers, with the excellent government resthouse at Nakpanduri forming the most obvious base for exploration, as well as boasting some fantastic traditional architecture in the form of sprawling *kraals* – extended family homesteads in which each nuclear family unit has its own hut and courtyard area enclosed within one walled compound.

Mamprusi is widely regarded to be the oldest of the Mole-Dagbani states; the Dagomba chief, or Nayiri, is still sometimes called upon to settle internal disputes in neighbouring Mossi and Dagomba. It is also probable that Mamprusi is the oldest extant political unit in Ghana. All Mole-Dagbani traditions agree that it was founded before AD1200 by the descendants of a light-skinned chief remembered by the name Toha-jie ('The Red Warrior'), who led his people from somewhere further east to Pusiga on what is now the Ghana–Burkina Faso border. Toha-jie's grandson, Naa Gbewa, is thought to have been the first true Mamprusi chief, settling first at a place called Mamprugu (from which the name Mamprusi derives), then at Gambaga, where he forged a union with the indigenous people by assuming political control, but allowing religious power to remain in the hands of traditional *Tengdana* priests.

The section that follows describes in an anticlockwise direction a loop through the Gambaga region, departing from the main Tamale–Bolgatanga road at Walewale, then running through Gambaga and Nalerigu to Nakpanduri, from where you could either turn back directly towards Walewale or else continue north via Garu, Bawku and Zebila to Bolgatanga.

Walewale

Situated at the junction to Nakpanduri, Walewale lies some 40km south of Bolgatanga and 120km north of Tamale, and although at least one (seriously dilapidated) bus runs daily in either direction between Nakpanduri and each of Tamale and Bolgatanga, you can also do the trip in short hops. Coming from Tamale, it's probably worth paying the extra to catch a tro-tro heading directly to Bolgatanga and then asking to be dropped at Walewale. Coming from Bolgatanga, look for a tro-tro that terminates in Walewale itself. At the junction, you'll find a couple of bars selling chilled drinks. Directly opposite, there's an intriguing mosque, notable for its Moorish tower, and built in 1961 on the site of an ancient mud-and-stick mosque. Should the need arise, there's also a small private guesthouse in Walewale, a short distance back from the junction towards Bolgatanga.

Gambaga

You're unlikely to wait too long at the junction for a lift of some sort, at least as far as Gambaga, 45km along the dirt road leading east from Walewale. It is difficult to determine the historical relationship between Gambaga and Nalerigu 8km to the east: most sources refer to Gambaga as the ancient capital of Mamprusi, and it was certainly the colonial capital of the Northern Territory until 1907 (it remains district capital to this day), but Nalerigu appears to be the older settlement and it houses the palace of the Mamprusi Nayiri. Gambaga itself isn't much of a place today, and assuming that your vehicle is continuing to Nalerigu you may as well stay on board.

Nalerigu

Of passing interest in **Nalerigu** are the attractive dam and pretty, sandstone church as you enter town from the Gambaga side. More ambitiously, ask a local guide to show you traces of the so-called 'Nigeria Walls' that surround the town, the remains of 16th-century fortifications that relate to the Sahelian slave trade. You'll probably also need a guide to locate the government resthouse, where for less than US$1 you'll be offered a bare room with no mattress, no lock, and not much of a ceiling to form a barrier between you and the several hundred bats that roost in the roof. Ask instead to be shown the government *guesthouse*, which is a little more expensive but reasonably habitable, consisting of three mud-walled rooms around a central courtyard, at least one of which might lock, definitely has a foam mattress, and seems entirely bat-free (the caretaker adamantly refused to let us look in another room after poking his own head round the door, so goodness knows what evil lurks inside). Be warned, too, that you should look at the accommodation only if you're reasonably serious about staying over, or you might well find yourself victim to a conspiracy of misinformation aimed to keep you in town overnight – it's a long story...! If you do have to wait around a while, check out the small garden bar next to the bus station (cool but not chilled drinks). Right next to that, a chop stall sells deliciously spicy guinea fowl stew.

Nakpanduri

The main draw in the region is **Nakpanduri**, perched on the edge of the highest point on the Gambaga escarpment, roughly 25km east of Nalerigu and connected to it by reasonably regular transport. There's little in the way of prescribed sightseeing in the area, but the combination of an excellent guesthouse, attractive surroundings and a relatively cool climate makes it a pleasant place to settle in for a few days. The town itself is a quite striking collection of sprawling, traditionally built compounds interspersed with massive baobab trees, while the area around the guesthouse affords great views to the northern plains, and is excellent for birdwatching. A good day's walk would be to follow the Bawku road through a forest reserve to the base of the escarpment, where a bridge crosses a forest-fringed tributary of the Volta River. There's also supposedly a seasonal waterfall nearby, worth asking directions to if you are there in the rainy season.

As for practicalities, the first thing you'll want to do upon arrival in Nakpanduri is make certain of a room at the government resthouse, where a comfortable double room with a fan (but no electricity within a 25km radius!) costs US$2, and there is plenty of water for bucket showers. To get to the resthouse from the main circle (which is where most tro-tros and buses stop), walk along the Bawku road for about ten minutes until you pass the Agricultural Rehabilitation Centre for the Blind to your right and see a three-way fork to your left opposite a signpost reading 'Caution: Slow Down'. The guesthouse is about 200m down the central fork. For food, either ask the caretaker about using the kitchen or head back to the main circle where there are several chop stalls. Spicy guinea fowl stew is the local speciality, sold from mid-afternoon until late evening, and stale bread is sold at all times, but on the basis of our experience *kenkey* (or whatever other hot starchy accompaniment is available) evidently sells out well before nightfall.

Bawku

Heading on from Nakpanduri, your options more or less amount to beating a retreat back to Walewale or striking on northwards to Bawku, a large and busy market town that can be rather absorbing on market days (every third day), but is less than memorable the rest of the time, unless perhaps you want to buy a sample of the attractive *fugu* shirts that are characteristic of the far northeast. Before you go clothes shopping, however, you'll need to find transport from Nakpanduri through to Bawku, apparently a more hit-and-miss affair than local advice ('you get lorry any time') might have you believe – we waited about seven hours for a lift on market day. As compensation, once you finally get going the 60km road offers some magnificent views. Accommodation in Bawku appears to be limited to the seedy but reasonably central Paradise Guest House, and the Hollywood Hotel, 3km out of town just off the Bolgatanga road, which has unexpectedly smart rooms with a fan for US$5, bucket showers, and a fridge loaded with ice-cold drinks. The best place to eat in the town centre is the Him Restaurant, next to the Mobil garage, while those staying at the Hollywood Hotel will find tasty grilled guinea fowl served outside the open-air bar on the junction 200m away. The only sightseeing in the area that I'm aware of is the ancient shrine to Naa Gbewa, the founder of the Mamprusi state, at nearby Pusiga.

Heading west from Bawku isn't a problem: not only do tro-tros to Bolgatanga leave from in front of the Mobil garage every half hour or so, but there's also a daily STC bus to Kumasi and Accra, leaving at 13.00, which you can use to hop as far as Bolgatanga or Tamale, assuming seats are available. You could also do the trip to Bolgatanga in hops, with the main attraction being the geometrically painted family compounds around **Zebilla** and **Amkwalaga**, better examples of which can be seen by 'dropping' from a tro-tro at an appropriate spot along the road than by actually getting off in one of these small towns.

NAVRONGO

This quiet, rustic town, situated close to the main border crossing into Burkina Faso, is notable for its many traditional homesteads, which are typical of northern Ghana, though angular where those in Gambaga curve, and often painted in monochrome geometric patterns. Should you arrive in Navrongo from Tamale or Bolgatanga, your first impression is likely to be how neat, orderly and shady it feels by comparison; this, despite the large number of uncompleted concrete buildings dotting the small town centre, skeletal relics of an absurdly over-ambitious development plan initiated by the short-lived Acheampong government of 1972–75.

Historically, Navrongo's claim to fame is as the home of Catholicism in northern Ghana. The Catholic Mission on the outskirts of town was founded in 1906 by pioneering 'White Fathers' under the French-Canadian missionary Oscar Morin, who travelled to this then little-known part of West Africa overland via what is now Burkina Faso. Definitely worth a visit is the Cathedral of Our Lady of the Seven Sorrows: consecrated by Father Morin in 1919, this large, traditionally constructed building is notable above all for the simple, but beautiful frescos that were painted on the pillars by local women using kerite oil and soil-based pigments. Also in the mission grounds is a remarkable grotto, reportedly a replica of the one at Lourdes, protected by a high stone wall constructed in a manner reminiscent of the Zimbabwe ruins in the country of the same name.

Getting there and away

Regular tro-tros connect Navrongo to Bolgatanga, and there are shared taxis running back and forth throughout the day to Paga. To get to nearby Lake Tono, the turn-off to which lies 3km along the Wa road, you'll probably have to charter a taxi for around US$3.

If you're heading towards Wa, the City Express buses from Bolgatanga do pass through Navrongo, but seats are generally full by that time, which means standing at least as far as Tumu, three hours away. Far better to go to Bolgatanga and pick up the bus at the terminus.

Where to stay and eat

The most central accommodation is at the **Hotel Mayaga**, a likeable little place clearly signposted about 500m from the lorry station along the Wa road. A spacious s/c room with fan and running water costs US$4/5 single/double, while an AC double costs US$10. The restaurant is better than you'd expect and not too expensive, and the outdoor bar serves chilled beer and cold drinks.

Less centrally, another option is the **Catholic Church Social Centre Guesthouse**, which faces the cathedral about 10–15 minutes' walk from the lorry station. There's nothing much wrong with the rooms here, but they seem relatively overpriced at US$10 for a non-s/c double with fan. To get there, follow the main road past the Ghana Commercial Bank and Bach Supermarket, and after the second big tree to your left turn into a vehicle-width track. After perhaps 500m you'll pass a conspicuous, blue water tower, then after another 100m reach a road with the cathedral in front of you – turn right into the road and the guesthouse is immediately on your right.

Even further out of town, the **Tono Guesthouse** is the only accommodation in the vicinity of Lake Tono, an artificial body of water that forms an important source of irrigation for the region, as well as offering good birding for visitors. The problem is that the guesthouse is often full, it's a good 2km from the lake itself, and without private transport you'll need to charter a taxi, or hitch. For those with vehicles, follow the Wa road out of town for roughly 3km, then turn right on to a surfaced turn-off, which after 5km leads directly to the guesthouse. Rooms cost around US$8 and meals can be arranged by advance request. Two men are not permitted to share a room.

There are several bars and chop houses in Navrongo; we had a wonderful plate of spicy guinea fowl and lettuce for little more than US$1 at the **Crossroads Bar**.

PAGA

The most frequently used border crossing between Ghana and Burkina Faso, Paga attracts a fair number of visitors owing to the sacred crocodile pools that lie within five minutes' walk from the main road through town. There are two such pools, Chief Pond on the main road near the Burkina Faso border, and Zenga Pond which is located along a clear footpath running at 45 degrees from behind the market next to the taxi station. Until recently, visitors to Paga were greeted by a dragnet of 'guides' and 'caretakers' who hung around the station waiting for custom, and organising a visit involved protracted negotiations and a fair amount of hustle. Recent reports, however, suggest that the fee has been formalised – inclusive of the cost of the chicken with which it's customary to feed one of the crocodiles – and the hassle factor minimised. When we visited, we still felt rather for the crocodiles – for centuries revered and protected as vassals for the ancestral spirits, they now suffer the indignity of being leaped on, prodded about and shooed off with a familiarity that might lead a more sceptical observer than myself to form the conclusion they are preserved solely for the money they generate. Nevertheless, it is a rare treat to be able to touch and photograph crocodiles at such close quarters.

Once show time is over, you'll probably be taken around one of the extended family homesteads that characterise this Burkina Faso border region – fantastic, labyrinthine, almost fortress-like complexes that share much architecturally with the more famous Dogon homesteads in Mali. The homestead we visited, one of the largest in the region and said to be well over a century old, is inhabited by roughly 100 people in ten separate households, each with its own living quarters and courtyard. The flat roofs are used not only for drying crops, but also as a place to sleep in hot weather. Some of the whitewashed mud walls are for some reason covered in labelled paintings of animals, a crocodile with a chicken in its mouth being a particular favourite. The graves of important family members actually lie within the courtyards of their former quarters. If you do visit a house, you'll be expected to make a small donation, but the whole thing is handled with a warmth and dignity that couldn't be more of a contrast to the mood at the crocodile pool down the road! Also of interest in Paga is a slave camp, where the slaves would rest during the slave trade before going to market. Unfortunately, like a lot of African history, it wasn't documented but is reputedly very interesting. At the Paga Pio Palace, you will see traditional mud huts with traditional writing. In a few of the mud huts you can see pottery that is hundreds of years old. Ask if you want to meet the Paga Pio or the chief.

So far as travel practicalities go, Paga is connected to Navrongo by regular shared taxis, and it's an easy day trip from either Navrongo or Bolgatanga. There's no formal accommodation in the main part of Paga, though doubtless you'd be able to arrange to sleep out on one of the roofs for a small fee. About 4km from town, close to the border, the **Paga Hotel** has clean doubles for US$8.50. At the Alahassan compound, a family provides bicycles for rent, and offers refreshments under a newly built summer hut. A suggestion box is available here, which the Paga Ecotourism Committee will review and act on.

Wa and the Upper West

The most remote and little-visited of Ghana's administrative regions, the Upper West boasts little in the way of formal tourist development, though in the right frame of mind, this absence is amply compensated for by its timeless frontier atmosphere and deep sense of removal from the rest of modern Ghana. The regional capital, Wa, is a sleepily appealing small town, studded with some fine examples of Sudanese-style mud-and-stick architecture, notably the striking Wa-Na's palace and lovely mosque in nearby Nakori. Many similar constructions are found elsewhere in the region, for instance at Bole, on the junction to the main western access point to Mole National Park. A more recent development, one which has received lavish praise from several quarters since its inception in early 1999, is the under-utilised Wechiau Community Hippo Sanctuary on the Black Volta, which not only protects a herd of 50-odd hippos, but also harbours a wide variety of birds, and lies in an area rich in traditional Sahelian cultures.

WA

The unimposing capital of Upper West Region, Wa is one of the oldest cities in the Ghanaian interior, founded in the mid-17th century by an offshoot of the Dagomba state. For several centuries the seat of the Wa-Na (the title given to the chief of Wa), Wa was one of the first parts of the country to adopt the Islamic faith, as evidenced by the extraordinarily high number of mosques dotted around the town centre. Of particular interest to tourists are two disused but reasonably well-preserved mud-and-stick mosques in the west Sudanese-style situated next to each other behind the modern Great Mosque. The same architectural style has been used to construct the 19th-century Wa-Na's palace, a large and striking building close to the main circle. In front of the palace lie the graves of five former Wa-Nas, starting with Pelpua III, who ruled from 1920 to 1935. The last Wa-Na died in January 1998, and his successor has yet to be decided. The palace is currently vacant, and under armed guard: one reader reports that visitors may be allowed to look around, another that the guards are touchy about photography. Once a new Wa-Na has been enstooled, it is customary for him to receive visitors when he's in town – the Wa-Na may not be spoken to directly, but the caretaker outside the palace will put you in the picture.

A worthwhile short excursion from Wa takes you to Nakori, where there's a very striking mud-and-stick mosque, taller than the one at Larabanga and of a similar vintage. The friendly chief of Nakori, to whom you'll probably be required to pay a call of respect, claims that the mosque was constructed in the 15th century and will sometimes let visitors climb to the roof and take photographs. Nakori lies within easy walking or cycling distance of Wa, roughly 4km from the town centre along the road passing the Upland Hotel. A taxi charter shouldn't cost more than US$4 for the round trip.

Getting there and away

Coming from the direction of Bolgatanga, the only public transport consists of two bus services run by City Express. Both these services stop at Navrongo, but there are usually no seats left by the time it gets there.

The first service is a direct bus between Bolga and Wa, leaving at 07.00 daily in either direction and arriving ten hours later – be at the station by 05.30 to be sure of getting a seat and take food because little is available along the way. The only scheduled stop is at Tumu, where you can buy chilled soft drinks and (assuming you're brave enough to enter a nominee for the category 'Most Disgusting Toilets that I've seen in Africa') make use of the public conveniences behind the vast and normally empty lorry station.

The second service from the Bolga area is the 'sleeper', so called because it involves an overnight stay in Tumu, 140km from Bolga and 120km from Wa. This trip actually consists of two separate services: a bus leaving Bolga for Tumu at around 14.00 daily and one leaving Tumu for Wa at roughly 12.00 daily. In the opposite direction, the bus from Wa to Tumu leaves at around 07.00 daily, as does the bus from Tumu to Bolga. Should you decide to use this service, there is cheap accommodation in Tumu at Lims Hotel (around US$1.50 per person), while nicer – and not much more expensive rooms can be found at the Department of Water and Sewage Works Guesthouse. There are plenty of nice places to eat, with spiced guinea fowl being the local speciality. You might also want to visit the Department of Game and Wildlife office in town to enquire about the possibility of investigating the 565km^2 Gbele Resource Area, which reportedly lies some 15–20km from Tumu along the Walembele road, and is home to significant numbers of roan antelope as well as a wide variety of birds.

Coming to or from Wa in other directions, plenty of buses run directly between Wa and Kumasi, and the main towns along this route are also connected to each other by localised tro-tro services. Two OSA buses daily run directly between Wa and Tamale, stopping at Larabanga for Mole National Park.

Where to stay and eat

The best budget option is the **Hotel du Pond**, which is very central and close to all the bus and lorry stations. An adequate double room with a fan costs US$3, and the communal showers have running water. It may be noisy on the rare occasions when there's live music, but otherwise it's great value for money. The only other cheap accommodation in the centre appears to be the similarly priced but more run-down **Hotel Seinu**.

Stepping up a bit in standard, the new **Kanateh Lodge** has rooms for US$2.50/4.50 single/double. It has a shared toilet, but the shower has good water pressure and the place is clean.

In a different league altogether, the **Upland Hotel** lies in attractive grounds some 10–15 minutes' walk from the town centre. Rooms here start at US$10 for a single with fan, US$16 for a s/c double with fan and US$22 for one with air-conditioning.

The restaurant at the Upland Hotel is the best in Wa, serving generously proportioned main dishes for around US$4 per plate. There are several cheaper chop houses and bars scattered in the town centre, and the usual street food is sold around the market.

WECHIAU COMMUNITY HIPPO SANCTUARY

A new sanctuary, developed in collaboration with the NCRC, Wechiau protects a 40km stretch of the Volta River west of Wa, and makes for a worthwhile and relatively straightforward excursion for anybody who makes it to this rather remote corner of Ghana. The sanctuary harbours a population of roughly 50 hippo – the second largest in the country after Bui – which are most readily seen from a canoe. The surrounding savannah and riparian forest also supports small populations of terrestrial mammals, though these are unlikely to be observed by casual visitors, and an impressive tally of 250 bird species have been recorded since the sanctuary was founded in February 1999. Among the more interesting species likely to be seen are exclamatory paradise whydah, malachite kingfisher, Senegal parrots, Abyssinian roller, and breeding colonies of red-throated bee-eater. In July 2000, the *Independent* newspaper in the UK ranked Wechiau as the third-best conservation holiday in the world!

Wechiau, the closest village to the sanctuary, and springboard from which it is visited, is also of some cultural and architectural interest. The centuries-old palace here is constructed in typical Sudanese mud-and-stick style. The main ethnic groups in the area are the Wala, Lobi and Biri, the last two still often to be seen wearing traditional lip-plugs. An added incentive to visit is that this is one of the first community-managed ecotourist ventures to be established in the far north of Ghana, and all profits are returned to the local community. A minimum stay of two nights is recommended to be reasonably certain of seeing hippos, and several day walks are offered, as well as canoe trips.

Activities are included in the bed price for overnight visitors (see *Where to Stay*), while day visitors are charged an entrance fee of around US$4.50 inclusive of a land guide and river safari. There will be a slight discount for Ghanaians.

Getting there and away

Tro-tros from Wa to Wechiau take roughly one hour. On arrival at Wechiau, visit the tourist office, where you must pay your fees, and will be given a guide to take you to the closer of the two lodges. Bicycles can also be hired to get to the lodges, for less than US$1 per day.

Where to stay and eat

Two low-key lodges have been constructed within the sanctuary, both of them set about 1km back from the river. **Tokali Lodge** lies 6km from Wechiau along a forest trail, while **Tankara Lodge** lies a further 5km from Tokali Lodge. A rate of roughly US$10 per person includes entrance, one night's accommodation, a river safari with guide, land guide, and cooking services (you provide the ingredients). Additional nights cost around US$8 per person.

BOLE

This small town on the main Kumasi–Wa road is of interest primarily for its beautiful mud-and-stick mosque, regarded locally to be the second oldest of its type in the country, but it also boasts some interesting traditional houses. The ancient mosque isn't visible from the main road, but it's easy enough to find, situated about 50m from the modern mosque, a major landmark with its five-storey parapet. A significant attraction of Bole over Larabanga is that the set-up is so much more casual: the Imam seems to be very relaxed about women visitors and photography, and he may well offer to take you inside the mosque and up to the roof. We were asked for a donation, which is only proper – the critical thing is that once we had paid we were left alone to take our time absorbing the atmosphere and photographing the mosque, a far cry from the incessant hassle and chit-chat that characterises the Larabanga experience.

Bole serves as a convenient overnight stop for travellers heading between Kumasi and Mole (see also *Getting there and away* under *Mole National Park*). Coming from Wa, there are at least three tro-tros daily to Bole. The only place to stay in town is the **Motel Eureka**, a clean, friendly, family-run establishment where a double with fan costs US$3. There's an outdoor bar on the main road, easily recognised by the tell-tale blue-and-white fence, which serves a good selection of refrigerated drinks as well as tasty chop on some evenings, but not at weekend (when you may have difficult finding cooked food other than basic chop). For those with private transport, we were told that there's superior accommodation a few kilometres out of town at the **Cocoa Research Centre Guesthouse**.

Two further mud-and-stick mosques are clearly visible from the road between Bole and Kumasi, evidence that the modern road approximates a much older Islamic trade route. Both these mosques are fenced, making them less photogenic than the one at Bole. The first mosque is on the east side of the main road through Maluwe, a forest-fringed village which might well hold some interesting walking possibilities. The second mosque, at Banda Nkwanta, lies on the west side of the road, and is notable for having very tall parapets relative to the size of the rest of the building. There's no formal accommodation in either of these villages, but it's unlikely you'd have a problem pitching a tent or finding a room in a private house.

Those with an insatiable desire to see mosques might be interested to know that we were told by everybody we asked in the region that the above (along with the mosques at Larabanga, Bole and Wa) are the only buildings of their sort in Ghana. A few weeks later, in Ho Museum, at the other side of the country, we saw a photograph of a similar mosque at a place called Dondoli, which I can find on no map ... so who knows how many other mud-and-stick mosques await discovery by travellers?

Appendix

LANGUAGE

English is the official language of Ghana, widely spoken in those parts of the country likely to be visited by travellers, to a standard that is matched in few other anglophone African countries. This means that there is little need for short-stay travellers to try to familiarise themselves with any local tongues, though as always knowing a few words or greetings in a local language will often help open doors and break through barriers, particularly in rural areas.

Numerous different languages and dialects are spoken in Ghana, but you'll find that most people belonging to one or other of the Akan groups – and that means more than half of the population and practically everybody in southern and central Ghana – will speak Twi (pronounced rather like Chwee) as a first or second language. Twi is the Ghanaian language taught to most Peace Corps and other volunteers spending a lengthy period of time in the country, and it may help travellers to know a few basic words and phrases. Those who speak Twi will also be able to understand Fante, another widely spoken Akan language.

Note that pronunciation of the words listed below, as of most place name in Ghana, is phonetic (for example *ache* is pronounced as *ah-chee* rather than the English word *ache*), and that spellings have been simplified to make sense to English speakers (as one example, 'ch' is often spelt 'ky' in Ghana, while 'dz' is pronounced 'j'). Note, too, that vowel sounds are closer to the soft French vowels than hard English ones:

Those who want to learn more could try getting hold of a copy of *Learning Ghanaian Languages*, available from the University Book Shop at Legon University in Accra.

a   similar to the 'a' in 'father'
e   as the 'e' in 'wet'
i   as the 'ee' in 'free' but less drawn out
o   somewhere between the 'o' in 'no' and the word 'awe'
u   similar to the 'oo' in 'food'

Basic words and phrases

Do you speak English?	*Wote Borofo ana?*
Equal to	*Ya anua*
friend	*madanfo*
Good afternoon	*Mma aha* (response *yemu*)
Good evening	*Mma ajo* (response *yemu*)
Good morning	*Mma ache* (response is *yemu*)

Goodbye	*Nanti ye*
How are you?	*Wo ho te sen?* (response me *ho ye*)
How much?	*Sain Me*
I'd like...	*Me pe*
man	*oberima*
No	*Dabe*
Please	*Me pawocheo*
Thank you	*Meda ase*
Today	*Enne*
Tomorrow	*Echina*
Water	*Nsuo*
We	*Ye*
Welcome	*Akwaaba* (response: *Ya eja* (to older man); *Ya ema* (to older woman)
What's your name? My name is...	*Ye frewo sen?/Ye fre me...*
What is the cost?	*Eyesen?*
Where is ....?	*... wo hin?*
woman	*obaa*
Yes	*Nyew* (Fante) *or aane* (Ashanti)
Yesterday	*Enra*

Numbers

1	*Baako*	30	*Aduasa*
2	*Mienu*	40	*Aduanang*
3	*Miensa*	50	*Aduonum*
4	*Enang*	60	*Aduosia*
5	*Enoum*	70	*Aduosong*
6	*Nsia*	80	*Aduowotwe*
7	*Nsong*	90	*Aduokrong*
8	*Nwotwe*	100	*Oha*
9	*Nkrong*	1,000	*Apem*
10	*Edu*	10,000	*Pemdu*
11, 12 etc	*Dubaako, dumienu* etc	100,000	*Mpemba*
20	*Aduono*	1,000,000	*Opepe*
21	*Aduono baako*		

Days of the week

Monday	*Uzoada*	Friday	*Fiada*
Tuesday	*Blada*	Saturday	*Memleda*
Wednesday	*Akuada*	Sunday	*Kuasiada*
Thursday	*Yawada*		

Appendix

FURTHER READING
History and background
I consulted quite a number of books while researching the general and local history sections included in this guide, all of which I was able to buy in Ghana, though I can't guarantee you'll be able to do the same. I've listed them all below, but it would be pushing it to class most of them as recommended further reading. Buah's *History of Ghana* would be the obvious starting point for those seeking deeper insight into the country's historical background; readable, informative and of manageable length, without really propelling you to turn to the next page. More compelling, oddly enough, is Agbodeka's *Economic History*, while Gadzekpo's otherwise rather flimsy *History of Ghana* is especially strong on prehistory. Best of all in my opinion – certainly the only substantial book in the collection that I could think about reading from start to finish for pleasure – is *A Thousand Years of West African History*, a collection of essays covering most aspects of the region's history, probably a bit dated by now but of great value for the lively, questioning style throughout.

Of the more focused titles, Danzig's *Forts and Castles* offers a good introduction to coastal history, brought to life by the final chapter on living conditions in and around the forts, and it's readily available in Accra and Cape Coast. Anquandah's *Castles & Forts of Ghana*, sold at the Accra Museum and at Cape Coast and Elmina Castles, covers similar ground with less substantial but more readable text and some wonderful photographs. Debrah's *Asante Traditional Buildings*, also sold at most museums, is a lightweight but beautiful production well worth buying for further detail on the shrines at Besease and elsewhere in Ashanti.

Superficially somewhat esoteric, Schweizer's *Survivors on the Gold Coast* relates the story of the foundation of the Basel Missionaries, but is of greater interest for its 80-plus pages of monochrome photographs, which date from 1860 onwards and document subjects as diverse as the Asantehene in exile in the Seychelles to Accra street scenes - all in all, a fascinating document.

Agbodeka, F *An Economic History of Ghana* (Ghana University Press 1992)
Ajayi, F & Espie, E (eds) *A Thousand Years of East African History* (Thomas Nelson 1965)
Amate, C O C *The Making Of Ada* (Woeli Publishing Services, 1999)
Anquandah, K J *Castles & Forts of Ghana* (Ghana Museums & Monuments Board, 1999)
Arhin, K (ed) *The Cape Coast and Elmina Handbook* (University of Ghana)
Buah, F *West Africa Since AD1000* (Macmillan 1974)

Buah, F *A History of Ghana* (Macmillan 1980)
Davidson, B *A History of West Africa 1000–1800* (Longman 1977)
Debrah, I N (ed), *Asante Traditional Buildings* (Ghana Museums & Monuments Board 1999)
Gadzekpo, A *History of Ghana* (Royal Crown Press 1997)
Graham, J *Cape Coast in History* (Anglican Printing Press 1994)
Kwadwo, O *An Outline of Asante History* (O Kwadwo Enterprises 1994)
Kyeremateng, K *The Akans of Ghana* (Sebewie Publishers 1996)
Moxon, J *Volta: Man's Greatest Lake* (Andre Deutsch 1969)
Obeng, E *Ancient Ashanti Chieftaincy* (Ghana Publishing Corporation 1984)
Onwubiko, K *History of West Africa 1000–1800* (Africana FEP 1982)
Onwubiko, K *History of West Africa 1800–Present Day* (Africana FEP 1985)
Packenham, T *The Scramble for Africa* (Jonathan Ball 1991)
Sampson, M *Makers of Modern Ghana Volume One* (Anowuo Publications 1969)
Sarpong, P *Ghana in Retrospect* (Ghana Publishing Corporation 1974)
Schweizer, P A *Survivors on the Gold Coast* (Smartline Publishing 2000)
Tufuo, J & Donkor, C *Ashantis of Ghana* (Anowuo Publications 1989)
van Dantzig, A *Forts and Castles of Ghana* (Sedco 1980)
Ward, W *Short History of Ghana* (Longman 1957)

Field guides

My favourite mammal field guide is Jonathon Kingdon's superb and dauntingly comprehensive *Field Guide to African Mammals* (Academic Press 1997). A cheaper and more handy volume, just as useful to most visitors whose interest is confined to large mammals, is Chris and Tilde Stuart's *Field Guide to the Larger Mammals of Africa* (Struik, South Africa, 1997). If you have difficulty locating these, several other inferior guides are more widely available, most visibly those published by Collins. Once in Ghana, you should be able to get hold of Happold's *Large Mammals of West Africa* (Longman 1973) which, despite being rather dated in some respects, is a very handy, lightweight volume with adequate pictures and descriptions.

The best starting point for dedicated birders visiting Ghana is Lesley Grimes' *The Birds of Ghana*, which includes a systematic list of all 712 species found in the country, together with details of favoured habitat, relative abundance, and distribution. For identification, however, you'll need to supplement this with a field guide. The most useful title available at present is Serle, Morel and Hatwig's *Field Guide to the Birds of West Africa* (HarperCollins 1977), though even this has a great many flaws, most seriously that full descriptions and illustrations are supplied for only half the species recorded in the region, while almost 400 species are relegated to one line each in an appendix. That said, you should be able to positively identify at least 80% of what you might see with this guide. Serious birdwatchers might also want to carry Ber van Perlo's *Illustrated Checklist to the Birds of East Africa* (HarperCollins, 1995), comprehensive for a region which has considerable overlap into West Africa, though you need to be alert to the numerous instances where the two books give different common names (and sometimes even Latin binomials) for the same species.

Travel guides

Highly recommended to those who are spending a while in the capital, is the North American Women's Association's *No Worries: The Indispensable Insiders'*

Guide to Accra, an excellent source of advice and contacts in Accra. Also worth buying, though more as a souvenir than a guide, is Mylene Remy's *Ghana Today* (Jaguar 1977 & 1992), a 30cm-long hardback book packed with good photos but textually tending towards whimsy and hyperbole. Jojo Cobbinah's *Ghana* (Peter Meyer, 1995 & 1999) is an established German-language guide written by a Ghanaian resident in Germany. It is popular with Germans, and contains lots of useful information, but the recently published English version has been ill-served by the translator.

Those travelling further afield in West Africa are pointed to one of two guides to the region: Jim Hudgens and Richard Trillo's *West Africa: The Rough Guide* (Rough Guides 1999 edition) and Alex Newton and David Else's *West African Travel Survival Kit* (Lonely Planet 1999 edition). If the Ghana chapters are representative, neither guide inspires total confidence, but for what it's worth the Lonely Planet guide is generally more accurate regarding accommodation and eating recommendations, while the Rough Guide is more engagingly written and tends to push more towards off-the-beaten-track travel.

Fiction and biography

Ghana has one of the strongest English literary traditions to be found anywhere in Africa, dating back to 1911 and the publication of what is regarded as West Africa's first novel, *Ethiopia Unbound*, by the barrister and nationalist politician Joseph Casely Hayford. A fair selection of local novels are available in most bookshops around the country, generally at very reasonable prices. A few better-known novels include B Kojo Laing's *Search Sweet Country*, Ayi Kwei Armah's *The Beautiful Ones Are Not Yet Born* and *Healers*, Ama Ata Aidoo's *Dilemma of a Ghost* and *Our Sister Killjoy*, and Amma Darko's *Beyond the Horizon*.

Maya Angelou's *All God's Children Need Travelling Shoes* (Virago 1987) recounts the story of this American author's return to Ghana to search out her roots. *The Narrow Path* by Francis Selormey (Heinemann African Writers Series) is a vivid and very readable account of a Ghanaian boy's upbringing in the 1920s.

Websites

Three websites worth checking out before you travel to Ghana are www.africaonline.com.gh (general tourist information), www.ncrc.org.gh (currently under development but potentially a highly worthwhile resource for information about ecotourist and community development tourist sites) and www.wildlife.gov.gh (details of national parks).

342

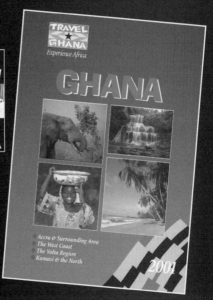

MEASUREMENTS AND CONVERSIONS

To convert	Multiply by
Inches to centimetres	2.54
Centimetres to inches	0.3937
Feet to metres	0.3048
Metres to feet	3.281
Yards to metres	0.9144
Metres to yards	1.094
Miles to kilometres	1.609
Kilometres to miles	0.6214
Acres to hectares	0.4047
Hectares to acres	2.471
Imperial gallons to litres	4.546
Litres to imperial gallons	0.22
US gallons to litres	3.785
Litres to US gallons	0.264
Ounces to grams	28.35
Grams to ounces	0.03527
Pounds to grams	453.6
Grams to pounds	0.002205
Pounds to kilograms	0.4536
Kilograms to pounds	2.205
British tons to kilograms	1016.0
Kilograms to British tons	0.0009812
US tons to kilograms	907.0
Kilograms to US tons	0.000907

5 imperial gallons are equal to 6 US gallons
A British ton is 2,240 lbs. A US ton is 2,000 lbs.

Temperature conversion table

The bold figures in the central columns can be read as either centigrade or fahrenheit.

°C		°F	°C		°F
−18	0	32	10	50	122
−15	5	41	13	55	131
−12	10	50	16	60	140
−9	15	59	18	65	149
−7	20	68	21	70	158
−4	25	77	24	75	167
−1	30	86	27	80	176
2	35	95	32	90	194
4	40	104	38	100	212
7	45	113	40	104	219

NOTES

Akosombo ⟶ Yeji

¢ 196,000

from 9am ⟶ 16.00

by 12pm

VOLTA REGION:

- Tafi Atome
- Wli falls
- Liate Wote
- Amedzofe
- Bialcpa

NOTES

NOTES

BOLGATANGA:

Nsamini Guest House
40,000 non-s/c

ACCRA: (20,000-)

Kokomlemle G/House 45,000 s/c
(Lemon Lodge - no s/c) 9,000 B/fast

TESI: 47,250

Nifanifa Hotel 30,000
(Ambassador Htl). non s/c

KUMASI:

Menka Memorial 40,000 non-s/c
50,000 s/c

Presbyterian G/House
(non-s/c) 100,000

WENCHI:

Drah Hotel 25,000 s/c
15,000 non-s/c

BUI NP:

Bui Camp, etc... 20,000

HOHOE:

Taste Lodge Complex
Fridge phone W/water 90,000 (s/c, a/c)

TAFI ATOME 70,000 each

TAKORADI:

Amenla Hotel 43,000 non s/c
53,000 s/c

Hotel You 84 60,000 fan
81,000 fan
TV. Fridge Phone 100,000 a/c
H/water 120,000 a/c

BRENU:

Beach Resort. 60,000 single
80,000 fan
100,000

CAPE COAST:

125,000 s/c fam

Mighty Victory Hotel.

Black Star Hotel (?)
10,000 - 40,000

The Blue Cheese.

dishes 10,000 - 25,000

Palace Hotel SHUT
G now residence

NOTES

NOTES

NOTES

NOTES

Index

Entries in italic indicate maps.